Anatomy of Literary Criticism

Anatomy of Literary Criticism

Attied Khawar Balwan
and
Ranbir Kaur

RANDOM

RANDOM PUBLICATIONS
NEW DELHI (INDIA)

Anatomy of Literary Criticism

ISBN 978-93-5111-577-9

Published in 2015 in India by

RANDOM PUBLICATIONS

4376-A/4B, Gali Murari Lal, Ansari Road
New Delhi-110 002
Phone : +9111-43580356, 011-23289044, 011-43142548
e-mail: sales@randompublications.com,
info@randompublications.com, randomexports@gmail.com

Reprinted 2025

Type Setting by : Friends Media, Delhi-110089
Digitally Printed at: Replika Press Pvt. Ltd.

Preface

Literary criticism is the study, evaluation, and interpretation of literature. Modern literary criticism is often influenced by literary theory, which is the philosophical discussion of its methods and goals. Though the two activities are closely related, literary criticsare not always, and have not always been, theorists.

The literary criticism of the Renaissance developed classical ideas of unity of form and content into literary neoclassicism, proclaiming literature as central to culture, entrusting the poet and the author with preservation of a long literary tradition.

Today interest in literary theory and Continental philosophy coexists in university literature departments with a more conservative literary criticism of which the New Critics would probably have approved. Disagreements over the goals and methods of literary criticism, which characterized both sides taken by critics during the "rise" of theory, have declined. Many critics feel that they now have a great plurality of methods and approaches from which to choose.

The aim of the Book is to make accessible in clear and concise form a body of material that has become overwhelm-ing. We hope it will continue to have a wide audience in the academy, an audience composed not only of professors and graduate students in literary studies.

I would like to thank my team for standing beside me throughout my career and writing this book. My special thanks go to "Random Publications" who have published the book.

– Attied Khawar Balwan and Ranbir Kaur

Contents

1

Introduction

INTRODUCTION TO LITERARY CRITICISM

Literary criticism is the study, evaluation, and interpretation of literature. Modern literary criticism is often influenced by literary theory, which is the philosophical discussion of its methods and goals. Though the two activities are closely related, literary criticsare not always, and have not always been, theorists.

Whether or not literary criticism should be considered a separate field of inquiry from literary theory, or conversely from book reviewing, is a matter of some controversy. For example, the *Johns Hopkins Guide to Literary Theory and Criticism* draws no distinction between literary theory and literary criticism, and almost always uses the terms together to describe the same concept. Some critics consider literary criticism a practical application of literary theory, because criticism always deals directly with particular literary works, while theory may be more general or abstract.

Literary criticism is often published in essay or book form. Academic literary critics teach in literature departments and publish inacademic journals, and more popular critics publish their criticism in broadly circulating periodicals such as the *Times Literary Supplement*, the *New York Times Book Review*, the *New York Review of Books*, the *London Review of Books*, *The Nation*, and *The New Yorker*.

HISTORY OF LITERARY CRITICISM

Aristotle's Poetics clearly defines aspects of literature and introduces many literary terms still used today.

CLASSICAL AND MEDIEVAL CRITICISM

Literary criticism has probably existed for as long as literature. In the 4th century BC Aristotle wrote the *Poetics*, a typology and description of literary forms with many specific criticisms of contemporary works of art. *Poetics* developed for the first time the concepts of mimesis and catharsis, which are still crucial in literary study. Plato's attacks on poetryas imitative, secondary, and false were formative as well. Around the same time, Bharata Muni, in his *Natya Shastra*, wrote literary criticism on ancient Indian literature and Sanskrit drama.

Later classical and medieval criticism often focused on religious texts, and the several long religious traditions of hermeneutics and textual exegesis have had a profound influence on the study of secular texts. This was particularly the case for the literary traditions of the three Abrahamic religions: Jewish literature, Christian literature and Islamic literature.Literary criticism was also employed in other forms of medieval Arabic literature and Arabic poetry from the 9th century, notably by Al-Jahiz in his *al-Bayan wa-'l-tabyin* and *al-Hayawan*, and by Abdullah ibn al-Mu'tazzb in his *Kitab al-Badi*.

Key texts

- Plato: *Ion, Republic, Cratylus*
- Aristotle: *Poetics, Rhetoric*
- Horace: *Art of Poetry*
- Longinus: *On the Sublime*
- Plotinus: *On the Intellectual Beauties*
- St. Augustine: *On Christian Doctrine*
- Boethius: *The Consolation of Philosophy*
- Aquinas: *The Nature and Domain of Sacred Doctrine*
- Dante: *The Banquet, Letter to Can Grande Della Scala*
- Boccaccio: *Life of Dante, Genealogy of the Gentile Gods*
- Christine de Pizan: *The Book of the City of Ladies*
- Bharata Muni: *Natya Shastra*
- Al-Jahiz: *al-Bayan wa-'l-tabyin, al-Hayawan*
- Abdullah ibn al-Mu'tazz: *Kitab al-Badi*
- Rajashekhara: *Inquiry into Literature*
- Valmiki: *The Invention of Poetry* (from the *Ramayana*)
- Anandavardhana: *Light on Suggestion*
- Cao Pi: *A Discourse on Literature*
- Lu Ji: *Rhymeprose on Literature*
- Liu Xie: *The Literary Mind*
- Wang Changling: *A Discussion of Literature and Meaning*
- Sikong Tu: *The Twenty-Four Classes of Poetry*

RENAISSANCE CRITICISM

The literary criticism of the Renaissance developed classical ideas of unity of form and content into literary non-classicism, proclaiming literature as central to culture, entrusting the poet and the author with preservation of a long literary tradition. The birth of Renaissance criticism was in 1498, with the recovery of classic texts, most notably, Giorgio Valla's Latin translation of Aristotle's *Poetics*.

The work of Aristotle, especially *Poetics*, was the most important influence upon literary criticism until the late eighteenth century.Lodovico Castelvetro was one of the most influential Renaissance critics who wrote commentaries on Aristotle's *Poetics* in 1570.

Key texts

- Lodovico Castelvetro: *The* Poetics *of Aristotle Translated and Explained*
- Philip Sidney: *An Apology for Poetry*
- Jacopo Mazzoni: *On the Defence of the Comedy of Dante*
- Torquato Tasso: *Discourses on the Heroic Poem*
- Francis Bacon: *The Advancement of Learning*
- Henry Reynolds: *Mythomystes*
- John Mandaville: *Composed in the mid-14th century—most probably by a french physician*

ENLIGHTENMENT CRITICISM

Key texts

- Thomas Hobbes: *Answer to Davenant's preface to* Gondibert
- Pierre Corneille: *Of the Three Unities of Action, Time, and Place*
- John Dryden: *An Essay of Dramatic Poesy*
- Nicolas Boileau-Despréaux: *The Art of Poetry*
- John Locke: *An Essay Concerning Human Understanding*
- John Dennis: *The Advancement and Reformation of Modern Poetry*
- Alexander Pope: *An Essay on Criticism*
- Joseph Addison: *On the Pleasures of the Imagination* (*Spectator* essays)
- Giambattista Vico: *The New Science*
- Edmund Burke: *A Philosophical Inquiry into the Origins of Our Ideas of the Sublime and the Beautiful*
- David Hume: *Of the Standard of Taste*
- Samuel Johnson: *On Fiction*, *Rasselas*, *Preface to* Shakespeare
- Edward Young: *Conjectures on Original Composition*
- Gotthold Ephraim Lessing: *Laocoön*
- Joshua Reynolds: *Discourses on Art*
- Richard "Conversation" Sharp Letters and Essays in Prose and Verse
- James Usher :*Clio: or a Discourse on Taste (1767)*
- Denis Diderot: *The Paradox of Acting*
- Immanuel Kant: *Critique of Judgement*
- Mary Wollstonecraft: *A Vindication of the Rights of Woman*
- William Blake: *The Marriage of Heaven or Hell*, *Letter to Thomas Butts*, *Annotations to Reynolds' Discourses*, *A Descriptive Catalogue*, *A Vision*

of the Last Judgement,On Homer's Poetry

- Friedrich Schiller: *Letters on the Aesthetic Education of Man*
- Friedrich Schlegel: *Critical Fragments, Athenaeum Fragments, On Incomprehensibility*

19TH-CENTURY CRITICISM

The British Romantic movement of the early nineteenth century introduced new aesthetic ideas to literary study, including the idea that the object of literature need not always be beautiful, noble, or perfect, but that literature itself could elevate a common subject to the level of the sublime. German Romanticism, which followed closely after the late development of German classicism, emphasized an aesthetic of fragmentation that can appear startlingly modern to the reader of English literature, and valued *Witz* – that is, "wit" or "humor" of a certain sort – more highly than the serious Anglophone Romanticism. The late nineteenth century brought renown to authors known more for critical writing than for their own literary work, such as Matthew Arnold.

Key texts

- William Wordsworth: *Preface to the Second Edition of* Lyrical Ballads
- Anne Louise Germaine de Staël: *Literature in its Relation to Social Institutions*
- Friedrich Wilhelm Joseph Schelling: *On the Relation of the Plastic Arts to Nature*
- Samuel Taylor Coleridge: *Shakespeare's Judgement Equal to His Genius, On the Principles of Genial Criticism, The Statesman's Manual, Biographia Literaria*
- Wilhelm von Humboldt: *Collected Works*
- John Keats: letters to Benjamin Bailey, George and Thomas Keats, John Taylor, and Richard Woodhouse
- Arthur Schopenhauer: *The World as Will and Idea*
- Thomas Love Peacock: *The Four Ages of Poetry*
- Percy Bysshe Shelley: *A Defence of Poetry*
- Johann Wolfgang von Goethe: *Conversations with Eckermann, Maxim No.279*
- Georg Wilhelm Friedrich Hegel: *The Philosophy of Fine Art*
- Thomas Carlyle: *Symbols*
- John Stuart Mill: *What is Poetry?*
- Ralph Waldo Emerson: *The Poet*
- Charles Augustin Sainte-Beuve: *What Is a Classic?*
- Edgar Allan Poe: *The Poetic Principle*
- Matthew Arnold: *Preface to the 1853 Edition of* Poems, *The Function of Criticism at the Present Time, The Study of Poetry*

- Hippolyte Taine: *History of English Literature*
- Charles Baudelaire: *The Salon of 1859*
- Karl Marx: *The German Ideology, A Contribution of the Critique of Political Economy*
- Søren Kierkegaard: *Two Ages: A Literary Review*, *The Concept of Irony*
- Friedrich Nietzsche: *The Birth of Tragedy from the Spirit of Music*, *Truth and Falsity in an Ultramoral Sense*
- Walter Pater: *Studies in the History of the Renaissance*
- Émile Zola: *The Experimental Novel*
- Anatole France: *The Adventures of the Soul*
- Oscar Wilde: *The Decay of Lying*
- Stéphane Mallarmé: *The Evolution of Literature*, *The Book: A Spiritual Mystery,Mystery in Literature*
- Leo Tolstoy: *What is Art?*

THE NEW CRITICISM

However important all of these aesthetic movements were as antecedents, current ideas about literary criticism derive almost entirely from the new direction taken in the early twentieth century. Early in the century the school of criticism known as Russian Formalism, and slightly later the New Criticism in Britain and in the United States, came to dominate the study and discussion of literature, in the English-speaking world.

Both schools emphasized the close reading of texts, elevating it far above generalizing discussion and speculation about either authorial intention (to say nothing of the author's psychology or biography, which became almost taboo subjects) or reader response. This emphasis on form and precise attention to "the words themselves" has persisted, after the decline of these critical doctrines themselves.

THEORY

In 1957 Northrop Frye published the influential *Anatomy of Criticism*. In his works Frye noted that some critics tend to embrace an ideology, and to judge literary pieces on the basis of their adherence to such ideology. This has been a highly influential viewpoint among modern conservative thinkers. E. Michael Jones, for example, argues in his*Degenerate Moderns* that Stanley Fish was influenced by his adulterous affairs to reject classic literature that condemned adultery.

In the British and American literary establishment, the New Criticism was more or less dominant until the late 1960s. Around that time Anglo-American university literature departments began to witness a rise of a more explicitly philosophical literary theory, influenced by structuralism, then post-structuralism, and other kinds of Continental philosophy. It continued until the mid-1980s, when interest in "theory" peaked. Many later critics, though undoubtedly still influenced by theoretical work, have been comfortable simply interpreting literature rather than writing explicitly about methodology and philosophical presumptions.

HISTORY OF THE BOOK

Related to other forms of literary criticism, the history of the book is a field of interdisciplinary inquiry drawing on the methods of bibliography, cultural history, history of literature, and media theory. Principally concerned with the production, circulation, and reception of texts and their material forms, book history seeks to connect forms of textuality with their material aspects.

Among the issues within the history of literature with which book history can be seen to intersect are: the development of authorship as a profession, the formation of reading audiences, the constraints of censorship and copyright, and the economics of literary form.

THE CURRENT STATE OF LITERARY CRITICISM

Today interest in literary theory and Continental philosophy coexists in university literature departments with a more conservative literary criticism of which the New Critics would probably have approved. Disagreements over the goals and methods of literary criticism, which characterized both sides taken by critics during the "rise" of theory, have declined. Many critics feel that they now have a great plurality of methods and approaches from which to choose.

Some critics work largely with theoretical texts, while others read traditional literature; interest in the literary canon is still great, but many critics are also interested in minority andwomen's literatures, while some critics influenced by cultural studies read popular texts like comic books or pulp/genre fiction. Ecocritics have drawn connections between literature and the natural sciences. Darwinian literary studies studies literature in the context of evolutionary influences on human nature. Many literary critics also work in film criticism or media studies. Some write intellectual history; others bring the results and methods of social history to bear on reading literature.

QUESTIONS TO THE VALUE OF ACADEMIC CRITICISM

The value of literary criticism has been questioned by some prominent artists. Vladimir Nabokov argued that good readers don't read books, and particularly literary masterpieces, "for the academic purpose of indulging in generalizations". Stephen J. Joyce, grandson of James Joyce, at a 1986 academic conference of Joyceans in Copenhagen, said "If my grandfather was here, he would have died laughing ... *Dubliners* and *A Portrait of the Artist as a Young Man* can be picked up, read, and enjoyed by virtually anybody without scholarly guides, theories, and intricate explanations, as can *Ulysses*, if you forget about all the hue and cry." And he questioned whether anything has been added to the legacy of Joyce's art by the 261 books of literary criticism stored in the Library of Congress.

NEW CRITICISM

New Criticism is a name applied to a varied and extremely energetic effort among Anglo-American writers to focus critical attention on literature itself. Like Russian Formalism, following Boris Eikhenbaum and Victor Shklovskii, the New Critics developed speculative positions on techniques of reading that provide a vital complement to the literary and artistic emergence of modernism.

In the specific context of Anglo-American literary study, however, the New Criticism appears, in retrospect, as part of an epochal project to create the curricular and pedagogical institutions by which the study of literature moved from the genteel cultivation of taste to an emerging professional academic discipline. In this respect, the New Criticism exhibits many similarities to Structuralism, just as it had an impact on the development of the French nouvelle critique and later, structuralist literary criticism as exemplified in the early work of Roland Barthes. In general, the far-reaching influence of New Criticism stems less from theoretical or programmatic coherence than from the practical (and pedagogical) appeal of a characteristic way of reading and its pervasive influence on the academic culture of Anglophone literary study.

The theoretical differences among the critics commonly described as New Critics (not necessarily by themselves)- I. A. RICHARDS, WILLIAM EMPSON, F. R. LEAVIS, KENNETH BURKE, John Crowe Ransom, Allen Tate, YVOR WINTERS, Cleanth Brooks, R. P.BLACKMUR, W. K. Wimsatt, Jr., RENÉ WELLEK-are sometimes so great as to leave little apparent ground for agreement. The New Critics tended to be eclectic on matters of theory, concentrating instead on what Blackmur called the critic's "job of work." For most of the New Critics that job was PRACTICAL CRITICISM or "close reading," in which the poem or literary text is treated as a self-sufficient verbal artifact.

In this general orientation, the literary text as such was generally viewed as a privileged site for shaping and disseminating cultural values held to be essential attribute of the aesthetic specificity of poetry. By careful attention to language, the text is presumed to be a unique source of meaning and value, sharply distinguished from other texts or other uses of language (particularly scientific language). Accordingly, the meaning of the poem is not conveyed by any prose paraphrase and is valued as the source of an experience (for the reader) available in no other way. For this among other reasons, opponents of the New Critics have frequently charged that they ignore history, ideology, politics, philosophy, or other factors that shape literary experience.

While such charges are not entirely fair, they arise because New Criticism in practice came to focus almost exclusively on problems of interpreting individual texts. Partly for this reason, New Criticism can still be considered a movement, beginning after World War I with the critical work of modern poets and critics, especially T. S. ELIOT, Richards, and somewhat later John Crowe

Ransom, culminating some 30 years later in the work o f explicitly academic critics, such as Wellek, Wimsatt, and Brooks.

The institutional dimension of the New Criticism is particularly clear in this respect, in the creation of enormously influential textbooks, the writing of histories not merely of literature but of criticism itself, and the practical working out of paradigmatic models for publishing literary criticism which could readily be taught to graduate students, and adapted to professional purposes, including (but not limited to) the granting of tenure and promotion. More explicitly, however, the force of the New Criticism as a movement is evident in the pervasive sense that literary study was strongly implicated in the formation and continuation of cultural values, precisely at a time when those values were perceived to be in peril.

This, as one of the major unifying motifs of diverse modernisms, provides a kind of background for the importance of a critical agenda carried out in professional, reasoned terms, not in what might otherwise seem the high-energy ranting of partisans— as, for example, in the emergence of the New Humanism under the leadership of Irving Babbitt, or other similar polemical attempts to re-argue the distinction between Romanticism and Classicism. It is of interest that the first use of the term, "The New Criticism" was in an essay of that title in Creative Criticism (1917) by Joel Spingarn, specifically as an antidote to the excesses of the New Humanist debates of that era.

The debt of the New Critics to T.S. Eliot was pervasive, but two germinal ideas from his essays shaped both New Critical theory and practice. In "Tradition and the Individual Talent" (1917), Eliot argued that the literature of Western Europe could be viewed as a "simultaneous order" of works, where the value of any new work depended on its relation to the order of the tradition. Thus, the work of the "individual talent" does not so much express a personality as it affects and is affected by the literature of the past.

Eliot was responding in part to complaints that modem poetry was too hard to understand, too austere, metaphysical, or unfamiliar. Eliot's essay asserts that difficult language reflects an equally difficult modern historical and psychological predicament. The point, however, is general: poetry as an historical process and a response to human predicaments is difficult, especially as the literature of any age is also a response to previous literature as a whole.

In "Hamlet and His Problems" (1919) Eliot further proposed that the effects of poetry stem from a relation between the words of the text and events, states of mind, or experiences that offer an "objective correlative". Eliot suggests that there is a unique experience to which the language of the poem corresponds: the poem means just what it says, but it is the "objective correlative" in experience that makes the intellectual and emotional value of the poem intelligible. Ironically, Eliot propounds this idea while arguing that Hamlet is a less than satisfactory play because no sufficient correlative (or too many correlatives) can be found.

A more encompassing irony is that both the origin and the collapse of New Criticism are contained in this point, where the precision of language demanded of the poem cannot be shown to determine a correlative meaning, "Objective" or otherwise. In suggesting that literature could be treated as a simultaneous order, a system, Eliot opened the way to more explicitly speculative and theoretical studies of literature, while in focusing attention on the fundamental operations by which literary works create intelligible structure, he provided an analytical example for critics that went well beyond traditional protocols for assigning critical praise or blame.

While Eliot himself evinces no strong inclination to pursue either explicit theory or critical technique, Richards pursued both, partly in an attempt to appraise the value of modem poets such as Eliot in explicitly theoretical terms and quite explicitly to advance the cause of English Studies, first at Cambridge and later, at other universities as far removed as China. Other critics, notably Leavis, pursued the questions as opportunities to re-evaluate literary history, explicitly as a "great tradition," continuing into the modem age, though far less in terms of the establishment of university departments and programmes than in a kind of stubborn, amateur pursuit of issues of taste.

I. A. Richards's Principles of Literary Criticism (1924) is arguably the first book in English that attempted to develop a comprehensive theory of criticism, a view Richards himself took in describing all previous speculation about literature as a "chaos" consisting of "random aperçues" and "brilliant guesses". According to Richards, a theory in criticism must offer both a theory of value and a theory of communication, on the assumption that poems communicate value, grounded on the reconciliation of conflicting "impulses" in the experience of the poet.

In Science and Poetry (1926) Richards elaborated his theory as it applied to the modem crisis of values. Following MATTHEW ARNOLD, Richards presumed that poetry could be an intellectually respectable substitute for religion in an emerging age of science. As an advocate for such a substitution, Richards urged that poetry; should be regarded as presenting, not statements, but rather "pseudo-statements" valued for an "emotive" meaning that could change our attitudes without requiring us to believe in what he called the "Magical View" as found in myth or traditional religion.

For the New Critics, however, Richards's most influential book was Practical Criticism (1929). The book reports in detail an experiment in critical reading in which students were presented with the texts of poems without their titles or the names of their authors. Put simply, this experiment represents a severe complication for Richards's theory of poetic communication, which he had assumed in his previous work to be relatively unproblematic and based almost entirely on "emotive" effects. In the experiment, students were given the texts of the poems and asked to write brief commentaries on them. For the most part, the experiment showed that poetry (as typically read or misread) did not reconcile conflicts but induced them, that instead of communicating valuable experience it provoked confusion and incomprehension.

The student responses, or "protocols," show a wide, sometimes bewildering range of irrelevant associations, "doctrinal adhesions," and confusions or uncertainties about sense, feeling, tone, and intent. Practical Criticism turned attention to the importance of teaching as it disclosed a problem that had largely escaped critical investigation: how do readers actually read? What do they actually understand, or fail to understand, and why? This work also crystallized what would become, for the New Critics, the central problems of poetic language and form.

One of Richards's students, the poet William Empson, pursued these problems with stunning effect in Seven Types of Ambiguity (1930), introducing many of the techniques of close reading that later became the hallmark of New Criticism. The book does not develop a systematic taxonomy of "types" but, rather, gives seven illustrations of increasingly complex ways in which poetry can be ambiguous or polysemous. In sometimes uncanny readings, Empson points out semantic relationships that a reader might miss habitually or systematically. In the United States, Richards's work prior to Practical Criticism (and prior to Empson's Seven Types) had relatively little effect. But as Allen Tate later remarked in (Essays o f Four Decades, 1970), "Nobody who read I. A. Richards' Practical Criticism when it appeared in 1929 could read any poem as he had read it before" (xi).

For a group of critics generally associated with the Agrarian Revival in the southern United States, many of whom taught at the University of the South, Vanderbilt University, and later Kenyon College, Practical Criticism offered a technical example that could be adapted to a quite different concern with the value of poetry in the modem world. Tate, John Crowe Ransom, and other agrarians viewed science not as a way out of mystification but as a direct threat to human values. While Richards saw poetry as a way to reconcile us to a brave new world, these critics recommended a conservative return to religion and, more particularly, a return to an agrarian style of life that set itself in deliberate opposition to industrialization.

Similar concerns were expressed by critics who did not share the ideological views of the agrarians, critics whom MURRAY KRIEGER has called "apologists for poetry" (New Apologists for Poetry, 1956). Yvor Winters, for example, argued for reading poetry as moral statement (especially in In Defence of Reason, 1949) while Kenneth Burke, in some ways following Richards, viewed literature as "equipment for living" (The Philosophy of Literary Form, 1941). In one of his most influential essays, "Poetry: A Note in Ontology" (in The World's Body, 1934), Ransom insisted on the priority in poetry of attention to the concrete image as natural object, in opposition to what he called "Platonism," or the impulse to render the world in terms of abstract ideas. This Platonism, for Ransom, is "always sciencing and devouring" and thereby represents both the force of scientific reason and the threat of industrialism. While this distinction recalls Richards's distinction between scientific and emotive uses of language, the difference of attitude is profound. Where Richards viewed the rise of science and "modernity" as generally beneficial, it represented for Ransom and many of his associates (especially Allen Tate) a form of oppression to be vigorously opposed. Tate, however, insisted that the field of knowledge must not be so easily surrendered—as it appears to be in the work of both Richards and Ransom (Tate).

To see poetry as a form of knowledge, however, requires renewed attention to the meaning of poetry and its relation to poetic language, generally treated as if it were merely technical problem. In later essays, Ransom modified his position so far as to admit that poetic language was the union of "logical structure" and "local texture," without compromising his insistence on the "rich contingent materiality" of poetry (Stauffer). As he later said in his essay "The Literary Criticism of Aristotle," "the critic never ceases to be impressed with his fine object" and, as a literary man himself, "starts with a spontaneous surge of piety, and is inducted by the contagion of art into a composition of his own" But.

Ransom also saw the value of academic criticism and the virtues of more precise abstract argument and literary scholarship. Increasingly, he moved away from the conservative ideology of his earlier essays to a position of mediation and acceptance of a wider range of critical practice by other critics who did not share his political or cultural views but were nevertheless encouraged by him and published in journals with which he was associated, such as the Southern Review, the Sewanee Review, and the Kenyon Review.

An important factor in the reputation of New Criticism as a movement is that it was, especially in the period just before and after World War II, a phenomenon of periodical journals, such as those just mentioned, together with Leavis's Scrutiny in England. Thriving in a climate of vitality for "little magazines," prevalent in the cultural scene in both America and England since the 1920s, New Criticism attracted younger critics by the exampl e of dist inc t iv e essays with a t l e as t a rhetoric i c a l and thematic family resemblance, in which a concentration on literary form made a wide range of cultural and aesthetic topics available for treatment in shorter critical articles.

While the variations are as rich as the literature examined, the New Critical essay is generally characterized by a close attention to the language of the text, to show a pattern of formal and thematic features that the critic commonly argues are fundamental to understanding the meaning of the work as a whole but that are expressed in terms that foreground the formal unity or balance of the work. Essays by Blackmur in particular reflect an increasing degree of sophisticated concentration on matters of poetic form, technique, and value. Blackmur's criticism (like his poetry) reflects his conviction that "literature is the bearer... of all the modes of understanding of which words are capable; and not only that: it also bears, sets in motion or life, certain modes which words merely initiate and symbolize." In this respect, literature was "always specific and unique; never general and repeated" and thus not really amenable to formal theoretical explanation (The Lion and the Honeycomb: Essays in Solicitude and Critique, 1955).

Although resolutely independent, and not a follower of any group, Blackmur is in many ways the paradigmatic New Critic as essayist. He approached criticism as the necessary expression of the man of letters contemplating the modes of words and their value. In contrast, the impact of one of Ransom's later students, Cleanth Brooks, on academic criticism has been a good deal more specific, both in practice and in theory. Brooks's influential textbook Understanding Poetry (1939), written with Robert Penn Warren, provided practical and teachable examples.

The Well Wrought Urn (1947) presented both exemplary instances of New Critical practice and a central account of New Critical doctrines that in many ways appears as a synthesis of ideas from Ransom, Eliot, Richards, and Empson. Following arguments begun in Modern Poetry and the Tradition (1939), Brooks set out to demonstrate that the tension, paradox, and ambiguity of much modern (and metaphysical) poetry—of just the sort exemplified by Eliot's poetry and explicated by Empson—was fundamental to the nature of poetry. In The Well Wrought Urn Brooks showed that in every age, in diverse styles, a quality of dramatic tension or paradox was essential to poetic meaning, so much so as to warrant the claim that poetry and paradox are all but identical.

Like Blackmur, however, Brooks's persuasiveness lay in the essays on individual texts and authors, while explicit theoretical speculation tended to take a secondary role. For Brooks, the term "paradox" calls attention to the finding that no easy distinction between "form" and "content" can be maintained without distorting the overall meaning of the poem: the form of the poem uniquely embodies its meaning, which may itself seem "paradoxical" within a commonsense notion of literal or referential "meaning". More particularly, Brooks asserted that the language of the poem itself effects the reconciliation of opposites or contraries and that the result is the meaning of the poem. In this way, Brooks replaced the psychologism of Richards's theory of reconciling and balancing experiential "impulses" by claiming that the effect was embodied in poetic language itself.

Brooks concluded The Well Wrought Urn by describing what he called the "Heresy of Paraphrase," arguing that any attempt to reduce poetic meaning to a prose statement of a theme or a description of a plot was a betrayal of the poem as a poem.

By using the term "heresy" when in truth there was no proper orthodoxy of interpretation from which to depart, Brooks virtually guaranteed polemical replies to his position, just as he called attention to a pervasive perplexity about how to construct a viable theory—which may seem to the individual theorist to be a direct description of a literary reality, but appears to others as saturated with an incompletely examined ideology or system of values.

While critics such as Blackmur had regarded explicit theory as either redundant or irrelevant, the increasingly vigorous practice of critical interpretation led to frequently irresolvable conflicts over rival interpretations that seemed mutually exclusive. Thus, the very success of New Critical practice called attention to theoretical problems that had never been adequately addressed, just as its practical strength in producing intelligible readings is the source of a persistent anomaly of incompatible readings that no available postulates appear able to resolve. A similar mixture of theory and polemic is evident in two influential essays by W. K. Wimsatt, Jr., and Monroe Beardsley, "The Intentional Fallacy" and "The Affective Fallacy" (Wimsatt,), which argued, respectively, that reports of an author's original intention are not germane to judging a work of art, which either succeeds or fails according to what is actually expressed in its words, and that the meaning of a poem cannot be equated with how it affects a reader.

A "heresy" may be more damning than a "fallacy," but both imply that there is a correct position and that it is in some way securely sanctioned. In this case, however, the supposition that one could accurately interpret texts without reference to authorial intention presents so severe a test of the reader that a strict avoidance of the intentional fallacy almost forces the reader into the affective fallacy, since the reader of the text is, by default, the only judge-as post-New Critical theorists, such as Norman Holland, David Bleich, or Stanley Fish, advocating different versions of Readerresponse thory and criticism, have not hesitated to assert. In perhaps the most ambitious (and least polemical) attempt to articulate a theory for New Criticism, Theory of Literature (1949), René Wellek and Austin Warren distinguish between the "intrinsic" and "extrinsic" study of literature.

The former concentrates on the work as a "stratified system of norms," whereas the latter relegates literary biography, history, psychology, and sociology to the "extrinsic" domain, a move that incurred the ire of literary historians, scholars, sociologists, and so on. In all of these major postwar efforts to consolidate theoretical gains, the same general problem persists: there is no well-grounded way to ascertain the validity of any particular interpretation.

Thus, E. D. Hirsch argued in Validity in Interpretation (1967) that the proliferation of incommensurable interpretations required a return to historical evidence ("extrinsic," according to Wellek and Warren) to buttress appeals to the author's intention (pronounced a "fallacy" by Wimsatt and Beardsley). Unfortunately, the historical documents from which Hirsch presumed authorial intention could be ascertained are themselves subject to a similar interpretive dilemma. While most of the early New Critics were no strangers to controversy, one of the most serious attacks came from R. S. Crane, who had earlier been welcomed by John Crowe Ransom as one of the most important "new critics."

In the late 1940s, Crane and his colleagues at the University of Chicago had been included in Robert Stallman's very influential anthology, Critiques and Essays in Criticism (1949) which defined New Criticism by default as what contemporary critics were actually doing.

Crane and his colleagues at Chicago had also argued strenuously for making criticism central in the English curriculum, and with Ransom, Tate, and Brooks, they had emphasized the issue of poetic form, but the CHICAGO CRITICS followed ARISTOTLE and Richard McKeon instead of SAMUEL TAYLOR COLERIDGE, Arnold, Eliot, and Richards. Crane edited a collection of essays by various hands, Critics and Criticism: Ancient and Modern (1952), which, like Brooks's The Well Wrought Urn, sought to demonstrate the coherence of an approach to poetic form across a broad range of periods and styles. But included within the volume were a series of highly polemical attacks on Richards, Empson, and Brooks, who had, according to the Chicago critics, impoverished criticism by concentrating on only one element of form, its language, or "diction."

In "The Critical Monism of Cleanth Brooks" Crane argues that Brooks and other New Critics impoverish theory by making irony or paradox a unique principle of structure, and he points out with sharp effect that the balancing and reconciliation of opposites that Brooks ' held to be the sole differentia of "poetic" language was in fact the characteristic of all connected discourse. By Brooks's own criteria, the best example of a modern "ironic" poem was Einstein's formula E = mc2, asserting the paradoxical identity of matter and energy (104).

Crane, however, treated this result as a reductio ad absurdum, deriving from the New Critics' "morbid obsession" with trying differentiate poetry from science by looking merely at its language—which Crane reduces, after Aristotle, to poetic "diction", the least important "element" in defining poetry. In Crane's view, the proper place to start was with "concrete poetic wholes of various kinds" (105), ignoring the fact that a poetic whole is not in any meaningful way "concrete," but verbal, and that any idea of its wholeness required some interpretation of its language.

Perhaps inadvertently, however, Crane's polemic locates a fundamental problem in formalism and structuralism of all varieties, including his own and that of the logical positivists, whom the New Critics since Ransom had regarded as irreconcilable enemies. In this sense, what might have been a family quarrel among American academic critics turns out to be especially helpful for understanding the demise of New Criticism as well as its genetic relation to the archetypal structuralism of NORTHROP FRYE and to later, poststructuralist criticism.

The central premise in this dispute is that literature ought to be definable (and thereby differentiated from science) by reference to formal properties of its language, an assumption shared by all parties to this dispute, including the logical positivists (who may have thought they had already won this battle) and by other theorists and critics for whom form and structure were decisive concerns. In a striking example of Coleridge's favourite maxim, "Extremes meet," the New Critics and the logical positivists, appearing as opposites, are so only because of a common commitment to the proposition that there must be some fundamental opposition between the referential language of science and the expressive, which I. A. Richards had decisively characterized as the "emotive" language of poetry.

Rudolph Carnap embraced this distinction in his first English publication, Philosophy and Logical Syntax (1935), which appeared in the Psyche Miniatures series edited by Richards's colleague and frequent collaborator, C. K. Ogden. Carnap used the distinction, however, as a grounds for rejecting metaphysical propositions because they assert nothing verifiable but have, like lyric poems, "no assertorial sense, no theoretical sense... [and do] not contain knowledge". In the same work, for similar reasons, he adopts Richards's disastrous notion of the "pseudo statement" in order to guard against any unwary acceptance of abstract entities (*e.g.*, numbers) as if they existed In a material mode.

The ironic importance of this connection is played out in Crane's major effort to launch a "newer criticism" in his much less polemical book, The Languages of Criticism and the Structure of Poetry (1953), calling for a radical "pluralism" in critical theory, in which the relativity between the "kind of questions" one poses about literature and the kind of answers that thereby appear to be appropriate leads Crane to borrow terms explicitly from Carnap. According to Crane, this matrix of questions and answers constitutes a critical "framework," which is chosen not because it captures an incontrovertible reality but because, on "practical" grounds, it reflects what a group of critics may be interested in pursuing. But Crane's acknowledged source for this idea is Carnap's classic essay, "Empiricism, Semantics, and Ontology" (1950, reprinted from Meaning and Necessity, 1956), in many ways a last-ditch effort to save logical positivism from accepting the reality of "metaphysical" entities.

Carnap had argued that one introduces and accepts a "framework" in order to be able to speak about such "entities" as numbers, space-time coordinates, and so on, without having to commit to a belief in their existence. The artifice of the "framework" then protects statements made within it, allowing them to be construed and evaluated for truth and theoretical cogency, without metaphysical compromises.

Crane, however, construed this as a warrant for theoretical pluralism, in which there may be many "incommensurable" frameworks—*i.e.* "theories"—for discussing poetry.

In this vision of critical laissez-faire, it is up to the critic to persuade others to accept one framework rather than another, on the practical basis of what a given framework will allow one to say and do. What Carnap proposed, however, is strikingly different, since the existence of "incommensurable" frameworks for numbers, for example, would only indicate that no "framework" had in fact been accepted, thereby preventing the development of any arithmetic theory to which mathematicians could assent. Carnap identified the "practical" problem with the acceptance of a framework, as the necessary condition for making statements that could be evaluated as true or false. The apposite analogy for literary study is that the existence of multiple incommensurable "frameworks" for the poem indicates that there is no general agreement about why or whether it is useful to talk about literature, and hence, no "framework" at all in Carnap's sense, to guarantee that statements about literature could be theoretically consistent and consequential.

Given the increasing evidence that New Critical readings of texts could proliferate indefinitely without the prospect of resolving mutually exclusive readings of the same poem, critical pluralism may have existed by default. It is therefore not surprising that Crane's argument did not succeed either in quelling the errors he had found in New Criticism or in establishing a new Aristotelian "framework".

On the contrary, it led to yet another round of polemical argument, now led by Wimsatt. In his essay "The Chicago Critics: The Fallacy of the non-classic Species" (1953, reprinted in T h e Verbal Icon) Wimsatt imagines a stage on which stands the contemporary critic, a composite, let us say, of Richards, Eliot, Empson, Brooks and Warren, and Tate. He is wearing the mask of his role in the drama to be enacted, a tolerably good, clean, bright critic's mask, though, let us say, it has some smudges on it (the psychologism of Richards, for instance, the excessive ingenuities of Empson). Enter: Professor Crane. He walks up to the critic and, taking a piece of burnt cork from his pocket, proceeds to blacken the mask all over.

"There now," he says, "that is what you really look like." The scene concludes with Crane reclaiming the mask, partially cleaning it, then writing "Aristotle" on the forehead to announce, "This looks a lot better on me than it did on you" (45- 46). Pluralism in this guise is hard to distinguish from bickering, and one could say that by the mid-1950s, while New Critical practice was still thriving in journal articles and classrooms, New Critical theorizing had come to an un resolvable impasse. Literary historians such as' Douglas Bush and Frederick Pottle continued the complaint that New Critical practice impoverished literary understanding by giving inadequate attention to historical specificity.

Critics such as Murray Krieger and Philip Wheelwright sought a way beyond the impasse by a more systematic and intensive alignment of criticism with aesthetic theory and with philosophical studies of language and metaphor, while attempting to preserve the characteristic qualities of New Critical practice. Clearly the boldest theorist to emerge in the aftermath of the polemical quarrels of the late 1950s was Northrop Frye, whose Anatomy of Criticism (1957) turned back to Eliot and to an Inductive survey of the literary field to view the "masterpieces of literature" as "phenomena to be explained in terms of a conceptual framework which criticism alone possesses".

In using Carnap's metaphor (quite probably drawn from Crane), Frye attempted to articulate a framework of precisely the kind Carnap had recommended. In, place of Eliot's "simultaneous order" of works, Frye proposed a total "order of words" in which literature "imitates the total dream of man", structured in and through literary archetypes. In writing an anatomy of criticism, Frye set out explicitly to integrate all of his more or less contentious critical ancestors, including Aristotle, WILLIAM BLAKE, Coleridge and Arnold, Eliot and Richards, Brooks and Crane, into a theory of literature as cultural communication drawing from Romantic theories of symbolism and the medieval fourfold theory of interpretation. The result is a syncretic and encyclopedic survey that marks a passage from formalism to an indigenous Anglo-American literary structuralism.

Where CLAUDE LEVI-STRAUSS focused on myth, Frye focused on the archetype; where Levi-Strauss drew upon FERDINAND DE SAUSSURE, Frye exploited T. S. Eliot's idea of a total order of words. From this point of view, Free can be seen as both the point of highest achievement of the modem tradition of New Criticism and the point of its irreversible collapse. For "myth" and "structure",in Levi-Strauss, like the "archetype" and "analogy" in Frye, are both subject to the same radical critique.

The "myth or the "archetype" appears to posit a form of transcendental agency that brings it into being, without having any way to explain that agency or to explain how it is that semantic or semiological differences arise. To see Frye as the culmination of New Criticism, however, is to see in his work both what is of enduring value in the movement and what is most vulnerable on theoretical grounds. New Criticism, from Eliot to Frye, sponsored a project in the reformation of critical reading that first called attention to the radical specificity of poetic language and dramatically widened the scope for poetic interpretation. Its theoretical frustrations represent less a failure than a gradual realization that a radical rethinking would be required, on a wide range of philosophical and metaphysical issues, and thus prepared the way for a more general pursuit of theory by later critics.

If the common belief of the New Critics in a fundamental linguistic opposition between poetry and science is untenable, and all uses of language reflect an intrinsic degree of freedom in the production of meaning, then the history of New Criticism may mark at once the end of a philosophical epoch and the beginning of a brave new world of speculative criticism. In precisely that spirit, moreover, subsequent critiques of the New Criticism have centered on the underlying cultural ideology, to some degree masked by the technical concentration on the aesthetic dimension of language, where the overriding issue lies in clarifying the purpose of literary work, as a form of cultural practice and a form of reasoning that may have the capacity to even more radically disrupt the philosophical heritage that began with Plato's attempt to exile the unpredictable creativity of the poetic as a disruption to a metaphysical pursuit of incontrovertible Truth.

Thus, the dilemmas of the New Criticism remain deeply implicated in such movements as the New Historicism, quarrels over the literary canon (see especially in this regard John Guillory's Cultural Capital), and the emergence of diverse forms of cultural studies. The enduring importance of the New Criticism in this regard lies in its institutional importance and its insistence on the practice of close reading, whatever conceptual justifications may be involved in putting it to use.

2

Historical Criticism

INTRODUCTION TO HISTORY OF CRITICISM

The history of criticism may be taken to mean either of two things: The history of the practice of criticism, or the history of critical theory. While the two are intimately related, they have not always advanced at the same rate of progress, nor developed along lines which are exactly parallel. For purposes of study and investigation, therefore, they may be regarded as measurably distinct.

Origin of Criticism

For the origin of criticism we must go back to very early times. Expressions of approval or disapproval that may be looked upon as primitive critical utterances, are found in some of the oldest monuments of literature. According to Mr. Bosanquet the following passage from the Iliad on the shield of Achilles, is one of the earliest aesthetic judgements in Western literature: "The earth looked dark behind the plough, and like to ground that had been ploughed, although it was made of gold; that was a marvellous piece of work." Whether the Homeric poems contain criticisms of literature, as well as criticisms of art, is a question the student should investigate for himself. The Vedas, the Nibelungen Lied, Old-English poetry, the Kalevala, and other early literatures may be examined with the same end in view.

The causes, psychological or social, which give rise to expressions of criticism may also be explored. These may be brought out by questions such as the following: Of what is criticism the outcome. Of curiosity, as held by Mr. Arnold. Of curiosity and self-expression combined, as suggested by Mr. Robertson. Of egotism. Of wonder. Of admiration. Of the competition of poets or schools of poets. Of a universal spirit of denial or pessimism. Or of "a divine discontent".

An interesting subject for investigation is the question whether criticism in literature, as in philosophy, is preceded by dogmatism and skepticism.These are questions to be asked in specific cases when the student has the evidence before him.

The principle of development in the practice of criticism should be examined both deductively and inductively. Working deductively, we may inquire whether the nature of criticism is such that in its history a law of evolution, or of progression, or of rhythmical alternation, is likely to be exemplified. Is it not so bound up with its object-matter, literature, that independent development is impossible.

Working inductively, we must first determine what shall be regarded as a sign of advance in criticism, whether increase in intellectual activity; in amount of production; in ability to deal adequately with past literature; in ability to estimate the value of current literature; in ability to forecast the literary future; in catholicity of appreciation; or in rationality of critical judgement. Furnished with a provisional test of this kind, we may examine in chronological order the critical utterances of a period or a people, noting, as we read, the signs of progress, of retrograde, or of rhythmical ebb and flow. The relation of criticism to the character of the age and the spirit of the people should also receive attention, as well as the influence of a preceding age on a following, and of one people upon another.

Questions which should be kept in view are: Whether the same principle of growth is observed in all countries and at all times; and whether this principle of growth is independent of, or intimately related to, the principle which determines the growth of literature.

Stages Of Growth

Critical practice, if it develops in an orderly way, should exhibit well-marked stages of progression. One kind or phase of criticism should come into being, rise, flourish, decay, and pass into another kind or phase. As a fact, do such stages appear in the history of criticism. If so, the student should note at what points the lines of demarcation occur, and the reasons why they occur where they do.

He should observe whether criticism tends to pass from negative to positive, from abstract to concrete; and where a succession of stages has been discovered he should endeavor to arrive at the leading characteristic of each. Such orders of succession as are indicated by the terms (a) Synthetic, (b) Analytic, (c) Organic; or the terms (a) Clan, (b) Individual, (c) Social, may be suggested as helpful; but the student should not adopt them as working bases without careful, independent research. It may not be unnecessary to suggest the following simple and convenient chronological division: 1. Ancient, including (a) Oriental, (b) Greek, (c) Roman; 2. Mediaeval; 3. Renaissance; 4. Modern.

Demarcation

A comparison may be made of different countries to determine whether the different kinds of criticism develop everywhere in similar fashion. The student should note whether activity in one kind of criticism is always accompanied by activity in other kinds. The question should also be asked whether the various types of literary criticism, as judicial and inductive, appear contemporaneously. Most writers who touch upon them assume that one follows and grows out of the other, *e.g.*, inductive follows judicial criticism. But is this borne out by the facts.

Certain periods in literary history are distinguished as periods of great critical activity. Examples are the Alexandrian age of Greek literature, the eighteenth century in English literature, the present century in French literature.

They are often set over against periods of great creative activity, such as the age of the tragic poets of Greece and the Elizabethan age of England. An age of criticism is often said to alternate with an age of creation. Matthew Arnold holds that critics set in motion the ideas, which the creative writer makes, use of when his turn comes. It will be well to examine the critical literature of so-called creative periods, in order to determine the amount and value of it. In some cases it will be found more extensive and of much greater importance than is generally supposed.

Criticism And Literature

Criticism, according to some writers, can hasten, retard, or divert the currents of literary energy. It can get the ear of the public for an author who would otherwise remain obscure; it can hold back for many years the recognition due to genius; it can lead or drive a writer into modes of expression which, if he were left to his own impulses, he would not choose to cultivate. By others all these statements are denied. Indeed, the fact's that are brought forward by one side to prove the critic's power, are sometimes regarded by the other side as evidences of his impotence.

It may be that both extremes are wrong, and that the truth lies somewhere between them. Thus, it may be that different kinds of criticism are of different degrees of effectiveness. If negative criticism has no deterrent influence, constructive criticism may yet have power to hasten. Inductive criticism may prevail after judicial criticism has spent itself in vain.

Under the second head, the influence of literature on criticism, an interesting question is as to the effect which a new and splendid work of genius exerts upon critical opinion. The effect of Shakespeare's plays, of Milton's Paradise Lost, of Goethe's Faust, of the novels of Scott, Dickens, Thackeray, and George Eliot, upon the movement of European criticism, may be studied in contemporary pamphlets, essays, and reviews. Another question is whether critical practice lags behind literary creation. It has been said that the critic can do no more than convince his generation. Is this true. Has not criticism at times outstripped creative literature, so called. Has not some critic in each epoch foreseen the course of literary development.

Development of Criticism Theory

By criticism as theory we mean the principles which critics have brought forward as the ground of their judgements or as the basis of their methods of procedure. As grounds of judgement they may or may not be the same as the principles of artistic or literary practice. The critic may work upon one principle, the artist whom he criticises upon another. Again, the critic's practice may not conform to his theory. Most of the questions upon criticism as practice will apply to critical theory as well.

First Appearance

(a) To be discovered by an examination of early literatures. What writer first gives reasons for his expressions of approval or disapproval. (b) What principles underlie the earliest criticisms, and why should these principles get the start of the rest.

Provenience

Where and when did the various principles of criticism come into being. Many of them have been handed down from early times, and transmitted from nation to nation with the progress of culture. Many are known to be of recent origin. Possibly examples may be found of independent rediscovery of old principles.

Laws of Development

Does the body of critical theory grow by accretion. By the development of contradictions, which, destroying one another, give place to new principles. By the development of specialized forms, or members with specific functions, like a plant or an animal. Where seek for the principle of critical evolution — in psychology, anthropology, philosophy, sociology, or biology. Mr. Robertson suggests Herbert Spencer's law of economy as a fundamental principle according to which divergent opinions tend to unanimity.

Stages of development

The stages of development in arttheory outlined in the general histories of aesthetics, such as Schasler's and Bosanquet's, may be applied with little change to the history of criticism. The same may be said of the periods or movements indicated in the standard histories of literature. How far do these divisions correspond to the stages of criticism as such.

Critical Theory and Literature

Does criticism lay down laws and principles for literature, or does literature give laws and principles to criticism. In the works of reputable writers probably every critical theory is exemplified; but which came first, the theory or the work. The question should be answered by a comparative study of the literatures of several periods or of several nationalities.

Science and Critical Theory

The effect of the scientific spirit upon recent critical theories and methods, as in the case of Taine, Sainte-Beuve, Brunetière, and Moulton, is a striking phenomenon. It will be interesting to note what each of the scientific critics understands by the term science, and the use each makes of it. Are these theories really scientific or only quasi-scientific. Or perhaps pseudo-scientific.

Critical Theory and Critical Practice

The main question to be asked under this head is the following: In the case of any particular critic, how far is his critical theory adequate to the task which he has undertaken. A similar question may be asked with regard to the critical literature of a given period, or of a nation.

HISTORICIST CRITICISM

New Historicist Criticism took shape in the late 1970s and early 1980s as opposed to New Criticism and to the critical deconstruction. It is also new and differ markedly from its former (old) historicism to view literature as a stable events which can be used as "background" of an era, or simply as a "reflection" that refer to material condition (as in early Marxism) of particular epoch of literature. Instead, it views literary texts as "situated" and "negotiated" the oft-disregard fragmentary view lies beyond a work. How relevant the concepts and procedures of New Historicism to the development of literary criticism in the department? What may New Historicism offer either to students or lecturers? What is implied within its use? In order to answer those critical questions, thus, it is critical to put the basic concepts, themes, and procedures of New Historicism within the context of its method so as to fulfill a fair basic assumption on the criticism and its relevance.

As suggested, profoundly configure those fragmentary presumptions on concepts which can be used as the basic themes on New Historicism reading procedures. In essence, the use of the method on literary works would be dependent and be flexible, as it suggested (within New Historicism) that no claim for exclusiveness on theories by means that every work develops its greatness on the background of the epoch that it evolved from. This flexibility is accordingly determined by the problems that occurred and resolved with the provision of theories, as it is inferred within the basic concept of New Historicism that there is no master discourse (theory).

WHAT IS NEW IN NEW HISTORICISM

New Historicism is first introduced by Stephen Greenblatt in 1980s, as he often refers this term to be a set of practices of 'cultural poetics'. The first appearance of New Historicism; its concepts, themes and procedures were most presumed by the scholar of the English Renaissance in the late of 1970s and early of 1980s. They stressed their attention to the literary form of drama, and alert within such texts the voices of the oppressed, the marginalized, and the dispossessed. In advanced, students and historicists of the English Romantic redeveloped parallel conceptions of the inter-textuality of literature, history and politics.

They suggested that the representations in literary texts are not simply as reflectors of reality but concretized the absence of history in order to uncover the literature and political contradictions. In 1990s, it viewpoints and practices have displaced deconstruction as the reigning mode of avant-garde critical theory and practice, that it stressed the embeddedness of literature in historical circumstances. New Historicism, then, becomes one of several theories and approach in literary theory within almost these three decades of the 20th century. What is new within this 'theory'?

As Hitchcock posits in his Theory for Classics that:

- Like so many words in the English language, theory comes from the Greek theoria, which means "a viewing" or "spectacle" and offers a way of seeing. In this way, theory serves like a pair of conceptual spectacles that you use to frame and focus on what you're looking at. It can serve as a tool for discerning, deciphering, and making sense. Alternatively, theory can provide a position from which to engage in a critique of the status quo.

Even so, the connection and its relevancy of interdisciplinary methods or theories provide readers and critics to see that such principal or one basic theory can be no longer appropriate on presenting interpretation. In fact, several researches precisely unpacked several approaches to uncover its problems. It demands conceptual basics of interdisciplinary approaches and theories. New Historicism, therefore, provides needs on that fragmentary view instead of one ultimate interpretation which is an illusionary exploitation of the unitary work. This exploitation is considerably discriminations between literature and non-literary texts to be a construct of one ultimate ideology of discursive formations. The nature of representation is the most important issue in our understanding of what is history.

This nature simply elaborated within these illustrations that, an author always present his/her (literary) work through several ways, and, it is readers/critics who represent the author's objectives within numerous method(s). Old Historicism had failed to see that history as 'background' of literary overview, that literary works is not only the production of history but it also produces the history, norms, conventions and cultural values of an era. Neither formalism nor New Criticism critics succeed to ensure the autonomous of the text itself as the method. Texts can be manipulated, to see history simply within its text is sometimes ambiguous and often conflicting textual representations, it bears the marks of repeated emendations additions, deletions, embellishments, translations. New historicism, however, adjust these approaches of formalism and history described in oft-quoted phrase by Louise Montrose, as "a reciprocal concern with the historicity of texts and the textuality of history." That is, history is an interaction of texts to be interpreted, and any text is conceived as a discourse in which consists of what we called representations.

THE TERMS, THEORY AND PRACTICE: MICHEL FOUCAULT

- Whenever one can describe, between a number of statements, such a system of dispersion, whenever, between objects, types of statement, concepts, or thematic choices, one can define a regularity (an order, correlations, positions and functionings, transformations), as suggested, say, for the sake of convenience, that we are dealing with a discursive formation.

Michel Foucault (1926–84) was a French philosopher, social and intellectual historian, and renowned cultural critic. The methodology of exploring the relation between discourse and reality of an era puts Foucault into account on leading New Historicists viewpoint. Foucault defines a discourse as language practice, which is language as it is used by various constituencies (the law, the medicine, the church, etc) for purposes to do power relationships between people. As he posits in The Archaeology of Knowledge that 'discourse' refer to 'the general domain of all statements, sometimes as an individualized group of statements, and sometimes as a regulated practice that accounts for a number of statements'. Moreover, Foucault asserts, discourse brought us into accounts of its discursive regularities, [to apprehend] that there are some external and internal exclusions (Foucault's terms) when discourses are being produced, such a complex system of multiple constraints acts which bring discourse into existence. There are some external exclusions overcome the set of discourse procedures, they are: the taboo, the distinction between mad and sane, and the distinction between true and false.

In addition, Foucault asserts another four internal exclusions within the discourse procedures, they are: commentary, author, disciplines, and the rarefaction of speaking subject. Thus, discourses should be seen as groups of statements which are associated with institutions, which are authorized in some sense and which have some unity of function at a fundamental level. Let us merely put this pattern of discourses into a very example we often found daily, which supported Foucault ideas into our society and comprehension. The taboo, wherever it defined, is a kind of prohibition (of statement) that make us difficult or restricted to say something more about it, for example, sexuality, religion, death, etc. The distinction between mad and sane, indeed, considered as universal agreement that only the statements of those considered sane are attended to, the speech of insane is treated as if it did not exist, as if it just the phantasm. This is related closely with the third external exclusion that those in position of authority who are seen as 'expert' are those who can 'only' speak the truth, otherwise, they are considered as insane (for instance), not-proper-person-yet, or any discriminative judgements. Foucault shows in his work how truth is something which is supported materially by a whole range of practices and institutions: universities, government departments, publishing houses, scientific bodies and so on. As Sara Mills posits in his statement: 'Thus, even if we are asserting something which as far as we know it is 'the truth', our statements will only be judged to be 'true' if they accord with, and fit in with, all of other statements which are authorized within our society. Commentary regards to literary terms is simply defined as writing about another's statement.

Thus, literary criticism can be considered to be commentary. The idea of commentary is that discourses (statements) will vanish as soon as they have been pronounced, it demonstrates that this kind of speech acts (commentary) bring discourse into existences by its formulation. Author function is (used) as an organizing principle of the texts, when we regard the author as the core of the works' meaning then we need to be alert that his/her discourse is something to be interpreted, something to be elaborated into other statements, that is why discourses are sometimes called emergent, it comes out from one (author) 'presents' into others' (critics) 'represents'. Disciplines are the other exclusions which Foucault asserted, that everything is reduced into categorical disciplines, the limits which we place on subject areas into disciplinary boundary.

For example, if we work within economy, as suggested, generally approach them on a particular range of methods and theoretical tools (*e.g.* Marxism). Or else we work within the same subject but different perspectives, for example structuralism and colonialism, as suggested, approach them and delimit those subjects in different ways and tools (as if to focus). In fact, these practices/boundaries exclude knowledge which might challenge them, any discourses (*e.g.* Deconstruction and Orientalism). The rarefaction of speaking subject could be simply showed within practical institutions, the government, for instance, along with its hierarchical department there will be unwritten rules which is explained that only those in higher positions of authority who can speak without restraint.

He also employs the idea of the episteme to indicate a particular group of knowledge and discourses which operate as the dominant discourses for ideological purposes, which take place from period to period in any given historical epoch. The episteme connects all the separate discourse (religious, scientific, historical, and medical, etc) into more or less coherent structure of thought, a discursive formation. Therefore, drawing from one partiality (discourse) to a bigger fragment (episteme), it can always be related back to a bigger unit so as to configure what called archives, which indicates a mode of analysis or methodology of discursive formations and statements, the archeology. This methodology is apparently applied in New Historicism spirit that the contexts of representations are inevitably entailed the appropriations of those discursive practices.

FOUCAULT AND NEW HISTORICISM

They have reduced liberty, beauty and risk. Liberty, beauty and risk may be reclaimed, if at all, in the techniques that people are able to apply to the shaping of their own existence. This is Foucault's way of becoming not an anti-humanist but a post-humanist, not a writer on the left but a post-revolutionary writer. Foucault's shift has been absorbed into "new historicism" within academic literary studies, nevertheless, without maintaining the concrete ethical and political interests that drove his work. Without maintaining the concrete ethical and political interest that drove Foucault's work, made Foucault as one of the prominent critics of New Historicism.

As it mingled with and embraced every aspects of life. This is the appropriation of interdisciplinary framework of New Historicist criticism, on which presented hand-in hand the pragmatic consequences on theoretical fragmentary viewpoints. Some factors at a certain point of time influencing the creation of a text: New Historicists argue that all levels of society share in the circulation of power through the production and distribution of the most elementary cultural and social text; include literature, laws, and sciences. The New Historicism theory and practice can be simply showed below:

Thus, New Historicists encompasses every single thing regarding to its discursive practices. It suggests that it would be clearly defined when we see one work using one literary theory, as if only for tactical convenience in conducting critical discussion. The illustration below may fit the explanation: We may put anything (theory and literary work), and we may start our own master discourse or our own interest, and it will shows us clearly that the illustration will say the relevancies about our knowledge and truth.

Everyone can say and explain about their own truth and understanding, because everything is interrelated and relative. Supposed that we start with several theories and one work in hand, the representation will be clearly enough to endorse the relativity of interpretation. What theory, then, can be applied within this circumscribe?

We have these theories in advanced:

- Moral/philosophical Literary Criticism
- Historical/biographical Literary Criticism
- French Structuralism, American New Criticism, Russian Formalism
- Psychoanalytic Literary Criticism
- Reader-response Literary Criticism
- Deconstructive Literary Criticism
- Marxist Literary Criticism
- Feminist Literary Criticism
- Postcolonial Literary Criticism

However, poststructuralist transformed and expanded this viewpoint of "theory", as it posits: "when common experience in the use or interpretation of language does not accord with what the theory entails, such experience is rejected as unjustified and illusory, or else is accounted an ideologically imposed concealment of the actual operation of the signifying system." Thus, poststructuralists expressly "challenge" and undertake to "destabilize," and in many instances to "undermine" and "subvert" what they identify as the foundational assumptions, concepts, procedures and findings in traditional modes of discourse.

Foucault's work on discourse and the provision of New Historicist Literary Criticism is exceedingly useful for students, lecturer, and theorists in order to be able to trace the way that we accept as 'true', how discourse enables us to think 'differently' and analyse the potential answer for the arbitrariness. As Simon During suggests to endorse literature 'obviously' (especially) for 'those who take Foucault's contribution as seriously as it deserves' that those scholars 'will feel the demand to elaborate and move past it, but perhaps' he puts forward that 'its real challenge lies in the question: "can it continue to be used to break down the limits of academic professionalism?" and that requires real changes in our methods and topics of study.'

Nietzsche puts 'cynicism' implied in his lecture "Homer and Classical Philology" in relation to theoretism that: "we may consider antiquity from a scientific point of view; we may try to look at what has happened with the eye of a historian, or to arrange and compare the linguistic forms of ancient masterpieces, to bring them at all events under a morphological law; but we always lose the wonderful creative force, the real fragrance, of the atmosphere of antiquity; we forget that passionate emotion which instinctively drove our meditation and enjoyment back to the Greeks.

HEGELIAN HISTORICISM

The historicist position by Hegel suggests that any human society and all human activities such as science, art, or philosophy, are defined by their history, so that their essence can be sought only through understanding that. The history of any such human endeavor, moreover, not only builds upon but also reacts against what has gone before; this is the source of Hegel's famous dialectic teaching usually summed up by the slogan "thesis, antithesis, and synthesis".

(Hegel did not use these terms, although Fichte did.) Hegel's famous aphorism, "Philosophy is the history of philosophy," describes it bluntly. Hegel's position is perhaps best illuminated when contrasted against the atomistic and reductionist view of human societies and social activities self-defining on an ad hoc basis through the sum of dozens of interactions.

Yet another contrasting model is the persistent metaphor of a social contract. Hegel sees the relationship between individuals and societies as organic, not atomic: even their social discourse is mediated by language, and language is rooted in etymology and unique character. It thus preserves the culture of the past in thousands of half-forgotten frozen metaphors. To understand why a person is the way he is, you must put that person in a society: and to understand that society, you must understand its history, and the forces that shaped it.

The Zeitgeist, the "Spirit of the Age," is the concrete embodiment of the most important factors that are acting in human history at any given time. This contrasts with teleological theories of activity, which suppose that the end is the determining factor of activity, as well as those who believe in a tabula rasa, or blank slate, view, where individuals are defined by their interactions.

These ideas can be taken in several directions. The Right Hegelians, working from Hegel's opinions about the organicism and historically determined nature of human societies, took Hegel's historicism as a justification of the unique destiny of national groups and the importance of stability and institutions. Hegel's conception of human societies as entities greater than the individuals who constitute them influenced nineteenth century romantic nationalism and its twentieth century excesses. The Young Hegelians, by contrast, took Hegel's thoughts on societies shaped by the forces of social conflict for a doctrine of progress, and attempted to chart a course that would manipulate these forces to lead to various improved outcomes.

Karl Marx's doctrine of "historical inevitabilities" and historical materialism is one of the more influential reactions to this side of Hegel's thought. Significantly, Karl Marx's theory of alienation comes full circle to the thought of the Hegelian right, arguing among other things that capitalism disrupts the rooted nature of traditional relationships between workers and their work.

Hegelian historicism is related to his ideas on the means by which human societies progress, specifically the dialectic and his conception of logic as reflecting the inner essential nature of reality. Hegel attributes the change to the "modern" need to interact with the world, whereas ancient philosophers were self-contained, and medieval philosophers were monks.

In his History of Philosophy Hegel writes:

- In modern times things are very different; now we no longer see philosophic individuals who constitute a class by themselves. With the present day all difference has disappeared; philosophers are not monks, for we find them generally in connection with the world, participating with others in some common work or calling. They live, not independently, but in the relation of citizens, or they occupy public offices and take part in the life of the state. Certainly they may be private persons, but if so, their position as such does not in any way isolate them from their other relationship. They are involved in present conditions, in the world and its work and progress. Thus their philosophy is only by the way, a sort of luxury and superfluity. This difference is really to be found in the manner in which outward conditions have taken shape after the building up of the inward world of religion. In modern times, namely, on account of the reconciliation of the worldly principle with itself, the external world is at rest, is brought into order—worldly relationships, conditions, modes of life, have become constituted and organized in a manner which is conformable to nature and rational. We see a universal, comprehensible connection, and with that individuality likewise attains another character and nature, for it is no longer the plastic individuality of the ancients. This connection is of such power that every individuality is under its dominion, and yet at the same time can construct for itself an inward world. This view that entanglement in society creates an indissoluble bond with expression, would be an influential question in philosophy going forward, namely, the requirements for individuality. It would be taken up by Nietzsche, John Dewey and Michel Foucault directly, as well as in the work of numerous artists and authors. There have been various responses to Hegel's challenge. The Romantic period focused on the ability of individual genius to transcend time and place, and use the materials from their heritage to fashion works which were beyond determination. The modern would advance versions of John Locke's infinite malleability of the human animal. Post-structuralism would argue that since history is not present, but only the image of history, that while an individual era or power structure might focus on a particular history, that the contradictions within the story would hinder the very purposes that the history was constructed to advance.

ANTHROPOLOGICAL HISTORICISM

Within anthropology and other sciences which study the past, historicism has a different meaning. It is associated with the work of Franz Boas. His theory took the diffusionist concept that there were a few "cradles of civilization" which grew outwards in circles, and merged it with the idea that societies would adapt to their circumstances, which is called historical particularism. The school of historicism grew up in response to unilinear theories that social development reflected adaptive fitness, and therefore existed on a spectrum. While these theories were espoused by Charles Darwin and many of his students, their application as applied in Social Darwinism and General Evolution characterized in the theories of Spencer and White, historicism was neither anti-selection, nor anti-evolution, as Darwin never attempted nor offered an explanation for cultural evolution.

However, it attacked the notion that there was one normative spectrum of development, instead focusing on how local conditions would create adaptations to the local environment. Steward refuted the viability of globally and universally applicable adaptive standards proposing that culture was honed adaptively in response to the idiosyncrasies of the local environment, the cultural ecology, by specific evolution. What was adaptive for one region might not be so for another. This conclusion has likewise been adopted by modern forms of biological evolutionary theory. The primary method of historicism was empirical, namely that there were so many requisite inputs into a society or event, that only by focusing on the data available could a theory of the source be determined. In this view, grand theories are unprovable, and instead intensive field work would determine the most likely explanation and history of a culture, and hence it is named Historicism. Boas would later teach at Columbia University and this would produce a school of thought based on his ideas.

This view would produce a wide range of definition of what, exactly, constituted culture and history, but in each case the only means of explaining it was in terms of the historical particulars of the culture itself.

HISTORY OF TEXTUAL CRITICISM

FROM ANTIQUITY TO THE RENAISSANCE

Until the 20th century the development of textual criticism was inevitably dominated by classical and biblical studies. The systematic study and practice of the subject originated in the 3rd century bc with the Greek scholars of Alexandria. Literary culture had before that time been predominantly oral, though books were in common use by the 5th century, and many texts had suffered damage because the idea of precise textual accuracy and reproduction was unfamiliar. The aim of the librarians of Alexandria was to collect and catalogue every extant Greek book and to produce critical editions of the most important together with textual and interpretative commentaries. Many such editions and commentaries did in fact appear. Alexandrian editing was distinguished above all by respect for the tradition; the text was constituted from the oldest and best copies available, and conjectural emendation was rigidly confined to the commentary, which was contained in a separate volume.

An elaborate battery of critical signs was used to refer from text to commentary. These techniques were applied, though on a less ambitious scale, by Roman scholars to Latin texts. Fidelity to tradition was the chief legacy of ancient textual scholarship to later ages; the copyist was expected to reproduce his exemplar as exactly as he could, and correction was based on comparison with other copies, not on the unaided conjectural sagacity of the scribe. Such was the practice of the best monastic scriptoria such as that of Tours, or of the best scholars, such as Lupus of Ferrières (fl. 850). From about 1350, however, a change in attitude is evident, particularly in the West. What is often called the revival of learning was in reality a practical movement to enlist the heritage of classical antiquity in the service of the new Christian humanism. In order to make them usable (*i.e.,* readable), texts were corrected freely and often arbitrarily by scholars, copyists, and readers (the three categories being in fact hardly distinguishable). At its best, as seen in the activities of a scholar like Demetrius Triclinius, later medieval and early Renaissance criticism verges on scientific scholarship, but such cases are exceptional.

For the most part the correction of texts was a purely subjective display of taste, sometimes right but much more often wrong, and resting as a rule on nothing more solid than a superficial sense of elegance. In consequence, by the 1470s, when the first printed editions (*editiones principes*) of classical texts began to appear, most Greek and Latin authors were circulating in a textually debased condition, and it was manuscripts of this character that almost always served as copy for the early printers. Very little editing in any real sense of the word was done; the scholars who saw the *editiones principes* through the press generally confined themselves to superficial improvements.

From Politian to Cobet

This state of affairs entailed that down to the 19th century most critics were engaged not in establishing and emending texts on scientific principles but in correcting, in a necessarily unsystematic fashion, a vulgate or received text (*lectio recepta*) that was itself the product of an almost entirely haphazard process of variation and conjecture. The situation was aggravated by the fact that the manuscripts themselves, the basic materials of the investigation, were largely inaccessible to scholars. The Italian poet and scholar Politian, unlike most of his contemporaries, was aware that only through the identification and comparison of the best manuscripts could texts be improved; his notes and collations show that he understood the problem correctly as essentially one of control of the sources.

What might have been done in this field is shown by his work, cut short by his early death, on the Florentine codex of Justinian's Pandects. Many manuscripts were still privately owned, their very existence unknown to scholars; public libraries were few and published catalogues fewer; travel was difficult, expensive, and often dangerous. It was not until the twin disciplines of diplomatic and paleography were founded by the great Benedictine monks Mabillon and Montfaucon, and developed by their successors, that a critical use of the evidence became possible; and much of the evidence itself did not become available until after the Napoleonic Wars, when most of the private stock of manuscripts passed finally into public collections.

Some advances were taking place, slowly and unsystematically, in both the theory and practice of textual criticism. The history of critical method in this period is most profitably studied in the best editions of the best editors. The accepted method was to correct the text (*i.e.,* the text of the last printed edition) *codicum et ingenii ope*; *i.e.,* with the aid of the manuscript and printed sources and the critic's own ingenuity. Divination was subordinated to authority, and any reading found in a manuscript or printed text was accounted superior to any conjecture, whatever its intrinsic merits. The first important departure from this pattern is seen in the edition of Catullus by J.J. Scaliger (1577), in which the possibilities of the genealogical method, already understood in principle by Politian and other Renaissance scholars, were exemplified by the demonstration that all the extant copies derived from a lost manuscript, whose orthography and provenance Scaliger was prepared to reconstruct.

Almost equally significant was Richard Bentley's edition of Horace (1711), in which for the first time the role of conjecture in the critical and editorial process was recognized and the tradition of producing a corrected version of the text of previous editors was decisively rejected. Bentley's scholarship was greatly admired in the Netherlands, and the editions of the great Dutch Latinists J.F. Gronovius and N. Heinsius were informed by Bentleian principles. Under his influence there grew up what may be called an Anglo-Dutch school of criticism, the two most typical representatives of which were Richard Porson and C.G. Cobet. Its strength lay in sound judgement and good taste rooted in minute linguistic and metrical study; its weaknesses were an excessive reliance on analogical criteria and an indifference to German science and method. Its influence may still be seen in the empiricism that characterizes much critical work by English scholars.

From Bentley to Lachmann

The decisive influence on the editing of secular texts came from the New Testament critics of the 18th century. The printed text of the Greek New Testament in common use was still essentially that established in 1516 by Desiderius Erasmus. For his edition, produced in great haste, he had used such manuscripts, neither ancient nor good, as chanced to be accessible to him. Superficially revised, this was the text termed in the Elzevier edition of 1633 "now received by all," *nunc ab omnibus receptum*. Bentley proposed an edition on radical lines in which he engaged to give the text "exactly as it was in the best exemplars at the time of the Council of Nice. So that there shall not be twenty words, nor even particles, difference..." This project never materialized, but editions of the Greek text that did not reproduce the *textus receptus* were published in England by Daniel Mace (1729), William Bowyer, the Younger (1763), and Edward Harwood (1776). On the Continent, meanwhile, New Testament criticism was being developed on scientific and historical lines by a succession of distinguished scholars, notably J.A. Bengel, J.J. Wettstein, J.S. Semler, and J.J. Griesbach.

They shaped the genealogical method that was later refined by editors of classical texts. Wettstein also deserves commemoration as the first New Testament critic to use *sigla* systematically. This was important, since some at least of the deficiencies of classical editions at this time are attributable to the lack of suitable conventions for the presentation of critical information, together with a conservative and belletristic attitude to technical jargon by publishers, scholars, and users of books in general. Though *sigla* occur sporadically in editions as early as the 16th century and were used by S. Haverkamp in his Lucretius (1725) in something like the modern style, they did not become normal until the second half of the 19th century.

The genealogical, or stemmatic, method of recension has already been described. It is usually associated with the name of the German Karl Lachmann, but it had its origins in the work of J.A. Bengel and his successors, and almost every essential feature of it was already present in the work of Lachmann's precursors such as J.A. Ernesti, F.A. Wolf, K.G. Zumpt, F.W. Ritschl, and J.N. Madvig. Nevertheless Lachmann occupies a central position in the development of textual criticism because of the unusual power and penetration of his scholarship, the range of textual material on which he worked, and his immense contemporary and posthumous influence. His edition of the Greek New Testament (1831; 2nd ed. 1842–50) was intended primarily as a vindication of the principles of Bentley and Bengel and a demonstration that the *textus receptus* must be finally rejected. Similarly his famous edition of Lucretius (1850) is important as an exemplification of the method in action, since the tradition of Lucretius is peculiarly suitable for the purpose.

The demonstration fell short of completeness, for Lachmann had not fully grasped the problem and so failed to exploit the method fully. It has been suggested that Lachmann's best critical work was in his editions of medieval German texts; their influence will be considered below. The Lachmannian model of recension derived added authority from seemingly analogous models in other fields, especially that of comparative philology. As propagated by disciples, notably Moritz Haupt, it dominated textual studies for half a century.

Related Developments in the Late 19th Century

Possibly the most important technical advance in the latter part of the 19th century was the perfection of photography. Instead of travelling in search of his material, the paleographer or critic could now assemble and study it at relatively little expense and without leaving his desk.During the last quarter of the 19th century the tempo of archaeological discovery in classical and biblical lands was vastly increased, and many new texts were unearthed. Some of these were in previously unknown languages, setting new problems of decipherment. Specifically relevant to textual studies are the many Greek papyri recovered from Egypt.

These have thrown much light on the history and techniques of ancient book production and scholarship and hence, indirectly, on critical problems. Where the texts they contain are already known, their evidence has tended to emphasize our ignorance of the textual history of classical literature in antiquity itself. Being usually far older than the manuscripts already known, they often illuminate the "pre-traditional" state of the text; by sometimes offering readings that agree with those of late and "inferior" medieval copies they justify editors in a policy of cautious eclecticism. Papyrus discoveries have been of particular moment for the text of the New Testament.Editors of printed texts, having invariably received a classical education (no other being available), had naturally followed, with minor modifications, the methods of classical editing.

They would reprint the text of the last edition with such improvements as editorial taste and learning suggested but with no attempt to investigate the sources of the text. Since Lachmann's method was inapplicable to printed texts, this procedure continued until, by the end of the 19th century, the text of Shakespeare, for example, was in a state somewhat analogous to that of most classical writers at the time of the *editiones principes*. Much of the work of modern Shakespearean editors has consisted of undoing the damage inflicted by their predecessors.

The early 20th century saw the rise of a new school of "biblio-textual" criticism, most notably represented by A.W. Pollard, R.B. McKerrow, and W.W. Greg. Its object was to devise a style of recension appropriate to the special circumstances under which early printed texts were produced and propagated, and its methods were those of analytical bibliography. These developments are of direct importance for the criticism and editing of a large range of texts of the 16th, 17th, and 18th centuries, particularly those of the Elizabethan and Jacobean dramatists.

They have also engendered a discussion of general methodological interest on the role of bibliographical as opposed to historical and literary criteria in the editorial process. This debate continues. Critics and editors of medieval texts had also inevitably been influenced by developments in the classical field. Before Lachmann it had been usual to choose a single manuscript as the main basis for an edition. Because of the circumstances in which much medieval literature was composed and transmitted this was not necessarily unscientific, and the surviving bulk of texts was so large as to dictate that approach in many cases if they were to be edited at all. This had been the style of editing followed by the Belgian Jesuits known as Bollandists, the French Benedictines called Maurists, and the Italian scholar L.A. Muratori, and perpetuated in the indispensable *Patrologiae Cursus Completus* (edition of the Church Fathers) of the French priest Jacques-Paul Migne. At its best it is seen in the editions of medieval Latin chronicles by the 18th-century Oxford antiquary Thomas Hearne, some of which are still standard works.

A more scientific approach was adopted in the publications of the *Monumenta Germaniae Historica*, the later volumes of which (from about 1880) were produced by editors trained in the school of Lachmann. Similarly, editors of vernacular texts followed the lead that Lachmann had given in his editions of such early German poems as the *Nibelunge Not* (1826) and the *Iwein* (1827). An important development in the application of the method was due to the medievalists G. Gröber and G. Paris, who first emphasized the significance of common errors. But in the general uncritical enthusiasm for scientific method, the genealogical approach was too often used without regard for the special conditions under which medieval literature has been handed down.

Reaction against the Genealogical Method

Haupt had proclaimed in his lectures that his main object was to teach method. But confidence in method led to its misuse. The Lachmannian formula of recension was applied to texts, classical as well as medieval, for which it was unsuitable, often with grotesque results. Commonly this took the form of choosing on "scientific" (*i.e.,* stemmatic) grounds a "best manuscript" (*codex optimus*) and defending its readings as authoritative even where common sense showed that they could not be authentic.

This was the type of editing satirized by A.E. Housman in the brilliant prefaces to his editions of Manilius (1903) and Juvenal (1905) and in many reviews and articles. It flourished chiefly between 1875 and 1900, but the dangers of excessive methodological rigidity had already been foreseen. In 1841 H. Sauppe in his *Epistola Critica ad G. Hermannum* had emphasized the diversity of transmissional situations and the difficulty or actual impossibility of classifying the manuscripts in all cases. In 1843 Lachmann's pupil O. Jahn, in his edition of Persius, had repudiated the strict application of the genealogical method as unsuitable to the tradition of that poet. The most extreme position was taken by E. Schwartz, who in his edition of Eusebius' *Historia ecclesiastica* (1909) denied that "vertically" transmitted texts of Greek books existed at all.

The limitations of the stemmatic method have subsequently been stressed in a more temperate fashion by other writers. The modern tendency is to acknowledge the validity of the method in principle while recommending a cautious empiricism in its application. For the editor of a contaminated tradition—and most traditions are probably contaminated—the lesson of recent research is that authoritative evidence may survive even in late and generally corrupt or interpolated sources. More radical criticism of the method has come from medievalists.

In 1913 and again in 1928 the French scholar J. Bédier attacked the stemmatic method because the *stemmata* it produced for medieval texts almost invariably had only two branches. Subsequent investigation has shown that Bédier overrated the inherent improbability of this situation, and it is generally agreed that his criticisms had to do with improper application rather than with the method itself. The point taken by H. Quentin (1922) has already been mentioned: that the method entails argument in a circle, since it relies on the identification of errors at the beginning of a process designed to lead to that very end. This objection, more cogent in theory than in practice, applies with greater force to medieval than to classical texts.

The linguistic and stylistic canons of classical Greek and Latin are relatively strict and well defined, whereas the vocabulary, grammar, and usage of many medieval authors (especially when an oral prehistory is in question) is often not certain enough to allow reliable discrimination between variant and error. Classical texts, moreover, have passed through a series of bottlenecks in their history, which have simplified editorial problems by eliminating a high proportion of the evidence (*cf.* the remarks on papyri above). With a few exceptions, such as the commentary of Servius, only one version of each text remains to be reconstructed, whereas many medieval texts are extant in several redactions that cannot be winnowed by the stemmatic method so as to leave only one. Quentin's own method, which depended on the comparison of variants in groups of three, without prejudice as to their correctness, has not been generally adopted.

It is immensely laborious and does not in practice possess the objectivity that its inventor claimed for it. Bédier and Quentin have, however, done good service to textual criticism in enjoining caution. The best critics in all fields now agree in rejecting the "logical" (*i.e.,* the illogical) application of any method if the results conflict with common sense, and in stressing the necessity of judging variant readings and forms of a text on their intrinsic merits in the light of the information available.

Mechanical methods

Quentin also gave a lead to later investigators in calling attention to the possibility of basing recension on the variants themselves, and the more sophisticated methods of Greg (1927), Archibald Hill (1950), Vinton Dearing (1959), and J. Froger (1968) may be seen as a continuation of his work. It has already been suggested that methods of this type, so far as recension is concerned, have been of primarily theoretical interest. But the use of mechanical and computing techniques in this field is in its infancy, and assessment must be provisional. Certain practical applications seem to have proved themselves. Mechanical aids to collation have been successfully used in editing Shakespeare and Dryden. Computer storage and analysis of texts can provide information about authorial usage, such as stylistic and metrical patterns, and facilitate the production of concordances.

These aids are more relevant to conjectural emendation (as shown by their application to the Dead Sea Scrolls) and the "higher" criticism (*e.g.,* determination of authenticity) than to the recension of texts. The formula or machine that will do the critic's essential work for him still awaits discovery; the best texts are produced by the best scholars, whatever their method or lack of method. Lachmann observed that the establishment of a text according to its tradition is a strictly historical undertaking. Twentieth-century research into the composition and transmission of ancient, medieval, and modern texts has confirmed the truth of his pronouncement..

MODERN HISTORICISM

Within the context of 20th century philosophy, the conflict over whether a historical and immanent methodologies were sufficient to understand meaning—that is to say, "what you see is what you get" positivism—or whether context, background and culture are important beyond the mere need to decode words, phrases and references. While post-structural historicism is relativist in its orientation, that is, it sees each culture as its own frame of reference, a large number of thinkers have embraced the need for historical context, not because culture is self-referential, but because there is no more compressed means of conveying all of the relevant information except through history. This view is often seen as being rooted in the work of Benedetto Croce. Recent historians in this tradition include Thomas Kuhn.

ESCHATOLOGICAL HISTORICISM

In Christianity, the term historicism refers to the confessional Protestant form of prophetical interpretation which holds that the fulfillment of biblical prophecy has taken place throughout history and continues to take place today; as opposed to other methods which limit the time-frame of prophecy-fulfillment to the past or to the future. The historicist method is what led reformers throughout Europe to declare that the Pope was the man of sin sitting on the Seven Hills of Rome. Examples of famous Christians and Protestant denominations declaring the pope to be the antichrist include the Waldensians, Albigenses, Lollards, Lutherans, Calvinists, Hussians, and a host of individuals, including the father of the modern English Bible William Tyndale and even objects of faith such as the original Westminster Confession of Faith.

DOGMATIC AND ECCLESIASTIC HISTORICISM

There is also a particular view in ecclesiastical history and in the history of dogmas which has been described as historicist by Pope Pius XII in the encyclical Humani Generis. "They add that the history of dogmas consists in the reporting of the various forms in which revealed truth has been clothed, forms that have succeeded one another in accordance with the different teachings and opinions that have arisen over the course of the centuries."

3

Literary Criticism Development

CRITICISM DEVELOPMENT

In England, as elsewhere, criticism was a late birth of the literary spirit. English poets had sung and literary prose been written for centuries before it struck men to ask themselves, What is the secret of the power that these things have on our mind, and by what principles are they to be judged? And it could hardly have been otherwise. Criticism is a self-conscious art, and could not have arisen in an age of intellectual childhood. It is a derivative art, and could scarcely have come into being without a large body of literature to suggest canons of judgement, and to furnish instances of their application. The age of Chaucer might have been expected to bring with it a new departure.

It was an age of self-scrutiny and of bold experiment. A new world of thought and imagination had dawned upon it; and a new literature, that of Italy, was spread before it. Yet who shall say that the facts answer to these expectations? In the writings of Chaucer himself a keen eye, it is true, may discern the faint beginnings of the critical spirit. No poet has written with more nicely calculated art; none has passed a cooler judgement upon the popular taste of his generation. We know that Chaucer despised the "false gallop" of chivalrous verse; we know that he had small respect for the marvels of Arthurian romance. And his admiration is at least as frank as his contempt. What poet has felt and avowed a deeper reverence for the great Latins?

What poet has been so alert to recognize the master-spirits of his own time and his father's? De Meung and Granson among the FrenchDante, Petrarch and Boccaccio of the Italianseach comes in for his share of praise from Chaucer, or of the princely borrowings which are still more eloquent than praise. Yet, for all this, Chaucer is far indeed from founding the art of criticism. His business was to create, and not to criticise. And, had he set himself to do so, there is no warrant that his success would have been great. In many ways he was still in bondage to the mediaval, and wholly uncritical, tradition. One classic, we may almost say, was as good to him as another. He seems to have placed Ovid on a line with Virgil; and the company in his House of Fame is undeniably mixed.

His judgements have the healthy instinct of the consummate artist. They do not show, as those of his master, Petrarch, unquestionably do, the discrimination and the tact of the born critic. For this, or for any approach to it, English literature had to wait for yet two centuries more.

In the strict sense, criticism did not begin till the age of Elizabeth; and, like much else in our literature, it was largely due to the passion for classical study, so strongly marked in the poets and dramatists of Shakespeare's youth, and inaugurated by Surrey and others in the previous generation. These conditions are in themselves significant. They serve to explain much both of the strength and the weakness of criticism, as it has grown up on English soil. From the Elizabethans to Milton, from Milton to Johnson, English criticism was dominated by constant reference to classical models. In the latter half of this period the influence of these models, on the whole, was harmful. It acted as a curb rather than as a spur to the imagination of poets; it tended to cripple rather than give energy to the judgement of critics.

But in earlier days it was not so. For nearly a century the influence of classical masterpieces was altogether for good. It was not the regularity but the richness, not the self-restraint but the freedom, of the ancients that came home to poets such as Marlowe, or even to critics such as Meres. And if adventurous spirits, like Spenser and Sidney, were for a time misled into the vain attempt to graft exotic forms upon the homely growths of native poetry, they soon saw their mistake and revolted in silence against the ridiculous pedant who preferred the limping hexameters of the Arcadia to Sidney's sonnets, and the spavined iambics of Spenser to the Faerie Queene.

In the main, the worship of the classics seems to have counted at this time rather for freedom than restraint. And it is well that it was so. Yet restraint too was necessary; and, like freedom, it was found though in less ample measurethrough devotion to the classics. There can be little doubt that, consciously or no, the Elizabethans, with their quick eye for beauty of every kind, were swayed, as men in all ages have been swayed, by the finely chiselled forms of classical art. The besetting sin of their imagination was the tendency to run riot; and it may well be that, save for the restraining influence of ancient poetry, they would have sinned in this matter still more boldly than they did. Yet the chastening power of classical models may be easily overrated. And we cannot but notice that it was precisely where the classical influence was strongest that the force of imagination was the least under control. Jonson apart, there were no more ardent disciples of the ancients than Marlowe and Chapman.

And no poets of that age are so open to the charge of extravagance as they. It is with Milton that the chastening influence of the ancients first makes itself definitely felt. But Milton was no less alive to the fervour than to the self-mastery of his classical models. And it was not till the Restoration that "correctness" was recognized as the highest, if not the only, quality of the ancients, or accepted as the one worthy object of poetic effort. For more than a century correctness remained the idol both of poetry and of criticism in England; and nothing less than the furious onslaught of the Lyrical Ballads was needed to overthrow it. Then the floodgates were opened. A new era both of poetic and critical energy had dawned. Thus the history of English criticism, like that of English literature, divides itself roughly into three periods.

The first is the period of the Elizabethans and of Milton; the second is from the Restoration to the French Revolution; the third from the Revolution to the present day. The typical critic of the first period is Sidney; Dryden opens and Johnson closes the second; the third, a period of far more varied tendencies than either of the others, is perhaps most fitly represented by Lamb, Hazlitt, and Carlyle. It will be the aim of the following pages to sketch the broader outlines of the course that critical inquiry has taken in each. The first thing that strikes us in the early attempts of criticism is that its problems are to a large extent remote from those which have engrossed critics of more recent times.

There is little attempt to appraise accurately the worth of individual authors; still less, to find out the secret of their power, or to lay bare the hidden lines of thought on which their imagination had set itself to work. The first aim both of Puttenham and of Webbe, the pioneers of Elizabethan criticism, was either to classify writers according to the subjects they treated and the literary form that each had made his own, or to analyse the metre and other more technical elements of their poetry. But this, after all, was the natural course in the infancy of the study.

All science begins with classification; and all classification with the external and the obvious. The Greek critics could take no step forward until they had classified all poems as either lyric, epic, or dramatic. And how necessary that division was may be seen from the length at which Plato discusses the nature of the distinction in the second book of the Republic. Even Aristotle, in this as in other things the 'master of those who know', devotes no inconsiderable space of the Poetics to technical matters such as the analysis of vocal sounds, and the aptness of different metres to different forms of poetic thought. There is another matter in which the methods of Elizabethan critics run side by side with those of the early Greeks.

In Plato and Aristotle we are not seldom startled by the sudden transition from questions of form to the deepest problems suggested by imaginative art. The same is true of the Elizabethan critics. It is doubtless true that the latter give a proportionally larger space to the more technical sides of the subject than their Greek forerunners. They could not reasonably be expected to write with the width of view that all the world has admired in Aristotle and Plato. Moreover, they were from the first confronted with a practical difficulty from which the Greek critics were so fortunate as to be free. Was rhyme a "brutish" form of verse? and, if so, was its place to be taken by the alliterative rhythm, so dear to the older poets, or by an importation of classical metres, such as was attempted by Sidney and Spenser, and enforced by the unwearied lectures of Harvey and of Webbe?

This, however technical, was a fundamental question; and, until it was settled, there was but little use in debating the weightier matters of the law. The discussion, which might have raged for ever among the critics, was happily cut short by the healthy instinct of the poets. Against alliteration the question had already been given by default. Revived, after long disuse, by Langland and other poets of the West Midlands in the fourteenth century, it had soon again been swept out of fashion by the irresistible charm of the genius of Chaucer. The Tale of Gamelyn, dating apparently from the first quarter of the fifteenth century, is probably the last poem of note in which the once universal metre is even partially employed. And what could prove more clearly that the old metrical form was dead?

The rough rhythm of early English poetry, it is true, is kept; but alliteration is dropped, and its place is taken by rhyme. Nor were the efforts to impose classical measures on English poetry more blest in their results. The very men on whom the literary Romanizers had fixed their hopes were the first to abandon the enterprise in despair. If any genius was equal to the task of naturalizing hexameters in a language where strict quantity is unknown, it was the genius of Spenser. But Spenser soon ranged himself heart and soul with the champions of rhyme; his very name has passed down to us as a synonym for the most elaborate of all rhyming stanzas that have taken root in our verse. For the moment, rhyme had fairly driven all rivals from the field.

Over the lyric its sway was undisputed. In narrative poetry, where its fitness was far more disputable, it maintained its hold till the closing years of Milton. In the drama itself, where its triumph would have been fatal, it disputed the ground inch by inch against the magnificent instrument devised by Surrey and perfected by Marlowe. It was during the ten years preceding the publication of Webbe's Discourse (1586) that this controversy seems to have been hottest.

From the first, perhaps, it bulked more largely with the critics than with the poets themselves. Certainly it allowed both poets and critics sufficient leisure for the far more important controversy which has left an enduring monument in Sidney's Apologie for Poetrie. The historical bearing of Sidney's treatise has been too commonly overlooked.

It forms, in truth, one move in the long struggle which ended only with the restoration of Charles II.; or, to speak more accurately, which has lasted, in a milder form, to the present day. In its immediate object it was a reply to the Puritan assaults upon the theatre; in its ultimate scope, a defence of imaginative art against the suspicions with which men of high but narrow purpose have always, consciously or unconsciously, tended to regard it. It is a noble plea for liberty, directed no less against the unwilling scruples of idealists, such as Plato or Rousseau, than against the ruthless bigotry of practical moralists and religious partisans. From the first dawn of the Elizabethan drama, the stricter Protestants had declared war upon the stage.

Intrenched within the city they were at once able to drive the theatres beyond the walls (1575); just as seventy years later, when it had seized the reins of central government, the same party, embittered by a thousand insults and brutalities, hastened to close the theatres altogether. It would be an evident mistake to suppose that this was merely a municipal prejudice, or to forget that the city council was backed by a large body of serious opinion throughout the country. A proof of this, if proof were needed, is to be found in the circumstances that gave rise to the Apologie of Sidney. The attack on the stage had been opened by the corporation and the clergy.

It was soon joined by the men of letters. And the essay of Sidney was an answer neither to a town councillor, nor to a preacher, but to a former dramatist and actor. This was Stephen Gosson, author of the School of Abuse. The style of Gosson's pamphlet is nothing if not literary. It is full of the glittering conceits and the fluent rhetoric which the ready talent of Lyly had just brought into currency. It is euphuism of the purest water, with all the merits and all the drawbacks of the euphuistic manner. For that very reason the blow was felt the more keenly. It was violently resented as treason by the playwrights and journalists who still professed to reckon Gosson among their ranks. A war of pamphlets followed, conducted with the usual fury of literary men.

Gosson on the one side, Lodge, the dramatist, upon the other, exchanged compliments with an energy which showed that one at least of them had not in vain graduated in "the school of abuse". "Raw devises", "hudder mudder", "guts and garbage", such are the phrases hurled by Gosson at the arguments and style of his opponents; "bawdy charms", "the very butchery of Christian souls", are samples of the names fastened by him upon the cause which they defended. From this war of words Sidney turned loftily aside. Pointedly challenged at the outsetfor the first and second pamphlets of Gosson had, without permission, been dedicated to "the right noble gentleman, Maister Philip Sidney"he seldom alludes to the arguments, and never once mentions the name of Gosson. He wrote to satisfy his own mind, and not to win glory in the world of letters. And thus his Apologie, though it seems to have been composed while the controversy was still fresh in men's memory, was not published until nearly ten years after his death (1595). It was not written for controversy, but for truth. From the first page it rises into the atmosphere of calm, in which alone great questions can be profitably discussed.

The Apologie of Sidney is, in truth, what would now be called a Philosophy of Poetry. It is philosophy taken from the side of the moralist; for that was the side to which the disputants had confined themselves, and in whichaltogether apart from the example of othersthe interest of Sidney, as man of action, inevitably lay. It is philosophy as conceived by the mind of a poet. But, none the less, it pierces to the eternal problems which underlie the workings of all creative art, and presents them with a force, for the like of which we must go back to Plato and Aristotle, or look forward to the philosophers and inspired critics of a time nearer our own. It recalls the Phadrus and the Ion; it anticipates the utterance of a still more kindred spirit, the Defence of Poetry by Shelley. Philosopher as he was, Sidney arranges his thoughts in the loose order of the poet or the orator. It may be well, therefore, to give a brief sketch of his argument; and to do so without much regard to the arrangement of the Apologie itself. The main argument of the Apologie may indeed be called a commentary on the saying of Aristotle, cited by Sidney himself, that "Poetry is more philosophical and more studiously serious than History"that is, as Sidney interprets it, than the scientific fact of any kind; or again, on that yet more pregnant saying of Shelley, that "poets are the unacknowledged legislators of the world". Gosson had denounced poetry as "the vizard of vanity, wantonness, and folly"; or, in Sidney's paraphrase, as "the mother of lies and the nurse of abuse". Sidney replies by urging that of all arts poetry is the most true and the most necessary to men.

All learning, he pleads, and all culture begin with poetry. Philosophy, religion, and history herself, speak through the lips of poetry. There is indeed a sense in which poetry stands on higher ground than any science. There is no science, not even metaphysics, the queen of all sciences, that does not "build upon nature", and that is not, so far, limited by the facts of nature. The poet alone is "not tied to any such subjection"; he alone "freely ranges within the zodiac of his own wit".

This, no doubt, is dangerous ground, and it is enforced by still more dangerous illustrations. But Sidney at once guards himself by insisting, as Plato had done before him, that the poet too is bound by laws which he finds but does not make; they are, however, laws not of fact but of thought, the laws of the ideathat is, of the inmost truth of things, and of God. Hence it is that the works of the poet seem to come from God, rather than from man. They stand rather on a level with nature, the material of all sciences, than with the sciences themselves, which are nothing more than man's interpretation of nature. In some sense, indeed, they are above nature; they stand midway between nature and him who created nature. They are a first nature, "beyond and over the works of that second nature". For they are the self-revelation of that which is the noblest work of God, and which in them finds utterance at its best and brightest.

Thus, so far from being the "mother of lies", poetry is the highest form of truth. Avowedly so, in what men have always recognized to be the noblest poetry, the psalms and parables and other writings that "do imitate the inconceivable excellences of God". To a less degree, but still avowedly, in that poetry whose theme is philosophy or history. And so essentially, however men may overlook it, in that poetry which, professedly dealing with human life as we know it, does not content itself with reproducing the character of this man or that, but "reined only with learned discretion, ranges into the divine consideration of what may be and should be"of the universal and complete rather than the individual and imperfect. But, if truth be the essence of the poet's work, "the right describing note to know a poet by", it would seem that the outward form of it, the metre and the ornament, are of little moment. "There have been many most excellent poets that never versified."

And verse is nothing more than a means, and not the only means, of securing a "fitting raiment" for their matter and suiting their manner "according to the dignity of their subject". In this suggestionthat harmonious prose may, for certain forms of poetic thought, be hardly less suitable than verseSidney is at one with Shelley. And neither critic must be taken to disparage verse, or to mean more than that the matter, the conception, is the soul of poetry, and that the form is only of moment so far as it aidsas undoubtedly it does aidto "reveal the soul within". It is rather as a witness to the whole scope of their argument than as a particular doctrine, to be left or taken, that the suggestion is most profitably regarded.

THE SPECULATIVE BASE OF POETRY

Having settled the speculative base of poetry, Sidney turns to a yet more cherished theme, its influence upon character and action. The "highest end" of all knowledge, he urges, is "the knowledge of a man's self, with the end of well doing and not of well knowing only". Now by no artist is this end served so perfectly as by the poet. His only serious rivals are the moral philosopher and the historian. But neither of these flies so straight to his mark as the poet. The one gives precepts that fire no heart to action; the other gives examples without the precepts that should interpret and control them. The one lives in the world of ideas, the other in the world of hard and literal fact. Neither, therefore, has power to bridge the gulf that parts thought from action; neither can hope to take hold of beings in whose life, by its very nature, thought and action are indissolubly interwoven.

"Now doth the peerless poet perform both. For whatsoever the philosopher saith should be done, he giveth a perfect picture of it in some one, by whom he presupposeth it was done. So as he coupleth the general notion with the particular example.... Therein of all sciences is our poet the monarch." Once more we feel that Sidney is treading upon dangerous ground. But once more he saves himself by giving a wider definition both to thought and action, both to "well knowing and to well doing", than is common with moralists. By the former most moralists are apt to understand the bare "precept", thought as crystallized in its immediate bearing upon action. By the latter they commonly mean the passive rather than the active virtues, temperance and self-restraint rather than energy and resolve. From both these limitations Sidney, on the whole, is nobly free.

To him the "delight which is all the good fellow poet seemeth to promise", "the words set in delightful proportion and prepared for the well enchanting skill of music", "the tale which holdeth children from play and old men from the chimney corner"all these, its indefinable and purely artistic elements, are an inseparable part of the "wisdom" which poetry has to offer. In other words, it is the frame of mind produced by poetry, the "thought hardly to be packed into the narrow act", no less than the prompting to this action or to that, which Sidney values in the work of the poet. And if this be true, none but the most fanatical champion of "art for art's sake" will dispute the justice of his demands on poetry. None but such will deny that, whether by attuning the mind to beauty and nobleness, or by means yet more direct and obvious, art must have some bearing upon the life of man and on the habitual temper of his soul. No doubt, we might have wished that, in widening the scope of poetry as a moral influence, Sidney had been yet more explicit than in fact he is. We cannot but regret that, however unjustly, he should have laid himself open to the charge of desiring to turn poetry into sermons. But it is bare justice to point out that such a charge cannot fairly be brought against him; or that it can only be brought with such qualifications as rob it of its sting.

On the other matter the record of Sidney is yet clearer. By "well doing" he does not mean, as is too often meant, mere abstinence from evil, but the active pursuit of whatsoever things are manly, noble, and of good report. It is not only the "temperance of Diomedes" though temperance too may be conceived as an active virtuebut the wisdom of Ulysses, the patriotism of Aneas, "the soon repenting pride of Agamemnon", the valour of Achillesit is courage, above all courage, that stirs his soul in the great works of ancient poetry. It is the same quality that moves him in the ballads and romances of the moderns. "Certainly I must confess my own barbarousness; I never heard the old song of Percy and Douglas that I found not my heart moved more than with a trumpet." And again: "Truly I have known men that, even with reading Amadis de Gaule (which, God knoweth, wanteth much of a perfect poesy), have found their hearts moved to the exercise of courtesy, liberality, and especially courage." The man who wrote these words had no starved conception of what poetry should be. Once again. Sidney has small patience with those who would limit art by the banishment of all that recalls the baser side of life. "Now, as in geometry, the oblique must be known as well as the right. So in the actions of our life, who seeth not the filthiness of evil, wanteth a great foil to perceive the beauty of virtue. This doth the comedy handle so... as with hearing it we get, as it were, an experience....

So that the right use of comedy will, I think, by no body be blamed." No doubt, the moral aspect of comedy is here marked with what must be called immoderate stress. Here, too, as when he deals with the kindred side of tragedy, Sidney demands that the poet shall, in his villains, "show you nothing that is not to be shunned"; in other words, that, so far as it paints evil, comedy shall take the form of satire. But, even with this restriction, it must be allowed that Sidney takes a wider view than might appear at a hasty reading; wider, it is probable, than was at all common among the men of his generation. No

Shakespeare had yet arisen to touch the baser qualities of men with a gleam of heroism or to humanize the most stoical endurance with a strain of weakness.

And even Shakespeare, in turning from the practice to the theory of his art, could find no words very different from those of Sidney. To him, as to Sidney, the aim of the drama is "to show virtue her own image and scorn her own feature"; though by a saving clause, which Sidney perhaps would hardly have accepted, it is further defined as being to show "the very age and body of the time his form and pressure". Yet it must be remembered that Sidney is loud in praise of so unflinching a portraiture of life, base and noble, as Chaucer's Troilus and Cressida. And on the whole it remains true that the limitations of Sidney are the limitations of his age, while his generosity is his own.

The remainder of the Apologie is necessarily of slighter texture. Apart from the examination of Plato's banishment of the poetsa theme on which Harington also discourses, though with less weight than Sidneyit is concerned mainly with two subjects: an assertion that each form of poetry has its peculiar moral import, and a lament over the decay into which English poetry had fallen in the sixteenth century.

Such a lament sounds strangely to us, accustomed as we are to regard the age of Elizabeth, already half ended when Sidney wrote, as the most fruitful period of our literature. But, when the Apologie was composed, no one of the authors by whose fame the Elizabethan age is now commonly knownSidney himself and Spenser alone exceptedhad begun to write. English poetry was about to wake from the long night that lies between the age of Chaucer and the age of Shakespeare. But it was not yet fully awakened. And the want of a full and free life in creative art goes far to account for the shortcomings of Elizabethan criticism.

Vague the Elizabethan critics undeniably are; they tend to lose themselves either in far-fetched analogies or in generalities that have but a slight bearing upon the distinctive problems of literary appreciation. When not vague, they are apt to fritter their strength on technical details which, important to them, have long lost their significance for the student of literature. But both technicalities and vagueness may be largely traced to the uncertain practice of the poets upon whom, in the first instance, their criticism was based. The work of Surrey and of Sackville was tentative; that of Webbe and Puttenham was necessarily the same. It is the more honour to Sidney that, shackled as he was by conditions from which no man could escape altogether, he should have struck a note at once so deep and so strong as is sounded in the Apologie. In turning from Sidney to Dryden we pass into a different world. The philosophy, the moral fervour, the prophetic strain of the Elizabethan critic have vanished. Their place is taken by qualities less stirring in themselves, but more akin to those that modern times have been apt to associate with criticism. In fact, whatever qualities we now demand from a critic may be found at least foreshadowed, and commonly much more than foreshadowed, in Dryden. Dryden is master of comparative criticism: he has something of the historical method; he is unrivalled in the art of seizing the distinctive qualities of his author and of setting them before us with the lightest touch. His very style, so pointed yet so easy, is enough in itself to mark the gulf that lies between the age of Elizabeth and the age of the Restoration.

All the Elizabethan critics, Sidney himself hardly excepted, bore some trace of the schoolmaster. Dryden was the first to meet his readers entirely as an equal, and talk to them as a friend with friends. It is Dryden, and not Sainte-Beuve, who is the true father of the literary causerie; and he still remains its unequalled master. There may be other methods of striking the right note in literary criticism. Lamb showed that there may be; so did Mr. Pater. But few indeed are the critics who have known how to attune the mind of the reader to a subject, which beyond all others cries out for harmonious treatment, so skilfully as Dryden.

That the first great critic should come with the Restoration, was only to be expected. The age of Elizabeth was essentially a creative age. The imagination of men was too busy to leave room for self-scrutiny. Their thoughts took shape so rapidly that there was no time to think about the manner of their coming. Not indeed that there is, as has sometimes been urged, any inherent strife between the creative and the critical spirit. A great poet, we can learn from Goethe and Coleridge, may also be a great critic. More than that: without some touch of poetry in himself, no man can hope to do more than hack-work as a critic of others.

Yet it may safely be said that, if no critical tradition exists in a nation, it is not an age of passionate creation, such as was that of Marlowe and Shakespeare, that will found it. With all their alertness, with all their wide outlook, with all their zeal for classical models, the men of that time were too much of children, too much beneath the spell of their own genius, to be critics. Compare them with the great writers of other ages; and we feel instinctively that, in spite of their surroundings, they have far more of vital kindred with Homer or the creators of the mediaval epic, than with the Greek dramatistsAschylus exceptedor with Dante or with Goethe. The "freshness of the early world" is still upon them; neither they nor their contemporaries were born to the task of weighing and pondering, which is the birthright of the critic.

It was far otherwise with the men of the Restoration. The creative impulse of a century had at length spent its force. For the first time since Wyatt and Surrey, England deserted the great themes of literature, the heroic passions of Tamburlaine and Faustus, of Lear and Othello, for the trivial round of social portraiture and didactic discourse; for Essays on Satire and on Translated Verse, for the Tea-Table of the Spectator, for dreary exercises on the Pleasures of the Imagination and the Art of Preserving Health. A new era had opened. It was the day of small things. Yet it would be wrong to regard the new movement as merely negative. Had that been all, it would be impossible to account for the passionate enthusiasm it aroused in those who came beneath its spell; an enthusiasm which lived long after the movement itself was spent, and whichexcept in so far as it led to absurd comparisons with the Elizabethanswas abundantly justified by the genius of Butler and Dryden, of Congreve and Swift and Pope.

Negative, on one side, the ideal of Restoration and Augustan poetry undoubtedly was. It was a reaction against the "unchartered freedom", the real or fancied extravagances, of the Elizabethan poets. But, on the higher side, it was no less positive, though doubtless far less noble, than the ideal it displaced. The great writers of the eighty years following the Restoration were consumed by a passion for observationo- bservation of the men and things that lay immediately around them. They may have seen but little; but what they did see, they grasped with surprising force and clearness. They may not have gone far beneath the surface; but, so far as they went, their work was a model of acuteness and precision. This was the secret of their power. To this may be traced their victory in the various tasks that they undertook.

Hence, on the one hand, their success in painting the manners of their own daya task from which, with some notable exceptions, the greatest of the Elizabethans had been apt to shrink, as from something alien to their genius; and, on the other hand, the range and keenness of their satire. Hence, finally, the originality of their work in criticism, and their new departure in philosophy. The energies of these men were diverse: but all sprang from the same rootfrom their invincible resolve to see and understand their world; to probe life, as they knew it, to the bottom.

Thus the new turn given to criticism by Dryden was part of a far- reaching intellectual movement; a movement no less positive and self- contained than, in another aspect, it was negative and reactionary. And it is only when taken as part of that movement, as side by side with the philosophy of Locke and the satire of Swift or Pope, that its true meaning can be understood. Nor is it the least important or the least attractive of Dryden's qualities, as a critic, that both the positive and the negative elements of the prevailing tendencyboth the determination to understand and the wish to bring all things under ruleshould make themselves felt so strongly and, on the whole, so harmoniously in his Essays.

No man could have felt more keenly the shortcomings of the Elizabethan writers. No man could have set greater store by that "art of writing easily" which was the chief pride of the Restoration poets. Yet no man has ever felt a juster admiration for the great writers of the opposite school; and no man has expressed his reverence for them in more glowing words. The highest eulogy that has yet been passed on Milton, the most discriminating but at the same time the most generous tribute that has ever been offered to Shakespeareboth these are to be found in Dryden. And they are to be found in company with a perception, at once reasoned and instinctive, of what criticism means, that was altogether new to English literature.

The finest and most characteristic of Dryden's critical writingsbut it is unfortunately also the longestis without doubt the Essay of Dramatic Poesy. The subject was one peculiarly well suited to Dryden's genius. It touched a burning question of the day, and it opened the door for a discussion of the deeper principles of the drama. The Essay itself forms part of a long controversy between Dryden and his brother-in-law, Sir Robert Howard. The dispute was opened by Dryden's preface to his tragi-comedy, The Rival Ladies, published probably, as it was certainly first acted, in 1664; and in the beginning Dryden, then first rising into fame as a dramatist, confines himself to pleading the cause of rhyme against blank verse in dramatic writing.. But, from the general drift of the argument, it seems probable that Dryden was speaking of the drama in general.

At a later stage of the dispute, however, he distinguishes between tragedy and comedy, and allows that the arguments in favour of rhyme apply only to the formera curious inversion of the truth, as it would appear to the modern mind.Ib., pp. 561, 566. Howardwho, it may reasonably be guessed, had had some brushes with Dryden over their joint tragedy, The Indian Queenat once took up the cudgels. He had written rhymed plays himself, it is true; the four plays, to which his attack on rhyme was prefixed, were such; but he saw a chance of paying off old scores against his brother-in-law, and he could not resist it. Dryden began his reply at once; but three years passed before it was published.

And the world has no reason to regret his tardiness. There are few writings of which we can say with greater certainty, as Dryden himself said of a more questionable achievement, 'T is not the hasty product of a day, But the well-ripened fruit of wise delay. The very form of the Essay bears witness to the spirit in which it is written. It is cast as a dialogue, "related"as Dryden truly says"without passion or interest, and leaving the reader to decide in favour of which part he shall judge most reasonable". The balance between opposing views is held as evenly as may be.

It is a search for truth, carried out in the "rude and undigested manner" of a friendly conversation. Roughly speaking, the subjects of the Essay are two. The first, and the more slightly treated, is the quarrel of rhyme against blank verse. The second is the far more important question, How far is the dramatist bound by conventional restrictions? The formera revival under a new form of a dispute already waged by the Elizabethansleads Dryden to sift the claims of the "heroic drama"; and his treatment of it has the special charm belonging to an author's defence of his artistic hearth and home. The latter is a theme which, under some shape or other, will be with us wherever the stage itself has a place in our life.

This is not the place to discuss at length the origin or the historical justification of the Heroic Drama. There is perhaps no form of art that so clearly marks the transition from the Elizabethan age to that of the Restoration. Transitional it must certainly be called; for, in all vital points, it stands curiously apart from the other forms of Restoration literature. It has nothing either of the negative or the positive qualities, nothing of the close observation and nothing of the measure and self-restraint, that all feel to be the distinctive marks of the Restoration temper. On the other hand the heroic drama, of which Dryden's Conquest of Granada and Tyrannic Love may be taken as fair samples, has obvious affinities with the more questionable side of the Elizabethan stage. It may be defined as wanting in all the virtues and as exaggerating all the vices of the Elizabethan dramatists.

Whatever was most wild in the wildest of the Elizabethan playsthe involved plots, the extravagant incidents, the swelling metaphors and similesall this reappears in the heroic drama. And it reappears without any of the dramatic force or of the splendid poetry which are seldom entirely absent from the work of the Elizabethan and Jacobean dramatists. The term "heroic drama" is, in fact, a fraud. The plays of Dryden and his school are at best but moc-heroic; and they are essentially undramatic. The truth is that these plays take something of the same place in the history of the English drama that is held by the verse of Donne and Cowley in the history of the English lyric. The extravagant incidents correspond to the far-fetched conceits which, unjustly enough, made the name of Donne a by-word with the critics of the last century.

The metaphors and similes are as abundant and overcharged, though assuredly not so rich in imagination, as those of the "metaphysical" poets. And Dryden, if we may accept the admission of Bayes, "loved argument in verse"; a confession that Donne and Cowley would heartily have echoed. The exaggerations of the heroic drama are the exaggerations of the metaphysical poets transferred from the study to the stage; with the extravagance deepened, as was natural, by the glare of their new surroundings. And, just as the extravagance of the "metaphysicians" led to the reaction that for a hundred years stifled the lyric note in English song, so the extravagance of the heroic drama gave the death-blow to English tragedy.

Against this parallel the objection may be raised that it takes no reckoning of the enormous gulf that, when all is said, separates even the weakest of the Elizabethan plays from the rant and fustian of Dryden: a gulf wider, it must be admitted, than that which parts the metaphysical poets from the "singing birds" of the Elizabethan era. And, so far as we have yet gone, the objection undoubtedly has force. It is only to be met if we can find some connecting link; if we can point to some author who, on the one hand, retains something of the dramatic instinct, the grace and flexibility of the Elizabethans; and, on the other hand, anticipates the metallic ring, the declamation and the theatrical conventions of Dryden.

Such an author is to be found in Shirley; in Shirley, as he became in his later years; at the time, for instance, when he wrote The Cardinal (1641). The Cardinal is, in many respects, a powerful play. It is unmistakably written under the influence of Webster; and of Webster at his most sombre and his bestthe Webster of the Duchess of Malfi. But it is no less unmistakably wanting in the subtle strength, the dramatic grip and profound poetry, of its model. The villainy of the Cardinal is mere mechanism beside the satanic, yet horribly human, iniquity of Ferdinand and Bosolo. And, at least in one scene, Shirley sinksit is true, in the person of a subordinate characterto a foul-mouthed vulgarity which recalls the shameless bombast of the heroes and heroines of Dryden.

Yet, with all his shortcomings, Shirley preserves in the main the great tradition of the Elizabethans. A further step downwards, a more deadly stage in the history of decadence, is marked by Sir William Davenant. That arch-impostor, as is well known, had the effrontery to call himself the "son of Shakespeare": a phrase which the unwary have taken in the physical sense, but which was undoubtedly intended to mark his literary kinship with the Elizabethans in general and with the greatest of Elizabethan dramatists in particular.

So far as dates go, indeed, the work of Davenant may be admitted to fall within what we loosely call the Elizabethan period; or, more strictly, within the last stage of the period that began with Elizabeth and continued throughout the reigns of her two successors. His first tragedy, Albovine, King of the Lombards, was brought out in 1629; and his earlier work was therefore contemporary with that of Massinger and Ford. But much beyond this his relation to the Elizabethans can hardly claim to go. Charity may allow him some faint and occasional traces of the dramatic power which is their peculiar glory; and this is perhaps more strongly marked in his earliest play than in any of its successors. What strikes us most forcibly, howeverand that, even in his more youthful workis the obvious anticipation of much that we associate only with the Restoration period. The historical plot, the metallic ring of the verse,the fustian and the bombast we have here every mark, save one, of what afterwards came to be known as the heroic drama. The rhymed couplet alone is wanting.

And that was added by Davenant himself at a later stage of his career. It was in The Siege of Rhodes, of which the first part was published in 1656, that the heroic couplet, after an interval of about sixty years, made its first reappearance on the English stage. It was garnished, no doubt, with much of what then passed for Pindaric lyric; it was eked out with music. But the fashion was set; and within ten years the heroic couplet and the heroic drama had swept everything before them. The above dates are enough to disprove the common belief that the heroic drama, rhymed couplet and all, was imported from France. Albovine, as we have seen, has every mark of the heroic drama, except the couplet; and Albovine was written seven years before the first masterpiece of Corneille, one year before his first attempt at tragedy.

A superficial likeness to the drama of Corneille and, subsequently, of Racine may doubtless have given wings to the popularity of the new style both with Davenant and his admirers. But the heroic drama is, in truth, a native growth: for good or for evil, to England alone must be given the credit of its birth. Dryden, no doubt, more than once claims French descent for the literary form with which his fame was then bound up. In a well-known prologue he describes his tragic-comedy, The Maiden Queen, as a mingled chime Of Jonson's humour and Corneille's rhyme.

But the fact is that of Corneille there is no more trace in Dryden's tragedy than there is of Jonson in his comedy; that is, just none at all. The heroic temper, which was at once the essence of Corneille's plays and true to the very soul of the man, was mere affectation and mise-en-scene with Dryden. The heroes of Corneille reflect that nobility of spirit which never entirely forsook France till the days of the Regency; those of Dryden give utterance to nothing better than the insolent swagger of the Restoration.

To the peculiar spirit of the heroic dramato its strength as well as to its weaknessno metrical form could have been more closely adapted than the heroic couplet. It was neither flexible nor delicate; but in the hands of Dryden, even more than in those of Davenant, it became an incomparably vigorous and effective weapon of declamation. As the most unmistakable and the most glaring mark of the new method it was naturally placed in the forefront of the battle waged by Dryden in defence of the heroic drama. It seems, indeed, to have struck him as the strongest advantage possessed by the Restoration drama over the Elizabethan, and as that which alone was wanting to place the Elizabethan drama far ahead both of the Greek and of the French.

The claims of rhyme to Dryden's regard would seem to have been twofold. On the one hand, he thought that it served to "bound and circumscribe" the luxuriance of the poet's fancy. On the other hand, it went to "heighten" the purely dramatic element and to "move that admiration which is the delight of serious plays" and to which "a bare imitation" will not suffice. Both grounds of defence will seem to the modern reader questionable enough. Howard at once laid his finger upon the weak spot of the first. "It is", he said, "no argument for the matter in hand. For the dispute is not what way a man may write best in; but which is most proper for the subject he writes upon. And, if this were let pass, the argument is yet unsolved in itself; for he that wants judgement in the liberty of his fancy may as well shew the want of it in its confinement." Besides, he adds in effect on the next page, so far from "confining the fancy" rhyme is apt to lead to turgid and stilted writing.

The second argument stands on higher ground. It amounts to a plea for the need of idealization; and, so far, may serve to remind us that the extravagances of the heroic drama had their stronger, as well as their weaker, side. No one, however, will now be willing to admit that the cause of dramatic idealization is indeed bound up with the heroic couplet; and a moment's thought will show the fallacy of Dryden's assumption that it is. In the first place, he takes for granted that, the further the language of the drama is removed from that of actual life, the nearer the spirit of it will approach to the ideal. An unwarrantable assumption, if there ever was one; and an assumption, as will be seen, that contains the seeds of the whole eighteenth-century theory of poetic diction. In the second placebut this is, in truth, only the deeper aspect of the former pleaDryden comes perilously near to an acceptance of the doctrine that idealization in a work of art depends purely on the outward form and has little or nothing to do with the conception or the spirit.

The bond between form and matter would, according to this view, be purely arbitrary. By a mere turn of the hand, by the substitution of rhyme for proseor for blank verse, which is on more than "measured" or harmonious prosethe baldest presentment of life could be converted into a dramatic poem. From the grosser forms of this fallacy Dryden's fine sense was enough to save him. Indeed, in the remarks on Jonson's comedies that immediately follow, he expressly rejects them; and seldom does he show a more nicely balanced judgement than in what he there says on the limits of imitation in the field of art. But in the passage before usin his assertion that "the converse must be heightened with all the arts and ornaments of poetry"it is hard to resist a vision of the dramatist first writing his dialogue in bald and skimble-skamble prose, and then wringing his brains to adorn it "with all the arts" of the dramatic gradus.

DOMINATED THE CRITICISM AND PERVERTED THE ART OF THE EIGHTEENTH CENTURY

Here again we have the seeds of the fatal theory which dominated the criticism and perverted the art of the eighteenth century; the theory which, finding in outward form the only distinction between prose and poetry, was logically led to look for the special themes of poetic art in the dissecting-room or the pulpit, and was driven to mark the difference by an outrageous diction that could only be called poetry on the principle that it certainly was not prose; the theory which at length received its death-blow from the joint attack of Wordsworth and Coleridge.

It remains only to note the practical issue of the battle of the metres. In the drama the triumph of the heroic couplet was for the moment complete; but it was short-lived. By 1675, the date of Aurungzebe, Dryden proclaimed himself already about to "weary of his long-loved mistress, Rhyme"; and his subsequent plays were all written in blank verse or prose. But the desertion of "his mistress" brought him little luck; and the rest of his tragedies show a marked falling off in that splendid vigour which went far to redeem even the grossest absurdities of his heroic plays.

A more sensitive, though a weaker, genius joined him in the rejection of rhyme; and the example of Otwaywhose two crucial plays belong to 1680 and 1682did perhaps more than that of Dryden himself, more even than the assaults of The Rehearsal, to discredit the heroic drama. With the appearance of Venice Preserved, rhyme ceased to play any part in English tragedy. But at the same time, it must be noted, tragedy itself began to drop from the place which for the last century it had held in English life. From that day to this no acting tragedy, worth serious attention, has been written for the English stage.

The reaction against rhyme was not confined to the drama. The epic, indeedor what in those days passed for suchcan hardly be said to have come within its scope. In the Essay of Dramatic Poesy Drydenand this is one of the few judgements in which Howard heartily agrees with himhad denounced rhyme as "too low for a poem"; by which, as the context shows, is meant an epic. This was written the very year in which Paradise Lost, with its laconic sneer at rhyme as a device "to set off wretched matter and lame metre", was given to the world. That, however, did not prevent Dryden from asking, and obtaining, leave to "tag its verses" into an opera; nor did it deter Blackmoreand, at a much later time, Wilkie from reverting to the metre that Milton had scorned to touch. It is not till the present century that blank verse can be said to have fairly taken seisin of the epic; one of the many services that English poetry owes to the genius of Keats.

In the more nondescript kinds of poetry, however, the revolt against rhyme spread faster than in the epic. In descriptive and didactic poetry, if anywhere, rhyme might reasonably claim to hold its place. There is much to be said for the opinion that, in such subjects, rhyme is necessary to fix the wandering attention of the reader. Yet, for all that, the great efforts of the reflective muse during the next century were, with hardly an exception, in blank verse.

It is enough to recall the Seasons of Thomson, the discourses of Akenside and Armstrong, and the Night Thoughts of the arch-moralist Young. In the case of Youngas later in that of Cowperthis is the more remarkable, because his Satires show him to have had complete command of the mechanism of the heroic couplet. That he should have deliberately chosen the rival metre is proofa proof which even the exquisite work of Goldsmith is not sufficient to gainsaythat, by the middle of the eighteenth century the heroic couplet had been virtually driven from every field of poetry, save that of satire. We may now turn to the second of the two themes with which Dryden is mainly occupied in the Essay of Dramatic Poesy. What are the conventional restrictions that surround the dramatist, and how far are they of binding force?

That the drama is by nature a conventionmore than this, a convention accepted largely with a view to the need of idealizationthe men of Dryden's day were in no danger of forgetting. The peril with them was all the other way.

The fashion of that age was to treat the arbitrary usages of the classical theatre as though they were binding for all time. Thus, of the four men who take part in the dialogue of the Essay, three are emphatically agreed in bowing down before the three unities as laws of nature.

Dryden himself (Neander) is alone in questioning their divinity: a memorable proof of his critical independence; but one in which, as he maliciously points out, he was supported by the greatest of living dramatists. Corneille could not be suspected of any personal motive for undertaking the defence of dramatic license. Yet he closed his Discourse of the Three Unities with the admission that he had "learnt by experience how much the French stage was constrained and bound up by the observance of these rules, and how many beauties it had sacrificed". When the two leading masters of the 'Classical Drama', the French and the English, joined hands to cast doubt upon the sacred unities, its opponents might well feel easy as to the ultimate issue of the dispute.

Dryden was not the man to bound his argument by any technical question, even when it touched a point so fundamental as the unities. Nothing is more remarkable in the Essay, as indeed in all his critical work, than the wide range which he gives to the discussion. And never has the case againstwe can hardly add, forthe French drama been stated more pointedly than by him. His main charge, as was to be expected, is against its monotony, and, in close connection with that, against its neglect of action and its preference for declamation. Having defined the drama as "a just and lively image of human nature, in its actions, passions and traverses of fortune", he proceeds to test the claims of the French stage by that standard.

Its characters, he finds, are wanting in variety and nature. Its range of passion and humour is lamentably narrow. Its declamations "tire us with their length; so that, instead of grieving for their imaginary heroes, we are concerned for our own trouble, as we are in the tedious visits of bad company; we are in pain till they are gone". The best tragedies of the FrenchCinna and Pompey"are not so properly to be called Plays as long discourses of Reason of State". Upon their avoidance of action he is hardly less severe. "If we are to be blamed for showing too much of the action"one is involuntarily reminded of the closing scene of Tyrannic Love and of the gibes in The Rehearsal"the French are as faulty for discovering too little of it ".

Given the definition with which he startsbut it is a definition that no Frenchman of the seventeenth or eighteenth century would have admittedit is hard to see how Dryden could have reached a substantially different result. Nor, if comparisons of this sort are to be made at all, is there muchso far, at least, as Shakespeare is concernedto find fault with in the verdict with which he closes. Yet it is impossible not to regret that Dryden should have failed to recognize the finer spirit and essence of French tragedy, as conceived by Corneille: the strong-tempered heroism of soul, the keen sense of honour, the consuming fire of religion, to which it gives utterance. The truth is that Dryden stood at once too near, and too far from, the ideals of Corneille to appreciate them altogether at their just value. Too near because he instinctively associated them with the heroic drama, which at the bottom of his heart he knew to be no better than an organized trick, done daily with a view to "elevate and surprise". Too far, because, in spite of his own candid and generous temper, it was well-nigh impossible for the Laureate of the Restoration to comprehend the highly strung nature of a man like Corneille, and his intense realization of the ideal.

But, if Dryden is blind to the essential qualities of Corneille, he is at least keenly alive to those of Shakespeare. It is a memorable thing that the most splendid tribute ever offered to the prince of Elizabethans should have come from the leading spirit of the Restoration. It has often been quoted, but it will bear quoting once again.

"Shakespeare was the man who, of all modern and perhaps ancient poets, had the largest and most comprehensive soul. All the images of nature were still present to him; and he drew them not laboriously, but luckily. When he describes anything, you more than see it, you feel it too. Those who accuse him to have wanted learning give him the great commendation. He was naturally learned. He needed not the spectacles of books to read nature; he looked inwards and found her there. I cannot say he is everywhere alike. Were he so, I should do him injury to compare him with the greatest of mankind. He is many times flat, insipid; his comic wit degenerating into clenches, his serious swelling into bombast. But he is always great when some great occasion is presented to him. No man can say, he ever had a fit subject for his wit, and did not then raise himself as high above the rest of poets, Quantum lenta solent inter viburna cupressi."

The same keenness of appreciation is found in Dryden's estimate of other writers who might have seemed to lie beyond the field of his immediate vision. Of Milton he is recorded to have said: "He cuts us all out, and the ancients too".On Chaucer he is yet more explicit. "As he is the father of English poetry, so I hold him in the same degree of veneration as the Grecians held Homer, or the Romans Virgil. He is a perpetual fountain of good sense; learned in all sciences, and therefore speaks properly on all subjects.

As he knew what to say, so he knows also when to leave off, a continence which is practised by few writers, and scarcely by any of the ancients, excepting Virgil and Horace... Chaucer followed nature everywhere, but was never so bold to go beyond her." This points to what was undoubtedly the most shining quality of Dryden, as a critic: his absolute freedom from preconceived notions, his readiness to "follow nature" and to welcome nature in whatever form she might appear. That was the more remarkable because it ran directly counter both to the general spirit of the period to which he belonged and to the prevailing practice of the critics who surrounded him. The spirit of the Restoration age was critical in the invidious, no less than in the nobler, sense of the word. It was an age of narrow ideals and of little ability to look beyond them. In particular, it was an age of carping and of fault-finding; an age within measurable distance of the pedantic system perfected in France by Boileau, and warmly adopted by a long line of English critics from Roscoromon and Buckinghamshire to the Monthly Reviewers and to Johnson. Such writers might always have "nature" on their lips; but it was nature seen through the windows of the lecture room or down the vista of a street.

With Dryden it was not so. With him we never fail to get an unbiassed judgement; the judgement of one who did not crave for nature "to advantage dressed", but trusted to the instinctive freshness of a mind, one of the most alert and open that ever gave themselves to literature. It is this that puts an impassable barrier between Dryden and the men of his own day, or for a century to come. It is this that gives him a place among the great critics of modern literature, and makes the passage from him to the schoolmen of the next century so dreary a descent. Dryden's openness of mind was his own secret. The comparative method was, in some measure, the common property of his generation. This, in fact, was the chief conquest of the Restoration and Augustan critics. It is the mark that serves to distinguish them most clearly from those of the Elizabethan age. Not that the Elizabethans are without comparisons; but that the parallels they saw were commonly of the simplest, not to say of the most childish, cast. Every sentence of Meres' critical effortor, to be rigorously exact, every sentence but oneis built on "as" and "so"; but it reads like a parodya schoolmaster's parodyof Touchstone's improvement on Orlando's verses in praise of Rosalind. Shakespeare is brought into line with Ovid, Elizabeth with Achilles, and Homer with William Warner.

This, no doubt, is an extreme instance; but it is typical of the artless methods dear to the infancy of criticism. In Jonson's Discoveries, such comparisons as there are have indisputable point; but they are few, and, for the most part, they are limited to the minuter matters of style. It is with the Restoration that the comparative method first made its way into English criticism; and that both in its lawful and less lawful use. The distinction must be jealously made; for there are few matters that lend themselves so readily to confusion and misapprehension as this. Between two men, or two forms of art, a comparison may be run either for the sake of placing the one above the head of the other, or for the sake of drawing out the essential differences between the one and the other. The latter method is indispensable to the work of the critic. Without reference, express or implied, to other types of genius or to other ways of treatment it is impossible for criticism to take a single step in definition either of an author, or a movement, or a form of art.

In a vague and haphazard fashion, even the Elizabethans were comparative. Meres was so in his endless stream of classical parallels; Sidney, after a loftier strain, in his defence of harmonious prose as a form of poetry. And it is the highest achievement of modern criticism to have brought science and order into the comparative method, and largely to have widened its scope. In this sense, comparison is criticism; and to compare with increased intelligence, with a clearer consciousness of the end in view, is to reform criticism itself, to make it a keener weapon and more effective for its purpose.

A comparison of qualities, however, is one thing, and a comparison between different degrees of merit is quite another. The former is the essence of criticism; the latter, one of the most futile pastimes that can readily be imagined. That each man should have his own preferences is right enough. It would be a nerveless and unprofitable mind to which such preferences were unknown. More than that, some rough classification, some understanding with oneself as to what authors are to be reckoned supreme masters of their craft, is hardly to be avoided. The mere fact that the critic lays stress on certain writers and dismisses others with scant notice or none at all, implies that in some sense he has formed an estimate of their relative merits. But to drag this process from the backgroundif we ought not rather to say, from behind the scenesto the very foot-lights, to publish it, to insist upon it, is as irrelevant as it would be for the historian and he, too, must make his own perspectiveto explain why he has recorded some events and left others altogether unnoticed. All this is work for the dark room; it should leave no trace, or as little as may be, upon the finished picture. Criticism has suffered from few things so much as from its incurable habit of granting degrees in poetry with honours. "The highest art", it has been well said, "is the region of equals." It must be admitted that the Restoration critics had an immoderate passion for classing authors according to their supposed rank in the scale of literary desert.

A glance at The Battle of the Booksa faint reflection of the quarrel between the ancients and the modernsis enough to place this beyond dispute. Dryden himself is probably as guilty as any in this matter. His parallel between Juvenal and Horace, his comparison of Homer with Virgil, are largely of the nature of an attempt to show each poet to his proper place, to determine their due order of precedence in the House of Fame. In the early days of criticism this was perhaps to be expected. Men were feeling their way to the principles; and the shortest road might naturally seem to lie through a comparative table of the men. They were right in thinking that the first step was to ascertain what qualities, and what modes of treatment, give lasting pleasure in poetry; and, to do this, they could not but turn to compare the works of individual poets. But they were wrong in supposing that they could learn anything by striking the balance between the merits of one poet, as a sum total, and the merits of another. The fault was, no doubt, largely in the Restoration critics themselves; and it is a fault which, so long as the competitive instinct holds sway with men, will never be entirely unknown.

But its hold on the men of Dryden's day was in great measure due to the influence of the French critics, and to the narrow lines which criticism had taken in France. No one can read Boileau's Art Poetique, no one can compare it with the corresponding Essay of Pope, without feeling that the purely personal element had eaten into the heart of French criticism to a degree which could never have been natural in England, and which, even in the darkest days of English literature, has seldom been approached. But at the same time it will be felt that never has England come nearer to a merely personal treatment of artistic questions than in the century between Dryden and Johnson; and that it was here, rather than in the adoption of any specific form of literaturerather, for instance, than in the growth of the heroic dramathat the influence of France is to be traced. Side by side, however, with the baser sort of comparisons, we find in the Restoration critics no small use of the kind that profits and delights. Rymer's Remarks on the Tragedies of the Former Age are an instance of the comparative method, in its just sense, as employed by a man of talent. The essays of Dryden abound in passages of this nature, that could only have been written by a man of genius. They may have a touch of the desire to set one form of art, or one particular poet, in array against another.

But, when all abatements have been made, they remain unrivalled samples of the manner in which the comparative vein can be worked by a master spirit. To the student of English literature they have a further interestnotably, perhaps, the comparison between Juvenal and Horace and the eulogy of Shakespeareas being among the most striking examples of that change from the Latinized style of the early Stuart writers to the short, pointed sentence commonly associated with French; the change that was inaugurated by Hobbes, but only brought to completion by Dryden. Once again. As Dryden was among the earliest to give the comparative method its due place in English criticism, so he was the first to make systematic use of the historical method. Daniel, indeed, in a remarkable essay belonging to the early years of the century, had employed that method in a vague and partial manner.

He had defended rhyme on the score of its popularity with all ages and all nations. Celts, Slavs, and HunsParthians and Medes and Elamitesare all pressed into the service. That is, perhaps, the first instance in which English criticism can be said to have attempted tracing a literary form through the various stages of its growth. But Daniel wrote without system and without accuracy. It was reserved for Drydenavowedly following in the steps of the French critic Dacierto introduce the order and the fulness of knowledgein Dryden's case, it must be admitted, a knowledge at second handwhich are indispensable to a fruitful use of the historical method. In this sense, tooas in his use of the comparative method, as in the singular grace and aptness of his styleDryden was a pioneer in the field of English criticism.

Over the century that parts Dryden from Johnson it is not well to linger. During that time criticism must be said, on the whole, to have gone back rather than to have advanced. With some reservations to be noticed later, the critics of the eighteenth century are a depressing study. Their conception of the art they professed was barren; their judgements of men and things were lamentably narrow. The more valuable elements traceable in the work of Drydenthe comparative and the historical treatmentdisappear or fall into the background. We are left with little but the futile exaltation of one poet at the expense of his rivals, or the still more futile insistence upon faults, shortcomings, and absurdities. The Dunciad, the most marked critical work of the period, may be defended on the ground that it is the Dunciad; a war waged by genius upon the fool, the pedant, and the fribble. But, none the less, it had a disastrous influence upon English criticism and English taste. It gave sanction to the habit of indiscriminate abuse; it encouraged the purely personal treatment of critical discussions. Its effects may be traced on writers even of such force as Smollett; of such genius and natural kindliness as Goldsmith. But it was on Johnson that Pope's influence made itself most keenly felt.

THE LIVES OF THE POETS

And The Lives of the Poets, though not written till the movement that gave it birth had spent its force, is the most complete and the most typical record of the tendencies that shaped English literature and gave the law to English taste from the Restoration to the French Revolution: a notable instance of the fact so often observed, and by some raised to the dignity of a general law, that both in philosophy and in art, the work of the critic does not commonly begin till the creative impulse of a given period is exhausted.

What, then, was Johnson's method? and what its practical application? The method is nothing if not magisterial. It takes for granted certain fixed lawswhether the laws formulated by Aristotle, or by Horace, or the French critics, is for the moment beside the questionand passes sentence on every work of art according as it conforms to the critical decalogue or transgresses it. The fault of this method is not, as is sometimes supposed, that it assumes principles in a subject where none are to be sought; but that its principles are built on a miserably narrow and perverted basis. That there are principles of criticism, that the artist's search for beauty must be guided by some idea, is obvious enough.

It can be questioned only by those who are prepared to deny the very possibility of criticism; who would reduce the task both of critic and of artist to a mere record of individual impressions. It need hardly be said that the very men who are most ready to profess such a doctrine with their lips, persistently, and rightly, give the lie to it in their deeds. No creative work, no critical judgement, either is or can be put forward as a mere impression; it is the impression of a trained mindthat is, of a mind which, instinctively or as a conscious process, is guided by principles or ideas.

So far, then, as he may be held to have borne witness to the need of ideas, Johnson was clearly in the right. It was when he came to ask, What is the nature of those ideas, and how does the artist or the critic arrive at them? that he began to go astray. Throughout he assumes that the principles of artand that, not only in their general bearing (proportion, harmony, and the like), but in their minuter details-are fixed and invariable. To him they form a kind of case-law, which is to be extracted by the learned from the works of a certain number of "correct writers", ancient and modern; and which, once established, is binding for all time both on the critic and on those he summons to his bar.

In effect, this was to declare that beauty can be conceived in no other way than as it presented itself, say, to Virgil or to Pope. It was to lay the dead hand of the past upon the present and the future. More than this. The models that lent themselves to be models, after the kind desired by Johnson, were inevitably just those it was most cramping and least inspiring to follow. They were the men who themselves wrote, to some degree, by rule; in whom "correctness" was stronger than inspiration; who, however admirable in their own achievement, were lacking in the nobler and subtler qualities of the poet. They were not the Greeks; not even, at first hand, the Latins; though the names both of Greek and Latin were often on Johnson's lips. They were rather the Latins as filtered through the English poets of the preceding century; the Latins in so far as they had appealed to the writers of the "Augustan age", but no further; the Latins, as masters of satire, of declamation, and of the lighter kinds of verse. It was Latin poetry without Lucretius and Catullus, without the odes of Horace, without the higher strain of the genius of Virgil. In other words, it was poetry as conceived by Boileau or Addison-or Mr. Smith.

Yet again. In the hands of Johnsonand it was a necessary consequence of his critical methodpoetry becomes more and more a mere matter of mechanism. Once admit that the greatness of a poet depends upon his success in following certain models, and it is but a short stepif indeed it be a stepfurther to say that he must attempt no task that has not been set him by the example of his forerunners. It is doubtless true that Johnson did not, in so many words, commit himself to this absurdity. But it is equally true that any poet, who overstepped the bounds laid down by previous writers, was likely to meet with but little mercy at his hands.

Milton, Cowley, Grayfor all had the audacity to take an untrodden path in poetry-one after another are dragged up for execution. It is clear that by example, if not by precept, Johnson was prepared to "make poetry a mere mechanic art"; and Cowper was right in saying that it had become so with Pope's successors. Indeed Johnson himself, in closing his estimate of Pope, seems half regretfully to anticipate Cowper's verdict. "By perusing the works of Dryden, he discovered the most perfect fabrick of English verse, and habituated himself to that only which he found the best.

New sentiments and new images others may produce; but to attempt any further improvement of versification will be dangerous. Art and diligence have now done their best, and what shall be added will be the effort of tedious toil and needless curiosity". But Johnson failed to see that his own view of poetry led inevitably to this lame and impotent conclusion. To adopt Johnson's method is, in truth, to misconceive the whole nature of poetry and of poetic imagination.

The ideas that have shaped the work of one poet may act as guide and spur, but can never be a rulefar less a lawto the imagination of another. The idea, as it comes to an artist, is not a law imposing itself from without; it is a seed of life and energy springing from within. This, however, was a truth entirely hidden from the eyes of Johnson and the Augustan critics. To assert it both by word and deed, both as critics and as poets, was the task of Coleridge, and of those who joined hands with Coleridge, in the succeeding generation. Apart from the undying beauty of their work as artists, this was the memorable service they rendered to poetry in England.

It remains to illustrate the method of Johnson by its practical application. As has already been said, Johnson is nothing if not a hanging judge; and it is just where originality is most striking that his sentences are the most severe. If there was one writer who might have been expected to win his favour, it was Pope; and if there is any work that bears witness to the originality of Pope's genius, it is the imitations of Horace. These are dismissed in a disparaging sentence.

There is no adequate recognition of Congreve's brilliance as a dramatist; none of Swift's amazing powers as a satirist. Yet all these were men who lived more or less within the range of ideas and tendencies by which Johnson's own mind was moulded and inspired. The case is still worse when we turn to writers of a different school. Take the poets from the Restoration to the closing years of the American war; and it is not too much to say that, with the exception of Thomsonsaved perhaps by his "glossy, unfeeling diction"there is not one of them who overstepped the bounds marked out for literary effort by the prevailing taste of the Augustan age, in its narrowest sense, without paying the price for his temerity in the sneers or reprobation of Johnson.

Collins, it is true, escapes more lightly than the rest; but that is probably due to the affection and pity of his critic. Yet even Collins, perhaps the most truly poetic spirit of the century between Milton and Burns, is blamed for a "diction often harsh, unskillfully laboured, and injudiciously selected"; for "lines commonly of slow motion"; for "poetry that may sometimes extort praise, when it gives little pleasureThe poems of Grayan exception must be made, to Johnson's honour, in favour of the Elegy are slaughtered in detail; the man himself is given dog's burial with the compendious epitaph: "A dull fellow, sir; dull in company, dull in his closet, dull everywhere".

But most astonishing of all, as is well known, is the treatment bestowed on Milton. Of all Milton's works, Paradise Lost seems to have been the only one that Johnson genuinely admired. That he praises with as little of reservation as was in the nature of so stern a critic. On Paradise Regained he is more guarded; on Samson, more guarded yet. But it is in speaking of the earlier poems that Johnson shows his hand most plainly. Comus "is a drama in the epic style, inelegantly splendid and tediously instructive". As for the sonnets, "they deserve not any particular criticism. For of the best it can only be said that they are not bad; and perhaps only the eighth and twenty-first are truly entitled to this slender commendation.... These little pieces may be dismissed without much anxiety".

It would be hardly worth while to record these ill-tempered judgements if they were not the natural outcome of a method which held unquestioned sway over English taste for a full centuryin France for nearly twoand which, during that time, if we except Gray and his friends, was not seriously disputed by a single man of mark. The one author in whose favour the rules of "correct writing" were commonly set aside was Shakespeare; and perhaps there is no testimony to his greatness so convincing as the unwilling homage it extorted from the contemporaries of Pope, of Johnson, and of Hume. Johnson's own notes and introductions to the separate plays are at times trifling enough; but his general preface is a solid and manly piece of work. It contrasts strangely not only with the verdicts given above, but with his jeers at Chevy Chase One more instance, and we may leave this depressing study in critical perversity.

Among the great writers of Johnson's day there was none who showed a truer originality than Fielding; no man who broke more markedly with the literary superstitions of the time; none who took his own road with more sturdiness and self-reliance. This was enough for Johnson, who persistently depreciated both the man and his work. Something of this should doubtless be set down to disapproval of the free speech and readiness to allow for human frailty, which could not but give offence to a moralist so unbending as Johnson. But that will hardly account for the assertion that "Harry Fielding knew nothing but the outer shell of life"; still less for the petulant ruling that he "was a barren rascal".

The truth isand Johnson felt it instinctivelythat the novel, as conceived by Fieldingthe novel that gloried in painting all sides of life, and above all in drawing out the humour of its "lower spheres"dealt a fatal blow not only at the pompous canons which the Rambler was pleased to call "the indispensable laws of Aristotelian criticism", but also at the view which found "human life to be a state where much is to be endured and little to be enjoyed". It would be hard to say whether Johnson found more in Fielding to affront him, as pessimist or as critic. And it would be equally hard to say in which of the two characters lay the greater barrier to literary insight. Even Richardsonno less revolutionary, though in a different way, than Fieldingwas only saved so as by fire; by the undying hatred which he shared with Johnson for his terrible rival. It was rather as moralist than as artist, rather for "the sentiment" than for the tragic force of his work, that Richardson seems to have won his way to Johnson's heart.

Is not the evidence conclusive? Is it a harsh judgement to say that no critic so narrow, so mechanical, so hostile to originality as Johnson has ever achieved the dictatorship of English letters? The supremacy of Johnson would have been impossible, had not the way been smoothed for it by a long succession of critics like-minded with himself. Such a succession may be traced from Swift to

Addison, from Addison to Pope, andwith marked reservationsfrom Pope to Goldsmith. It would be unjust to charge all, or indeed any, of these with the narrowness of view betrayed in Johnson's verdicts on individual writers.

To arrive at this perfection of sourness was a work of time; and the nature of Addison and Goldsmith at least was too genial to allow of any approach to it. But, with all their difference of temperament, the method of the earlier critics is hardly to be distinguished from that of Johnson. There is the same orderliness of treatmentfirst the fable, then the characters, lastly the sentiment and the diction; the same persistency in applying general rules to a matter which, above all others, is a law to itself; the same invincible faith in "the indispensable laws of Aristotelian criticism". It is this that, in spite of its readiness to admire, makes Addison's criticism of Paradise Lost so dreary a study; and this that, in an evil hour, prompted Goldsmith to treat the soliloquy of Hamlet as though it were a schoolboy's exercise in rhetoric and logic. And yet it is with Goldsmith that we come to the first dawn of better things. The carping strain and the stiffness of method, that we cannot overlook in him, were the note of his generation. The openness to new ideas, the sense of nature, the fruitful use of the historical method, are entirely his own. There had been nothing like them in our literature since Dryden.

In criticism, as in creative work, Goldsmith marks the transition from the old order to the new. Perhaps the clearest indication of this is to be found in his constant appeal to nature. In itself, as we have seen, this may mean much or little. "Nature" is a vague word; it was the battle-cry of Wordsworth, but it was also the battle-cry of Boileau.

And, at first sight, it might seem to be used by Goldsmith in the narrower rather than in the wider sense. "It is the business of art", he writes, "to imitate nature, but not with a servile pencil; and to choose those attitudes and dispositions only which are beautiful and engaging." But a glance at the context will show that what Goldsmith had in mind was not "nature to advantage dressed", not nature with any adornments added by man; but nature stripped of all that to man has degrading associations; nature, to adopt the words used by Wordsworth on a kindred subject, "purified from all lasting or rational causes of dislike or disgust". It may well be that Goldsmith gave undue weight to this reservation. It may well be that he did not throw himself on nature with the unwavering constancy of Wordsworth.

But, none the less, we have hereand we have it worked out in detail the germ of the principle which, in bolder hands, gave England the Lyrical Ballads and the Essays of Lamb. In an essay not commonly reprinted, Goldsmith, laying his finger on the one weak spot in the genius of Gray, gives the poet the memorable adviceto "study the people". And throughout his own critical work, as in his novel, his comedies, and his poems, there is an abiding sense that, without this, there is no salvation for poetry. That in itself is enough to fix an impassable barrier between Goldsmith and the official criticism of his day. The other main service rendered by Goldsmith was his return to the historical method. It is true that his knowledge is no more at first hand, and is set out with still less system than that of Dryden a century before. But it is also true that he has a far keener sense of the strength which art may draw from history than his great forerunner.

Dryden confines himself to the history of certain forms of art; Goldsmith includes the history of nations also in his view. With Dryden the past is little more than an antiquarian study; with Goldsmith it is a living fountain of inspiration for the present. The art of the pastthe poetry, say, of Teutonic or Celtic antiquityis to him an undying record of the days when man still walked hand in hand with nature. The history of the past is at once a storehouse of stirring themes ready to the hand of the artist, and the surest safeguard against both flatness and exaggeration in his work.: It offers, moreover, the truest schooling of the heart, and insensibly "enlists the passions on the side of humanity". "Poetry", Byron said, "is the feeling of a former world, and future"; and to the first half of the statement Goldsmith would have heartily subscribed.

For the historical method in his hands is but another aspect of the counsel he gave to Gray: "Study the people". It is an anticipationvague, no doubt, but still unmistakableof the spirit which, both in France and England, gave birth to the romantic movement a generation or two later. That zeal for the literature of the past was in the air when Goldsmith wrote is proved by works so different as those of Gray and Percy, of Chatterton and MacPherson, of Mallet and Warton.But it may be doubted whether any one of them, Gray excepted, saw the true bearing of the movement more clearly than Goldsmith, or did more to open fresh springs of thought and beauty for the poetry of the next age, if not of his own. It would be unpardonable to turn from the writers of the eighteenth century with no notice of a book which, seldom now read, is nevertheless perhaps the most solid piece of work that modern Europe had as yet to show in any branch of literary criticism. This is Burke's treatise On the Sublime and the Beautiful.

Few will now be prepared to accept the material basis which Burke finds for the ideas of the imagination. But none can deny the skill with which he works out his theory, nor the easy mastery with which each part is fitted into its place. The speculative power of the book and the light it throws on the deeper springs of the imagination are alike memorable.

The first is not unworthy of the Reflections or the Appeal from the New to the Old Whigs; the second shows that fruitful study of the Bible and the poets, English and classical, to which his later writings and speeches bear witness on every page. If the originality and depth of Burke's treatise is to be justly measured, it should be set side by side with those papers of Addison which Akenside expanded in his dismal Pleasures of the Imagination. The performance of Addison, grateful though one must be to him for attempting it, is thin and lifeless. That of Burke is massive and full of suggestion.

At every turn it betrays the hand of the craftsman who works with his eye upon his tools. The speculative side of criticism has never been a popular study with Englishmen, and it is no accident that one of the few attempts to deal seriously with it should have been made at the only time when philosophy was a living power among us, and when the desire to get behind the outward shows of things was keener than it has ever been before or since. But for Burke's treatise, a wide gap would have been left both in the philosophy and the criticism of the eighteenth century; and it is to be wished that later times had done more to work the vein which he so skilfully explored.

As it is, the writers both of France and Germanyabove all, Hegel in his Aesthetikhave laboured with incomparably more effect than his own countrymen, Mr. Ruskin excepted, upon the foundations that he laid. IV. Johnson's Lives of the Poets was the last word of the school which the Restoration had enthroned; the final verdict of the supreme court which gave the law to English letters from the accession of Anne to the French Revolution.

Save in the splenetic outbursts of Byronand they are not to be taken too seriouslythe indispensable laws of Aristotelian criticism fell silent at Johnson's death. A time of anarchy followed; anarchy plus the policeman's truncheon of the Edinburgh and the Quarterly. The ill-fame of these Reviews, as they were in their pride of youth, is now so great that doubts may sometimes suggest themselves whether it can possibly be deserved. No one who feels such doubts can do better than turn to the earlier numbers; he will be forced to the conclusion that, whatever their services as the journeymen of letters and of party politics, few critics could have been so incompetent to judge of genius as the men who enlisted under the standard of Jeffrey or of Gifford.

There is not, doubtless, in either Review the same iron wall of reasoned prejudice that has been noted in Johnson, but there is a plentiful lack of the clear vision and the openness to new impressions which are the first necessity of the critic. What Carlyle says of Jeffrey and the Edinburgh may be taken as the substantial truth also about Gifford and the Quarterly, and it is the most pregnant judgement that has yet been passed upon them. "Jeffrey may be said to have begun the rash, reckless style of criticising everything in heaven and earth by appeal to Moliere's maid: 'Do you like it?' 'Don't you like it?' a style which, in hands more and more inferior to that sound-hearted old lady and him, has since grown gradually to such immeasurable length among us; and he himself is one of the first that suffers by it. If praise and blame are to be perfected, not in the mouth of Moliere's maid only but in that of mischievous, precocious babes and sucklings, you will arrive at singular judgements by degrees."

Carlyle has much here to say of Jeffrey's "recklessness", his defiance of all rules, his appeal to the chance taste of the man in the crowd. He has much also to say of his acuteness, and the unrivalled authority of his decrees. But he is discreetly silent on their severity and short-sightedness.Yet this is the unpardonable sin of both Reviews: that mediocrity was applauded, but that, whenever a man of genius came before them, the chances were ten to one that he would be held up to ridicule and contempt. The very first number of the Edinburgh lays this down as an article of faith. Taking post on the recent appearance of Thalaba, the reviewer opens fire by a laboured parallel between poetry and religion. With an alteration of names it might have been written by a member of the English Church Union, or of the Holy Inquisition. "The standards of poetry have been fixed long ago by certain inspired writers, whose authority it is no longer lawful to call in question. Many profess to be entirely devoted to poetry, who have no good works to produce in support of their pretensions. The Catholic poetical Church too... has given birth to an infinite variety of heresies and errors, the followers of which have hated and persecuted each other as heartily as other bigots."

Then, turning to business, the writer proceeds to apply his creed to Southey and all his works, not forgetting the works also of his friends. "The author belongs to a sect of poets that has established itself in this country within these ten or twelve years"it would be hard to say for whose benefit in particular this date was taken"and is looked upon as one of its chief champions and apostles". "The doctrines of this sect"the Reviewer continues, with an eye upon the Alien Act"are of German origin, or borrowed from the great apostle of Geneva". Rousseau is then "named" for expulsion, together with a miscellaneous selection of his following: Schiller and Kotzebue (the next number includes Kant under the anathema), Quarles and Donne, Ambrose Phillips and Cowperperhaps the most motley crew that was ever brought together for excommunication.

It is not, however, till the end of the essay that the true root of bitterness between the critic and his victims is suffered fully to appear. "A splenetic and idle discontent with the existing institutions of society seems to be at the bottom of all their serious and peculiar sentiments." In other words, the Edinburgh takes up the work of the Anti-Jacobin; with no very good grace Jeffrey affects to sit in the seat of Canning and of Frere. So much for the "principles" of the new venture; principles, it will be seen, which appear to rest rather upon a hatred of innovation in general than upon any reasoned code, such as that of Johnson or the "Aristotelian laws", in particular. On that point, it must be clearly realized, Carlyle was in the right. It is that which marks the essential difference of the Reviewerswe can hardly say their advanceas against Johnson. We may now turn to watch the Reviewers, knife in hand, at the dissecting-table. For the twenty-five years that followed the foundation of the Edinburgh, England was more full of literary genius than it had been at any time since the age of Elizabeth. And it is not too much to say that during that period there was not one of the men, now accepted as among the chief glories of English literature, who did not fall under the lash of one, or both, of the Reviews. The leading cases will suffice.

And first, the famous attacknot altogether undeserved, it must be allowedof the Edinburgh upon Byron. "The poetry of this young lord belongs to the class which neither gods nor men are said to permit", and so on for two or three pages of rather vulgar and heartless merriment at the young lord's expense. The answer to the sneer, as all the world knows, was English Bards and Scotch Reviewers. The author of the article had reason to be proud of his feat. Never before did pertness succeed in striking such unexpected fire from genius. And it is only fair to say that the Review took its beating like a gentleman. A few years later, and the Edinburgh was among the warmest champions of the "English Bard". It was reserved for Southey, a pillar of the Quarterly, to rank him as the "Goliath" of the "Satanic school". Let us now turn to the Quarterly upon Keats. Endymion, in spite of the noble self-criticism of its preface, is denounced as "Cockney poetry" a stupid and pointless vulgarismand is branded as clothing "the most incongruous ideas in the most uncouth language".

The author is dismissed with the following amenities: "Being bitten by Leigh Hunt's insane criticism, he more than rivals the insanity of his poetry"; and we are half-surprised not to find him told, as he was by Blackwood, to "go back to the shop, Mr. John; back to the plasters, pills, and ointment-boxes". With this insolence it is satisfactory to contrast the verdict of the Edinburgh: "We have been exceedingly struck with the genius these poemsEndymion, Lamia, Isabella, The Eve of St. Agnes, and c.display, and the spirit of poetry which breathes through all their extravagance.... They are at least as full of genius as absurdity." Of Hyperion the Reviewer says: "An original character and distinct individuality is bestowed upon the poet's mythological persons.... We cannot advise its completion. For, though there are passages of some force and grandeur, it is sufficiently obvious that the subject is too far removed from all the sources of human interest to be successfully treated by any modern author". A blundering criticism, which, however, may be pardoned in virtue of the discernment, not to say the generosity, of the foregoing estimate. It would have been well had the Edinburgh always written in this vein. But Wordsworth was a sure stumbling-block to the sagacity of his critics, and he certainly never failed to call forth the insolence and flippancy of Jeffrey. Two articles upon him remain as monuments to the incompetence of the Edinburgh; the first prompted by the Poems of 1807, the second by the Excursion.

The former pronounces sentence roundly at the very start: "Mr. Wordsworth's diction has nowhere any pretence to elegance or dignity, and he has scarcely ever condescended to give the grace of correctness or dignity to his versification". From this sweeping condemnation four poemsBrougham Castle, and the sonnets on Venice, Milton, and Bonaparteare generously excepted. But, as though astonished at his own moderation, the reviewer quickly proceeds to deal slaughter among the rest. Of the closing lines of Resolution and Independence he writes: "We defy Mr. Wordsworth's bitterest enemy to produce anything at all parallel to this from any collection of English poetry, or even from the specimens of his friend, Mr. Southey". Of the stanzas to the sons of Burns, "never was anything more miserable". Alice Fell is "trash"; Yarrow Unvisited, "tedious and affected". The lines from the Ode to Duty.

"Thou dost preserve the stars from wrong, And the most ancient heavens through thee are fresh and strong," are "utterly without meaning". The poem on the Cuckoo is "absurd". The Ode on Immortality is "the most illegible and unintelligible part of the whole publication". "We venture to hope that there is now an end of this folly." But the hope is doomed to disappointment. The publication of the Excursion a few years later finds the reviewer still equal to his task. "This will never do", he begins in a fury; "the case of Mr. Wordsworth is now manifestly hopeless. We give him up as altogether incurable and beyond the power of criticism." The story of Margaret, indeed, though "it abounds, of course, with mawkish sentiment and details of preposterous minuteness, has considerable pathos".

But the other passage which one would have thought must have gone home to every heartthat which describes the communing of the wanderer with nature is singled out for ridicule; while the whole poem is judged to display "a puerile ambition of singularity, grafted on an unlucky predilection for truisms". It would be idle to maintain that in some of these slashing verdicts criticisms they cannot be calledthe reviewer does not fairly hit the mark. But these are chance strokes; and they are dealt, as the whole attack is conceived, in the worst style of the professional swash- buckler. Yet, low as is the deep they sound, a lower deep is opened by the Quarterly in its article on Shelley; an article which bears unmistakable marks of having been written under the inspiration, if not by the hand, of Southey. It is impossible to know anything about Southey without feeling that, both in character and in intellect, he had many of the qualities that go to make an enlightened critic. But his fine nature was warped by a strain of bigotry; and he had what, even in a man who otherwise gave conclusive proof of sincerity and whole-heartedness, must be set down as a strong touch of the Pharisee.

After every allowance has been made, no feeling other than indignation is possible at the tone which he thought fit to adopt towards Shelley. He opens the assault, and it is well that he does so, by an acknowledgment that the versification of the Revolt of Islam, the corpus delicti at that moment under the scalpel, is "smooth and harmonious", and that the poem is "not without beautiful passages, free from errors of taste". But the "voice of warning", as he himself would too generously have called it, is not long in making itself heard. "Mr. Shelley, with perfect deliberation and the steadiest perseverance, perverts all the gifts of his nature, and does all the injury, both public and private, which his faculties enable him to perpetrate....He draws largely on the rich stores of another mountain poet, to whose religious mind it must be matter of perpetual sorrow to see the philosophy, which comes pure and holy from his pen, degraded and perverted by this miserable crew of atheists and pantheists."

So far, perhaps, the writer may claim not to have outstepped the traditional limits of theological hatred. For what follows there is not even that poor excuse. "If we might withdraw the veil of his private life and tell what we now know about him, it would be indeed a disgusting picture that we should exhibit, but it would be an unanswerable comment on our text...Mr. Shelley is too young, too ignorant, too inexperienced, and too vicious to undertake the task of reforming any world but the little world within his own breast."For the credit of both Reviews it must be said that it would be difficult to find another instance of so foul a blow as this: Non ragioniam di lui, ma guarda e passa. Apart from their truculence, the early numbers of the Edinburgh and Quarterly are memorable for two reasons in the history of English literature. They mark the downfall of the absolute standard assumed by Johnson and others to hold good in criticism. And they led the way, slowly indeed but surely, to the formation of a general interest in literature, which, sooner or later, could not but be fatal to their own haphazard dogmatism. By their very nature they were an appeal to the people; and, like other appeals of the kind, they ended in a revolution.

Of the men who fixed the lines on which this revolution was to run, four stand out taller from the shoulders upwards than their fellows. These are Coleridge, Lamb, Hazlitt, and Carlyle. The critical work of all four belongs to the first thirty years or so of the present century; and of the four it is probable that Carlyle, by nature certainly the least critical, had the greatest influence in changing the current of critical ideas. Space forbids any attempt to treat their work in detail. All that can be done is to indicate what were the shortcomings of English criticism as it came into their hands, and how far and in what manner they modified its methods and its aims. Till the beginning of the present century, criticism in England had remained a very simple thing. When judgement had once been passed, for good or evil, on an individual work or an individual writer, the critic was apt to suppose that nothing further could reasonably be expected of him. The comparative method, foreshadowed but only foreshadowed by Dryden, had not been carried perceptibly further by Dryden's successors. The historical method was still more clearly in its infancy. The connection between the two, the unity of purpose which alone gives significance to either, was hardly as yet suspected. It may be saidan English critic of the eighteenth century would undoubtedly have saidthat these, after all, are but methods; better, possibly, than other methods; but still no more than means to an end the eternal end of criticism, which is to appraise and to classify.

CRITICISM OF LITERATURE AND ARTHAS

The view is disputable enough. It leaves out of sight all that criticismthe criticism of literature and arthas done to throw light upon the dark places of human thought and history, upon the growth and subtle transformations of spiritual belief, upon the power of reason and imagination to mould the shape of outward institutions. All these things are included in the scope of the historical and comparative methods; and all of them stand entirely apart from the need to judge or classify the works of individual poets.

But, for the moment, such wider considerations may be put aside, and the objection weighed on its own merits. It must then be answered that, without comparison and without the appeal to history, even to judge and classify reasonably would be impossible; and hence that, however much we narrow the scope of criticism, these two methodsor rather, two aspects of the same methodmust still find place within its range. For, failing them, the critic in search of a standardand without some standard or criterion there can be no such thing as criticismis left with but two possible alternatives. He must either appeal to some absolute standardthe rules drawn from the "classical writers", in a sense wider or narrower, as the case may be; or he must decide everything by his own impression of the moment, eked out by the "appeal to Moliere's maid". The latter is the negation of all criticism. The former, spite of itself, is the historical method, but the historical method applied in an utterly arbitrary and irrational way. The former was the method of Johnson; the latter, of the Edinburgh and the Quarterly. Each in turn, as we have seen, had ludicrously broken down.

In the light of recent inventions, it might have been expected that some attempt would be made to limit the task of the critic to a mere record of his individual impressions. This, in fact, would only have been to avow, and to give the theory of what the Edinburgh and the Quarterly had already reduced to practice. But the truth is that the men of that day were not strong in such fine-spun speculations. It was a refinement from which even Lamb, who loved a paradox as well as any man, would have shrunk with playful indignation. It was in another direction that Coleridge and his contemporaries sought escape from the discredit with which criticism was threatened.

This was by changing the issue on which the discussion was to be fought. In its most general form, the problem of criticism amounts to this: What is the nature of the standard to be employed in literary judgements? Hithertoat least to the Reviewersthe question may be said to have presented itself in the following shape: Is the standard to be sought within or without the mind of the critic? Is it by his own impression, or by the code handed down from previous critics, that in the last resort the critic should be guided? In the hands of Coleridge and others, this was replaced by the question: Is the touchstone of excellence to be found within the work of the poet, or outside of it?

Are we to judge of a given work merely by asking: Is it clearly conceived and consistently carried out? Or are we bound to consider the further question: Is the original conception just, and capable of artistic treatment; and is the workmanship true to the vital principles of poetry? The change is significant. It makes the poet, not the critic, master of the situation. It implies that the critic is no longer to give the law to the poet; but that, in some sense more or less complete, he must begin, if not by putting himself in the place of the individual writer as he was when at work on the individual poem, at least by taking upon himselfby making his own, as far as may bewhat he may conceive to be the essential temperament of the poet.

This, indeed, is one of the first things to strike us in passing from the old criticism to the new. The Edinburgh and Quarterly plunge straight into the business of the moment. From the first instantwith "This will never do"the Reviewer poses as the critic, or rather as the accuser. Not so Coleridge and Hazlitt. Like the Edinburgh and Quarterly, they undertake to discourse on individual poets.

Unlike them, each opens his enquiry with the previous question-a question that seems to have found no lodgment in the mind of the ReviewersWhat is poetry? Further than this. Hazlitt, in a passage of incomparably greater force than any recorded utterance of Coleridge, makes it his task to trace poetry to the deepest and most universal springs of human nature; asserts boldly that it is poetry which, in the strictest sense, is "the life of all of us"; and calls on each one of us to assert his birthright by enjoying it. It is in virtue of the poet latent in him, that the plain man has the power to become a critic. Starting then from the question as just stated: Is it within the mind of the individual poet, or without it, that the standard of judgement should be sought?neither Coleridge nor Hazlitt could have any doubt as to the answer.

It is not, they would tell us, in the individual work but in the nature of poetryof poetry as written large in the common instincts of all men no less than in the particular achievement of exceptional artiststhat the test of poetic beauty must be discovered. The opposite view, doubtless, finds some countenance in the precepts, if not the example, of Goethe. But, when pressed to extremes, it is neither more nor less than the impressionist conception of criticism transferred to the creative faculty; and, like its counterpart, is liable to the objection that the impression of one poet, so long as it is sincerely rendered, is as good as the impression of another. It is the abdication of art, as the other is the abdication of criticism.

Yet Hazlitt alsofor, leaving Coleridge, we may now confine ourselves to himis open to attack. His fine critical powers were marred by the strain of bitterness in his nature. And the result is that his judgement on many poets, and notably the poets of his own day, too often sounds like an intelligent version of the Edinburgh or the Quarterly. Or, to speak more accurately, he betrays some tendency to return to principles which, though assuredly applied in a more generous spirit, are at bottom hardly to be distinguished from the principles of Johnson. He too has his "indispensable laws", or something very like them. He too has his bills of exclusion and his list of proscriptions. The poetry of earth, he more than suspects, is for ever dead; after Milton, no claimant is admitted to anything more substantial than a courtesy title. This, no doubt, was in part due to his morose temper; but it was partly also the result of the imperfect method with which he started.

The fault of his conceptionand it was that which determined his methodis to be too absolute. It allows too much room to poetry in the abstract; too little to the ever-varying temperament of the individual poet. And even that is perhaps too favourable a statement of the case. His idea of poetry may in part be drawnand its strength is to have been partly drawndirect from life and nature. But it is also taken, as from the nature of the case it must be with all of us, from the works of particular poets. And, in spite of his appeal to Dante and the Bible, it is clear that, in framing it, he was guided too exclusively by his loving study of the earlier English writers, from Chaucer to Milton.

The model, so framed, is laid with heavy hand upon all other writers, who naturally fare ill in the comparison. Is it possible to account otherwise for his disparagement of Moliere, or his grudging praise of Wordsworth and of Coleridge? It was here that Carlyle came in to redress the balance. From interests, in their origin perhaps less purely literary than have moved any man who has exercised a profound influence on literature, Carlyle was led to quicken the sense of poetic beauty, and by consequence to widen the scope of criticism, more than any writer of his day. He may have sought German literature more for its matter than for its artistic beautyhere, too, he brought a new, if in some ways a dangerous, element into criticismbut neither he nor his readers could study it, least of all could they study the work of Goethe, without awakening to a whole world of imagination and beauty, to which England had hitherto been dead. With all its shortcomings, the discovery of German literature was a greater revelation than any made to Europe since the classical Renaissance.

The shockfor it was nothing lesscame at a singularly happy moment. The blow, given by Carlyle as critic, was closely followed up by the French Romantiques, as creative artists. Nothing could well have been more alien to English taste, as understood by the Edinburgh and Quarterly, than the early works, or indeed any works, of Hugo and those who owned him for chiefif it were not the works of Goethe and the countrymen of Goethe. Different as these were from each other, they held common ground in uniting the most opposite prejudices of Englishmen against them. The sarcasms of Thackeray on the French writers speak to this no less eloquently than the fluent flippancies of De Quincey upon the Germans.Yet, in the one case as in the otherthanks, in no small measure, to Matthew Arnold and Mr. Swinburnegenius, in the long run, carried the day.

And the same history has been repeated, as the literatures of Russia and of Scandinavia have each in turn been brought within our ken. These discoveries have all fallen within little more than half a century since Carlyle, by the irony of fate, reviewed Richter and the State of German Literature in the pages of the Edinburgh. And their result has been to modify the standards of taste and criticism in a thousand ways. They have opened our eyes to aspects of poetry that we should never otherwise have suspected, and unveiled to us fields of thought, as well as methods of artistic treatment which, save by our own fault, must both have widened and deepened our conception of poetry. That is the true meaning of the historical method. The more we broaden our vision, the less is our danger of confounding poetry, which is the divine genius of the whole world, with the imperfect, if not misshapen idols of the tribe, the market-place and the cave. Of this conquest Carlyle must in justice be reckoned as the pioneer. For many years he stood almost single-handed as the champion of German thought and German art against the scorn or neglect of his countrymen. But he knew that he was right, and was fully conscious whither the path he had chosen was to lead. Aware that much in the work of Goethe would seem "faulty" to many, he forestalls the objection at the outset.

"To see rightly into this matter, to determine with any infallibility whether what we call a fault is in very deed a fault, we must previously have settled two points, neither of which may be so readily settled. First, we must have made plain to ourselves what the poet's aim really and truly was, how the task he had to do stood before his own eye, and how far, with such means as it afforded him, he has fulfilled it. Secondly, we must have decided whether and how far this aim, this task of his accordednot with us and our individual crotchets, and the crotchets of our little senate where we give or take the lawbut with human nature and the nature of things at large; with the universal principles of poetic beauty, not as they stand written in our text-books, but in the hearts and imaginations of all men. Does the answer in either case come out unfavourable; was there an inconsistency between the means and the end, a discordance between the end and the truth, there is a fault; was there not, there is no fault."

Nothing could ring clearer than this. No man could draw the line more accurately between the tendency to dispense with principles and the tendency to stereotype them, which are the twin dangers of the critic. But it is specially important to note Carlyle's relation, in this matter, to Hazlitt He insists with as much force as Hazlitt upon the need of basing all poetry on "human nature and the nature of things at large"; upon the fact that its principles are written "in the hearts and imaginations of all men". But, unlike Hazlitt, he bids us also consider what the aim of the individual poet was, and how far he has taken the most fitting means to reach it. In other words, he allows, as Hazlitt did not allow, for the many-sidedness of poetry, and the infinite variety of poetic genius. And, just because he does so, he is able to give a deeper meaning to "nature" and the universal principles of imagination than Hazlitt, with all his critical and reflective brilliance, was in a position to do. Hazlitt is too apt to confine "nature" to the nature of Englishmen in general and, in his weaker moments, of Hazlitt in particular.

Carlyle makes an honest attempt to bound it only by the universal instincts of man, and the "everlasting reason" of the world. Thus, in Carlyle's conception, "it is the essence of the poet to be new"; it is his mission "to wrench us from our old fixtures"; for it is only by so doing that he can show us some aspect of nature or of man's heart that was hidden from us before. The originality of the poet, the impossibility of binding him by the example of his forerunners, is the necessary consequence of the infinity of truth. That Carlyle saw this, and saw it so clearly, is no doubt partly due to a cause, of which more must be said directly; to his craving for ideas. But it was in part owing to his hearty acceptance of the historical method. Both as critic and as historian, he knewat that time, no man so wellthat each nation has its own genius; and justly pronounced the conduct of that nation which "isolates itself from foreign influence, regards its own modes as so many laws of nature, and rejects all that is different as unworthy even of examination", to be "pedantry". This was the first, and perhaps the most fruitful consequence that he drew from the application of historical ideas to literature. They enlarged his field of comparison; and, by so doing, they gave both width and precision to his definition of criticism.

But there is anotherand a more usual, if a narrowersense of the historical method; and here, too, Carlyle was a pioneer. He was among the first in our country to grasp the importance of studying the literature of a nation, as a whole, and from its earliest monuments, its mythological and heroic legends, downwards to the present. The year 1831a turning-point in the mental history of Carlyle, for it was also the year in which Sartor Resartus took shape "among the mountain solitudes"was largely devoted to Essays on the history of German literature, of which one, that on the Nibelungenlied, is specially memorable. And some ten years later (1840) he again took up the theme in the first of his lectures on Heroes, which still remains the most enlightening, because the most poetic, account of the primitive Norse faith, or rather successive layers of faith, in our language. But what mainly concerns us here is that Carlyle, in this matter as in others, had clearly realized and as clearly defines the goal which the student, in this case the student of literary history, should set before his eyes.

"A History... of any national Poetry would form, taken in its complete sense, one of the most arduous enterprises any writer could engage in. Poetry, were it the rudest, so it be sincere, is the attempt which man makes to render his existence harmonious, the utmost he can do for that end; it springs, therefore, from his whole feelings, opinions, activity, and takes its character from these. It may be called the music of his whole manner of being; and, historically considered, is the test how far Music, or Freedom, existed therein; how the feeling of Love, of Beauty, and Dignity, could be elicited from that peculiar situation of his, and from the views he there had of Life and Nature, of the Universe, internal and external.

Hence, in any measure to understand the Poetry, to estimate its worth and historical meaning, we ask, as a quite fundamental inquiry: What that situation was? Thus the History of a nation's Poetry is the essence of its History, political, economic, scientific, religious. With all these the complete Historian of a national Poetry will be familiar; the national physiognomy, in its finest traits and through its successive stages of growth, will be dear to him: he will discern the grand spiritual Tendency of each period, what was the highest Aim and Enthusiasm of mankind in each, and how one epoch naturally evolved itself from the other. He has to record the highest Aim of a nation, in its successive directions and developments; for by this the Poetry of the nation modulates itself; this is the Poetry of the nation."

Never has the task of the literary historian been more accurately defined than in this passage; and never do we feel so bitterly the gulf between the ideal and the actual performance, at which more than one man of talent has since tried his hand, as when we read it. It strikes perhaps the first note of Carlyle's lifelong war against "Dryasdust". But it contains at least two other points on which it is well for us to pause. The first is the inseparable bond which Carlyle saw to exist between the poetry of a nation and its history; the connection which inevitably follows from the fact that both one and the other are the expression of its character.

This is a vein of thought that was first struck by Vico and by Montesquieu; but it was left for the German philosophers, in particular Fichte and Hegel, to see its full significance; and Carlyle was the earliest writer in this country to make it his own. It is manifest that the connection between the literature and the history of a nation may be taken from either side. We may illustrate its literature from its history, or its history from its literature. It is on the necessity of the former study that Carlyle dwells in the above.

And in the light of later exaggerations, notably those of Taine, it is well to remember, what Carlyle himself would have been the last man to forget, that no man of genius is the creature of his time or his surroundings; and, consequently, that when we have mastered all the circumstances, in Carlyle's phrase the whole "situation", of the poet, we are still only at the beginning of our task. We have still to learn what his genius made out of its surroundings, and what the eye of the poet discovered in the world of traditional belief; in other words, what it was that made him a poet, what it was that he saw and to which all the rest were blind. We have studied the soil; we have yet to study the tree that grew from it and overshadows it.

In reversing the relation, in reading history by the light of literature, the danger is not so great. The man of genius may, and does, see deeper than his contemporaries; but, for that very reason, he is a surer guide to the tendencies of his time than they. He is above and beyond his time; but, just in so far as he is so, he sees over it and through it. As Shakespeare defined it, his "end, both at the first and now, was and is... to show the very age and body of the time his form and pressure". Some allowance must doubtless be made for the individuality of the poet; for the qualities in which he stands aloof from his time, and in which, therefore, he must not be taken to reflect it. But to make such allowance is a task not beyond the skill of the practised critic; and many instances suggest themselves in which it has, more or less successfully, been done. Witness not a few passages in Michelet's Histoire de France, and some to be found in the various works of Ranke.Witness, again, Hegel's illustration of the Greek conception of the family from the Antigone and the Oedipus of Sophocles; or, if we may pass to a somewhat different field, his "construction" of the French Revolution from the religious and metaphysical ideas of Rousseau.

So far as it employs literature to give the key to the outward history of a nation or to the growth of its spiritual faith, it is clear that the historical method ceases to be, in the strict sense of the word, a literary instrument. It implies certainly that a literary judgement has been passed; but, once passed, that judgement is used for ends that lie altogether apart from the interests of literature. But it is idle to consider that literature loses caste by lending itself to such a purpose. It would be wiser to say that it gains by anything that may add to its fruitfulness and instructiveness.

In any case, and whether it pleases us or no, this is one of the things that the historical method has done for literature; and neither Carlyle, nor any other thinker of the century, would have been minded to disavow it. This brings us to the second point that calls for remark in the foregoing quotation from Carlyle. Throughout he assumes that the matter of the poet is no less important than his manner. And here again he dwells on an aspect of literature that previous, and later, critics have tended to throw into the shade.

That Carlyle should have been led to assert, and even at times to exaggerate, the claims of thought in imaginative work was inevitable; and that, not only from his temperament, but from those principles of his teaching that we have already noticed. If the poetry of a nation be indeed the expression of its spiritual aims, then it is clear that among those aims must be numbered its craving to make the world intelligible to itself, and to comprehend the working of God both within man and around him. Not that Carlyle shows any disposition to limit "thought" to its more abstract forms; on the contrary, it is on the sense of "music, love, and beauty" that he specially insists. What he does demand is that these shall be not merely outward adornments, but the instinctive utterance of a deeper harmony within; that they shall be such as not merely to "furnish a languid mind with fantastic shows and indolent emotions, but to incorporate the everlasting reason of man in forms visible to his sense, and suitable to it". The "reason" is no less necessary to poetry than its sensible form; and whether its utterance be direct or indirect, that is a matter for the genius of the individual poet to decide. Gott und Welt, we may be sure Carlyle would have said, is poetry as legitimate as Der Erlkonig or the songs of Mignon.

In this connection he more than once appeals to the doctrine of Fichte, one of the few writers whom he was willing to recognize as his teachers. "According to Fichte, there is a 'divine idea' pervading the visible universe; which visible universe is indeed but its symbol and sensible manifestation, having in itself no meaning, or even true existence independent of it. To the mass of men this divine idea of the world lies hidden; yet to discern it, to seize it, and live wholly in it, is the condition of all genuine virtue, knowledge, freedom; and the end, therefore, of all spiritual effort in every age.

Literary men are the appointed interpreters of this divine idea; a perpetual priesthood, we might say, standing forth, generation after generation, as the dispensers and living types of God's everlasting wisdom, to show it in their writings and actions, in such particular form as their own particular times require it in. For each age, by the law of its nature, is different from every other age, and demands a different representation of the divine idea, the essence of which is the same in all; so that the literary man of one century is only by mediation and reinterpretation applicable to the wants of another."

The particular form of Fichte's teaching may still sound unfamiliar enough. But in substance it has had the deepest influence on the aims and methods of criticism; and, so far as England is concerned, this is mainly due to the genius of Carlyle. Compare the criticism of the last century with that of the present, and we at once see the change that has come over the temper and instincts of Englishmen in this matter.

When Johnson, or the reviewers of the next generation, quittedas they seldom did quitthe ground of external form and regularity and logical coherence, it was only to ask: Is this work, this poem or this novel, in conformity with the traditional conventions of respectability, is it such as can be put into the hands of boys and girls? To them this was the one ground on which the matter of literature, as apart from the beggarly elements of its form, could come under the cognizance of the critic. And this narrowness, a narrowness which belonged at least in equal measure to the official criticism of the French, naturally begot a reaction almost as narrow as itself. The cry of "art for art's sake", a cry raised in France at the moment when Carlyle was beginning his work in England, must be regarded as a protest against the moralizing bigotry of the classical school no less than against its antiquated formalities.

The men who raised it were themselves not free from the charge of formalism; but the forms they worshipped were at least those inspired by the spontaneous genius of the artist, not the mechanical rules inherited from the traditions of the past. Nor, whatever may be the case with those who have taken it up in our own day, must the cry be pressed too rigorously against the men of 1830. The very man, on whom it was commonly fathered, was known to disavow it; and certainly in his own works, in their burning humanity and their "passion for reforming the world", was the first to set it at defiance. The moralist and the formalist still make their voice heard, and will always do so. But since Carlyle wrote, it is certain that a wider, a more fruitful, view of criticism has gained ground among us. And, if it be asked where lies the precise difference between such a view and that which satisfied the critics of an earlier day, the answer must be, that we are no longer contented to rest upon the outward form of a work of art, still less upon its conventional morality. We demand to learn what is the idea, of which the outward form is the harmonious utterance; and which, just because the form is individual, must itself too have more or less of originality and power. We are resolved to know what is the artist's peculiar fashion of conceiving life, what is his insight, that which he has to teach us of God and man and nature. "Poetry", said Wordsworth, "is the breath and finer spirit of all knowledge; it is the impassioned expression which is in the countenance of all Science." And Wordsworth is echoed by Shelley. But it is again to Carlyle that we must turn for the explicit application of these ideas to criticism:

"Criticism has assumed a new form...; it proceeds on other principles, and proposes to itself a higher aim. The grand question is not now a question concerning the qualities of diction, the coherence of metaphors, the fitness of sentiments, the general logical truth, in a work of art, as it was some half-century ago among most critics; neither is it a question mainly of a psychological sort, to be answered by discovering and delineating the peculiar nature of the poet from his poetry, as is usual with the best of our own critics at present: but it isnot indeed exclusively, but inclusively of those two other questionsproperly and ultimately a question on the essence and peculiar life of the poetry itself. The first of these questions, as we see it answered, for instance, in the criticisms of Johnson and Kames, relates, strictly speaking, to the garment of poetry: the second, indeed, to its body and material existence, a much higher point; but only the last to its soul and spiritual existence, by which alone can the body... be informed with significance and rational life.

The problem is not now to determine by what mechanism Addison composed sentences and struck out similitudes; but by what far finer and more mysterious mechanism Shakespeare organized his dramas, and gave life and individuality to his Ariel and his Hamlet? Wherein lies that life; how have they attained that shape and individuality? Whence comes that empyrean fire, which irradiates their whole being, and pierces, at least in starry gleams, like a diviner thing, into all hearts? Are these dramas of his not verisimilar only, but true; nay, truer than reality itself, since the essence of unmixed reality is bodied forth in them under more expressive symbols? What is this unity of theirs; and can our deeper inspection discern it to be indivisible, and existing by necessity, because each work springs, as it were, from the general elements of all thought, and grows up therefrom into form and expansion by its own growth?

Not only who was the poet, and how did he compose; but what and how was the poem, and why was it a poem and not rhymed eloquence, creation and not figured passion? These are the questions for the critic." And, a few pages later: "As an instance we might refer to Goethe's criticism of Hamlet.... This truly is what may be called the poetry of criticism: for it is in some sort also a creative art; aiming, at least, to reproduce under a different shape the existing product of the poet; painting to the intellect what already lay painted to the heart and the imagination."

Instances of criticism, conceived in this spirit, are unhappily still rare. But some of Coleridge's on Shakespeare, and some of Lamb's on the Plays of the Elizabethan Dramatistsin particular The Duchess of Malfi and The Broken Heartmay fairly be ranked among them. So, and with still less of hesitation, may Mr. Ruskin's rendering of the Last Judgement of Tintoret, and Mr. Pater's studies on Lionardo, Michaelangelo, and Giorgione. Of these, Mr. Pater's achievement is probably the most memorable; for it is an attempt, and an attempt of surprising power and subtlety, to reproduce not merely the effect of a single poem or picture, but the imaginative atmosphere, the spiritual individuality, of the artist. In a sense still higher than would be true even of the work done by Lamb and Ruskin, it deserves the praise justly given by Carlyle to the masterpiece of Goethe; it is "the very poetry of criticism".

We have now reviewed the whole circle traversed by criticism during the present century, and are in a position to define its limits and extent. We have seen that a change of method was at once the cause and indication of a change in spirit and in aim. The narrow range of the eighteenth century was enlarged on the one hand by the study of new literatures, and on the other hand by that appeal to history, and that idea of development which has so profoundly modified every field of thought and knowledge.

In that lay the change of method. And this, in itself, was enough to suggest a wider tolerance, a greater readiness to make allowance for differences of taste, whether as between nation and nation or as between period and period, than had been possible for men whose view was practically limited to Latin literature and to such modern literatures as were professedly moulded upon the Latin. With such diversity of material, the absolute standard, absurd enough in any case, became altogether impossible to maintain. It was replaced by the conception of a common instinct for beauty, modified in each nation by the special circumstances of its temperament and history.

EXTENT OF THE REVOLUTION IN CRITICAL IDEAS

But even this does not cover the whole extent of the revolution in critical ideas. Side by side with a more tolerantand, it may be added, a keenerjudgement of artistic form, came a clearer sense of the inseparable connection between form and matter, and the impossibility of comprehending the form, if it be taken apart from the matter, of a work of art. This, too, was in part the natural effect of the historical method, one result of which was to establish a closer correspondence between the thought of a nation and its art than had hitherto been suspected. But it was in part also a consequence of the intellectual and spiritual revolution of which Rousseau was the herald and which, during fifty years, found in German philosophy at once its strongest inspiration and its most articulate expression.

Men were no longer satisfied to explain to themselves what Carlyle calls the "garment" and the "body" of art; they set themselves to pierce through these to the soul and spirit within. They instinctively felt that the art which lives is the art that gives man something to live by; and that, just because its form is more significant than other of man's utterances, it must have a deeper significance also in substance and in purport. Of this purport Criticism of lifethe phrase suggested by one who was at once a poet and a criticis doubtless an unhappy, because a pedantic definition; and it is rather creation of life, than the criticism of it, that art has to offer. But it must be life in all its fulness and variety; as thought, no less than as action; as energy, no less than as beauty As power, as love, as influencing soul.

This is the mission of art; and to unfold its working in the art of all times and of all nations, to set it forth by intuition, by patient reason, by every means at his command, is the function of the critic. To have seen this, and to have marked out the way for its performance, is not the least among the services rendered by Carlyle to his own generation and to ours. Later critics can hardly be said to have yet filled out the design that he laid. They have certainly not gone beyond it.

Sir Philip Sidney . (1554-1586.)

4

Principles of Literary Criticism

PRINCIPLES OF LITERARY CRITICISM' ON THE NATURE OF POETRY

A. Richards believes that sometimes the impulses of man respond to a situation in such an organised way that the mind has a unique experience. Poetry is the representation of this experience, this organised and happy play of impulses and a true reader ought to feel the same in his own self. The poet, says Richards, does not tell the literal truth about the real world, but suggests attitudes which represent a proper balance of the nervous system and which are absorbed by the properly qualified reader.

In his *Science and Poetry* (1926), Richards says that much labour has been done to explain the high place of poetry in human affairs, with, on the whole, few satisfactory or convincing results. The reason is that both a passionate knowledge of poetry and a capacity for dispassionate psychological analysis are required if poetry is to be properly understood and interpreted.

To understand the real nature of poetry, we have to understand clearly "how the mind works in an experience, and what sort of stream of events the experience is." There are conflicting instincts and desires, or appetencies,as he calls them, in the human mind. Man is often between conflicting pulls from different directions and consequently he suffers from mental uneasiness. The main function of art is to enable human mind to organize itself more quickly and completely than it could do otherwise. In short, art (poetry) is a means whereby we can gain emotional balance, mental equilibrium, peace and rest.

Illustrating his point by an image of a magnetic compass, I. A. Richards says that the systematization of impulses is necessary for the poise and balance. Emotions make experiences, and emotions are better realized and expressed through poetry. The poet does all this with the help of words. Misunderstanding and under-estimation of poetry is mainly due to over estimation of the thought in it. "It is never what a poem *says* which matters, but what it *is*. The poet is not writing as a scientist. He uses these words because the interest which the situation calls into play combine to bring them, just in this form, into his consciousness as a means of ordering, controlling, and consolidating the whole experience."

WHAT, ACCORDING TO I. A. RICHARDS, IS THE VALUE OF POETRY?

Richards defines the poem as "the artist's experience." He examines poetry as a stimulus-response proposition. The poem can be a communication in the broad sense that it communicates an experience. Some experience must naturally be good and some bad. It is only the good ones that can be said to be valuable. What are they like. It has frequently been emphasized by Richards that an experience results from theplay of impulses. The mind is ever engaged in the unconscious process of reconciling their conflicting claims in such a way that success is obtained for the greater number or mass of them, for the most important and the weightiest set. In the very exercise of this choice the mind unconsciously decided which impulses are valuable for it and should therefore be satisfied U the full, and which not and should therefore be suppressed.

In order to answer the questions—"Of what use is poetry?" "Why and how is it valuable?" Richards develops a general theory of value— general in the sense that it applies to all human activities and not especially to poetry— and then shows how poetry is valuable on the basis of this general standard. Poetry is valuable because it produces man's moral improvement. Richards seems to support Sidney's observations about poetry and also Shelley from whom Richards quotes in his *Principles of*

Literary Criticism " poetry acts in a divine manner. It awakens and the mind itself by rendering it the receptacle of a thousand unapprehended combinations of thought. Whatever strengthens and purifies the affections, enlarges the imagination, and adds spirit to sense, is useful". We may look upon *Principles of Literary Criticism* as an attempt to chisel this doctrine into the marble of positivism."

I. A. Richards has explained his views on the value of poetry in the chapter 'Art and Morals' in *Principles of Literary Criticism.* He begins, the chapter by saying : "From this excursion let us return to our proper task, the attempt to outline a morality which will change its values as circumstances alter, a morality free from occultism, absolutes and arbitrariness, a morality which will explain, as no morality has yet explained, the place and value of the arts in human affairs. What is good or valuable, we have said, is the exercise of impulses and the satisfaction of their appetencies." And poetry does this task. Poetry does the reconciliation of impulses.

David Daiches comments : "Poetry," wrote Shelley, "is the record of the best and happiest moments of the happiest and best minds." This is precisely Richards' position, though Richards would define "best" and "happiest" in his own way. Whether the psychological humanism on which Richards bases his view of what is good in poetry as in any other human

Activity is really adequate to account for the special nature and value of,poetry is argueable. To many of his readers there seems to be a gap between his perceptive, detailed discussion of particular poems and his generalizations about the value of poetry, which are inlarge measure based on psychological notions which no important contemporary psychologist accepts."

However, Richards, like Arnold, is of the opinion that poetry is a central means of saving civilization. He concludes the essay *Science and Poetry* with a general statement which expresses his view very clearly : "It is very probable that the Hindenburg Line to which the defence of our traditions retired as a result of the onslaughts of the last century will be blown up the near future. If this should happen a moral chaos such as man has never experienced may be expected. We shall then be thrown back, as Matthew Arnold foresaw, upon poetry. It is capable of saving us; it is perfectly possible means of overcoming chaos."

This is Richard's reply to the attack made on poetry by Thomas Love Peacock in 1820 in the half-serious essay, *The Four Ages of Poetry.* While the other branches of learning, he had complained, were steadily marching towards a fuller knowledge or reality, poetry by its love of myth and legend was 'wallowing in the rubbish of departed ignorance.' Whence he concluded : 'A poet in our times is a semi-barbarian in a civilized community. He lives in the ways that ate past.

His ideas, thoughts, feelings, associations, are all with barbarious manners, obsolete customs, and exploded superstitions. The march of his intellect if like that of a crab, backward.' Richards's analysis of poetry, if it is accepted as true, shows how even in this age of scientific enlightenment poetry has a vital role to play in the life of the individual and society. In the mind ordered in the poetic way lies the hope of civilization.

AESTHETIC PRINCIPLES OF LITERARY CRITICISM

AEsthetics. The science of beauty in general is called AEsthetics, to which we have to look for some of the principles that are to guide our critical judgement. Unfortunately for us, the science of beauty has not yet been fully and satisfactorily wrought out, and the ablest writers, from Aristotle to Herbert Spencer, exhibit great diversity of view. There are two main theories of beauty: the one makes beauty subjective, or an emotion of the mind; the other makes it objective, or a quality in the external object. Without entering into the intricacies and difficulties of the discussion, beauty will here be regarded as that quality in literature which awakens in the cultivated reader a sense of the beautiful. This sense of the beautiful is a refined and pleasurable feeling; and, as we shall see, it is traceable to a variety of sources.

Literary Taste. Literary taste is that power or faculty of the mind which apprehends and appreciates what is beautiful and artistic in literature. It embraces two elements: first, the apprehension of the aesthetic quality; and secondly, an appreciation or emotional response to its appeal. These two elements are not always equally developed in the critic; and it frequently happens that an artistic literary production affords exquisite pleasure without a clear apprehension of the aesthetic elements from which the pleasure springs. In literary criticism, as has already been shown, the standard of taste is the ideal, developed by an application of necessary and recognized principles, which the intelligent critic is able to form in every department of literature.

The capacity of taste is a natural gift; but, like other powers of the mind, it is capable of great development. It is cultivated by a study of the principles of beauty and by a contemplation of beautiful objects in nature and art. Bad taste exhibits itself in a failure to apprehend and appreciate what is genuinely beautiful; it often mistakes defects for excellences. A refined taste responds to what is delicate in beauty, and a catholic taste recognizes and responds to beauty of every kind. The critic who would do honour to his office must have a taste both refined and catholic.

AEsthetic Elements. Literary beauty may pertain either to the form or to the content. Deferring to subsequent chapters the elements of external beauty, we here consider the elements of internal beauty. Though beauty of form and beauty of content may thus be distinguished, they are always combined in works of the highest excellence. Both alike have their source in the cultivated, creative spirit of the writer. They cannot be effectually learned by rule; and the best training for successful authorship is the development of the intellectual and moral faculties. Vividness of description is a frequent source of literary beauty. Scenes, objects, and events are sometimes so presented as to become visible to the inner eye. Thus Tennyson describes the flinging of Arthur's sword:

"The great brand
Made lightnings in the splendor of the moon."

Carlyle was a master of graphic description, and in a few touches he thus brings De Quincey before us: "One of the smallest man figures I ever saw; shaped like a pair of tongs, and hardly above five feet in all. When he sate, you would have taken him by candlelight for the beautifullest little child; blue-eyed, sparkling face, had there not been something, too, which said, 'Eccovithis child has been in hell!'"

Meditative reflection, when aptly associated with circumstance or occasion, may become a pleasing source of beauty. When employed by way of introduction, it may, as frequently in Irving and Hawthorne, strike the keynote of what follows. Sometimes it gives natural expression to the vague thought or feeling that had been produced in the reader by the preceding narrative and that would otherwise have remained unsatisfied. In the darkness and silence of night the poet hears the striking of a deep-toned bell. Naturally he thinks of the flight of time.

"The bell strikes one. We take no note of time
But from its loss: to give it then a tongue
Is wise in man. As if an angel spoke,

I feel the solemn sound. If heard aright,
It is the knell of my departed hours."

A meditation may, as a conclusion, impart a satisfying completeness to a piece. Nothing could be finer, for example, than Addison's reflections at the close of his essay on the tombs of Westminster Abbey: "When I look upon the tombs of the great, every emotion of envy dies in me; when I read the epitaphs of the beautiful, every inordinate desire goes out; when I meet with the grief of parents upon a tombstone, my heart melts with compassion; when I see the tomb of the parents themselves, I consider the vanity of grieving for those whom we must quickly follow.

When I see kings lying by those who deposed them, when I consider rival wits placed side by side, or the holy men that divided the world with their contests and disputes, I reflect with sorrow and astonishment on the little competitions, factions, and debates of mankind. When I read the several dates of the tombs, of some that died yesterday, and some six hundred years ago, I consider that great day when we shall all of us be contemporaries, and make our appearance together."

Harmony of thought and expression is another source of excellence. The thought should be clothed in a perfect body, so that nothing can be added or subtracted without marring the beauty. The following stanza from Holmes's "The Last Leaf" will serve for illustration:

"The mossy marbles rest
On the lips that he has prest
In their bloom;
And the names he loved to hear
Have been carved for many a year
On the tomb."

When, in addition to perfect harmony between spirit and form, the sound re-enforces the sense, there is an added element of beauty. The intellect is thus assisted in imaging or realizing the scene. As the heroine returns to her palace in Tennyson's "Godiva,"

"All at once
With twelve great shocks of sound, the shameless noon
Was clashed and hammered from a hundred towers."

A well-known illustration is furnished in Pope's "Essay on Criticism":

"Soft is the strain when Zephyr gently blows,
And the smooth stream in smoother numbers flows;
But when loud surges lash the sounding shore,
The hoarse, rough verse should like the torrent roar."

The felicitous expression of some well-known truth or experience is always pleasing. In its happiest form such an expression is received as the final embodiment of its truth. It is henceforth taken up by the multitude and quoted as having the authority of a sacred text. Pope tells us, for example, that

"To err is human; to forgive, divine";
and also that
"Fools rush in where angels fear to tread."

But no other English writer has equaled Shakespeare in the number of felicitous expressions that have passed into current use. His works are a veritable mine of jeweled phrases. We often feel, for example, that somehow there is a mysterious power controlling our lives; and this experience he voices in the well-known lines,

"There's a divinity that shapes our ends,
Rough-hew them how we will."

Yet at the same time, recognizing the truth of human freedom, he declares,

"Our remedies oft in ourselves do lie,
Which we ascribe to heaven; the fated sky
Gives us free scope, only doth backward push
Our slow designs when we ourselves are dull."

High spiritual truth, in fitting expression, is a source of great beauty. There are three great provinces of thought,man, nature, and God. The last is the greatest of all; and the highest achievement of literature is to lead us to a new or fuller appreciation of his character. As we look upon the irrepressible and unending conflict between good and evil in this world, we are sometimes tempted to doubt a favorable issue; but Lowell tells us, in self-evidencing words, that "Behind the dim unknown Standeth God within the shadow, keeping watch above his own." To Ruskin the various phenomena of nature brought a sweet message: "All those passings to and fro of fruitful shower and grateful shade, and all those visions of silver palaces built about the horizon, and voices of moaning winds and threatening thunders, and glories of colored robe and cloven ray, are but to deepen in our hearts the acceptance, and distinctness, and dearness of the simple words, 'Our Father, which art in heaven.'"

Another principal source of literary beauty is found in a worthy expression of noble thought and sentiment. This may be regarded as the soul of enduring literature, and it is as exhaustless as the human mind itself. The dauntless love of liberty that breathes through Patrick Henry's famous speech is thrilling in its eloquence: "What is it that gentlemen wish? What would they have? Is life so dear, or peace so sweet, as to be purchased at the price of chains and slavery? Forbid it, Almighty God! I know not what course others may take, but, as for me, give me liberty, or give me death!" Carlyle conceived of nature as the vesture of God; and, as he speaks of the universe, this thought lifts his style to great majesty: "Oh, could I transport thee direct from the beginnings to the endings, how were thy eyesight unsealed, and thy heart set flaming in the Light-sea of celestial wonder! Then sawest thou that this fair Universe, were it in the meanest province thereof, is in very deed the star-domed City of God; that through every star, through every grass-blade, and most, through every Living Soul, the glory of a present God still beams. But Nature, which is the Time-vesture of God, and reveals Him to the wise, hides Him from the foolish."

Love is a perennial inspiration both in prose and poetry. It partakes of the divine, for "God is love." Its highest manifestations, whether in the family, among relatives and friends, or between lovers, are always beautiful; and perhaps Browning was not far wrong when he sang,

"There is no good in life but lovebut love!
What else looks good, is some shade flung from love;
Love yields it, gives it worth."

The portrayal of noble character is always inspiring. It appeals to the better side of our nature, and strengthens our confidence in humanity.

No literary art can confer immortality on what is ignoble. The fiction that is devoted to obscene realism, whatever may be the prestige of its authors or its current vogue, is surely doomed. Only that which is morally good is destined to live through the ages. The genial Dickens will always be more popular than the satirical Thackeray. Boswell's "Life of Johnson" owes its principal charm not to any trick of style, but to the honest, rugged piece of manhood it brings before us. Only a man of Luther's heroic spirit could have inspired this magnificent tribute in Carlyle's "Heroes and Hero-Worship": "I will call this Luther a true great man; great in intellect, in courage, affection, and integrity; one of our most lovable and precious men.

Great, not as a hewn obelisk, but as an Alpine mountain,so simple, honest, spontaneous, not setting up to be great at all; there for quite another purpose than being great! Ah yes, unsubduable granite, piercing far and wide into the heavens; yet in the clefts of it fountains, green, beautiful valleys with flowers! A right spiritual hero and prophet; once more, a true son of nature and fact, for whom these centuries, and many that are to come yet, will be thankful to Heaven."

Heroic self-sacrifice strongly appeals to us. Whenever a man or woman gives up self for the good of others, we intuitively admire and honour the deed. The story of Thermopylae, the leap of Curtius into the yawning chasm, the charge of the Light Brigade, "... though the soldier knew Some one had blundered," are instances of heroic self-sacrifice which the world is unwilling to forget.

There is a charm in Tennyson's "Godiva" or his "Enoch Arden" beyond the reach of mere art; it is found in the noble spirit of the heroine who replies to the taunt of her husband, "But I would die"; and in the deep self-renunciation of the hero who, in heartbreaking anguish, prayed, "Help me not to break in upon her peace." The beauty of a life of simplicity and benevolence is seen in the immortal Vicar of Wakefield. His unaffected goodness has made him dear to successive generations. In like manner we pay a spontaneous tribute to Chaucer's "poure parson of a toune," and to the preacher of the

"Deserted Village":
"A man he was to all the country dear,
And passing rich with forty pounds a year;
Remote from towns he ran his godly race,
Nor e'er had changed, nor wished to change, his place.
Unskilful he to fawn, or seek for power,
By doctrines fashioned to the varying hour;
Far other aims his heart had learned to prize,
More bent to raise the wretched than to rise."

The fitting description of scenes and incidents of grandeur imparts dignity and charm to a production. Grandeur is of two kinds: first, the grandeur or sublimity of natural objects, such as the ocean, a storm, an earthquake, or other exhibitions of tremendous power; and secondly, the moral sublime, in which the heroic soul rises superior to dangers and death. Milton's "Paradise Lost" abounds in grave and sublime passages. Byron reaches the sublime in many of the descriptions of "Childe Harold," of which the following will serve for illustration:

"Far along
From peak to peak, the rattling crags among,
Leaps the live thunder! Not from one lone cloud,
But every mountain now hath found a tongue,
And Jura answers, through her misty shroud,
Back to the joyous Alps, who call to her aloud."

Perhaps no finer instance of the moral sublime is to be found than in the bearing of Luther before the Imperial Diet in the city of Worms. He was confronted by the chief dignitaries of Church and Empire. The emperor himself, Charles V, was present. "Will you, or will you not, retract?" solemnly demanded the speaker of the Diet. "Unless," replied the intrepid reformer, "unless I am convinced by the testimony of Holy Scripture or by clear and indisputable reasoning, I cannot, and will not, retract anything; for it is unsafe for a Christian to do anything against his conscience. Here I stand, I cannot do otherwise, God help me. Amen!"

Another source of beauty is found in tenderness and pathos. These feelings appeal to the gentler side of our nature. The pathos may arise from various causes,from bereaved affection, from fond memories, from sore disappointments, or from helpless suffering. Every one is familiar with Dickens's description of the death of little Nell in "Old Curiosity Shop." Irving's story of "The Broken Heart" is deeply pathetic.

The deathbed scene of Colonel Newcome in Thackeray's great novel is notable for its simple pathos: "At the usual evening hour the chapel bell began to toll, and Thomas Newcome's hands outside the bed feebly beat time. And just as the last bell struck, a peculiar sweet smile shone over his face, and he lifted up his head a little, and quickly said 'Adsum!' and fell back. It was the word used at school, when names were called; and lo, he, whose heart was that of a little child, had answered to his name, and stood in the presence of his Master." There is a tender regret in Hood's little poem, "I Remember":

"I remember, I remember,
The fir-trees dark and high;
I used to think their slender tops
Were close against the sky;
It was a childish ignorance,
But now 'tis little joy
To know I'm further off from heaven
Than when I was a boy."

The ludicrous often adds charm to literature. It is divided into two species,wit and humour. Wit consists in the discovery of remote analogies or relations, and produces an amusing surprise. It has various forms. In the pun, which is a rather low order of wit, there is a play on the meaning of words. Punning is an art easily acquired; but a pun is usually an impertinence to be excused only by its felicity. Hood was one of the most ingenious of punsters; and in his ballad, "Faithless Nelly

Gray," the wit of each stanza is found in a pun.
"Ben Battle was a soldier bold,
And used to war's alarms;
But a cannon-ball took off his legs,
So he laid down his arms."

Satire ridicules the follies and vices of men, and is frequent in both ancient and modern literature. Sometimes it is good-natured, but oftener it is bitter. Swift's "Tale of a Tub" is a fierce attack upon ecclesiastical divisions, while Pope's "Dunciad," which impales many of his contemporary writers, almost ruined the reputations it touched. Addison in the Spectator is genial in his satire. Byron is a master of powerful satire, and in the "English Bards and Scotch Reviewers" he indiscriminately lampoons his contemporaries. For example:

"Shall gentle Coleridge pass unnoticed here,
To turgid ode and tumid stanza dear?
Though themes of innocence amuse him best,
Yet still obscurity's a welcome guest.
If inspiration should her aid refuse
To him who takes a Pixy for a muse,
Yet none in lofty numbers can surpass
The bard who soars to elegize an ass.
How well the subject suits his noble mind!
'A fellow-feeling makes us wondrous kind!'"

A parody is a burlesque imitation and degradation of something serious. In his song, "Those Evening Bells," Moore wrote in pensive mood,

"And so 'twill be when I am gone;
That tuneful peal will still ring on,

While other bards shall walk these dells,
And sing your praise, sweet evening bells."

But in Hood's parody of the same title, this stanza is travestied as follows:

"And so 'twill be when she is gone;
That tuneful peal will still ring on,
And other maids with timely yells
Forget to stay those evening bells."

The other principal form of the ludicrous is humour. It is wit modified by a genial or sympathetic feeling. It has its origin in the disposition or character, while wit springs alone from the intellect. It often pervades an entire production. While wit generally breaks out in brief and sudden flashes, humour is frequently diffused through an entire work like a delicious fragrance. Addison's Sir Roger de Coverley papers in the Spectator are delightful examples of delicate humour. Hood's "Up the Rhine" is a rich commingling of wit and humour. Dickens's "Pickwick Papers" and Mark Twain's "Innocents Abroad" are humorous works of a broader type. Irving's minor writings are suffused with a delightful humour.

And no one who has read the humorous beginning of the "Vicar of Wakefield" is likely to forget it: "I was ever of opinion, that the honest man who married and brought up a large family, did more service than he who continued single and only talked of a population. From this motive, I had scarcely taken orders a year, before I began to think seriously of matrimony, and chose my wife, as she did her wedding-gown, not for a fine glossy surface, but for such qualities as would wear well."

5

The Function of Criticism

THE FUNCTION OF CRITICISM IN RECENT DEVELOPMENT

MANY objections have been made to a proposition which, in some remarks of mine on translating Homer, I ventured to put forth; a proposition about criticism, and its importance at the present day. I said: "Of the literature of France and Germany, as of the intellect of Europe in general, the main effort, for now many years, has been a critical effort; the endeavour, in all branches of knowledge, theology, philosophy, history, art, science, to see the object as in itself it really is." I added, that owing to the operation in English litera- ture of certain causes, "almost the last thing for which one would come to English literature is just that very thing which now Europe most desires—criticism;" and that the power and value of English literature was thereby impaired. More than one rejoinder declared that the importance I here assigned to criticism was excessive, and asserted the inherent superiority of the creative effort of the human spirit over its critical effort. And the other day, having been led by an excellent notice of Wordsworth published in the North British Review, to turn again to his biography, I found, in the words of this great man, whom I, for one, must always listen to with the profoundest respect, a sentence passed on the critic's business, which seems to justify every possible disparagement of it. Wordsworth says in one of his letters:—

> *"The writers in these publications" (the Reviews), "while they prosecute their inglorious employment, cannot be supposed to be in a state of mind very favourable for being affected by the finer influences of a thing so pure as genuine poetry."*

And a trustworthy reporter of his conversation quotes a more elaborate judgement to the same effect:—

> *"Wordsworth holds the critical power very low, infinitely lower than the inventive and he said to-day that if the quantity of time consumed in writing critiques on the works of others were given to original com-*

> *position, of whatever kind it might be, it would be much better employed; it would make a man find out sooner his own level, and it would do infinitely less mischief. A false or malicious criticism may do much injury to the minds of others; a stupid invention, either in prose or verse, is quite harmless."*

It is almost too much to expect of poor human nature, that a man capable of producing some effect in one line of literature, should, for the greater good of society, voluntarily doom himself to impotence and obscurity in another. Still less is this to be expected from men addicted to the composition of the "false or malicious criticism," of which Wordsworth speaks.

However, everybody would admit that a false or malicious criticism had better never have been written. Every- body, too, would be willing to admit, as a general propo- sition, that the critical faculty is lower than the inventive. But is it true that criticism is really, in itself, a baneful and injurious employment; is it true that all time given to writing critiques on the works of others would be much better employed if it were given to original composition, of whatever kind this may be? Is it true that Johnson had better have gone on producing more Irenes instead of writing his Lives of the Poets; nay, is it certain that Wordsworth himself was better employed in making his Ecclesiastical Sonnets, than when he made his celebrated Preface, so full of criticism, and criticism of the works of others?

Wordsworth was himself a great critic, and it is to be sincerely regretted that he has not left us more criticism; Goethe was one of the greatest of critics, and we may sincerely congratu- late ourselves that he has left us so much criticism. Without wasting time over the exaggeration which Wordsworth's judgement on criticism clearly contains, or over an attempt to trace the causes,—not difficult I think to be traced,—which may have led Wordsworth to this exaggeration, a critic may with advantage seize an occasion for trying his own conscience, and for asking himself of what real service, at any given moment, the practice of criticism either is, or may be made, to his own mind and spirit, and to the minds and spirits of others.

The critical power is of lower rank than the creative. True; but in assenting to this proposition, one or two things are to be kept in mind. It is undeniable that the exercise of a creative power, that a free creative activity, is the true function of man; it is proved to be so by man's finding in it his true happiness.

But it is un- deniable, also, that men may have the sense of exercising this free creative activity in other ways than in producing great works of literature or art; if it were not so, all but a very few men would be shut out from the true happiness of all men; they may have it in well-doing, they may have it in learning, they may have it even in criticising. This is one thing to be kept in mind.

Another is, that the exercise of the creative power in the production of great works of literature or art, however high this exercise of it may rank, is not at all epochs and under all conditions possible; and that therefore labour may be vainly spent in attempting it, which might with more fruit be used in preparing for it, in rendering it possible. This creative power works with elements, with materials; what if it has not those materials, those elements, ready for its use?

In that case it must surely wait till they are ready. Now in literature,—I will limit myself to literature, for it is about literature that the question arises,—the elements with which the creative power works are ideas; the best ideas, on every matter which literature touches, current at the time; at any rate we may lay it down as certain that in modern literature no manifestation of the creative power not working with these can be very important or fruitful.

And I say current at the time, not merely accessible at the time; for creative literary genius does not principally show itself in discovering new ideas; that is rather the business of the philosopher; the grand work of literary genius is a work of synthesis and exposition, not of analysis and discovery; its gift lies in the faculty of being happily inspired by a certain intellectual and spiritual atmosphere, by a certain order of ideas, when it finds itself in them; of dealing divinely with these ideas, presenting them in the most effective and attractive combinations, making beautiful works with them, in short. But it must have the atmosphere, it must find itself amidst the order of ideas, in order to work freely; and these it is not so easy to command.

This is why great creative epochs in literature are so rare; this is why there is so much that is unsatisfactory in the productions of many men of real genius; because for the creation of a master-work of literature two powers must concur, the power of the man and the power of the moment, and the man is not enough without the moment; the creative power has, for its happy exercise, appointed elements, and those ele- ments are not in its own control.

Nay, they are more within the control of the critical power. It is the business of the critical power, as I said in the words already quoted, "in all branches of know- ledge, theology, philosophy, history, art, science, to see the object as in itself it really is." Thus it tends, at last, to make an intellectual situation of which the creative power can profitably avail itself.

It tends to establish an order of ideas, if not absolutely true, yet true by comparison with that which it displaces; to make the best ideas prevail. Presently these new ideas reach society, the touch of truth is the touch of life, and there is a stir and growth everywhere; out of this stir and growth comes the creative epochs of literature. Or, to narrow our range, and quit these considerations of the general march of genius and of society, considera- tions which are apt to become too abstract and impalp- able,—every one can see that a poet, for instance, ought to know life and the world before dealing with them in poetry; and life and the world being, in modern times, very complex things, the creation of a modern poet, to be worth much, implies a great critical effort behind it; else it must be a comparatively poor, barren, and short- lived affair.

This is why Byron's poetry had so little endurance in it, and Goethe's so much; both Byron and Goethe had a great productive power, but Goethe's was nourished by a great critical effort providing the true materials for it, and Byron's was not; Goethe knew life and the world, the poet's necessary subjects, much more comprehensively and thoroughly than Byron. He knew a great deal more of them, and he knew them much more as they really are.

It has long seemed to me that the burst of creative activity in our literature, through the first quarter of this century, had about it, in fact, something premature; and that from this cause its productions are doomed, most of them, in spite of the sanguine hopes which accompanied and do still accompany them, to prove hardly more lasting than the productions of far less splendid epochs. And this prematureness comes from its having proceeded without having its proper data, without sufficient materials to work with.

In other words, the English poetry of the first quarter of this century, with plenty of energy, plenty of creative force, did not know enough. This makes Byron so empty of matter, Shelley so incoherent, Words- worth even, profound as he is, yet so wanting in com- pleteness and variety. Wordsworth cared little for books, and disparaged Goethe.

I admire Wordsworth, as he is, so much that I cannot wish him different; and it is vain, no doubt, to imagine such a man different from what he is, to suppose that he could have been different; but surely the one thing wanting to make Wordsworth an even greater poet than he is,—his thought richer, and his influence of wider application,—was that he should have read more books, among them, no doubt, those of that Goethe whom he disparaged without reading him.

But to speak of books and reading may easily lead to a misunderstanding here. It was not really books and reading that lacked to our poetry, at this epoch; Shelley had plenty of reading, Coleridge had immense reading. Pindar and Sophocles,—as we all say so glibly, and often with so little discernment of the real import of what we are saying,—had not many books; Shakspeare was no deep reader.

True; but in the Greece of Pindar and Sophocles, in the England of Shakspeare, the poet lived in a current of ideas in the highest degree animating and nourishing to the creative power; society was, in the fullest measure, permeated by fresh thought, intelligent and alive; and this state of things is the true basis for the creative power's exercise, in this it finds its data, its materials, truly ready for its hand; all the books and reading in the world are only valuable as they are helps to this.

Even when this does not actually exist, books and reading may enable a man to construct a kind of semblance of it in his own mind, a world of knowledge and intelligence in which he may live and work; this is by no means an equivalent, to the artist, for the nationally diffused life and thought of the epochs of Sophocles or Shakspeare, but, besides that it may be a means of preparation for such epochs, it does really constitute, if many share in it, a quickening and sustaining atmosphere of great value.

Such an atmosphere the many-sided learning and the long and widely-combined critical effort of Germany formed for Goethe, when he lived and worked. There was no national glow of life and thought there, as in the Athens of Pericles, or the England of Elizabeth. That was the poet's weakness. But there was a sort of equivalent for it in the complete culture and unfettered thinking of a large body of Germans. That was his strength. In the England of the first quarter of this century, there was neither a national glow of life and thought, such as we had in the age of Elizabeth, nor yet a culture and a force of learning and criticism, such as were to be found in Germany.

Therefore the creative power of poetry wanted, for success in the highest sense, materials and a basis; a thorough interpretation of the world was necessarily denied to it. At first sight it seems strange that out of the immense stir of the French Revolution and its age should not have come a crop of works of genius equal to that which came out of the stir of the great productive time of Greece, or out of that of the Renaissance, with its powerful episode the Reformation. But the truth is that the stir of the French Revolution took a character which essentially distinguished it from such movements as these. These were, in the main, disinterestedly intellectual and spiritual movements; movements in which the human spirit looked for its satisfaction in itself and in the in- creased play of its own activity: the French Revolution took a political, practical character.

The movement which went on in France under the old régime, from 1700 to 1789, was far more really akin than that of the Revolution itself to the movement of the Renaissance; the France of Voltaire and Rousseau told far more powerfully upon the mind of Europe than the France of the Revolution. Goethe reproached this last expressly with having "thrown quiet culture back." Nay, and the true key to how much in our Byron, even in our Words- worth, is this!—that they had their source in a great movement of feeling, not in a great movement of mind.

The French Revolution, however,—that object of so much blind love and so much blind hatred,—found undoubtedly its motive-power in the intelligence of men and not in their practical sense;—this is what distinguishes it from the English Revolution of Charles the First's time; this is what makes it a more spiritual event than our Re- volution, an event of much more powerful and world-wide interest, though practically less successful;—it appeals to an order of ideas which are universal, certain, permanent. 1789 asked of a thing, Is it rational? 1642 asked of a thing, Is it legal? or, when it went furthest, Is it according to conscience?

This is the English fashion; a fashion to be treated, within its own sphere, with the highest respect; for its success, within its own sphere, has been prodigious. But what is law in one place, is not law in another; what is law here to-day, is not law even here tomorrow; and as for conscience, what is binding on one man's conscience is not binding on another's; the old woman who threw her stool at the head of the surpliced minister in St. Giles's Church at Edinburgh obeyed an impulse to which millions of the human race may be permitted to remain strangers. But the pre- scriptions of reason are absolute, unchanging, of universal validity; to count by tens is the simplest way of counting,*— *A writer in the Saturday Review, who has offered me some counsels about style for which I am truly grateful, suggests that this should stand as follows:— To take as your unit an established base of notation, ten being given as the base of notation, is, except for numbers under twenty, the simplest way of counting. I tried it so, but I assure him, without jealousy, that the more I looked at his improved way of putting the thing, the less I liked it.

It seems to me that the maxim, in this shape, would never make the tour of a world, where most of us are plain easy-spoken people. He forgets that he is a reasoner, a member of a school, a disciple of the great Bentham, and that he naturally talks in the scientific way of his school, with exact accuracy, philosophic propriety; I am a mere solitary wanderer in search of the light, and I talk an artless, un- studied, every-day, familiar language. But, after all, this is the language of the mass of the world.

The mass of Frenchmen who felt the force of that prescription of the reason which my reviewer, in his purified language, states thus:—to count by tens has the advantage of taking as your unit the base of an * that is a proposition of which every one, from here to the Antipodes, feels the force; at least, I should say so, if we did not live in a country where it is not impossible that any morning we may find a letter in the Times declaring that a decimal coinage is an absurdity. That a whole nation should have been pene- trated with an enthusiasm for pure reason, and with an ardent zeal for making its prescriptions triumph, is a very

** established system of notation, certainly rendered this, for themselves, in some such loose language as mine. My point is that they felt the force of a prescription of the reason so strongly that they legislated in accordance with it. They may have been wrong in so doing; they may have foolishly omitted to take other prescriptions of reason into account;—the non-English world does not seem to think so, but let that pass;—what I say is, that by legislating as they did they showed a keen susceptibility to purely rational, intellectual considerations. On the other hand, does my reviewer say that we keep our mone- tary system unchanged because our nation has grasped the intellec- tual proposition which he puts, in his masterly way, thus :* {{"}}*to count by twelves has the advantage of taking as your unit a number in itself far more convenient than ten for that purpose?" Surely not; but because our system is there, and we are too practical a people to trouble ourselves about its intellectual aspect.*

To take a second case. The French Revolutionists abolished

> *the sale of offices, because they thought (my reviewer will kindly allow me to put the thing in my imperfect, popular language) the sale of offices a gross anomaly. We still sell commissions in the army. I have no doubt my reviewer, with his scientific powers, can easily invent some beautiful formula to make us appear to be doing this on the purest philosophical principles; the principles of Hobbes, Locke, Bentham, Mr. Mill, Mr. Bain, and himself, their worthy disciple. But surely the plain unscientific account of the matter is, that we have the anomalous practice (he will allow it is, in itself, an anomalous practice?) established, and that (in the words of senatorial wisdom already quoted) "for a thing to be an anomaly we consider to be no objection to it whatever."*

remarkable thing, when we consider how little of mind, or anything so worthy and quickening as mind, comes into the motives which alone, in general, impel great masses of men. In spite of the extravagant direction given to this enthusiasm, in spite of the crimes and follies in which it lost itself, the French Revolution derives, from the force, truth, and universality of the ideas which it took for its law, and from the passion with which it could inspire a multitude for these ideas, a unique and still living power; it is,—it will probably long remain,—the greatest, the most animating event in history. And, as no sincere passion for the things of the mind, even though it turn out in many respects an unfortunate passion, is ever quite thrown away and quite barren of good, France has reaped from hers one fruit, the natural and legitimate fruit, though not precisely the grand fruit she expected; she is the country in Europe where the people is most alive.

But the mania for giving an immediate political and practical application to all these fine ideas of the reason was fatal. Here an Englishman is in his element: on this theme we can all go on for hours. And all we are in the habit of saying on it has undoubtedly a great deal of truth. Ideas cannot be too much prized in and for themselves, cannot be too much lived with; but to transport them abruptly into the world of politics and practice, violently to revolutionise this world to their bidding,—that is quite another thing.

There is the world of ideas and there is the world of practice; the French are often for suppressing the one and the English the other; but neither is to be suppressed. A member of the House of Commons said to me the other day: "That a thing is an anomaly, I consider to be no objection to it what- ever." I venture to think he was wrong; that a thing is an anomaly is an objection to it, but absolutely and in the sphere of ideas: it is not necessarily, under such and such circumstances, or at such and such a moment, an objection to it in the sphere of politics and practice.

Joubert has said beautifully: "C'est la force et le droit qui règlent toutes choses dans le monde; la force en attendant le droit." Force and right are the governors of this world; force till right is ready. Force till right is ready; and till right is ready, force, the existing order of things, is justified, is the legitimate ruler. But right is something moral, and implies inward recognition, free assent of the will; we are not ready for right,—right, so far as we are concerned, is not ready,—until we have attained this sense of seeing it and willing it. The way in which for us it may change and transform force, the existing order of things, and become, in its turn, the legitimate ruler of the world, will depend on the way in which, when our time comes, we see it and will it.

Therefore for other people enamoured of their own newly discerned right, to attempt to impose it upon us as ours, and violently to substitute their right for our force, is an act of tyranny, and to be resisted. It sets at nought the second great half of our maxim, force till right is ready. This was the grand error of the French Revolution, and its movement of ideas, by quitting the intellectual sphere and rushing furiously into the political sphere, ran, in- deed, a prodigious and memorable course, but produced no such intellectual fruit as the movement of ideas of the Renaissance, and created, in opposition to itself, what I may call an epoch of concentration.

The great force of that epoch of concentration was England; and the great voice of that epoch of concentration was Burke. It is the fashion to treat Burke's writings on the French Revolution as superannuated and conquered by the event; as the eloquent but unphilosophical tirades of bigotry and prejudice. I will not deny that they are often disfigured by the violence and passion of the moment, and that in some directions Burke's view was bounded, and his observation therefore at fault; but on the whole, and for those who can make the needful corrections, what distinguishes these writings is their profound, permanent, fruitful, philosophical truth; they contain the true philosophy of an epoch of concentration, dissipate the heavy atmosphere which its own nature is apt to engender round it, and make its resistance rational instead of mechanical.

But Burke is so great because, almost alone in England, he brings thought to bear upon politics, he saturates politics with thought; it is his accident that his ideas were at the service of an epoch of concentration, not of an epoch of expansion; it is his characteristic that he so lived by ideas, and had such a source of them welling up within him, that he could float even an epoch of concentration and English Tory politics with them.

It does not hurt him that Dr. Price and the Liberals were enraged with him; it does not even hurt him that George the Third and the Tories were enchanted with him. His greatness is that he lived in a world which neither English Liberal- ism nor English Toryism is apt to enter;—the world of ideas, not the world of catchwords and party habits. So far is it from being really true of him that he "to party gave up what was meant for mankind," that at the very end of his fierce struggle with the French Revolution, after all his invectives against its false pretensions, hollow- ness, and madness, with his sincere conviction of its mischievousness, he can close a memorandum on the best means of combating it, some of the last pages he ever wrote,—the Thoughts on French Affairs, in December, 1791,—with these striking words:—

> *"The evil is stated, in my opinion, as it exists. The remedy must be where power, wisdom, and information, I hope, are more united with good intentions than they can be with me. I have done with this subject, I believe, for ever. It has given me many anxious moments for the last two years. If a great change is to be made in human affairs, the minds of men be fitted to it; the general opinions and feelings will draw that way. Every fear, every hope will forward it; and then they who persist in opposing this mighty current in human affairs, will appear rather to resist the decrees of Providence itself, than the mere designs of men. They will not be resolute and firm, but perverse and obstinate."*

That return of Burke upon himself has always seemed to me one of the finest things in English literature, or indeed, in any literature. That is what I call living by ideas; when one side of a question has long had your earnest support, when all your feelings are engaged, when you hear all round you no language but one, when your party talks this language like a steam engine and can imagine no other,—still to be able to think, still to be irresistibly carried, if so it be, by the current of thought to the opposite side of the question, and, like Balaam, to be unable to speak anything but what the Lord has put in your mouth. I know nothing more striking, and I must add that I know nothing more un-English.

For the Englishman in general is like my friend the Member of Parliament, and believes, point-blank, that for a thing to be an anomaly is absolutely no objection to it whatever. He is like the Lord Auckland of Burke's day, who, in a memorandum on the French Revolution, talks of "certain miscreants, assuming the name of philosophers, who have presumed themselves capable of establishing a new system of society."

The Englishman has been called a political animal, and he values what is political and practical so much that ideas easily become objects of dislike in his eyes, and thinkers "miscreants," because ideas and thinkers have rashly meddled with politics and practice. This would be all very well if the dislike and neglect confined themselves to ideas transported out of their own sphere, and meddling rashly with practice; but they are inevitably extended to ideas as such, and to the whole life of intelligence; practice is everything, a free play of the mind is nothing.

The notion of the free play of the mind upon all subjects being a pleasure in itself, being an object of desire, being an essential provider of elements without which a nation's spirit, whatever compensations it may have for them, must, in the long run, die of inanition, hardly enters into an Englishman's thoughts.

It is noticeable that the word curiosity, which in other languages is used in a good sense, to mean, as a high and fine quality of man's nature, just this disinterested love of a free play of the mind on all subjects, for its own sake,—it is noticeable, I say, that this word has in our language no sense of the kind, no sense but a rather bad and disparaging one. But criticism, real criticism, is essentially the exercise of this very quality; it obeys an instinct prompting it to try to know the best that is known and thought in the world, irrespectively of practice, politics, and everything of the kind; and to value knowledge and thought as they approach this best, without the intrusion of any other considerations whatever.

This is an instinct for which there is, I think, little original sympathy in the practical English nature, and what there was of it has undergone a long benumbing period of blight and suppression in the epoch of concentration which followed the French Revolution. But epochs of concentration cannot well endure for ever; epochs of expansion, in the due course of things, follow them. Such an epoch of expansion seems to be opening in this country.

In the first place all danger of a hostile forcible pressure of foreign ideas upon our practice has long disappeared; like the traveller in the fable, therefore, we begin to wear our cloak a little more loosely. Then, with a long peace, the ideas of Europe steal gradually and amicably in, and mingle, though in infinitesimally small quantities at a time, with our own notions.

Then, too, in spite of all that is said about the absorbing and brutalising influence of our passionate material progress, it seems to me indisputable that this progress is likely, though not certain, to lead in the end to an apparition of intellectual life; and that man, after he has made himself perfectly comfortable and has now to determine what to do with himself next, may begin to remember that he has a mind, and that the mind may be made the source of great pleasure. I grant it is mainly the privilege of faith, at present, to discern this end to our railways, our business, and our fortune-making; but we shall see if, here as elsewhere, faith is not in the end the true prophet. Our ease, our travelling, and our un- bounded liberty to hold just as hard and securely as we please to the practice to which our notions have given birth, all tend to beget an inclination to deal a little more freely with these notions themselves, to canvass them a little, to penetrate a little into their real nature.

Flutterings of curiosity, in the foreign sense of the word, appear amongst us, and it is in these that criticism must look to find its account. Criticism first; a time of true creative activity, perhaps,—which, as I have said, must inevitably be preceded amongst us by a time of criticism, —here after, when criticism has done its work.

It is of the last importance that English criticism should clearly discern what rule for its course, in order to avail itself of the field now opening to it, and to pro- duce fruit for the future, it ought to take. The rule may be summed up in one word,—disinterestedness. And how is criticism to show disinterestedness? By keeping aloof from practice; by resolutely following the law of its own nature, which is to be a free play of the mind on all subjects which it touches; by steadily refusing to lend itself to any of those ulterior, political, practical con- siderations about ideas which plenty of people will be sure to attach to them, which perhaps ought often to be attached to them, which in this country at any rate are certain to be attached to them quite sufficiently, but which criticism has really nothing to do with.

Its busi- ness is, as I have said, simply to know the best that is known and thought in the world, and by in its turn making this known, to create a current of true and fresh ideas. Its business is to do this with inflexible honesty, with due ability; but its business is to do no more, and to leave alone all questions of practical consequences and applications, questions which will never fail to have due prominence given to them.

Else criticism, besides being really false to its own nature, merely continues in the old rut which it has hitherto followed in this country, and will certainly miss the chance now given to it. For what is at present the bane of criticism in this country? It is that practical considerations cling to it and stifle it; it subserves interests not its own; our organs of criticism are organs of men and parties having practical ends to serve, and with them those practical ends are the first thing and the play of mind the second; so much play of mind as is compatible with the prosecution of those prac- tical ends is all that is wanted.

An organ like the Revue des Deux Mondes, having for its main function to under- stand and utter the best that is known and thought in the world, existing, it may be said, as just an organ for a‘ free play of the mind, we have not; but we have the Edinburgh Review, existing as an organ of the old Whigs, and for as much play of mind as may suit its being that; we have the Quarterly Review, existing as an organ of the Tories, and for as much play of mind as may suit its being that; we have the British Quarterly Review, exist- ing as an organ of the political Dissenters, and for as much play of mind as may suit its being that; we have the Times, existing as an organ of the common, satisfied, well-to-do Englishman, and for as much play of mind as may suit its being that.

And so on through all the various fractions, political and religious, of our society; every fraction has, as such, its organ of criticism, but the notion of combining all fractions in the common pleasure of a free disinterested play of mind meets with no favour. Directly this play of mind wants to have more scope, and to forget the pressure of practical considerations a little, it is checked, it is made to feel the chain; we saw this the other day in the extinction, so much to be regretted, of the Home and Foreign Review; perhaps in no organ of criticism in this country was there so much knowledge, so much play of mind; but these could not save it; the Dublin Review subordinates play of mind to the prac- tical business of English and Irish Catholicism, and lives. It must needs be that men should act in sects and par- ties, that each of these sects and parties should have its organ, and should make this organ subserve the interests of its action;

but it would be well, too, that there should be a criticism, not the minister of these interests, not their enemy, but absolutely and entirely independent of them. No other criticism will ever attain any real authority or make any real way towards its end,—the creating a current of true and fresh ideas.

It is because criticism has so little kept in the pure intellectual sphere, has so little detached itself from practice, has been so directly polemical and controversial, that it has so ill accomplished, in this country, its best spiritual work; which is to keep man from a self- satisfaction which is retarding and vulgarising, to lead him towards perfection, by making his mind dwell upon what is excellent in itself, and the absolute beauty and fitness of things.

A polemical practical criticism makes men blind even to the ideal imperfection of their practice, makes them willingly assert its ideal perfection, in order the better to secure it against attack; and clearly this is narrowing and baneful for them. If they were reassured on the practical side, speculative considerations of ideal perfection they might be brought to entertain, and their spiritual horizon would thus gra- dually widen. Adderley says to the Warwickshire farmers:—

"Talk of the improvement of breed! Why, the race we ourselves represent, the men and women, the old Anglo-Saxon race, are the best breed in the whole world. ... The absence of a too enervating climate, too unclouded skies, and a too luxurious nature, has produced so vigorous a race of people, and has rendered us so superior to all the world."

Mr. Roebuck says to the Sheffield cutlers:—

"I look around me and ask what is the state of England? Is not property safe? Is not every man able to say what he likes? Can you not walk from one end of England to the other in perfect security? I ask you whether, the world over or in past history, there is anything like it? Nothing. I pray that our unrivalled happiness may last."

Now obviously there is a peril for poor human nature in words and thoughts of such exuberant self-satisfaction, until we find ourselves safe in the streets of the Celestial City.

"Das wenige verschwindet leicht deln Blicke Der vorwärts sieht, wie viel noch übrig bleibt—" says Goethe; the little that is done seems nothing when we look forward and see how much we have yet to do. Clearly this is a better line of reflection for weak humanity, so long as it remains on this earthly field of labour and trial. But neither Mr. Adderley nor Mr. Roebuck are by nature inaccessible to considerations of this sort.

They only lose sight of them owing to the controversial life we all lead, and the practical form which all specu- lation takes with us. They have in view opponents whose aim is not ideal, but practical, and in their zeal to uphold their own practice against these innovators, they go so far as even to attribute to this practice an ideal perfection. Somebody has been wanting to introduce a six-pound franchise, or to abolish church-rates, or to collect agricultural statistics by force, or to diminish local self-government. How natural, in reply to such pro- posals, very likely improper or ill-timed, to go a little beyond the mark, and to say stoutly: "Such a race of people as we stand, so superior to all the world!

The old Anglo-Saxon race, the best breed in the whole world! I pray that our unrivalled happiness may last! I ask you whether, the world over or in past history, there is anything like it!" And so long as criticism answers this dithyramb by insisting that the old Anglo-Saxon race would be still more superior to all others if it had no church-rates, or that our unrivalled happiness would last yet longer with a six-pound franchise, so long will the strain, "The best breed in the whole world!" swell louder and louder, everything ideal and refining will be lost out of sight, and both the assailed and their critics will remain in a sphere, to say the truth, perfectly unvital, a sphere in which spiritual progression is impossible.

But let criticism leave church-rates and the franchise alone, and in the most candid spirit, without a single lurking thought of practical innovation, confront with our dithyramb this paragraph on which I stumbled in a news- paper soon after reading Mr. Roebuck:— "A shocking child murder has just been committed at Nottingham. A girl named Wragg left the workhouse there on Saturday morning with her young illegitimate child.

The child was soon afterwards found dead on Mapperly Hills, having been strangled. Wragg is in custody." Nothing but that; but, in juxtaposition with the absolute eulogies of Mr. Adderley and Mr. Roebuck, how elo- quent, how suggestive are those few lines!" Our old Anglo-Saxon breed, the best in the whole world!"—how much that is harsh and ill-favoured there is in this best! Wragg!

If we are to talk of ideal perfection, of "the best in the whole world," has anyone reflected what a touch of grossness in our race, what an original short-coming in the more delicate spiritual perceptions, is shown by the natural growth amongst us of such hideous names,—Higginbottom, Stiggins, Bugg! In Ionia and Attica they were luckier in this respect than "the best race in the world;" by the Ilissus there was no Wragg, poor thing! And "our unrivalled happiness;"—what an element of grimness, bareness, and hideousness mixes with it and blurs it; the workhouse, the dismal Map- perly Hills,—how dismal those who have seen them will remember;—the gloom, the smoke, the cold, the strangled illegitimate child!"

I ask you whether, the world over or in past history, there is anything like it?" Perhaps not, one is inclined to answer; but at any rate, in that case, the world is very much to be pitied. And the final touch,—short, bleak, and inhuman:

Wragg is in custody. The sex lost in the confusion of our unrivalled happiness; or, shall I say? the superfluous Christian name lopped off by the straightforward vigour of our old Anglo-Saxon breed!

There is profit for the spirit in such contrasts as this; criticism serves the cause of perfection by esta- blishing them. By eluding sterile conflict, by refusing to remain in the sphere where alone narrow and relative conceptions have any worth and validity, criticism may diminish its momentary importance, but only in this way has it a chance of gaining admittance for those wider and more perfect conceptions to which all its duty is really owed. Mr. Roebuck will have a poor opinion of an adversary who replies to his defiant songs of triumph only by murmuring under his breath, Wragg is in custody; but in no other way will these songs of triumph be induced gradually to moderate themselves, to get rid of what in them is excessive and offensive, and to fall into a softer and truer key.

It will be said that it is a very subtle and indirect action which I am thus prescribing for criticism, and that by embracing in this manner the Indian virtue of detach- ment and abandoning the sphere of practical life, it condemns itself to a slow and obscure work. Slow and obscure it may be, but it is the only proper work of criticism. The mass of mankind will never have any ardent zeal for seeing things as they are; very inadequate ideas will always satisfy them.

On these inadequate ideas reposes, and must repose, the general practice of the world. That is as much as saying that whoever sets himself to see things as they are will find himself one of a very small circle; but it is only by this small circle resolutely doing its own work that adequate ideas will ever get current at all.

The rush and roar of practical life will always have a dizzying and attracting effect upon the most collected spectator, and tend to draw him into its vortex; most of all will this be the case where that life is so powerful as it is in England. But it is only by remaining collected, and refusing to lend himself to the point of view of the practical man, that the critic can do the practical man any service; and it is only by the greatest sincerity in pursuing his own course, and by at last convincing even the practical man of his sincerity, that he can escape misunderstandings which perpetually threaten him.

For the practical man is not apt for fine distinctions, and yet in these distinctions truth and the highest culture greatly find their account. But it is not easy to lead a practical man,—unless you reassure him as to your practical intentions you have no chance of leading him,—to see that a thing which he has always been used to look at from one side only, which he greatly values, and which, looked at from that side, more than deserves, perhaps, all the prizing and admiring which he bestows upon it,—that this thing, looked at from another side, may appear much less beneficent and beautiful, and yet retain all its claims to our practical allegiance. Where shall we find lan- guage innocent enough, how shall we make the spotless purity of our intentions evident enough, to enable us to say to the political Englishman that the British Constitu- tion itself, which, seen from the practical side, looks such a magnificent organ of progress and virtue, seen from the speculative side,—with its compromises, its love of facts, its horror of theory, its studied avoidance of clear thoughts,—that, seen from this side, our august Consti- tution sometimes looks,—forgive me, shade of Lord Somers!—a colossal machine for the manufacture of Philistines?

How is Cobbett to say this and not be mis- understood, blackened as he is with the smoke of a life- long conflict in the field of political practice? how is Mr. Carlyle to say it and not be misunderstood, after his furious raid into this field with his Latter-day Pamphlets how is Mr. Ruskin, after his pugnacious political economy? I say, the critic must keep out of the region of immediate practice in the political, social, humanitarian sphere, if he wants to make a beginning for that more free specu- lative treatment of things, which may perhaps one day make its benefits felt even in this sphere, but in a natural and thence irresistible manner.

Do what he will, however, the critic will still remain exposed to frequent misunderstandings, and nowhere so much as in this country. For here people are particu- larly indisposed even to comprehend that without this free disinterested treatment of things, truth and the highest culture are out of the question. So immersed are they in practical life, so accustomed to take all their notions from this life and its processes, that they are apt to think that truth and culture themselves can be reached by the processes of this life, and that it is an impertinent singularity to think of reaching them in any other.

"We are all terræ filii," cries their eloquent advocate; "all Philistines together. Away with the notion of proceed- ing by any other course than the course dear to the Philistines; let us have a social movement, let us organise and combine a party to pursue truth and new thought, let us call it the liberal party, and let us all stick to each other, and back each other up. Let us have no nonsense about independent criticism, and intellectual delicacy, and the few and the many; don't let us trouble our- selves about foreign thought; we shall invent the whole thing for ourselves as we go along; if one of us speaks well, applaud him; if one of us speaks ill, applaud him too; we are all in the same movement, we are all liberals, we are all in pursuit of truth."

In this way the pursuit of truth becomes really a social, practical, pleasureable affair, almost requiring a chairman, a secretary, and advertisements; with the excitement of an occasional scandal, with a little resistance to give the happy sense of difficulty overcome; but, in general, plenty of bustle and very little thought. To act is so easy, as Goethe says; to think is so hard! It is true that the critic has many temptations to go with the stream, to make one of the party of movement, one of these terræ filii; it seems ungracious to refuse to be a terræ filius, when so many excellent people are; but the critic's duty is to refuse, or, if resistance is vain, at least to cry with Obermann: Périssons en résistant.

How serious a matter it is to try and resist, I had ample opportunity of experiencing when I ventured some time ago to criticise the celebrated first volume of Bishop Colenso. * The echoes of the storm which was then raised I still, from time to time, hear grumbling round me. That storm arose out of a misunderstanding almost inevitable.

It is a result of no little culture to attain to a clear perception that science and religion are two wholly different things; the multitude will for ever confuse them, but happily that is of no great real im- portance, for while the multitude imagines itself to live by its false science, it does really live by its true religion. Dr. Colenso, however, in his first volume did all he could to strengthen the confusion, and to make it dangerous.

** So sincere is my dislike to all personal attack and controversy, that I abstain from reprinting, at this distance of time from the occasion which called them forth, the essays in which I criticised the Bishop of Natal's book; I feel bound, however, after all that has passed, to make here a final declaration of my sincere impenitence for having published them. The Bishop of Natal's subsequent volumes are in great measure free from the crying fault of his first; he has at length succeeded in more clearly separating, in his own thoughts, the idea of science from the idea of religion; his mind appears to be opening as he goes along, and he may perhaps end by becoming a useful biblical critic, though never, I think, of the first order. Still, in here taking leave of him at the moment when he is publishing, for popular use, a cheap edition of his work, I cannot forbear repeating yet once more, for his benefit and that of his readers, this sentence from my original remarks upon him: There is truth of science and truth of religion; truth of science does not become truth of religion till it is made religious. And I will add: Let us have all the science there is from the men of science; from the men of religion let us have religion.*

It has been said I make it "a crime against literary criticism * He did this with the best intentions, I freely admit, and with the most candid ignorance that this was the natural effect of what he was doing; but, says Joubert, "Ignorance, which in matters of morals extenuates the crime, in itself, in intellectual matters, a crime of the first order." I criticised Bishop Colenso's speculative confusion. Im- mediately there was a cry raised: "What is this? here a liberal attacking a liberal. Do not you belong to the movement? are not you a friend of truth? Is not Bishop Colenso in pursuit of truth? then speak with proper respect of his book. Dr. Stanley is another friend of truth, and you speak with proper respect of his book; why make these invidious differences? both books are excellent, admirable, liberal; Bishop Colenso's perhaps the most so, because it is the boldest, and will have the best practical consequences for the liberal cause. Do you want to encourage to the attack of a brother liberal his, and your, and our implacable enemies, the Church and State Review or the Record,—the High Church rhinoceros and the Evangelical hyæna?

Be silent, therefore; or rather speak, speak as loud as ever you can, and go into ecstasies over the eighty and odd pigeons." But criticism cannot follow this coarse and indiscriminate method. It is unfortunately possible for a man in pur- suit of truth to write a book which reposes upon a false conception. Even the practical consequences of a book are to genuine criticism no recommendation of it, if the book is, in the highest sense, blundering. I see that a

**and the higher culture to attempt to inform the ignorant." Need I point out that the ignorant are not informed by being confirmed in a confusion?*

lady who herself, too, is in pursuit of truth, and who writes with great ability, but a little too much, perhaps, under the influence of the practical spirit of the English liberal movement, classes Bishop Colenso's book and M. Renan's together, in her survey of the religious state of Europe, as facts of the same order, works, both of them, of "great importance;" "great ability, power and skill;" Bishop Colenso's, perhaps, the most powerful; at least, Miss Cobbe gives special expression to her gratitude that to Bishop Colenso "has been given the strength to grasp, and the courage to teach truths of such deep import."

In the same way, more than one popular writer has compared him to Luther. Now it is just this kind of false estimate which the critical spirit is, it seems to me, bound to resist. It is really the strongest possible proof of the low ebb at which, in England, the critical spirit is, that while the critical hit in the religious literature of Germany is Dr. Strauss's book, in that of France M. Renan's book, the book of Bishop Colenso is the critical hit in the religious literature of England. Bishop Colenso's book reposes on a total misconcep- tion of the essential elements of the religious problem, as that problem is now presented for solution.

To cri- ticism, therefore, which seeks to have the best that is known and thought on this problem, it is, however well meant, of no importance whatever. M. Renan's book attempts a new synthesis of the elements furnished to us by the four Gospels. It attempts, in my opinion, a synthesis, perhaps premature, perhaps impossible, cer- tainly not successful. Up to the present time, at any rate, we must acquiesce in Fleury's sentence on such recastings of the Gospel story : Quiconque s'imagine la pouvoir mieux écrire, ne l'entend pas.

M. Renan had himself passed by anticipation a like sentence on his own work, when he said: "If a new presentation of the character of Jesus were offered to me, I would not have it; its very clearness would be, in my opinion, the best proof of its insufficiency." His friends may with perfect justice rejoin that at the sight of the Holy Land, and of the actual scene of the Gospel-story, all the current of M. Renan's thoughts may have naturally changed, and a new casting of that story irresistibly suggested itself to him; and that this is just a case for applying Cicero's maxim: Change of mind is not inconsistency— nemo doctus unquam mutationem consilii inconstantiam dixit esse.

Nevertheless, for criticism, M. Renan's first thought must still be the truer one, as long as his new casting so fails more fully to commend itself, more fully (to use Coleridge's happy phrase about the Bible) to find us. Still M. Renan's attempt is, for criticism, of the most real interest and importance, since, with all its difficulty, a fresh synthesis of the New Testament data,— not a making war on them, in Voltaire's fashion, not a leaving them out of mind, in the world's fashion, but the putting a new construction upon them, the taking them from under the old, adoptive, traditional, un- spiritual point of view and placing them under a new one,—is the very essence of the religious problem, as now presented; and only by efforts in this direction can it receive a solution.

Again, in the same spirit in which she judges Bishop Colenso, Miss Cobbe, like so many earnest liberals of our practical race, both here and in America, herself sets vigorously about a positive reconstruction of religion, about making a religion of the future out of hand, or at least setting about making it; we must not rest, she and they are always thinking and saying, in negative criti- cism, we must be creative and constructive; hence we have such works as her recent Religious Duty, and works still more considerable, perhaps, by others, which will be in everyone's mind.

These works often have much ability; they often spring out of sincere convictions, and a sincere wish to do good; and they sometimes, perhaps, do good. Their fault is (if I may be permitted to say so) one which they have in common with the British College of Health, in the New Road. Everyone knows the British College of Health; it is that building with the lion and the statue of the Goddess Hygeia before it; at least, I am sure about the lion, though I am not absolutely certain about the Goddess Hygeia. This building does credit, perhaps, to the resources of Dr. Morrison and his disciples; but it falls a good deal short of one's idea of what a British College of Health ought to be.

In England, where we hate public inter- ference and love individual enterprise, we have a whole crop of places like the British College of Health; the grand name without the grand thing. Unluckily, credit- able to individual enterprise as they are, they tend to impair our taste by making us forget what more grandiose, noble, or beautiful character properly belongs to a public institution. The same may be said of the religions of the future of Miss Cobbe and others. Creditable, like the British College of Health, to the resources of their authors, they yet tend to make us forget what more grandiose, noble, or beautiful character properly belongs to religious constructions.

The historic religions, with all their faults, have had this; it certainly belongs to the religious sentiment, when it truly flowers, to have this; and we impoverish our spirit if we allow a religion of the future without it. What then is the duty of criticism here? To take the practical point of view, to applaud the liberal movement and all its works,—its New Road religions of the future into the bargain,—for their general utility's sake? By no means; but to be perpetually dis- satisfied with these works, while they perpetually fall short of a high and perfect ideal.

For criticism, these are elementary laws; but they never can be popular, and in this country they have been very little followed, and one meets with immense obstacles in following them. That is a reason for asserting them again and again. Criticism must maintain its independence of the practical spirit and its aims. Even with well-meant efforts of the practical spirit it must express dissatisfaction, if in the sphere of the ideal they seem impoverishing and limiting.

It must not hurry on to the goal because of its practical importance. It must be patient, and know how to wait; and flexible, and know how to attach itself to things and how to withdraw from them. It must be apt to study and praise elements that for the fulness of spiritual perfection are wanted, even though they belong to a power which in the prac- tical sphere may be maleficent.

It must be apt to discern the spiritual shortcomings or illusions of powers that in the practical sphere may be beneficent. And this with- out any notion of favouring or injuring, in the practical sphere, one power or the other; without any notion of playing off, in this sphere, one power against the other. When one looks, for instance, at the English Divorce Court,—an institution which perhaps has its practical conveniences, but which in the ideal sphere is so hideous;*

**A critic, already quoted, says that I have no right, on my own principles, to "object to practical measures on theoretical grounds," and that only "when a man has got a theory which will fully explain all the duties of the legislator on the matter of marriage, will he have a right to abuse the Divorce Court." In short, he wants me to produce a plan for a new and improved Divorce Court, before I call the present one hideous. But God forbid that I should thus enter into competition with the Lord Chancellor! It is just this invasion of the practical sphere which is really against my principles; the taking a practical measure into the world of ideas, and seeing how it looks there, is, on the other hand, just what I am recom- mending. It is because we have not been conversant enough with ideas that our practice now falls so short; it is only by becoming more conversant with them that we shall make it better. Our present Divorce Court is not the result of any legislator's meditations on the subject of marriage; rich people had an anomalous privilege of getting divorced; privileges are odious, and we said everybody should have the same chance. There was no meditation about marriage here; that was just the mischief.*

If my practical critic will but himself accompany me, for a little while, into the despised world of ideas;—if, renouncing any attempt to patch hastily up, with a noble disdain for transcendentalists, our *present Divorce law, he will but allow his mind to dwell a little, first on the Catholic idea of marriage, which exhibits marriage as indissoluble, and then upon that Protestant idea of marriage, which exhibits it as a union terminable by mutual consent,—if he will meditate well on these, and afterwards on the thought of what married life, according to its idea, really is, of what family life really is, of what social life really is, and national life, and public morals, —he will find, after a while, I do assure him, the whole state of his**

an institution which neither makes divorce impossible nor makes it decent, which allows a man to get rid of his wife, or a wife of her husband, but makes them drag one another first, for the public edification, through a mire of unutterable infamy,—when one looks at this charming institution, I say, with its crowded benches, its newspaper-reports, and its money-compensations, this institution in which the gross unregenerate British Philis- tine has indeed stamped an image of himself,—one may be permitted to find the marriage-theory of Catholicism refreshing and elevating. Or when Protestantism, in virtue of its supposed rational and intellectual origin, gives the law to criticism too magisterially, criticism may and must remind it that its pretensions, in this respect, are illusive and do it harm; that the Reformation was a moral rather than an intellectual event; that Luther's theory of grace no more exactly reflects the mind of the spirit than Bossuet's philosophy of history reflects it; and that there is no more antecedent probability of the Bishop of Durham's stock of ideas being agreeable to- perfect reason than of Pope Pius the Ninth's. But criticism will not on that account forget the achievements of Protestantism in the practical and moral sphere; nor that, even in the intellectual sphere, Protestantism,

*spirit quite changed; the Divorce Court will then seem to him, if he looks at it, strangely hideous; and he will at the same time discover in himself, as the fruit of his inward discipline, lights and resources for making it better, of which now he does not dream. He must make haste, though, for the condition of his "practical measure" is getting awkward; even the British Philistine begins to have qualms as he looks at his offspring; even his "thrice-battered God of Palestine" is beginning to roll its eyes convulsively. though in a blind and stumbling manner, carried forward the Renaissance, while Catholicism threw itself violently across its path.

I lately heard a man of thought and energy contrasting the want of ardour and movement which he now found amongst young men in this country with what he re- membered in his own youth, twenty years ago. "What reformers we were then!" he exclaimed; "what a zeal we had! how we canvassed every institution in Church and State, and were prepared to remodel them all on first principles!" He was inclined to regret, as a spiritual flagging, the lull which he saw. I am disposed rather to regard it as a pause in which the turn to a new mode of spiritual progress is being accomplished. Everything was long seen, by the young and ardent amongst us, in inseparable connexion with politics and practical life; we have pretty well exhausted the benefits of seeing things in this connexion, we have got all that can be got by so seeing them.

Let us try a more dis- interested mode of seeing them; let us betake ourselves more to the serener life of the mind and spirit. This life, too, may have its excesses and dangers; but they are not for us at present. Let us think of quietly enlarging our stock of true and fresh ideas, and not, as soon as we get an idea or half an idea, be running out with it into the street, and trying to make it rule there. Our ideas will, in the end, shape the world all the better for maturing a little.

Perhaps in fifty years time it will in the English House of Commons be an objection to an institution that it is an anomaly, and my friend the member of Parliament will shudder in his grave. But let us in the meanwhile rather endeavour that in twenty years time it may, in English literature, be an objection to a proposition that it is absurd. That will be a change so vast, that the imagination almost fails to grasp it.

If I have insisted so much on the course which criticism must take where politics and religion are con- cemed, it is because, where these burning matters are in question, it is most likely to go astray. In general, its course is determined for it by the idea which is the law of its being; the idea of a disinterested endeavour to learn and propagate the best that is known and thought in the world, and thus to establish a current of fresh and true ideas.

By the very nature of things, as England is not all the world, much of the best that is known and thought in the world cannot be of English growth, must be foreign; by the nature of things, again, it is just this that we are least likely to know, while English thought is streaming in upon us from all sides and takes excellent care that we shall not be ignorant of its existence; the English critic, therefore, must dwell much on foreign thought, and with particular heed on any part of it, which, while significant and fruitful in itself, is for any reason specially likely to escape him. Again, judging is often spoken of as the critic's one business; and so in some sense it is; but the judgement which almost insensibly forms itself in a fair and clear mind, along with fresh knowledge, is the valuable one; and thus knowledge, and ever fresh knowledge, must be the critic's great concern for himself; and it is by communicating fresh knowledge, and letting his own judgement pass along with it,—but insensibly, and in the second place not the first, as a sort of companion and clue, not as an abstract law-giver,—that he will generally do most good to his readers.

Sometimes, no doubt, for the sake of esta- blishing an author's place in literature, and his relation to a central standard (and if this is not done how are we to get at our best in the world?), criticism may have to deal with a subject-matter so familiar that fresh knowledge is out of the question, and then it must be all judgement; an enunciation and detailed application of principles. Here the great safeguard is never to let oneself become abstract, always to retain an intimate and lively con- sciousness of the truth of what one is saying, and, the moment this fails us, to be sure that something is wrong. Still, under all circumstances, this mere judgement and application of principles is, in itself, not the most satis- factory work to the critic; like mathematics it is tauto- logical, and cannot well give us, like fresh learning, the sense of creative activity.

But stop, some one will say; all this talk is of no practical use to us whatever; this criticism of yours is not what we have in our minds when we speak of criticism; when we speak of critics and criticism, we mean critics and criticism of the current English literature of the day; when you offer to tell criticism its function, it is to this criticism that we expect you to address yourself. I am sorry for it, for I am afraid I must disappoint these expectations. I am bound by my own definition of cri- ticism: a disinterested endeavour to learn and propagate the best that is known and thought in the world.

How much of current English literature comes into this "best that is known and thought in the world"? Not very much, I fear; certainly less, at this moment, than of the current literature of France or Germany. Well, then, am I to alter my definition of criticism, in order to meet the requirements of a number of practising English critics, who, after all, are free in their choice of a business?

That would be making criticism lend itself just to one of those alien practical considerations, which, I have said, are so fatal to it. One may say, indeed, to those who have to deal with the mass,—so much better disregarded,—of current English literature, that they may at all events endeavour, in dealing with this, to try it, so far as they can, by the standard of the best that is known and thought in the world; one may say, that to get anywhere near this standard, every critic should try and possess one great literature, at least, besides his own; and the more unlike his own, the better.

But, after all, the criticism I am really concerned with,—the criticism which alone can much help us for the future, the criticism which, through- out Europe, is at the present day meant, when so much stress is laid on the importance of criticism and the critical spirit,—is a criticism which regards Europe as being, for intellectual and spiritual purposes, one great confederation, bound to a joint action and working to a common result; and whose members have, for their proper outfit, a knowledge of Greek, Roman, and Eastern antiquity, and of one another. Special, local, and tempo- rary advantages being put out of account, that modern nation will in the intellectual and spiritual sphere make most progress, which most thoroughly carries out this programme. And what is that but saying that we too, all of us, as individuals, the more thoroughly we carry it out, shall make the more progress?

There is so much inviting us! what are we to take? what will nourish us in growth towards perfection? That is the question which, with the immense field of life and of literature lying before him, the critic has to answer; for himself first, and afterwards for others. In this idea of the critic's business the essays brought together in the following pages have had their origin; in this idea, widely different as are their subjects, they have, perhaps, their unity. I conclude with what I said at the beginning: to have the sense of creative activity is the great happiness and the great proof of being alive, and it is not denied to criticism to have it; but then criticism must be sincere, simple, flexible, ardent, ever widening its knowledge. Then it may have, in no contemptible measure, a joyful sense of creative activity; a sense which a man of insight and conscience will prefer to what he might derive from a poor, starved, fragmentary, inadequate creation. And at some epochs no other creation is possible.

Still, in full measure, the sense of creative activity belongs only to genuine creation; in literature we must never forget that. But what true man of letters ever can forget it? It is no such common matter for a gifted nature to come into possession of a current of true and living ideas, and to produce amidst the inspira- tion of them, that we are likely to underrate it. The epochs of Æschylus and Shakspeare make us feel their pre-eminence.

In an epoch like those is, no doubt, the true life of a literature; there is the promised land, towards which criticism can only beckon. That pro- mised land it will not be ours to enter, and we shall die in the wilderness: but to have desired to enter it, to have saluted it from afar, is already, perhaps, the best distinction among contemporaries; it will certainly be the best title to esteem with posterity.

THE FUNCTION OF CRITICISM: T. S. ELIOT

Writing several years ago on the subject of the relation of the new to the old in art, I formulated a view to which I still adhere, in sentences which I take the liberty of quoting, because the present paper is an application of the principle they express: 'The existing monuments form an ideal order among themselves, which is modified by the introduction of the new (the really new) work of art among them.

The existing order is complete before the new work arrives; for order to persist after the supervention of novelty, the *whole* existing order must be, if ever so slightly, altered; and so the relations, proportions, values of each work of art towards the whole are readjusted; and this is conformity between the old and the new.

Whoever has approved this idea of order, of the form of European, of English literature, will not find it preposterous that the past should be altered by the present as much as the present is directed by the past.' I was dealing then with the artist, and the sense of tradition which, it seemed to me, the artist should have; but it was generally a problem of order; and the function of criticism seems to be essentially a problem of order too. I thought of literature then, as I think of it now, of the literature of the world, of the literature of Europe, of the literature of a single country, not as a collection of the writings of individuals, but as 'organic wholes', as systems in relation to which, and only in relation to which, individual works of literary art, and the works of individual artists, have their significance. There is accordingly something outside of the artist to which he owes allegiance, a devotion to which he must surrender and sacrifice himself in order to earn and to obtain his unique position.

A common inheritance and a common cause unite artists consciously or unconsciously: it must be admitted that the union is mostly unconscious. Between the true artists of any time there is, I believe, an unconscious community. And, as our instincts of tidiness imperatively command us not to leave to the haphazard of unconsciousness what we can attempt to do consciously, we are forced to conclude that what happens unconsciously we could bring about, and form into a purpose, if we made a conscious attempt.

The second-rate artist, of course, cannot afford to surrender himself to any common action; for his chief task is the assertion of all the trifling differences which are his distinction: only the man who has so much to give that he can forget himself in his work can afford to collaborate, to exchange, to contribute. If such views are held about art, it follows that *a fortiori* whoever holds them must hold similar views about criticism.

When I say criticism, I mean of course in this place the commentation and exposition of works of art by means of written words; for of the general use of the word 'criticism' to mean such writings, as Matthew Arnold uses it in his essay, I shall presently make several qualifications. No Exponent of criticism (in this limited sense) has, I presume, ever made the preposterous assumption that criticism is an autotelic activity. I do not deny that art may be affirmed to serve ends beyond itself; but art is not required to be aware of these ends, and indeed performs its function, whatever that may be, according to various theories of value, much better by indifference to them.

Criticism, on the other hand, must always profess an end in view, which, roughly speaking appears to be the elucidation of works of art and the correction of taste. The critic's task, therefore, appears to be quite clearly cut out for him; and it ought to be comparatively easy to decide whether he performs it satisfactorily, and in general, what kinds of criticism are useful and what are otiose.

But on giving the matter a little attention, we perceive that criticism, far from being a simple and orderly field of beneficent activity, from which impostors can be readily ejected, is no better than a Sunday park of contending and contentious orators, who have not even arrived at the articulation of their differences. Here, one would suppose, was a place for quiet co-operative labour. The critic, one would suppose, if he is to justify his existence, should endeavour to discipline his personal prejudices and cranks— tares to which we are all subject— and compose his differences with as many of his fellows as possible, in the common pursuit of true judgement.

When we find that quite the contrary prevails, we begin to suspect that the critic owes his livelihood to the violence and extremity of his opposition to other critics, or else to some trifling oddities of his own with which he contrives to season the opinions which men already hold, and which out of vanity or sloth they prefer to maintain. We are tempted to expel the lot. Immediately after such an eviction, or as soon as relief has abated our rage, we are compelled to admit that there remain certain books, certain essays, certain sentences, certain men, who have been 'useful' to us. And our next step is to attempt to classify these, and find out whether we establish any principles for deciding what kinds of book should be preserved, and what aims and methods of criticism should be followed.

VIEW OF THE RELATION OF THE WORK OF ART

The view of the relation of the work of art to art, of the work of literature to literature, of 'criticism' to criticism, which I have outlined above, seemed to me natural and self-evident. I owe to Mr. Middleton Murry my perception of the contentious character of the problem; or rather, my perception that there is a definite and final choice involved. To Mr. Murry I feel an increasing debt of gratitude. Most of our critics are occupied in labour of obnubilation; in reconciling, in hushing up, in patting down, in squeezing in, in glozing over, in concocting pleasant sedatives, in pretending that the only difference between themselves and others is that they are nice men and the others of very doubtful repute.

Mr. Murry is not one of these. He is aware that there are definite positions to be taken, and that now and then one must actually reject something and select something else. He is not the anonymous writer who in a literary paper several years ago asserted that Romanticism and Classicism arc much the same thing, and that the true Classical Age in France was the Age which produced the Gothic cathedrals and—Jeanne d'Arc. With Mr. Murry's formulation of Classicism and Romanticism I cannot agree; the difference seems to me rather the difference between the complete and the fragmentary, the adult and the immature, the orderly and the chaotic. But what Mr. Murry does show is that there are at least two attitudes towards literature and towards everything, and that you cannot hold both.

And the attitude which he professes appears to imply that the other has no standing in England whatever. For it is made a national, a racial issue. Mr. Murry makes his issue perfectly clear. 'Catholicism', he says, 'stands for the principle of unquestioned spiritual authority outside the individual; that is also the principle of Classicism in literature.' Within the orbit within which Mr. Murry's discussion moves, this seems to me an unimpeachable definition, though it is of course not all that there is to be said about either Catholicism or Classicism.

Those of us who find ourselves supporting what Mr. Murry calls Classicism believe that men cannot get on without giving allegiance to something outside themselves. I am aware that 'outside' and 'inside' are terms which provide unlimited opportunity for quibbling, and that no psychologist would tolerate a discussion which shuffled such base coinage; but I will presume that Mr. Murry and myself can agree that for our purpose these counters are adequate, and concur in disregarding the admonitions of our psycho- logical friends. If you find that you have to imagine it as outside, then it is outside.

If, then, a man's interest is political, he must, I presume, profess an allegiance to principles, or to a form of government, or to a monarch; and if he is interested in religion, and has one, to a Church; and if he happens to be interested in literature, he must acknowledge, it seems to me, just that sort of allegiance which I endeavoured to put forth in the preceding section. There is, nevertheless, an alternative, which Mr. Murry has expressed. 'The English writer, the English divine, the English statesman, inherit no rules from their forebears; they inherit only this: a sense that in the last resort they must depend upon the inner voice.'

This statement does, I admit, appear to cover certain cases; it throws a flood of light upon Mr. Lloyd George. But why '*in the last resort*'? Do they, then, avoid the dictates of the inner voice up to the last extremity? My belief is that those who possess this inner voice are ready enough to hearken to it, and will hear no other. The inner voice, in fact, sounds remarkably like an old principle which has been formulated by an elder critic in the now familiar phrase of 'doing as one likes'.

The possessors of the inner voice ride ten in a compartment to a football match at Swansea, listening to the inner voice, which breathes the eternal message of vanity, fear, and lust. Mr. Murry will say, with some show of justice, that this is a wilful misrepresentation. He says: 'If they (the English writer, divine, statesman) dig *deep enough* in their pursuit of self-knowledge—a piece of mining done not with the intellect alone, but with the whole man—they will come upon a self that is universal'—an exercise far beyond the strength of our football enthusiasts.

It is an exercise, however, which I believe was of enough interest to Catholicism for several handbooks to be written on its practice. But the Catholic practitioners were, I believe, with the possible exception of certain heretics, not palpitating Narcissi; the Catholic did not believe that God and himself were identical. 'The man who truly interrogates himself will ultimately hear the voice of God', Mr. Murry says. In theory, this leads to a form of pantheism which I maintain is not European—just as Mr. Murry maintains that 'Classicism' is not English.

For its practical results, one may refer to the verses of*Hudibras*. I did not realise that Mr. Murry was the spokesman for a considerable sect, until I read in the editorial columns of a dignified daily that 'magnificent as the representatives of the classical genius have been in England, they are not the sole expressions of the English character, which remains at bottom obstinately "humorous" and nonconformist'. This writer is moderate in using the qualification sole, and brutally frank in attributing this 'humorousness' to 'the unreclaimed Teutonic element in us'. But it strikes me that Mr. Murry, and this other voice, are either too obstinate or too tolerant.

The question is, the first question, not what comes natural or what conies easy to us, but what is*right*? Either one attitude is better than the other, or else it is indifferent. But how can such a choice be indifferent? Surely the reference to racial origins, or the mere statement that the French are thus, and the English otherwise, is not expected to settle the question: which, of two antithetical views, is right?

And I cannot understand why the opposition between Classicism and Romanticism should be pro- found enough in Latin countries (Mr. Murry says it is) and yet of no significance among ourselves. For if the French are*naturally* classical, why should there be any 'opposition' in France, any more than there is here! And if Classicism is not natural to them, but something acquired, why not acquire it here! Were the French in the year 1600 classical, and the English in the same year romantic? A more important difference, to my mind, is that the French in the year 1600 *had already a more mature prose*.

COMPARISON OF OUTSIDE AUTHORITY WITH THE INNER VOICE

This discussion may seem to have led us a long way from the subject of this paper. But it was worth my while to follow Mr. Murry's comparison of Outside Authority with the Inner Voice. For to those who obey the inner voice (perhaps 'obey' is not the word) nothing that I can say about criticism will have the slightest value. For, they will not be interested in the attempt to find any common principles for the pursuit of criticism. Why have principles, when one has the inner voice? If I like a tiling, that is all I want; and if enough of us, shouting all together, like it, that should be all that *you* (who don't like it) ought to want. The law of art, said Mr. Clutton Brock, is all case law. And we can not only like whatever we like to like but we can like it for any reason we choose. We are not, in fact, concerned with literary *perfection* at all—the search for perfection is a sign of pettiness, for it shows that the writer has admitted the existence of an unquestioned spiritual authority outside himself, to which he has attempted to*conform*.

We are not in fact interested in art. We will not worship Baal. 'The principle of classical leadership is that obeisance is made to the office or to the tradition, never to the man.' And we want, not principles, but men. Thus speaks the Inner Voice. It is a voice to which, for convenience, we may give a name: and the name I suggest is Whiggery.

THE CRITICAL DISCRIMINATION

Leaving, then, those whose calling and election are sure and returning to those who shamefully depend upon tradition and the accumulated wisdom of time, and restricting the discussion to those who sympathise with each other in this frailty, we may comment for a moment upon the use of the terms 'critical' and 'creative' by one whose place, on the whole, is with the weaker brethren. Matthew Arnold distinguishes far too bluntly, it seems to me, between the two activities: he overlooks the capital importance of criticism in the work of creation itself. Probably, indeed, the larger part of the labour of an author in composing his work is critical labour; the labour of sifting, combining, constructing, expunging, correcting, testing: this frightful toil is as much critical as creative. I maintain even that the criticism employed by a trained and skilled writer on his own work is the most vital, the highest kind of criticism; and (as I think I have said before) that some creative writers are superior to others solely because their critical faculty is superior.

There is a tendency, and I think it is a whiggery tendency, to decry this critical toil of the artist; to propound the thesis that the great artist is an unconscious artist, unconsciously inscribing on his banner the words Muddle Through. Those of us who are Inner Deaf Mutes are, however, sometimes compensated by a humble conscience, which, though without oracular expertness, counsels us to do the best we can, reminds us that our compositions ought to be as free from defects as possible (to atone for their lack of inspiration), and, in short, makes us waste a good deal of time.

We are aware, too, that the critical discrimination which comes so hardly to us has in more fortunate men flashed in the very heat of creation; and we do not assume that because works have been composed without apparent critical labour, no critical labour has been done. We do not know what previous labours have prepared, or what goes on, in the way of criticism, all the time in the minds of the creators. But this affirmation recoils upon us. If so large a part of creation is really criticism, is not a large part of what is called 'critical writing' really creative!

If so, is there not creative criticism in the ordinary sense? The answer seems to be, that there is no equation. I have assumed as axiomatic that a creation, a work of art, is autotelic; and that criticism, by definition, is*about* something other than itself. Hence you cannot fuse creation with criticism as you can fuse criticism with creation. The critical activity finds its highest, its true fulfilment in a kind of union with creation in the labour of the artist. But no writer is completely self-sufficient, and many creative writers have a critical activity which is not all discharged into their work.

Some seem to require to keep their critical powers in condition for the real work by exercising them miscellaneously; others, on completing a work, need to continue the critical activity by commenting on it. There is no general rule. And as men can learn from each other, so some of these treatises have been useful to other writers. And some of them have been useful to those who were not writers.

At one time I was inclined to take the extreme position that the *only* critics worth reading were the critics who practised, and practised well, the art of which they wrote. But I had to stretch this frame to make some important inclusions; and I have since been in search of a formula which should cover everything I wished to include, even if it included more than I wanted. And the most important qualification which I have been able to find, which ac- counts for the peculiar importance of the criticism of practitioners, is that a critic must have a very highly developed sense of fact.

This is by no means a trifling or frequent gift. And it is not one which easily wins popular commendations. The sense of fact is something very slow to develop, and its complete development means perhaps the very pinnacle of civilization. For there are so many spheres of fact to be mastered, and our outermost sphere of fact, of knowledge, of control, will be ringed with narcotic fancies in the sphere beyond.

To the member of the Browning Study Circle, the discussion of poets about poetry may seem arid, technical, and limited. It is merely that the practitioners have clarified and reduced to a state of fact all the feelings that the member can only enjoy in the most nebulous form; the dry technique implies, for those who have mastered it, all that the member thrills to; only that has been made into something precise, tractable, under control.

That, at all events, is one reason for the value of the practitioner's criticism—he is dealing with his facts, and he can help us to do the same. And at every level of criticism I find the same necessity regnant. There is a large part of critical writing which consists in 'interpreting' an author, a work. This is not on the level of the Study Circle either; it occasionally happens that one person obtains an understanding of another, or a creative writer, which he can partially communicate, and which we feel to be true and illuminating. It is difficult to confirm the 'interpretation' by external evidence. To any- one who is skilled in fact on this level there will be evidence enough. But who is to prove his own skill; And for every success in this type of writing there are thousands of impostures. Instead of insight, you get a fiction. Your test is to apply it again and again to the original, with your view of the original to guide you. But there is no one to guarantee your competence, and once again we find ourselves in a dilemma.

We must ourselves decide what is useful to us and what is not; and it is quite likely that we are not competent to decide. But it is fairly certain that 'interpretation' (I am not touching upon the acrostic element in literature) is only legitimate when it is not interpretation at all, but merely putting the reader in possession of facts which he would otherwise have missed. I have had some experience of Extension lecturing, and I have found only two ways of leading any pupils to like anything with the right liking: to present them with a selection of the simpler kind of facts ab.out a work—its conditions, its setting, its genesis—or else to spring the work on them in such a way that they were not prepared to be prejudiced against it.

There were many facts to help them with Elizabethan drama: the poems of T. E. Hulme only needed to be read aloud to have immediate effect. Comparison and analysis, I have said before, and Remy de Gourmont has said before me (a real master of fact—sometimes, I am afraid, when he moved outside of literature, a master illusionist of fact), are the chief tools of the critic.

It is obvious indeed that they are tools, to be handled with care, and not employed in an inquiry into the number of times giraffes are mentioned in the English novel. They are not used with conspicuous success by many contemporary writers. You must know what to compare and what to analyse. The late Professor Ker had skill in the use of these tools. Comparison and analysis need only the cadavers on the table; but interpretation is always producing parts of the body from its pockets, and fixing them in place. And any book, any essay, any note in *Notes and Queries*, which produces a fact even of the lowest order about a work of art is a better piece of work than nine-tenths of the most pretentious critical journalism, in journals or in books.

We assume, of course, that we are masters and not servants of facts, and that we know that the discovery of Shakespeare's laundry bills would not be of much use to us; but we must always reserve final judgement as to the futility of the research which has discovered them, in the possibility that some genius will appear who will know of a use to which to put them. Scholarship, even in its humblest forms, has its rights; we assume that we know how to use it, and how to neglect it. Of course the multiplication of critical books and essays may create, and I have seen it create, a vicious taste for reading about works of art instead of reading the works themselves, it may supply opinion instead of educating taste. But fact cannot corrupt taste; it can at worst gratify one taste—a taste for history, let us say, or antiquities, or biography—under the illusion that it is assisting another.

The real corrupters are those who supply opinion or fancy; and Goethe and Coleridge are not guiltless—for what is Coleridge's *Hamlet*: is it an honest inquiry as far as the data permit, or is it an attempt to present Coleridge in an attractive costume? We have not succeeded in finding such a test as anyone can apply; we have been forced to allow ingress to innumerable dull and tedious books; but we have, I think, found a test which, for those who are able to apply it, will dispose of the really vicious ones. And with this test we may return to the preliminary statement of the polity of literature and of criticism.

For the kinds of critical work which we have admitted, there is the possibility of cooperative activity, with the further possibility of arriving at something outside of ourselves, which may provisionally be called truth. But if anyone complains that I have not defined truth, or fact, or reality, I can only say apologetically that it was no part of my purpose to do so, but only to find a scheme into which, whatever they are, they will fit, if they exist.

THE FUNCTION OF CRITICISM AT THE PRESENT TIME BY MATTHEW ARNOLD

Arnold's essay, "The Function of Criticism at the Present Time" was published in his first collection of critical writings, *Essays in Criticism*, in 1865.

Prior to the publication of these essays, Arnold had just completed some lectures on the translation of Homer—works which bear, in a less developed form, some of Arnold's ideas on the need for new, intelligent criticism in England.

"The Function of Criticism at the Present Time" thus seems a bit of a turning point in Arnold's career; by the time Arnold began writing *Culture and Anarchy*, he had turned away from his career as a poet to focus on social and theological writings. The project which Arnold began with this essay—to make the reading, middle-class public of England understand the need for a critical spirit in order to provide society with fresh, intelligent ideas—would occupy him fully and it is for this new direction which Arnold takes that would make Arnold interesting to generations after him.

SUMMARY:

The central argument of the essay responds to what Arnold felt to be the prevailing attitude that the constructive, creative capacity was much more important than the critical faculty. Arnold's expanded definition of criticism, however—"the endeavour, in all branches of knowledge, theology, philosophy, history, art, science, to see the object as in itself it really is"—renders criticism a necessary prerequisite for truly valuable creation. Specifically, criticism is what generates "fresh" and "intelligent" ideas during a specific time and place in history, and Arnold claim that since literature works with current ideas (literature is "synthesis and exposition"), great works can only be generated in a climate of great ideas. Thus, Arnold argues that criticism prepares the way for creation.

Arnold pegs the work of the romantic poets after the French Revolution and in the earlier part of the century as creative, but without the quality of ideas necessary for truly great work. This is because, Arnold explains, the French Revolution devolved into an obsession with the political and practical, "quitting the intellectual sphere and rushing furiously into the political sphere." While Arnold praises the intellectual quality of the initial ideas, particularly Burke's, coming out of this "epoch of concentration," Arnold disparages the devolution of these ideas too manically into the political and practical.

In the present time, Arnold argues, criticism must maintain a position of "disinterestedness," keeping aloof from "the practical view of things" in order to "know the best that is known and thought in the world, and in its turn making this known, to create a current of true and fresh ideas." Its logic runs counter to that of self-satisfaction (what Arnold felt to be the problematic attitude of middle-class reformers) and thus leads men to desire greater perfection.

Arnold concedes, finally, that the work of the critic is "slow and obscure" and doesn't quite give an answer as to how the critic can make his work known to the so-called "practical" men. Arnold holds that the critic will be misunderstood, and English society is likely to be on the side of the likes of Bishop Colenso and Miss Cobbe, who offer "constructive" suggestions for living.

Nevertheless, Arnold seems deeply hopeful that the recent commentary on the youth of today having less "zeal" means that they are in fact thinking more, and cultivating a more disinterested, critical life and in doing so, coming up with fresh, intelligent ideas.

CRITICAL APPROACH

One of the most interesting aspects of Arnold's ideas on criticism for me is his direct association between the need for criticism and what he perceived to be an increasingly complex, modern, world. As abstract as many of Arnold's phrases seem, and given the absence of any sense of specific historicity in terms like "epoch of concentration" or "epoch of expansion," somehow, Arnold yet maintains that he means criticism for the *present time*, which, as it turns out, means "modernity."

In his own words, "the life and world being in modern times very complex things," it becomes necessary that an intellectual elite (transcending above all "practical" things—later, in *Culture and Anarchy,* "ordinary selves"—including class status, but problematically so as Hadley points out in her critique of Victorian liberalism) maintain clarity through determining what is true and what is socially constructed.

The emphasis in this essay on "modernity" in all its hefty, complex associations with industrialization, capitalism, secularization, institutional organization, and relatedly, the destruction of the so-called "individual" makes it a particularly interesting one to look at if one is to offer students of Victorian literature a framework for understanding *the* major clash between humanity and "modernity" perceived by so many.

Arnold's sweeping generalizations of the French Revolution and romanticism in this essay also offers an easy way into pointing out two rather different waves of historical anxiety: the first related to the violence of establishing new political orders, the second related to the mechanical complacency of the middle-class individual in the face of improved living conditions and general acceptance of "liberal" ideas.

Pragmatic theorists from Plato onwards have emphasized the impact which literature has on the reader. Here, Arnold, arguably England's most important cultural critic in the second half of the nineteenth century and someone who has exerted enormous influence on subsequent generations of critics even here in the Caribbean, focuses not on what literature does to the reader but what the reader or critic ought to do to the literary works which he reads. Influenced by Plato's belief that the objective, absolute truth can be known, Arnold offers a 'disinterested' model of reading that aspires to be objective about both the meaning and value of the work in question (*i.e.* both what the work is about and its moral impact) and which, even though it appears very dated today in the light of recent theoretical developments, was profoundly influential upon literary criticism until at least the 1960's.

Arnold begins by defending the role of the critic against the accusation that the role performed by the creative writer is far more important: they argue for the "inherent superiority of the creative effort of the human spirit over its critical effort". Arnold does not deny that a "free creative activity" is the "highest function of man" and that he finds in it his "true happiness". However, he argues that this activity can be exercised "in other ways than in producing great works of literature or art". Men may also express it, he contends, in "well-doing", "learning", and "criticising".

Moreover, he argues, the ability to write great works is not possible in all eras and "therefore labour may be vainly spent in preparing for it, in rendering it possible". Arguing that creative writers work with "elements, with materials" and that the elements in question are "ideas; the best ideas on every matter which literature touches, current at the time", Arnold contends that "creative literary genius" does not "principally show itself in discovering new ideas" (which is the province of the phil sopher) but in "synthesis and exposition, not of analysis and discovery": its gift lies in the faculty of being happily inspired by a certain intellectual and spiritual atmosphere, by a certain order of ideas,... of dealing divinely with these ideas, presenting them in the most effective and attractive combinations, – making beautiful work with them, in short. But it must have the atmosphere, it must find itself amidst the order of ideas, in order to work freely.

In short, the "creative power has... appointed elements, and those elements are not in its control". The "creative power" depends, Arnold claims, upon the "critical power". The goal of criticism, Arnold argues, is "to see the object as in itself it really is". Criticism consequently functions to establish an order of ideas, if not absolutely true, yet true by comparison with that which it displaces; to make the best ideas prevail.

Presently these new ideas reach society, the touch of truth is the touch of life, and there is stir and growths everywhere; out of this stir and growth come the creative epochs of literature. Because a poet "ought to know life and the world before dealing with them in poetry", the "creation of a modern poet... implies a great critical effort behind it".

The key quality on the part of the critic is, Arnold argues, "disinterestedness" which the critic accomplishes by: keeping aloof from what is called 'the practical view of things;' by resolutely following the law of its own nature, which is to be a free play of the mind on all subjects which it touches. By steadfastly refusing to lend itself to any of those ulterior, practical considerations about ideas, which plenty of people will be sure to attach to them... but which criticism has really nothing to do with.

Its business is... simply to know the best that is known and thought in the world, and in its making this known, to create a current of true and fresh ideas. Its business is to do with inflexible honesty, with due ability; but its business is to do no more, and to leave alone all questions of practical consequences, and applications. He defines such disinterestedness as, in short, the "free play of mind upon all subjects being a pleasure in itself, being an object of desire, being an essential provider of elements without which a nation's spirit... must, in the long run, die of inanition" The "bane of criticism" in England, he argues, is that practical considerations cling to it and stifle it. It subserves interests not its own. Our organs of criticism are organs of men and parties having practical ends to serve, and with them those practical ends are the first thing and the play of the mind the second. Disinterested criticism which confines itself to the "pure intellectual sphere" leads, by contrast, not to partisanship and biases but to objectivity and truth.

Its "best spiritual work" is to "keep man from a self-satisfaction which is retarding and vulgarising, to lead him towards perfection, by making his mind dwell upon what is excellent in itself, and the absolute beauty and fitness of things". Arnold acknowledges that the "virtue of detachment" is not attractive to the "mass of mankind" and that it is "not easy to lead a practical man... to see a thing which he has always been used to look at from one side only, that this thing looked at from another side, may appear much less beneficent and beautiful".

However, "without this free disinterested treatment of things, truth and the highest culture are out of the question". This is why criticism must "maintain its independence of the practical spirit and its aims". If we would think of "quietly enlarging our stock of true and fresh ideas", we must "betake ourselves to the serener life of the mind and spirit". Disinterestedness is not limited to the criticism of "politics and religion".

In literary criticism, he asserts, it is vital to adopt a similar attitude. If "judging" is the critic's business, the "judgement which almost insensibly forms itself in a fair and clear mind, along with fresh knowledge is the valuable one". This is why "fresh knowledge" must ever be the critic's greatest concern. It is in "communicating fresh knowledge, and letting his own judgement pass along with it – but insensibly", that is, not in a preachy way, that the critic will "do most good to his reader". Arnold argues that Romantic poetry was a failure. It possessed "plenty of energy, plenty of creative force", he admits, but "did not know enough" because, notwithstanding the impact of the French Revolution on the movement, their creative endeavour was not predicated upon sound and disinterested criticism.

The French Revolution provoked much thought, he admits, but is to be distinguished from earlier momentous historical events. Where the latter produced "disinterested intellectual and spiritual movements... in which the human spirit looked for its satisfaction in itself and in the increased play of its own activity", the French Revolution "took a political, practical character".

To be sure, he agrees, it animated a whole nation with an "enthusiasm for pure reason, and with an ardent zeal for making its prescriptions triumph" (no mean achievement given "how little of mind... comes into the motives which...

impel great masses of men"). It derived a "unique and still living power" from the "force, truth, and universality of its ideas" and from the "passion with which it could inspire a3 multitude for these ideas". As a result, France is the "country in Europe where the people is most alive".

However, he argues, the "mania for giving an immediate political and practical application for all these fine ideas of the reason was fatal". This is because ideas "cannot be too much prized in and for themselves" as a result of which it is simply wrong to "transport them abruptly into the world of politics, and practice, violently to revolutionise this world to their bidding". There is an immense gulf between the "world of ideas" and the "world of practice". The French Revolution made the fatal error of blindly "quitting the intellectual sphere and rushing furiously into the political sphere".

6

Literary Criticism and Theory

INTRODUCTION

The word critic, is derived from the ancient Greek word krites meaning a judge, is a person who offers a value judgement or an interpretation The word is sometimes used pejoratively especially by defenders of a critics object The term is used in particular for a professional who regularly judges or interprets performances or other work of other people such as artists, scientists, musicians or actors and publishes these judgements or interpretations in a periodical often a newspaper magazine or academic. The study of literary criticism may best be begun by an inquiry into the meaning of the term. The following questions then suggest themselves: What is the nature of the process called criticism. How many kinds of criticism are there, and what is the principle of classification. How is literary criticism distinguished from other varieties or types of criticism.

Definitions

These may be drawn from the usages of speech and writing, or framed in accordance with some theory; or, the two methods may be combined, one being used to correct and verify the other. In what follows we shall first consider popular usages of the term, then call attention to its theoretical aspects.

The following are some of the meanings commonly attached to the word:

Criticism is used in the sense of fault-finding or taking exception. The critic is one who takes a hostile attitude.

Of late years writers have attempted to give criticism a more genial function than it had formerly. Such writers maintain that the business of criticism is less to censure than to praise. Some even go so far as to say that the critic ought never to censure. Is not this going too far. May we apply the name critic to a man who sees only the good points of what he is criticising. or who registers what he sees without saying whether it is good or bad.

Another and more philosophic way of defining criticism is to say that it is a process, or the process, of passing judgement upon anything. Criticism is a process that goes on over all the field of human knowledge, being simply comparison or clash of opinion. All genuine criticism consists in comparison between two ways of doing something." Does comparison in these cases mean the same as judgement or as classifying with or without ranking. Do these definitions exclude from criticism the exercise of the imagination and the emotions.

A famous definition is that which Matthew Arnold gave in his essay, On the Function of Criticism, namely, "to see the object as in itself it really is." To this should be joined another phrase from the same essay, "the endeavor to learn and propagate the best that is known and thought in the world." Do the two definitions come to the same thing. Is not seeing a thing as in itself it really is, the same as judging it. If judging means making a comparison, with what do we compare a thing when we see it as in itself it really is. Again, what attitude does Mr. Arnold assume towards fault-finding or censuring. May his method be regarded as impartial appreciation. and would his definition exclude the destructive kind of criticism.

Theory

What is the Scientific Basis of criticism. Is criticism a science, or an art, or merely a method. If a science, may it be classed among the exact sciences. Does it belong to the descriptive sciences like psychology, or to the normative sciences like ethics and logic. Is it an inductive or a deductive process.

What is the Psychological Basis of criticism. Does criticism proceed from the emotions, or from the intellect. or do both combine in the critical process. If it is purely intellectual, how does it differ from other operations of the intellect, such as imagination and judgement. Is there a critical element in every mental process. If criticism is an act of the judgement, in what way does it differ from other judgements.

What is the Social Basis of criticism. Is criticism individual or social in its aim. Is the test which it applies an individual or a social test. What part does criticism play in the workings of the social body. How does it affect social progress.

What is the Philosophical Basis of criticism. Where in the division of the field of human knowledge and activity, is the place of criticism. Is it a principal or a subordinate division. Is it a process, or a principle, or is it both. Is it subjective or objective. May it deal with things of nature, or is it concerned only with things of art. Is it abstract or concrete. Is it analytic, or synthetic, or organic. Is it a positive force or a negative force.

Criticism and relative sciences

In philology and religion, and sometimes in law, it is customary to distinguish between criticism and hermeneutics. According to Boeckh, the purpose of hermeneutics is "to understand the object itself in its own nature," while the purpose of criticism is not to understand an object in and for itself, but "to establish a relation with some other object in such wise that the knowledge of the relation is the end in view". How is criticism related to such sciences as ethics, psychology, sociology, politics, anthropology. What is its relation to aesthetics.

Kinds of criticism

Although the difficulties of classification are as great as those of definition, we shall find upon careful examination that much of the confusion is due to the fact that two principles of classification have been commonly employed, one referring to the subject matter of the criticism, the other to the method of procedure.

According to the first principle of division, any critical process which deals with the facts of history is called historical criticism, any critical process which deals with science is scientific criticism; and so any critical process which deals with literature is called literary criticism. The kinds of criticism are as numerous as the kinds of subject matter.

According to the second principle of division, the name is determined by the method. If the historical method is pursued, the result is called historical criticism. In like manner the application of the principles of science is scientific criticism, and of philosophy is philosophical criticism, whether applied to history, philology, art, or literature.

Types of literary criticism

Literary criticism, it will be noticed, is named with reference to its subject matter. It is not a method which can be applied to other subjects. Its method may be scientific, historical, philosophical, psychological, or any other that answers the purpose. Some, it is true, hold that literature is a species of art and that only the methods of criticism appropriate to art are applicable to literature.

Two varieties or types of literary criticism which are often contrasted, are judicial criticism and inductive criticism.

Judicial criticism

The judicial method passes judgement on the work of literature, that is, evaluates it or appraises it. Of this class, Jeffrey with his famous "This will never do" is a striking example.

Inductive criticism

Inductive criticism, when employed in its simplicity, busies itself solely with the collection and arrangement of facts. It refuses to evaluate or appraise.

Under Inductive criticism we may point out two subdivisions. (i) The first occupies itself with the work in hand. It aims to examine the work and in a methodical way to describe the contents. Perhaps Mr. Moulton's method falls in this division. (ii.) The second kind of inductive criticism sees in the work an expression of external influences, and hence pays most attention to the environment. Its aim is to classify the work, to place it in its proper relation to other works of the same kind and time. Taine and Sainte-Beuve may serve as examples.

Many other divisions of literary criticism may be suggested, some of which are perhaps more philosophical than the division into judicial and inductive. Criticism may be divided into personal criticism, such as we find in the writings of Henry James, and impersonal or objective criticism, such as was advocated by Émile Hennequin; it may be classed as analytic and synthetic; as positive and negative; as higher, and lower; as internal and external; as static, dynamic, and organic; as scientific, philosophic, ethical, and aesthetic. Possibly no comprehensive and strictly logical classification has yet been made.

An interesting question is whether various types of criticism may not be combined; whether certain types are not complementary to one another. Thus, should not judicial criticism also be inductive. analytical criticism also be synthetic. Literary criticism so differs in different countries that it is possible to speak of British, American, French, German, Italian and Russian criticism.

Rationale

The object of criticism should be very closely related to its definition. As there are different opinions on the first point, we may expect to find different opinions on the second. The following are some of the objects which have been advanced as proper to criticism.

Like any other means of obtaining or imparting knowledge, criticism is interesting for its own sake. Since criticism is a kind of literature, its justification rests on the same basis as other literary forms. Criticism is a help to our appreciation of literature. It enhances the impression; it interprets and makes clear what is obscure in the thing criticised. (4) It teaches us what in literature is good, and what is bad, and thus saves our time and mental energy. It prepares the public for the author. It shows the author how to adapt himself to his public. It regulates and disciplines literary taste. It frees literature from the tyranny of prejudice or whim. It destroys morbidity in the author or the public. It gives people who have not time to read the originals information about new books and new ideas.

In connection with this topic the question may be raised whether in criticism the writer's character is a proper subject of praise or blame; also, whether the purpose of criticism is to convince or to persuade.

Relation of criticism to conception

It has been often maintained that criticism as a form of intellectual effort is lower than creation. If this is so, does the argument apply as well to inductive as to judicial criticism. The statement has also been made that critics are naturally hostile to authors and that the history of criticism has been a history of the triumph of the author over the critic. Is such in fact the case. Does criticism necessarily lag behind creation. Why should it. If it does, is its tardiness irremediable. or is it merely due to vicious methods of criticism employed by bad critics. Is "the judicial attitude unreceptive".

Again, it is sometimes said that criticism tends to crush out originality; yet according to Mr. Howells all criticism is futile; the literary movement is "never stayed in the least or arrested by criticism." Which is the sounder view. Another theory, a theory for which Macaulay is often given credit, is that an age of fine creation cannot also be an age of fine criticism. Was this true of the literary history of Greece and Rome.

Has it been true in the history of English literature. of the French, and German, and Italian literatures. A corollary is that a good poet cannot be a good critic. Is there anything in the nature of criticism and of creation to make the two incompatible. Have both ever reached a high degree of excellence in the same man. What shall be said of Shakespeare's critical powers of Dante's, of Goethe's, of Schiller's. Shenstone thought that "every good poet includes a critic," but he was careful to add, "the reverse will not hold." May not criticism itself be creative. May not criticism be even an advance upon the work which is criticised.

Qualities of the critic

Should the critic be in the main a man of intellect or a man of taste. Ought he to be a specialist. Can he be a good critic if he knows no literature but that of his own nation. Should he be disinterested.

Laws of criticism

Under this head the question may first be asked whether such things as laws of criticism exist. If they exist and have validity, on what principles, scientific, philosophic, psychological, ethical, or aesthetic, do they rest. Are they relative or absolute. Are they fixed and good for all time, or do they shift with the progress of intelligence and change of taste. What is the standard of taste. How far is it alike for all nations. How are individual differences of critical opinion to be accounted for and reconciled. Of what value are the classics as guides in matters of criticism.

Are they to be accepted as models. Is it possible to deduce from them all the laws of criticism. Is it possible for a literary work to violate the laws of criticism and yet be a masterpiece. What value should be attached to consensus of opinion. to the test of time.

The validity of such laws may be tested, first, by the success of those who have conformed to them; and, secondly, by comparison with the unformulated rules that may be gathered from the practice of more spontaneous, but perhaps none the less admirable, critics.

Philosophical Sense of Criticism

The term criticism is used in the history of philosophy to designate the philosophical system of Immanuel Kant. The meaning which Kant attached to the term has doubtless had considerable influence in shaping modern views upon the subject; hence it will be well for the advanced student to gain some acquaintance with the Kantian philosophy. Kant's three critiques are now available in good translations, and should, if possible, be read, especially the critique of Judgement; but if they seem too formidable, Wallace's Kant, or the histories of Ueberweg, Erdmann, or Windelband, will give the desired information in brief compass.

POSTCOLONIAL THEORY

Postcolonial criticism and theory alike comprise a variety of practices, performed within a range of disciplinary fields in a multitude of different institutional locations around the globe. Many of these long predate the period when the term'postcolonial' began to gain currency and have since been claimed retrospectively as continuous, or contiguous, with what are now commonly identified as postcolonial modes of cultural analysis.

Anyone with the temerity to write a history of these practices would probably have to start at least as early as the beginning of this century with the work of figures as different as the African-American thinker W. E. B. Du Bois and the South African Sol Plaatje (and, arguably, much further back). S/he would need to discuss cultural formations as diverse as the Harlem Renaissance of World War One and the 1920s and the négritude movement of the 1940s and 1950s.

Such a history would need to address figures as geographically, ideologically and culturally varied as the Trinidadian C. L. R. James, who lived much of his life in London, Frantz Fanon, originally from Martinique but a revolutionary activist in Algeria, African critics as different as Chinua Achebe and Anta Diop, and Ranajit Guha, the Indian historiographer long based in Australia.To do justice to what was never a smooth narrative of'influence and development', such a history would also have to examine the claims of some Latin-American criticism,'Commonwealth' literary studies of the 1960s and 1970s, and various kinds of aesthetic theory in non-European languages considered as precursors to, or variants of, what is now regarded as postcolonial criticism.

While postcolonial criticism has apparently had a long and complex history outside Europe and America, it arrived only belatedly in the Western academy and British university literature departments more particularly. (Much of the following account will be shaped by the fact that I am a literary critic working in Britain, though I shall try not to be too parochial in my range of reference.)

One mark of this belatedness is that it was not acknowledged as a separate category of analysis in a number of relatively recent and influential works of cultural description and critical theory in Britain, from Raymond Williams Keywords (1976, revised edition 1983), to Terry Eagleton Literary Theory (1983) and Raman Selden The Theory of Criticism (1988).

Indeed, reconsideration of the'crisis in English studies' engendered in British universities in the late 1970s and early 1980s indicates just how little part was played in rethinking the field of literary studies by what would now be described as postcolonial concerns and modes of criticism.

Thus neither of the Methuen New Accents volumes which sought to redefine the discipline at this moment of turmoil-- Peter Widdowson Re-Reading English (1982) and Janet Batsleer Rewriting English (1985)--found space to address in any detailed manner either the cluster of interests now identified with colonial discourse analysis or the already well-developed fields of'new' or postcolonial literatures in English.

It was not until 1989 that a preliminary survey of postcolonial criticism, Bill Ashcroft, Gareth Griffiths and Helen Tiffin The Empire Writes Back, appeared; the first critical reader in the field, Patrick Williams and Laura Chrisman Colonial Discourse and Post-Colonial Theory, was published as recently as 1993. Given its short history as a practice in the Western academy, and literature departments in Britain more specifically, postcolonial criticism has nonetheless had--on the face of it, at least--a major impact upon current modes of cultural analysis, bringing to the forefront of concern the interconnection of issues of race, nation, empire, migration and ethnicity with cultural production.

One measure of this impact is that while undergraduate courses on the new literatures in English or in areas such as'empire and literature' were only exceptionally on offer in Britain in the late 1960s, for instance at Leeds and Kent universities, options in postcolonial literature, criticism and theory are now available as part of the curriculum of English departments in all but the most traditional (and these are often, not coincidentally, the most prestigious) institutions.

By the middle of the 1970s, whole degree programmes combining English and the study of one or more of the'new' literatures came onstream, and a recent development has been the appearance of a range of taught Master's degrees, providing various configurations of'Postcolonial Studies', notably at the universities of Kent, Warwick and Essex. These transformations have been accompanied by new kinds and patterns of scholarly production. For instance, there is now a variety of journals dedicated to the investigation of postcolonial culture and critical problems, including The Journal of Commonwealth Literature, Ariel, Research in African Literatures, Kunapipi, The Journal of New Literatures in EnglishEnglish, World Literature Written in English, Third Text and Wasafiri.

The consolidation of the postcolonial field since the early 1980s is, moreover, reflected in the widespread attention being paid to it in special issues of non-'dedicated' journals: a by no means comprehensive list of examples would include Critical Inquiry (1985 and 1986), New Literary History and Cultural Critique (1987), Oxford Literary Review (1987 and 1991), Inscriptions and South Atlantic Quarterly (1988), Genders (1991), Public Culture and Social Text (1992), Yale French Studies, The Cambridge Review, History Workshop and PMLA (1993), New Formations and Literature and History (1994). Equally striking has been the proliferation of conferences which have engaged with various postcolonial concerns. In Britain alone, these range from the Roehampton Institute conference of 1983 on'Literature and Imperialism' and the Essex University conference of 1985 on'Europe and Its Others', to the University of Galway conference on'Gender and Colonialism' (1992), the South Bank University conference on black writing in Britain entitled'Out of the Margins' and the London University Institute of Commonwealth Studies conference on'Empire, Nation, Language' (both in 1993), the Warwick University conference on Edward Said in 1994, the London Institute of Contemporary Arts conference on Fanon in 1995 and the University of North London conference on'Border Crossings' in 1996.

Professional associations and networks servicing those involved in the field of postcolonial criticism have also expanded in range and number; they include the Association for Commonwealth Literature and Language Studies, the African Literature Association, the Association of Teachers of Caribbean, African and Associated Literatures, the Open University Group for the Study of Post-Colonial Literatures and the London Inter-University Post-Colonial Seminar.

All this activity has been partly enabled by important institutional developments outside the university, notably in publishing, which have made available much of the'primary' material to support many of these new activities. Heinemann started its African Writers series in 1962 and in the next decade launched a complementary Caribbean Writers series, which has been followed in turn by an Asian Writers series.

Also, in the 1970s, Longman introduced its Drumbeat Series of'Commonwealth' writing. More recently, the Women's Press launched a Black and Third World Women Writers Series. These initiatives have been complemented by the foundation by contemporary migrants of publishing houses specializing in postcolonial concerns like Karnak, New Beacon and Bogle L'Ouverture within the British context.

In mainstream academic publishing, too, the interest in postcolonial studies is reflected in the lists of an increasing number of firms, including Routledge, Manchester University Press and Verso. As the notes in this volume indicate, there has been a rapid expansion in the number of monographs (and an explosion of articles) dedicated to the issues raised by postcolonial criticism and cultural production. As much as by analysis and dissemination of the new literatures in English, postcolonial criticism has been increasingly preoccupied in investigating the complicity of a large part of Western culture, and the canon of

English literature more specifically, in the attitudes and values underpinning the process of expansion overseas.

From the more obvious figures like Defoe, Conrad and Kipling, attention has now spread to writers who were traditionally conceived of as having no immediately apparent connection to questions of empire. Attention is now being devoted, moreover, to consideration of the interconnections between empire and literary production in whole periods and movements.

Postcolonial perspectives have influenced many of the new interpretations of the Renaissance period and have helped to produce important new interpretations of Romantic literature. The traditional view of Victorian writing, represented by C. A. Bodelson's comment that'the part played by the colonies in mid-Victorian fiction is surprisingly small', is being radically reassessed and there is increasing investigation of the links between Modernism and imperialism.

Postcolonial criticism has not simply enlarged the traditional field of English studies, or refocused attention on neglected aspects or areas within it. It has also, in association with other relatively recent critical discourses as various as feminism and deconstruction, significantly altered the modes of analysis which were dominant within the discipline in the period from 1945 to 1980.

Most notably, perhaps, it has helped to undermine the traditional conception of disciplinary boundaries. Configura-tions such as'colonial discourse analysis' insist upon the importance of studying literature together with history, politics, sociology and other art forms rather than in isolation from the multiple material and intellectual contexts which determine its production and reception.

In related fashion, postcolonial criticism has challenged hitherto dominant notions of the autonomy of the aesthetic sphere, helping to gain acceptance for the argument, advanced on a number of fronts since the 1960s especially, that'culture' mediates relations of power as effectively, albeit in more indirect and subtle ways, as more public and visible forms of oppression.

For example, postcolonial critics have characteristically worked to break down the formerly fixed boundaries between text and context in order to show the continuities between patterns of representation of subject peoples and the material practices of (neo-)colonial power. Moreover, postcolonial criticism has contributed to the interrogation of received distinctions between'high' and'popular' culture which has been such a feature of cultural criticism more generally in recent decades.

For example, a recurrent concern for some postcolonial critics has been to challenge the assumptions governing traditional discriminations between literature and oral narratives, or orature. In colonial discourse analysis, meanwhile, there has been a proliferating interest in hitherto marginalized genres such as journalism and travel writing, a project initiated by Said Orientalism.

Such developments suggest an extensive and continuing, if belated, response from within the West to the complaint of Orientalism that the systematic study of the relations between metropolitan culture and questions of race, empire and ethnicity was still considered to be offlimits by the Western literary-cultural establishment: in the mid-1970s.

Indeed such has been the enthusiasm for postcolonial criticism in the two decades since then that it could be argued that it is now itself betraying a tendency to'colonize' an evergrowing number of historical periods, geographical locations and disciplinary fields.

As Aijaz Ahmad points out, the term was first used in the early 1970s in political theory to describe the predicament of nations which had thrown off the yoke of European empires after World War Two. By the time of Ashcroft, Griffiths and Tiffin The Empire Writes Back (1989), it was being used to describe'all the culture affected by the [European] imperial process from the moment of colonization to the present day'. 'Colonial discourse analysis' now operates across an ever broader range of fields, including the history of law, anthropology, political economy, philosophy, historiography, art history and psychoanalysis.

The perspectives and approaches associated with postcolonial criticism are also being used increasingly to address the histories and current predicaments of'internally colonized' cultures within the nation state in the'developed' world. In the case of Britain, for instance, Michael Hechter's Internal Colonialism (1975) inaugurated a new phase of analysis which stresses a continuing, essentially (neo-)colonial, relationship of subordination of the'peripheral' nations of Scotland, Wales and Ireland by the English'centre'.

Similarly, while Fanon The Wretched of the Earth (1961) disavowed the possibility of meaningful comparison between the historical and cultural predicaments of African America and the colonized peoples subject to European control, this same text, ironically, became an important reference point for the American Civil Rights and Black Nationalism movements of the 1960s.

A new generation of African-American critics, represented by figures like Henry Louis Gates, has drawn on the work of older African contemporares like Soyinka in attempting to elaborate both a'black' poetics and literary theory. And the migration of African intellectuals as diverse as Anthony Appiah and Toks Adewate to the United States has further blurred the kind of barriers which Fanon assumed to exist, leading to a profound cross-fertilization between African-American and postcolonial cultural perspectives.

Finally, as'Commonwealth' literary studies have largely reconce-ptualized itself since around 1975, so many of its proponents have increasingly claimed a postcolonial identity for the old'settler' colonies, formerly known as the British Dominions such as Australia, New Zealand or Canada. The example of Canada serves to suggest just how tangled and multifaceted the term'postcolonial' has now become in terms of its temporal, spatial, political and socio-cultural meanings. Here there are at least five distinct but often overlapping contexts to which the term might be applied.

First of all, as Mary Louise Pratt suggests in Imperial Eyes (1992), until the 1960s at least, white Canada saw itself to a large degree as in a dependent relationship, culturally and politically, to Britain; and the legacy of this relationship continues to have important repercussions for Canada's identity today. As a novel like Margaret Atwood Surfacing (1970) intimates, many Canadians now see themselves as having fallen under the economic and political sway of the United States.

A parallel process of subordination has been detected in especially as a consequence of US domination of the continent's mass media; this was already being volubly protested against in the 1960s, for example in the criticism of R. D. Mathews. Thirdly, there is the issue of Quebec, which has often been seen in recent times as an oppressed culture or, indeed, a nation within Canada--in a manner analogous to Atwood's conception of the relationship of Canada to the United States.

As Pierre Valti and re NU+1FCOgres Blancs d'Amirique (1968) suggests, for three decades at least Quebecois critics have been using what would now be considered as postcolonial frameworks and perspectives, in this case drawn from Fanon's work, to describe the predicament in which Quebec finds itself vis-à-vis Anglophone Canada.

However, as the bitter threeway conflict over land rights in the early 1990s between federal and state governments and the Mohawk people suggests, a state like Quebec (or, indeed, Canada as a whole) which seems to be postcolonial from one perspective can be simultaneously (neo-)colonial in its relationship to other groups within its jurisdiction.

The example of the Mohawk, then, points to a fourth such context in modern Canada, the predicament of the indigenous inhabitants who predated white colonization, sometimes described as the'First Nations' of Canada. As Julia Emberley

Thresholds of Difference suggests, the increasingly voluminous and selfassertive nature of the cultural production of these groups is fully amenable to analysis within postcolonial frameworks. A final context is provided by the arrival of significant numbers of''New Commonwealth' migrants to Canada, whose relocation has taken place since the formal decolonization of Britain's former empire and the relaxation of the'white Canada' policy which governed immigration strategies until the 1960s.

To these is now being added a new wave of a quite different kind of economic migrant from Hong Kong, whose arrival is having a significant impact on cities like Toronto and Vancouver in particular. As writers from Austin Clarke in the 1960s to Bharati Mukherjee in the 1980s suggest, Canada's treatment of such minorities raises many questions about its claims to be a genuinely pluralistic or'multi-cultural' society.

POSTCOLONIAL CRITICISM THEORY

What makes it impossible to dismiss the hostility of critics like MacKenzie and Jacoby as simply the product of traditional disciplinary jealousies, however, is that elements of their critique are repeated by others working within approximately the same discursive terrain as Said, Bhabha and Spivak. In fact, the interventions of MacKenzie and Jacoby have simply exacerbated an already heated'internal' debate over appropriate methods of analysis of the cultural production generated by the histories of (neo-)colonialism.

In focusing their attacks on postcolonial studies on the work of Said, Bhabha and Spivak, MacKenzie and Jacoby thus reinforce a divide between postcolonial criticism and postcolonial theory which was already becoming marked as a consequence of the publication of earlier texts as different in method, political affiliation and subject matter as Stephen Slemon and Helen Tiffin After Europe: Critical Theory and Post-Colonial Writing (1989) and Aijaz Ahmad In Theory: Classes, Nations, Literatures (1992).

To some degree, this apparent rift is the responsibility of Said, Bhabha and Spivak themselves. Aijaz Ahmad comments justifiably in In Theory that one is struck by the fact that neither the architecture of Orientalism nor the kind of knowledge the book generally represents has any room in it for criticisms of colonial cultural domination of the kind that have been available... on an expanding scale, since the late nineteenth century. Said's next major work of criticism, The World, the Text, and the Critic (1983), contains a single reference to Fanon, but it is not until"Orientalism Reconsidered" (1985) that he makes any extensive acknowledgement of the work of such predecessors: At bottom, what I said in Orientalism had been said before me by A. L. Tibawi, by Abdullah Laroui, by Anwar Abdel Malik, by Talal Asad, by S. H. Alatas, by Fanon and Césaire, by Pannikar, and Romila Thapar... who in challenging the authority, provenance, and institutions of the science that represented them to Europe, were also understanding themselves as something more than what this science said they were. While this is generous, if belated, recognition of the earlier critical tradition, it is only in the essays collected in Culture and Imperialism (1993) that Said engages in detail with any of these precursors. Similarly, while Bhabha addresses a limited range of Fanon's work with some consistency from the early 1980s, there is scarcely any citation of other predecessors in the field apart from Said himself in the initial phase of his career.

"Representation and the Colonial Text" (1980) alludes to Achebe"Colonialist Criticism", though this piece is omitted from the recent selection of essays comprising Bhabha The Location of Culture (1994).'Commonwealth' literary studies is the object of somewhat lazy jibes in both this chapter and in,'Signs Taken for Wonders', reinforcing the impression that Bhabha's methodology is shaped almost entirely by European'high' theory. The same pattern is discernible in Spivak's career.

The Post-Colonial Critic (1990) refers in passing to Ngugi Avriters in Politics, and there is a single reference to Achebe in In Other Worlds (1987). Moreover, while many of the interviews which make up ThePost-Colonial CriticPost-Colonial Critic were given in Australia, it is clear that for Spivak, the'white settler' histories of such countries make their presumption of a'postcolonial' identity, and consequently of a role in postcolonial criticism, deeply problematic.

Some of what has been written about these figures by their admirers also encourages the idea that a radical break exists between their work and the rest of postcolonial criticism. At times, indeed, such accounts suggest that postcolonial criticism is something which begins with Said. Thus in Colonial Discourse and Postcolonial Theory (1993), Williams and Chrisman make the following claim:'It is perhaps no exaggeration to say that Edward Said Orientalism, published in 1978, single-handedly inaugurates a new area of academic inquiry: colonial discourse, also referred to as colonial discourse theory or colonial discourse analysis.

'The looseness of this formulation apart (colonial discourse is not the same as colonial discourse analysis), it is apparent from the voluminous extracts which they themselves have so usefully collated that the analysis of colonial systems of representation and cultural description long predates Said's intervention in the field. What Said inaugurates, rather is an approach to such analysis from within methodological paradigm derived, as already suggested, from contemporary continental Euroean cultural theories.

Similar problems also beset what is still the best account of Said, Spivak and Bhabha, Robert Young White Mythologies: Writing History and the West (1990), a text to which all subsequent evaluations of postcolonial theory must express a debt. Young argues that the novelty of this trio's work is its engagement with'the discursive forms, representations and practices of contemporary racism, together with their relation to the colonial past'.

Young does recognize the importance of Fanon as a precursor to the work of these three critics, naming The Wretched of the Earth (1961) as the text which initiates the attempt to decolonize European philosophy and historiography. However, while this work is privileged in a somewhat arbitrary way (many of its concerns were anticipated in Black Skin, White Masks almost a decade earlier), Young's discussion of Fanon is extremely brief, barely longer than that devoted to Barthes, whose appearance in such company seems particularly contentious.

Fanon is certainly not given space on the scale deemed appropriate to Said, Spivak and Bhabha, the last of whom, at the time Young's book appeared, had written a bare handful of essays, as compared with several substantial and influential books by Fanon. In this sense, ironically, Young's account of the emergence of postcolonial criticism parallels the Marxist model of global history, deconstruction of which is a primary aim of White Mythologies. While Marxism, according to Young, only sees the periphery's history in a dependent and imitative relation to that of the metropolis, he seems unwittingly to imply that postcolonial analysis only'comes of age' once it becomes a practice of the Western academy and teams to theorize itself in ways which derive from a European context.

Moreover, it is arguable that Young does not question the claims of postcolonial theory with sufficient scepticism. For instance, in somewhat cursorily discounting the criticisms made of Bhabha's politics by Abdul JanMohamed, on the grounds that they result from a simple misunderstanding of his work, Young closes off important areas of debate, which this book seeks to reopen as a central concern.

JanMohamed"The Economy of Manichean Allegory" (1986) inaugurates the critique of postcolonial theory from a counter-hegemonic political perspective. He has been followed in this respect by a large number of critics, as diverse as Ketu Katrak, Stephen Slemon, Anne McClintock and Arif Dirlik. While other points of disagreement, for example over periodization of the'postcolonial', or the cultures to which it might be taken to refer, are by no means to be discounted, perhaps the most heated current debate concerns the political implications of the incorporation of Frenchderived'high" theory into postcolonial analysis.

Indeed the unity of what I have more narrowly defined as postcolonial criticism, rests to a surprisingly large measure on a shared hostility towards the supposedly reactionary politics of postcolonial theory, as a comparison of Aijaz Ahmad with some latter-day exponents of'Comnionwealth' literary studies suggests. The attack on postcolonial theory from within approximately the same discursive field has perhaps become most notoriously associated with Ahmad In Theory.

While Said's work has long been subject to modification and elaboration, both by himself and by'disciples' like Bhabha and Spivak, the effect of these revisions has generally been to reinforce rather than undermine his status as the pre-eminent figure in the field. By contrast, Ahmad's critique of Said is so hostile that Said's sympathizers have at times condemned In Theory in terms as violent as those in which Ahmad excoriates the work of Said.

Thus in The Times Higher, Bryan Cheyette expressed outrage at the appearance of what he described as'this extraordinarily offensive volume' and concluded:'It is to Verso's discredit that they have published a volume that will be grist to the mill of those who wish to dismiss out of hand any kind of theoretical thinking about"race" and"nation" in literary studies.'

The alarm evident in such pronouncements testifies to the scale of Ahmad's challenge, which is expressed in his desire to'break theoretical formation both methodologically and empirically' a formation for which he holds Said, despite generous personal praise, primarily responsible. In some ways, In Theory is as comprehensive an attack on postcolonial theory as MacKenzie's. In contrast to MacKenzie, however, Ahmad sees lpostcolonial theory not as politically radical or even'correct' but as deeply conservative in its ideas and effects.

In fact, Ahmad goes as far as to suggest that postcolonial theory is simply one more medium through which the authority of the West over the formerly imperialized parts of the globe is currently being reinscribed within a neo-colonial'new world order' and is, indeed, best understood as a new expression of the West's historical will to power over the rest of the world.

There are five main elements to Ahmad's critique, all of which are anticipated or repeated, albeit generally in more temperate terms, by others working in the field. First of all, In Theory explores the implications of the institutional location and affiliations of figures like Said.

From this perspective, Ahmad interprets postcolonial theory as the activity of a privileged and deracinated class fraction, which is cut off from the material realities of'Third World' Struggles, the dynamic energies of which are appropriated and domesticated into a chic but finally unchallenging intellectual commodity which circulates largely within the Western academy. In Ahmad's eyes, postcolonial theorists reproduce within the academic sphere the contemporary international division of labour authorized by global capitalism.

According to this argument, Third World cultural producers send'primary' material to the metropolis, which is then turned into a'refined' product by the likes of Said, principally for the metropolitan cultural elite, which they in fact regard as their primary audience; a certain amount of such work is in turn re-exported as'theory' to the Third World. Ahmad's conclusion is scornful:'The East, reborn and greatly expanded now as a"Third World", seems to have become, yet again, a career--even for the"Oriental" this time, and within the"Occident" too.'

Given his deep scepticism about'Commonwealth' literary studies, it is somewhat ironic that comparable criticisms of postcolonial theory were being articulated from within that critical sub-formation prior to Ahmad's intervention in the debate. For example, Slemon and Tiffin After Europe (1989) argues that postcolonial theory relegates other forms of postcolonial criticism, which do not rely on French-derived'high theory', to an inferior category of analysis which is assumed to be both an anterior, or more'primitive', stage in its own emergence and to b. c incapable of self-consciousness about its epistemological assumptions or methodological procedures.

Postcolonial theorists are, moreover, represented as having the tendency to appropriate to themselves the subversive energies which they have discovered in the postcolonial cultures that they mediate: When reading for textual resistance becomes entirely dependent on'theoretical' disentanglement of contradiction or ambivalence within the colonialist text--as it does in deconstructive or new historical readings of colonialist discourse,--then the actual locus of subversive agency is necessarily wrenched away from colonised or post-colonial subjects and resituated within the textual work of the institutionalised western literary critic. As primary evidence of postcolonial theory's reinscription of the West's traditional cultural authority, Ahmad points to the hierarchy which organizes its choice of objects for study. The favoured field for analysis in the work of Said and his followers is identified as colonial discourse.

In Ahmad's eyes, this privileges the Western canon over Third World culture and, moreover, represents a politically disabling shift of attention from the facts of current neo-colonialism to the less contentious area of fictions produced in an era of formal imperialism now safely past.

According to Ahmad, postcolonial theory subsequently favours the work of the migrant intelligentsia of Third World origin based in the West. Said and his followers are taken to task for assuming that writers like Salman Rushdie (to whom Ahmad is consistently hostile) represent the authentic voice of their countries of origin.

Instead, Ahmad locates them within the politically dominant class fraction of their host society, to which texts like Shame, like postcolonial theory itself, are in the first instance deemed to be addressed. Ultimately, Ahmad implies, a lot of such work needs to be placed within metropolitan discursive traditions such as Orientalism and Ahmad takes Said severely to task for failing to see how a text like Satanic Verses belongs to a long tradition of anti-Islamic sentiment in the West.

When Third World culture'proper' is addressed in postcolonial theory, Ahmad argues, most attention is given to those texts which'answer back' to imperial and neo-colonial culture--for instance, the fictional ripostes to Heart of Darkness by figures as diverse as Chinua Achebe, Wilson Harris and Tayib Salih. According to In Theory, this attention to work that has been, in a crucial sense, interpellated by Western culture simply reinforces the traditional relationship between centre and periphery which underlay all discourse, political and cultural, of the colonial period.

There is thus a damaging tendency'to view the products of the English-writing intelligentsia of the cosmopolitan cities as the central documents' of the national literature of the country in question. In the process those aspects of Third World culture which are most genuinely independent of metropolitan influences and of allegiance to the national bourgeoisie, such as literatures written in regional Indian languages, are either neglected or ignored.

Such objections are echoed in recent versions of'Commonwealth' literary studies. In"New Approaches to the New Literatures in English", for instance, Diana Brydon also argues that so much energy is expended by postcolonial theory on engaging with colonial discourse that the new cultural production of the postcolonial world is in danger of being overlooked or even silenced in a process which unwittingly replicates the operations of colonial discourse itself.

Objecting to'the narrowing of focus to the imperial/colonial relation as if it were all that there were', Brydon concludes that:'Deconstructing imperialism keeps us within imperialism's orbit.' Brydon also anticipates Ahmad in pointing to two other important lacunae in postcolonial theory which qualify its claim to be performing radical kinds of cultural analysis. She argues that postcolonial criticism addresses the areas of class and gender in a way that postcolonial theory characteristically fails to do.

Ahmad, by comparison, suggests that insofar as postcolonial theory does address non-Western cultures, its habitual focus on the problematics of the Third World nation overlooks these other important sites of mobilization against (neo-)colonialism--which may often be in conflict with nationalist discourse and programmes of liberation.

Ahmad detects similar shortcomings in postcolonial theory's approach to the work of metropolitan-based migrants. In his view, it persistently fails to recognize the customarily hostile representation by writers like Rushdie of'women, minorities, servants, and others who are not of the ruling class'.

Above all else, however, Ahmad organizes his attack on postcolonial theory around the argument that its methodological procedures derive from contemporary Euro-American critical theories which are politically regressive in a number of ways.

To Ahmad, Western cultural criticism in general has become increasingly detached from any concrete connection with popular political struggle, whether at home or abroad, since the 1960s. Post-structuralism is then represented as the most striking and debilitating instance of this divorce, especially in its American versions in which, according to Ahmad, material forms of activism are replaced by a textual engagement which sees'reading as the appropriate form of politics'.

Ahmad attaches Said's criticism to post-structuralism and consequently reads his model of postcolonial analysis as similarly cut off from any real engagement with popular liberation movements in the Third World. The prestige of postcolonial theory is then attributed to its emergence in the wake of post-structuralist theory which itself reached the peak of its influence at a particularly conservative historical and cultural conjuncture, the period'supervised by Reagan and Thatcher'.

In this respect, too, there are parallels between In Theory and texts like Slemon and Tiffin After Europe (1989), which is chiefly concerned with exploring how a'genuinely' postcolonial literary criticism may be developed, a preoccupation which runs through many of the contributions to the volume.

Integral to this inquiry is a critique of postcolonial theory as represented by Spivak and Bhabha in particular, who are arraigned for evading the real politics of the postcolonial predicament as a consequence of their obsession with'a set of philosophical questions whose cultural and historical specificity within postmodern AngloAmerican culture is rarely admitted'. In an essay published in the same year as In Theory, Helen Tiffin takes this argument further:

For all its potentially useful insights, post-structuralist philosophy remains the handmaiden of repression, and if I may mix metaphors, serves as District Commissioner of the 1980s, his book title now changed from The Pacification of the Primitive Tribes of the Lower Niger to Enjoying the Other: or Difference Domesticated.

Adapting some of the perspectives and terms of Said's critique of Derrida in The World, the Text, and the Critic to his followers, Slemon and Tiffin's volume attempts to recuperate a number of analytic concepts, strategies and figures which Spivak and Bhabha deconstruct, on what many of the essays see as the mistaken assumption that they articulate the epistemological or political values of the dominant order.

For many of the contributors to After Europe, the centred subject, the aesthetic sphere, foundational identities, the nation and nationalism,'master'-narratives of liberation and emancipation, and authorial intention are all variously and at different times considered to be legitimate means of organizing resistance to (neo-)colonialism, whether in the spheres of politics or cultural criticism.

More than anything else, After Europe seeks to recuperate the referential properties of language, which the volume presents as consistently side-lined by post-structuralism's characteristic fracturing of the traditional conception of the relationship between signifier and signified. In the view of many of the contributors, this theoretical priority leads to an occlusion of'the real' which constantly defers the attempted engagement of postcolonial culture with pressing social and political problems.

The strategic logic of such arguments is comparable, once more, with that which informs Ahmad's resistance to post-structuralism's'debunking of all myths of origin, totalizing narratives, determinate and collective historical agents -- even the state and political economy as key sites for historical narrativization'.

Finally, the surface discourse of postcolonial theory is often no more palatable to such critics than it is to the historians considered earlier in this introduction.

Like MacKenzie Orientalism, and in contradiction of Jacoby's claim that stylistic clarity and coherence are of concern only to'conservative' critics, Ahmad In Theory laments the'very arcane' nature of Homi Bhabha's style and the'inflationary rhetoric' of postcolonial theory more generally.

Likewise, from within the ambit of contemporary versions of'Commonwealth' literary studies, Graham Huggan complains of'the often mystificatory vocabulary' of European post-structuralism which subsequently seeps into postcolonial theory. For many within the field of postcolonial criticism, the complexity of the language of postcolonial theory is one more symptom of its will to power over other kinds of postcolonial analysis. Consequently such figures insist on the importance of writing in what Ketu Katrak describes as'a language lucid enough to inspire people to struggle and to achieve social change'.

THEORY OF ART

STUDY of the underlying principles of literature leads the student back inevitably to the principles of art. The principles of literature, he finds, are but special applications of the broader principles which lie at the base of all the arts.

It would seem desirable, therefore, that the student early in his course should gain clear and right notions regarding the fundamental conceptions of aesthetics. Familiar with the principles of the broader science, he should be better prepared to work within the limits of the narrower. From a study of writings on the theory of art he should gain a power to discriminate among writings on the theory of literature; he should be enabled to detect the hidden bases of literary principles or precepts; he should be enabled to judge independently of the source and value of traditional literary doctrines.

Aesthetics is a large subject. None but a specialist can hope to master it in all its extent, and but few can hope to keep abreast of the active discussions and investigations that are going on at present. Nevertheless, complex and difficult as the subject appears, its fundamental principles are simple and its main problems few. Further, as in many other branches of knowledge, a thorough study of some one problem or principle will put the student in possession of all the rest. The following are suggested as some of the important questions likely to arise in a search for the fundamental principle of art.

Elementary Problems

What is the relation of Art to Nature. (2) What is the relation of Art to Imitation. (3) What is Beauty. (4) Is Beauty subjective or objective, or both. (5) How is the Beautiful related to the Sublime, the Ludicrous, the Pathetic, the Comic, and the Tragic. (6) What is the function of the Imagination in Art. (7) What are the Aesthetic Emotions. (8) What is the purpose of Art. (9) What part is played in the theory of Art by Pleasure. By the Play-impulse. Rhythm. Harmony. Regularity. Economy. (10) What is the relation of Art to Science, Morals, and Religion. (11) Can Art be useful. (12) What are the principal classifications of Art. (13) Upon what basis of differentiation do these classifications rest. (14) If there is a hierarchy of the Arts, upon what principle does it rest. (15) What is the function of Taste. (16) What determines the validity and the limitations of canons of Art.

Scrutiny of Problems

For those who desire to go more profoundly into the subject the following analysis is presented.

The problems of aesthetics may be classified under four heads: (1) Physiological problems, (2) psychological problems, (3) speculative problems, (4) social problems. It is not easy, perhaps not desirable, to keep the four classes wholly distinct; consequently, in the statement of the problems, some overlapping may be expected.

Physiological Problems

The general problem of physiological aesthetics may be stated in this way: What is the origin, nature, and physical explanation of the aesthetic thrill.

As the inquiry usually proceeds upon the assumption that aesthetic feeling is a species of pleasurable feeling, the line of research is in the direction of differentiating this kind of sensuous pleasure from sensuous pleasure in general. Thus the following series of subsidiary problems arises:

What changes in the nervous system, resulting from the application of stimuli, produce the sensation of pleasure.

What class of objects supply these stimuli. What are the attributes of these objects. Do dissimilar qualities furnish the same result, or is there some one quality, existing in different forms, in all objects that occasion pleasure.

Is the relation between the stimulus and the pleasurable feeling necessary and invariable, or accidental and mutable.

How are pleasurable feelings related to the vital functions. What quality in the stimulus, or what modification of the neural process occasions the aesthetic quality of the feeling. What are the preëminently aesthetic senses.

Assuming that hearing and seeing are the only, or the preeminently, aesthetic senses, the physiologist may inquire:—

What in the nervous structure and function of the ear corresponds to the relations of tones constituting the musical scale. To the relations of tones constituting harmony or discord.

What are the exact mathematical relations of such tones.

What are the neural equivalents of rhythm and melody.

What colours and combinations of colours are pleasing to the eye.

What forms and proportions of objects are pleasing.

What movements of the eye and modifications of its neural processes correspond to pleasing forms and colours of objects.

What are the neural equivalents of contrast, climax, and effective anti-climax. Is pain a necessary accompaniment, or condition precedent, of aesthetic feeling.

Psychological

Aesthetics as psychology is most obviously concerned with the nature of aesthetic emotions, although it is bound to take into account all facts of consciousness involved in the production of such emotions. Calling, for convenience, all objects that can arouse aesthetic emotion aethetic objects, the psychologist may inquire:

Does the perception of the aesthetic object differ from that of other objects. And if so, how. This problem resolves itself into two subordinate problems: —

a. What sensations do the peculiar physical marks of the aesthetic object, as, *e.g.*, colour, symmetry, etc., produce.

b. How is this raw material of sensation worked up into consciousness through perception.

What is the nature and function of imagination in so far as it has to do with the aesthetic object.

Are there aesthetic pleasures which are separable from the imagination.

Characteristics of the different kinds of aesthetic imagination.

Are all aesthetic objects products of the aesthetic imagination.

Can the aesthetic imagination do anything more than combine what has been given it in experience.

Why does the mind take an interest in the aesthetic object. May the same object be at times aesthetic and at other times non-aesthetic.

Characteristics of aesthetic emotion. How related to sensation.

Is pleasurableness the essential characteristic of aesthetic emotion.

Kinds of aesthetic emotion.

Relations between aesthetic emotion and other kinds of emotion.

Are aesthetic pleasures sense-pleasures.

Is immediacy of pleasure-getting the distinction between ordinary emotion and aesthetic emotion.

Is all aesthetic emotion the revival of pleasurable emotion or of a pleasurable content.

What is the nature of the impulse that leads to the production of works of art. Is there a difference between 'expression' and 'discharge of emotion'.

Is the emotional state which is produced by a work of art, passive and receptive, or active.

What is the importance of sub-conscious processes as explanation of aesthetic effects. Aesthetic function of the Will.

Speculative Problems

The problem of aesthetics as philosophy may be said, in a general way, to be the relation of the subject-matter to human experience. As suggested by the parenthesis, the nature of the subject-matter is itself a part of the problem. Retaining the convenient term aesthetic object, we may inquire:—

What is it about things that makes them aesthetic objects.

The number of the answers which have been made to this question is very large. Among the qualities or characteristics posited of the aesthetic object are the following: Truth, Conflict, Reconciliation of Opposites, Repose, Growth, Life, Order, Symmetry, Fitness, Unity in Variety, Simplicity, Intricacy, Harmony, Usefulness, Expression, Suggestion, Personality, Novelty, Consistency, Proportion, Freedom, Economy, Rhythm. By most writers these and all similar characteristics are held to be summed up in the comprehensive term Beauty.

If it is necessary to posit some particular thing as the essence of the aesthetic object, it would perhaps be better to substitute for the ambiguous term beauty the term aesthetic value, which has at least the advantage of suggesting its question-begging character. Adopting this term as a matter of convenience, we may ask:—

Is aesthetic value subjective or objective, or both. 3. Kinds of aesthetic value, and relation of one kind to another. As examples of the different kinds, may be mentioned the Beautiful, the Sublime, the Ludicrous, the Pathetic, the Tragic, the Grotesque, etc.

Relation of the work of art to nature.

This question may take on a great diversity of forms, as, for example: —

Is art an imitation of nature, and if so, is that all that art is.

In what respect does the aesthetic value of art differ from that of nature.

Is there a higher and a lower aesthetic value, and if so, which is higher, that of nature or that of art.

Does nature, when it takes on aesthetic value, become art.

Character of the work of art.

In dealing with the work of art, we may inquire, (a) What is its essential principle. Or, taking into account the conditions of its production, may ask (b) Why works of art should be produced at all. Or, (c) What were the aims and motives of the producer of a particular work. Or, (d) By what processes and in obedience to what laws he gave embodiment to his idea. Or, (e) In what material he embodied it. Or, (f) What are the laws of the development of art in general. The answer to the first question will bring before us the theory of art; to the second, the genesis of art, or the art-impulse; to the third, the relations of art and the artist; to the fourth, the technique of art and the nature of genius; to the fifth, the classification of the arts; and to the sixth, the evolution of art as a historical growth.

Social Problems

These are such as relate to the communal origin and development of the aesthetic impulse, and the effect exerted upon the community by aesthetic productions. What part has sympathy or altruism played in the origin and development of aesthetic pleasure. In the production of works of art. Are aesthetic pleasures ever selfish pleasures.

What part has been played in aesthetic production by the imitative instinct — the instinct of one man to do what another has done or is doing.

To what extent does the law of supply and demand govern the production of art.To what extent is art individual, and to what extent is it social. Is art the possession of the whole people.

To what extent are the principles of coöperation and division of labour effective in art. Place of art in the theory of the State.

1. In what form of government does art best flourish.
2. Does inequality of condition promote or hinder the healthy development of art.

To what extent is art the expression of pleasure in the labour of production.

To what extent is freedom of the artist essential to good art.

What part is played by machinery in the production of works of art. Are machine-made articles necessarily bad art.

Does civilization inevitably bring ugliness with it.

Does art go hand in hand with luxury.

What effect has art upon social development.

What is the relation of art to morality. May art be non-moral.

Is the best art that which appeals to the people — the masses. Or that which appeals to an aristocracy of intellect and emotion.

What is the service which useful art renders to the community, and how does this differ from the service rendered by, fine art.

LITERARY THEORY AND CRITICISM

Subject and disciplines. Contemporary literary theory and criticism encompasses a complex and changing group of disciplines. There arethree main areas of study: literary theory, the history of literature, and literary criticism in the strict sense *(literaturnaia kritika).* The theory ofliterature investigates the general laws of the structure and development of literature. The history of literature studies the literary past as aprocess or one of the stages of this process. Literary criticism is concerned with the most recent, the "present" state of literature. It alsointerprets the literature of the past from the standpoint of modern social and artistic aims. Literary criticism in the strict sense is notuniversally accepted as being part of the scholarly discipline of literary theory and criticism.

The most important part of literary theory and criticism is poetics, the study of the structure of individual works and groups of works, forexample, all the works of a particular writer or the works of a literary school or epoch. Poetics may be related to each of the major areas ofliterary theory and criticism. In literary theory it provides knowledge of the structure of any literary work (general poetics). Within the scope ofliterary history, historical poetics investigates the development of artistic structures and their elements, such as genres, plots, and stylisticimages. The principles of poetics may also be applied in criticism in the strict sense. Stylistics occupies a similar position in literary theoryand criticism. Stylistics may be included in literary theory as part of general poetics; here stylistics is the study of one level of the structure,the stylistic and language level. In literary history stylistics treats the language and style of a particular current or school. The stylistic studyof contemporary works has almost always been one of the chief functions of literary criticism in the strict sense.

The three spheres of literary theory and criticism are closely related. Criticism, for example, is dependent on information derived from literaryhistory and theory, which in turn take into account and reveal the significance of criticism. Moreover, secondary disciplines have arisen inliterary theory and criticism, such as the theory and history of criticism in the strict sense, the history of poetics (as opposed to historicalpoetics), and the theory of the stylistics of artistic language. The various disciplines within literary theory and criticism also shift from onelevel to another: thus, criticism becomes material for the history of literature, for historical poetics, and for other studies. In addition to theprincipal disciplines already mentioned, there are many auxiliary disciplines, such as the study of archives relating to literary theory andcriticism, the compilation of bibliographies of literature and criticism, heuristics, paleography, textual criticism and commentary, and thetheory and practice of publishing. In the mid-20th century mathematical methods, especially those of statistics, were widely adopted inliterary theory and criticism, primarily in prosody, stylistics, textual criticism, and folklore study, where quantifiable structural segments canbe isolated more easily. The auxiliary disciplines are an indispensable foundation for the primary disciplines. As they develop and growincreasingly complex, however, they may set independent scholarly goals and acquire independent cultural functions.

Literary theory and criticism is in many ways linked to the humanities, some of which (philosophy, aesthetics) serve as its methodologicalbasis; other branches of the humanities resemble literary theory and criticism in their goals and subject of investigation (folklore studies, artstudies) or are related by a general humanistic orientation (history, psychology, sociology). The many links between literary theory andcriticism and linguistics are based not only on common material (language as a means of communication and as the raw material ofliterature) but also on the contiguity of the epistemological functions of words and images and on an analogy between the structure of wordsand images. The close relation between literary theory and criticism and the other humanities was formerly reflected in the concept ofphilology as a synthesizing branch of learning, studying culture in all its written manifestations, including literary works. In the mid-20thcentury the concept of philology suggests the affinity between literary theory and criticism and linguistics; in the strict sense philologydenotes textual criticism.

History of schools and trends. Literary theory and criticism originated in early antiquity in the form of mythological concepts, for example, thereflection in myths of the classical differentiation between the arts. Judgements about art are found in such ancient works as the Indian Vedas(tenth to second centuries B.C.), the Chinese *Book of Legends (Shu Ching,* 12th to fifth centuries B.C.), and the ancient Greek *Iliad* and*Odyssey* (eighth and seventh centuries B.C.).

In Europe the first concepts of art and literature were developed by the ancient thinkers. Plato dealt with aesthetic problems, including that ofthe beautiful, from the standpoint of objective idealism and examined the epistemological nature and educational function of art. He alsocontributed to the theory of art and literature, classifying literature as epic, lyric, or dramatic. Although Aristotle's works *Poetics, Rhetoric,* and *Metaphysics* preserve the general aesthetic approach to art, they introduce several disciplines of literary study, including the theory ofliterature, stylistics, and especially poetics. Aristotle's *Poetics,* containing the first systematic exposition of the fundamentals of poetics,initiated a long tradition of treatises on poetics. As time passed, however, these works became more normative, for example, Horace's *Art ofPoetry.* Along with classical poetics there developed rhetoric, initially the study of oratory and prose in general, for example, Aristotle's*Rhetoric,* the works of Isocrates and Cicero, and Quintilian's *The Training of an Orator.* The theory of prose and stylistics developed withinthe framework of rhetoric. The writing of treatises on rhetoric, as well as poetics, continued into modern times; in Russia M. V. Lomonosovpublished his *Short Manual on Eloquence* in 1748. Criticism in the strict sense also arose in Europe in antiquity, as may be seen from theearly philosophers' opinions about Homer and the comparison of the tragedies of Aeschylus and Euripides in Aristophanes' comedy *TheFrogs* (405 B.C.). Initially, criticism was inseparable not only from other areas of literary study but from art as a whole.

Significant differentiation in literary theory and criticism occurred in the Hellenistic age. During the period of Alexandrian philology (third andsecond centuries B.C.) literary theory and criticism, along with other studies, broke away from philosophy and formed its own disciplines,including biobibliography (the *Tablets* of Callimachus, the prototype of the literary encyclopedia), textual criticism to determine theauthenticity of a text, and textual commentary and the publication of texts (Zenodotus of Ephesus, Aristophanes of Byzantium, and laterAristarchus of Samothrace). Later, comparative historical studies arose, for example, comparisons of classical works from the standpoint of the sublime and the beginning of the section entitled "Being" in the treatise *On the Sublime,* written in the first century A.D. by an unidentified author known as Pseudo-Lon-ginus.

Profound concepts of art and literature also developed in the Oriental countries in ancient times. In China the doctrine of the social and educational function of art evolved within Confucianism (Hsiin-tsu, c. 298–238 B.C.). The Taoist school developed an aesthetic theory of the beautiful in conformity with Tao, the universal creative principle (Lao-tzu, sixth and fifth centuries B.C.). In India problems of artistic structure were worked out in relation to theories of the psychological perception of art, called *rasa* (in *Bharata's Natyasastra,* c. fourth century and later treatises), and theories of *dhvani,* the hidden meaning of works of art (in Anandavardhana's *Dhvanyaloka,* ninth century). Primary attention was given to style, that is, to the linguistic realization of artistic effects. In the Oriental countries general theoretical and aesthetic methods(alongside textual analysis and bibliographic work) predominated for many centuries. Research on the historical and evolutionary plane appeared only in the 19th and 20th centuries.

Byzantium and the Latin works of the Western European peoples were the links between ancient and modern literary theory and criticism. Stimulated by the study and collection of ancient works, literary study in Byzantium was primarily concerned with biobibliography andcommentary. Important Byzantine works included one of the first European encyclopedic collections of literary works, Photius' *Myriobiblon*(ninth century), containing paraphrases and evaluations of literary works; Suidas' biographic dictionary of ancient authors (c. tenth century);commentaries on Homer, Pindar, and other authors by Johannes Tzetzes (12th century) and Eustathius of Thessalonica (12th century); anda treatise on rhetoric by Michael Psellus (11th century). In Latin works, philological study stressed the writing of compendiums and textbookson rhetoric. At the same time, within a theological framework and often assimilating non-platonism and Aristotelianism, the philosophical andepistemological principles of literary theory and criticism were developed by St. Augustine in the fourth and fifth centuries and St. ThomasAquinas in the 13th century.

The Renaissance stimulated the creation of original poetics adapted to local and national conditions. The problem of language, extending beyond stylistics and rhetoric, became the general theoretical problem of establishing modern European languages as legitimate material ofpoetry. Important works on this subject include Dante's treatise *On Popular Speech* (1304–07) and Du Bellay's *Defence and Illustration of the French Language* (1549). The right of literary theory and criticism to deal with contemporary artistic phenomena was affirmed in Boccaccio's lectures on the *Divine Comedy* and his biography *The Life of Dante Alighieri* (c. 1360). The moral significance of contemporary literature was the subject of the Englishman P. Sidney's *Defence of Poesie* written in 1583. But inasmuch as modern literary theory and criticism was developing out of the "discovery of antiquity," the Renaissance faced the problem of originality in its full force. Solutions to thisproblem ranged from attempts to adapt elements of classical poetics to modern literature (the application of the norms of the Aristotelian theory of drama to the epic in T. Tasso's *Discourse on the Art of Poetry,* 1587) to the rejection of classical authorities (F. Patrizi's *On Poetry,* 1586). The view of the classical genres as "eternal" canons coexisted with the sense of dynamism and incompleteness that was characteristic of the Renaissance. The prevailing tripartite division of man's history into antiquity, the Middle Ages, and the Renaissance (theterm was first used by G. Vasari in his *Lives,* 1550) anticipated G. Vico's theory of cycles and the doctrine of stages of cultural development expressed by the romantics and found in the dialectical philosophical systems of the late 18th and early 19th centuries.

Beginning in the late 16th century and especially in the age of classicism, the trend towards systematizing artistic laws became more pronounced, and the normative and pragmatic character of artistic theory was emphasized. In his *Art of Poetry* (1674), N. Boileau relegated general epistemological and aesthetic problems to the background and concentrated on constructing a harmonious poetics imbued with Cartesianism and conceived as a system of genre, stylistic, and linguistic norms. The exclusive and obligatory nature of Boileau's normsmade his treatise and such related works as J. C. Gottsched's *Experiment With a Critical Poetics for Germans* (1730) and A. P. Sumarokov's *Epistle on Versification* (1748) literary codes. Rationalism also stimulated attempts to achieve a deductive knowledge of artand to reduce all its elements to "one principle," for example, imitation (C. Batteux's *The Fine Arts Reduced to One General Principle,* 1746).

However, the 17th and 18th centuries also saw a strong trend opposing the normative approach to literary types and genres. In defending the mixing of genres S. Johnson pointed to Shakespeare's works in his *Lives of the Most Outstanding English Poets* (1779–1781). D. Diderotadvocated middle-class drama, a genre between tragedy and comedy. Finally, with E. Joung *(Description of Original Works,* 1759) and G. E.Lessing *(Hamburg Dramaturgy,* 1767–69), this tendency grew into an attack on all normative poetics, thus opening the way for the aestheticand literary theories of the romantics. During the Enlightenment attempts were also made to explain the development of literature in terms of local conditions, particularly environment and climate (J. Dubos, *Critical Reflections on Poetry and Painting,* 1719; writings of Montesquieu and J. J. Winckelmann), which anticipated the later theories of determinism. In the 18th century the first courses in literary history were given, notably G. Tiraboschi's *History of Italian Literature* (1772–82), T. War-ton's *History of English Poetry* (1774–81), and J. La Harpe's *Lyceum, or Course in Ancient and Modern Literature* (1799–1805), based on a historical consideration of the types of poetry.

It is more difficult to date the appearance of literary criticism in the strict sense, which evolved in the course of more than a century, from F. Malherbe, Boileau, and J. Dryden (whom S. Johnson called the father of English criticism) to Lessing, Diderot, J. Marmontel, and N. M.Karamzin, who was the first Russian to include in his magazine a substantial section devoted to criticism and bibliography.

In the late 18th century an important change occurred in European literary thought, shaking the stable hierarchy of artistic values. The inclusion of folklore in the scholarly study of medieval European and Oriental literatures cast doubt on the validity of models, whether classical or Renaissance. There developed a strong sense of the intrinsic merit of artistic criteria of different ages which ought not to be compared. This attitude was best expressed by J. G. Herder in his *Shakespeare* (1773) and*Ideas Towards a Philosophy of Human History*(1784–91). The category of the "unique" came to denote the literature of a given people or period, possessing its own measure of perfection. Following J. Hamann in studying the Eastern sources of classical Greek literature and approaching the Bible as an artistic work of aparticular age, Herder created the preconditions for the comparative historical method.

The romantic view that different criteria existed developed into the concept of different cultural periods expressing the spirit of a particular people or era. Adhering to the classification of art forms proposed by J. F. Schiller *(On Naïve and Sentimental Poetry,* 1795), the romantics drew a distinction between classical (ancient) and modern (Christian) art forms. Recognizing the impossibility of restoring the classical form, the romantics stressed the endless mutability and capacity for renewal of art (F. Schlegel, *Fragments,* 1798). A. Schlegel applied this idea toliterary history in his Berlin lectures on literature and art (1801–03) and his *Lectures on Dramatic Art and Literature* (1809–11).

However, in establishing modern art as romantic, as imbued with the Christian symbolism of the spiritual and infinite, the romantics imperceptibly, and despite the dialectical tone of their doctrine, restored the category of model (historically medieval art and regionally Oriental art). At the same time, in the idealist philosophical systems, culminating in Hegel's philosophy, the idea of the development of art was embodied in a phenomenology of artistic forms dialectically replacing each other (Hegel's symbolic, classical, and romantic forms). The nature of the aesthetic and the distinction between it and the moral and cognitive were established philosophically by I. Kant. The inexhaustible, "symbolic" nature of the artistic image was expounded in philosophical terms by F. Schelling. Another important aspect of Hegel's philosophy was the right of mediated (discursive-scientific) knowledge to judge artistic phenomena since "art is not so disorderly thatit could not lend itself to philosophical elucidation" ; this view stood in opposition to the intuitivist tendencies that prevailed among the romantics.

The philosophical period of literary theory and criticism was a time of large-scale systems conceived as universal knowledge of art (and,more broadly, of all existence), which "crushed" beneath them the history of literature, poetics, and stylistics. The most important aspect of the speculative edifice was the conception of theory as knowledge of the laws of development of the concrete. As a result, the historical aspect of literary theory and criticism often coincided with the theoretical aspect, as N. Stan-kevich noted in his comment about Hegel: "The history of art, considered rationally, is also the theory of art".

A school of "philosophical criticism" represented by D. V. Venevitinov, N. I. Nadezhdin, and to some extent V. G. Belinskii, arose in Russiain the 1820's and 1830's, influenced by and growing out of German philosophical systems. The school also asserted the distinctive nature ofart and its changing forms, but in response to the vital needs of Russian literature, it devoted special attention to working out the new,realistic form. In the 1840's, after passing through a philosophical aesthetics phase, Belinskii related this aesthetics to his conception of thecivic function of art and to historicism ("social preoccupation") in an original manner. His series of articles on A. S. Pushkin (1843–46) wasessentially the first course devoted to the history of contemporary Russian literature. Belinskii linked his explanation of past phenomena totheoretical problems of realism in art. Despite the differentiation of disciplines that had occurred, the chief form of literary study in Russia (incontrast to Western Europe) and the one which was developing the richest content and incorporating the other branches of learning wasprecisely philosophical criticism. As N. G. Chernyshevskii noted later, "people who were engaged in aesthetic criticism . . . also did a greatdeal for the history of literature" .

In the first quarter of the 19th century the scope of literary study expanded in the European countries. Many new courses were offered inliterary history, notably those of F. Bouterwek in Germany, L. S. Sismondi in Switzerland, and A. Villemin in France. Disciplines arose thatstudied all aspects of the culture of a particular ethnic group, for example, the Slavic studies of J. Dobrovský, J. Kollár, and P. Šafa?ik. Withthe growing interest in literary history, attention shifted from great masters to the entire body of artistic facts and from world literature to thestudent's own national literature, for example, G. G. Gervinus' History of the Poetic National Literature of the Germans (1835-42). In Russianliterary studies the place of ancient Russian literature was affirmed; philosophical criticism had not viewed ancient Russian literature asbeing part of the mainstream of European literary development and had therefore excluded it from its aesthetic system. A greater interest inpre-Petrine literature was shown in M. A. Maksimovich's History of Ancient Russian Literature (1839), A. V. Nikitenko's Essay on theHistory of Russian Literature (1845), and especially S. P. Shevyrev's History of Russian Literature, Primarily Ancient (1846).

Several methodological schools arose in Europe, cutting across national boundaries. Among the first was the mythological school (itsphilosophical basis was the works on aesthetics of F. Schelling and the Schlegel brothers). Interest in mythology and folklore symbolism, which had been stimulated by romanticism , grew among German mythologists, who discerned an Aryan protomytholoy . The common features of primitive thought as recorded in language and legend were studied. In Russia the mythologist F. I. Buslaev did not restrict himself to studying mythology but traced its historical course, including the interaction of folk poetry and written works. Later the "youngmythologists"—M. Müller in England, W. Schwartz in Germany, and A. N. Afanas'ev in Russia—posed the problem of the sources of myth.

Under the influence of another aspect of romantic theory—the view that art was the self-expression of the creative spirit—the biographical method took shape. To some extent the biographical approach was included in all modern literary study, sometimes resembling the method of cultural history and at other times becoming frank impressionism. The biographical method also paved the way for the psychological theories of creativity of the late 19th and early 20th centuries.

In the second half of the 19th century the school of cultural history became prominent. It had evolved under the influence of many factors, including the deterministic trends in literary theory and criticism in the preceding century, the romantic interest in national and local "colour," and French historical science (F. Guizot, A. Thierry, and F. O. Mignet). Impressed by the successes of the natural sciences, the school ofcultural history attempted to reduce causality and determinism in literary study to precise, tangible factors, such as H. Taine's triune of race,milieu, and moment. The traditions of this school were developed by De Sanctis, W. Scherer, and M. Meléndezy Pelayo. In Russia its adherents included N. S. Tikhonravov, A. N. Pypin, and N. I. Storozhenko. As the cultural history method developed, it notonly underrated the artistic nature of literature, which was regarded primarily as a social document, but also revealed strong positivist tendencies that ignored the dialectical method and aesthetic criteria.

In Russian literary theory and criticism the positivist tendencies were opposed by revolutionary-democratic criticism. Drawing on Belinskii'slegacy, revolutionary-democratic criticism attempted to restore the broad philosophical and epistemological context of literary research: "If itis important to collect and study facts, it is equally important to try to grasp their meaning. . . . Thus, the question of what is art and what is poetry cannot but be extremely important" . Asserting the cognitive functions of art, the revolutionary democrats noted that works of art also often "serve to pass judgement on various aspects of life". N. A. Dobroliubov propounded the concept of "realistic criticism," whose main principle was the analysis of a literary work, insofar as it was true tolife, as a phenomenon of life in order to explain to the reader the spirit and problems of the times. In treating problems of the history ofliterature and criticism in the strict sense, the revolutionary democrats emphasized the link between the literary process and the socialstruggle, the interaction and opposition of different social groups, and the progress of the liberation movement .

In the mid-1840's, the study of folklore and ancient literature gave rise to the comparative historical method. Pypin came close to this methodin his *Essay on the Literary History of Old Russian Stories and Fairy Tales* (1857). Later, T. Benfey (*Panchatantra,* 1859) proposed themigration theory, attributing the similarity of plots of folk tales not to the common origin of peoples, but to later contacts among peoples andthe migration of plots from India. Benfey's theory stimulated both the historical approach to links among peoples and an interest in suchpurely poetic elements as plots and characters. However, the theory did not investigate the genesis of the poetic elements and often resultedin random and superficial comparisons. Parallel to the comparative historical school and correcting and elaborating its conclusions, therearose theories attributing the similarity of poetic forms to the uniformity of the human psyche (the ethnopsy-chology school of H. Steinthaland M. Lazarus) and to the animism common to all primitive peoples (E. B. Tylor). These theories in turn became the basis for the Scottishscholar A. Lang's theory of the spontaneous origin of plots, known as the anthropological theory.

The scholarly work of A. N. Veselovskii was based on the mingling of many 19th-century methodological traditions. Adopting themythologists' theory of the myth as the primary form of artistic creation, Veselovskii directed his investigations to concrete comparisons inliterary history. Unlike the migration school, however, he raised the question of the preconditions for borrowing, the problem of"countercurrents" in the literature experiencing the influence. Despite the positivistic tinge of his initial position, Veselovskii opened the wayfor historical-genetic studies of artistic forms. In his *Historical Poetics,* explaining the "essence of poetry based on its history," Veselovskiiturned to historical reality and investigated the "emotional experience of poetic imagery and the forms expressing it" . Thus, the subject of historical poetics was established as the study of the development of poetic forms and of the laws bywhich "a particular social content is embodied in certain inevitable poetic forms," such as genre, epithet, or plot. A. A. Potebnia approachedthe problem of imagery from another angle, from the standpoint of the structure of the work of art as a whole . Potebnia's study of the analogy between words and images with respect totheir social "applications" substantiates the ambiguity of the artistic work, which seems to contain a multiplicity of meanings, and reveals theimage's infinite capacity for renewal in the course of its historical life and the creative role of the reader in this change. Potebnia's idea of the"inner form" of the word stimulated the dialectical study of the problem of the artistic image and anticipated the later study of poetic structurein relation to its function.

In the last third of the 19th century the method of cultural history was further developed in Western European literary studies through thecomparative historical and, especially, the psychological approach . Representatives of the psychological school included W. Wundt, J.Volkelt, R. Müller-Freienfels, Potebnia (to some extent), and D. N. Ov-sianiko-Kulikovskii. The emphasis on comparative historical studiesled to the creation of a special discipline, comparative literary theory and criticism (F. Baldensperger and P. Van Tieghem in France). Thedevelopment of literary theory and criticism became worldwide, breaking down age-old barriers between East and West. The first histories ofnational literatures appeared in the Oriental countries, notably Haga Yaichi's *Ten Lectures on Japanese Literature* (1899) and, somewhatlater, histories of Indian literature and Lu Hsin's *Short History of Chinese Prose* (1923). This period saw the evolution of systematic literarycriticism in the strict sense.

At the turn of the 20th century an antipositivist trend based on idealist premises arose in Western literary theory and criticism. It assumedthree principal forms. First, mediated, intellectual knowledge was disparaged in favor of intuitive knowledge as applied to both the creativeact and to judgements about art (H. Bergson's *Laughter,* 1900). There were attempts not only to reject the system of traditional literarycategories (types of poetry, genres) but also to prove that they were fundamentally inapplicable to art. In his *Aesthetics* (1902), B. Crocestated that all traditional classifications and poetic terminology determined only the external structure of a work, not its artistic value. Inbringing intuition into conflict with reason and conceptual judgement, the intuitionists also questioned the scholarly validity of literary theoryand criticism.

Second, efforts were made to overcome the superficial determinism of the cultural history school and to construct a classification of literaturebased on deep-rooted psychological and intellectual distinctions. Such was F. Nietzsche's polarity of artistic types, derived from theclassical gods Apollo and Dionysus: the plastic and musical, the contemplative, mental, form-creating principle as opposed to "vital,"emotional-aesthetic, turbulent, and at the same time tragic elements (The Birth of Tragedy From the Spirit of Music, 1872). Stronglyinfluencing bourgeois and, especially, decadent aesthetics were the late Nietzsche's irrationalism, his "tragic" relativism denying social andhistorical progress, and his antirealist notion of "myth-creation" in art. The Geistesgeschichte, or cultural-philosophical, school attempted toexplain art in terms of deep-seated processes, above all the merging of the "epoch" (the "historical spirit") and the "psychic" (the spiritualintegrity of the individual). W. Dilthey, the leading representative of Geistesgeschichte posited three basic types of world view and artisticactivity (positivists, objective idealists, and dualists). Rendering more concrete the philosophical approach to art, R. Unger consideredgeneral philosophical problems to be of lesser importance than such specific problems as fate, freedom and necessity, spirit and nature, andlove and death (Philosophical Problems in Recent Literary Studies, 1908). Asserting the primacy of "emotional experience" (as a unity of the"psychic" and the "historical") in literature and its link with the world view of an epoch, the Geistesgeschichte school ignored the social andclass aspects of emotional experience. In developing the principle of histori-cism with respect to the alternation of artistic styles and forms,the school avoided explaining the lawlike regularities of the historical process and tended towards irrationalism and skepticism. It alsominimized the importance of artistic structure since art was dissolved in the general world view of an epoch.

Greater attention to form was shown in H. Wölfflin's theory of the structural differences between the art of the Renaissance and of thebaroque *(Principles of Art History,* 1915), which was subsequently applied to literature by the German theoretician O. Walzel. A shortcomingof this approach was its tendency towards rigid classification, reducing the diversity of literature to one of two forms and exaggerating thespontaneous development of artistic forms.

The third manifestation of the antipositivist tendencies was psychoanalysis (S. Freud), which introduced the unconscious into explanationsof art. The of Freudian psychoanalysis yielded meager results, such as explaining an artist's entire creative work in terms of an "Oedipuscomplex." Moreover, the psychoanalytic approach completely ignored social and ideological factors in literature. Applying psychoanalyticprinciples to art in a different manner, C. G. Jung formulated his theory of the collective unconscious (archetypes) in *On the RelationshipBetween Analytical Psychology and the Literary Work,* (1922).

The ritual-mythological school (N. Frye, M. Bodkin) developed under the influence of Jung's analytical psychology and the ritual-mythologicalapproach to the study of ancient cultures, represented by R. Smith and especially J. Frazer and his followers, the Cambridge school. Theexponents of the ritual-mythological approach attempted to identify certain rituals and archetypes of the collective unconscious in the worksof all ages, for example, initiation rituals corresponding to the psychological archetypes of birth and death. Similar views were held by E.Bjork in the United States, who attributed the symbolic effect of artistic works to magic rituals. Ritual-mythological criticism promotes studyof genres and poetic devices (metaphors, symbols), but in its subordination of literature to myth and ritual, it submerges literary studybeneath ethnology and psychoanalysis.

Currents based on existential philosophy occupied a special place in Western literary studies. Attempting to refute the view of history as aphenomenological process, these currents introduced the concept of existential time, to which great works of art correspond (M. Heidegger,*The Origin of the Work of Art,* 1935). E. Staiger made time the cornerstone of his classification of artistic styles and types of poetry, in whichlyric, epic, and dramatic poetry express, respectively, the past, present, and future (*Principles of Poetics,* 1946; *The Transformation of Style,* 1963). Treating poetic works as self-sufficient, self-contained truth and "prophesy," the existential "interpretation" avoids the traditionalgenetic approach and removes the work from its social and historical context.

In the 1920's the formalist school emerged in Russia, reacting against intuitionism and biographic impressionism and against the methodsthat ignored the distinctive features of art (the school of cultural history). The formalists attempted to transcend the dualism of form andcontent by proposing a new interrelationship, that of material (something antecedent to the artist) and form (the arrangement of material in thework). Thus they expanded the concept of form, previously reduced to style or randomly chosen elements, to include the arrangement ofartistic material as a whole. Such a view of form, however, left no room in the analysis and conception of art for epistemological andphilosophical interpretations of art or for social interpretation of artistic phenomena. Through the Prague linguistic circle the formalist schoolhad a significant influence on literary theory and criticism throughout the world, particularly on the "new criticism" and on structuralism, bothof which also subscribed to T. S. Eliot's ideas.

Alongside the further formalization and supplanting of epistemological and aesthetic aspects, there were attempts to bridge the dichotomy ofform and content, unresolved by the formalist method, with its non-positivist methodology. First, the artistic work was viewed as a complexsystem of levels including elements of both content and form (R. Ingarden). Second, attempts were made to create a "system of systems,"that is, principles of interrelationship between the literary and other levels. C. Lévi-Strauss and J. Muka?ovský studied the function of form. Inthe 1960's there also emerged the sociological approach of L. Gold-mann and P. Macherey, reacting against formalist methods andsubjective tendencies. Many of the exponents of this approach related literary phenomena directly to socioeconomic factors.

In general, contemporary literary theory and criticism has failed to resolve such key problems as literature's relation to public life and theinterrelationship between artistic form and content. Contemporary schools of literary theory and criticism in the West include the existential,the sociological, the ritual-mythological, and the structuralist. The various approaches both converge and conflict with one another; forexample, the sociological approach tends towards both structuralism and existentialism.

Marxist-Leninist literary studies represented a new stage in the history of modern literary theory and criticism. In accordance with theirdoctrine of dialectical and historical materialism, Marx and Engels described the basic problems of aesthetics and art. In the Marxist view ofart, the crucial factor is the tenet of historical materialism that states that the "mode of production of material life determines the social,political, and intellectual processes of life in general" . Like the entire intellectualprocess of life, aesthetic notions, literature, and art are considered by historical materialism to be the "ideal superstructure" above the realeconomic base of society . The development of aesthetic ideals cannot be considered apart from the life ofsociety as a whole, as an independent sphere obeying only its internal laws. The development of aesthetic ideals is ultimately determined inthe same manner as are all other aspects of the life of society—by the development of material production and by the resulting productionrelations. However, Marx noted that artistic flowering and the development of society's material base "by no means correspond to oneanother" . Whether a social system favors or hinders artistic development, the direction taken by artistic development,and the predominance of particular forms and genres—all are determined not merely by the level of the material base of an epoch but aboveall by the nature of the epoch's characteristic social relations: class or nonclass, antagonistic or non-antagonistic, and conducive or hostile tofostering man's individuality. Marx and Engels also concluded that capitalist production is inimical to art and poetry.

Among works influenced by Marx and Engels were F. Mehring's *The Legend of Lessing* (1893) and P. Lafargue's *The Origin of Romanticism*(1885–96). Marxist study of literature was fruitfully developed in Russia by G. V. Plekhanov, V. V. Vorovskii, and A. V. Lunacharskii.Plekhanov's writings on literature include *Unaddressed Letters* (1899–1900), articles on V. G. Belinskii and N. G. Chernyshevskii, *TheProletarian Movement and Bourgeois Art* (1905), and *Art and Public Life* (1912–13). Vorovskii is noted for his articles on the revolutionarydemocrats, M. Gorky, and the decadents; among Lunacharskii's works are *Marxism and Aesthetics: Dialogue on Art* (1905) and *Critical andPolemic Studies* (1905). Interpreting art from the point of view of historical materialism, Marxist literary study from the outset criticized notonly positivist (naturalistic) and subjective-idealist trends in modern literary theory and criticism but also the formalistic and antirealisticaesthetic notions of the decadents. However, as historians of culture and sociologists of art, Plekhanov, Mehring, and Lafargue borrowedextensively from the cultural history school, adopting the idea that literature is linked to social psychology, which they interpreted "from thepoint of view of the mutual relations and mutual influence of social classes" .

In the second decade of the 20th century, vulgar sociologism developed under the influence of the sociological interpretation of literature. Itgrew out of a one-sided and incomplete conception of Marxist sociology and became influential in Soviet literary studies in the 1920's and1930's. Opposing vulgar sociologism, Marxist literary theory and criticism demonstrated not only the distinctive nature of art and the laws ofits development but also the dialectical conception of the social and historical causality of art and its social function. Fundamental to theMarxist position was the tenet that "only in the final analysis" does the economic base determine the phenomena of intellectual life and thatthis determining trend can be discerned only as the most general resultant of a "parallelogram" formed by the stress of social forces andinfluences moving in different directions, not as a mechanical cause-effect link. Equally basic was the thesis of the "relative independence"of ideology.

Lenin's "In Memory of Herzen" (1912) and his articles on L. N. Tolstoy (1908–11) became vivid examples as well as methodological keys forthe dialectical materialist interpretation of the social causality of art and for the struggle against vulgar sociologism. Lenin's articlesemphasized the objective importance of the writer's works in the class struggle and offered models for the critical study of literature inrelation to its epoch. In "Leo Tolstoy as the Mirror of the Russian Revolution" (1908), Lenin wrote: "To identify the great artist with therevolution which he has obviously failed to understand, and from which he obviously stands aloof, may at first sight seem strange andartificial.. . . And if we have before us a really great artist, he must have reflected in his work at least some of the essential aspects of therevolution" . According to Lunacharskii, Lenin's theory of reflection took into account "not so much thewriter's origin as the manner in which he reflects social changes, not so much the author's subjective attachments and links with a particularsocial milieu as the extent to which he is objectively representative of a given historical situation" .

One of the complex and vital issues of 20th-century culture was that of cultural heritage. Guidelines for solving this problem in terms ofMarxist literary theory and criticism were provided by Lenin's doctrine of "two national cultures in each national culture" (that of the rulingclasses and democratic and socialist culture), as well as by his defence of the cultural heritage of the past, which he developed in the courseof his struggle against Proletkult. "Marxism," he wrote, "far from rejecting the most valuable achievements of the bourgeois epoch has, on thecontrary, assimilated and refashioned everything of value in the more than two thousand years of development of human thought and culture".

Lenin's article "The Party Organization and Party Literature" (1905) recognizes the importance of literature in the social and political life ofsociety. This article became the basis of one of the guiding principles of Marxist literary theory and criticism —the principle of party-mindedness *(partiinost')*. The key element of this principle is conscious service "to socialism and the toiling millions." Lenin's theory ofreflection, his principle of *partiinost'* in literature, and his doctrine of cultural heritage were fundamental for the creation of the theory ofsocialist realism.

Contemporary Soviet literary theory and criticism is a science that studies all aspects of literature and its origins and social ties. It studiesthe distinctive features of word-image artistic thinking, the nature and functions of artistic creativity, and the general and local lawlikeregularities of literary history. In recent decades research in poetics has aimed at identifying the form-creating, content aspects of literature.This has brought into focus the problem of the literary work as a complex system to be considered within the framework of a changinghistorical and social context.

Such an approach, which opposes the atomistic-metaphysical trends of positivist literary theory and criticism, establishes the hierarchicalnature of the work's inner organization and considers its components functionally, in their changing relationships to one another. Greaterattention is being given to the mathematical aspects of literary study, and structural-semiotic methods of research are developing. Includingartistic phenomena in the social-intellectual process, Soviet literary study investigates the place and functions of literature within othersystems— economic, social, and ideological. This enables Soviet literary theory and criticism to overcome the one-sidedness of certainforeign schools, for example, to determine the true role of the mythological and ritual elements in classical and medieval literature. During the1960's study of the historical destiny of artistic works—the history of their recognition and the problems of their origin and typology—were setas scholarly goals. Greater attention has been directed to the points of contact and the transitions in artistic epochs, periods, and styles—forexample, ancient and Byzantine literature, medieval Latin and modern European literature, the Enlightenment and romanticism, and ancientand modern Russian literature.

Comparative study attempts to go beyond external and occasional similarities and to deal with historically conditioned artistic and, morebroadly, general cultural contacts and analogies. The study of literary links in Soviet literary theory and criticism has become a typologicalstudy of the uniformity of the literary process, which passes through relatively similar artistic stages in different countries. Textual criticismhas expanded considerably, and various types of editions of the Russian classics, including scholarly ones, have been published. Thefoundations are being laid for the comprehensive study of literature in its relation to other art forms, ideology, and science.

Questions of *partiinost'* and national character in literature and theoretical problems of socialist realism are being explored. Many books andcollections of articles criticize contemporary bourgeois methodology and revisionist, sectarian, and vulgarizing trends in Marxist literarytheory and criticism. Party decisions on ideological questions exert a considerable influence on Soviet literary studies. The 1972 resolution ofthe Central Committee of the CPSU On Literary-Artistic Criticism emphasizes the importance of criticism in the strict sense *(kritika)* and ofliterary theory and criticism *(literaturovedenie)* in the cultural life of the Soviet people today. Marxist-Leninist doctrine must be applied inthoroughly analyzing the literary process, exposing "the reactionary essence of bourgeois 'mass culture' and decadent currents" andstruggling against "all types of non--Marxist views of literature and art and revisionist aesthetic conceptions" .

7

Rhetorical Criticism

INTRODUCTION

The present book employs a diagrammatic framework that has been used in poetics ever since Plato's time. This is the division of "the good" into three main areas, of which the world of art, beauty, feeling, and taste is the central one, and is flanked by two other worlds. One is the world of social action and events, the other the world of individual thought and ideas. Reading from left to right, this threefold structure divides human faculties into will, feeling, and reason. It divides the mental constructs which these faculties produce into history, art, and science and philosophy.

It divides the ideals which form compulsions or obligations on these faculties into law, beauty, and truth. Poe gives his version of the diagram (right to left) as Pure Intellect, Taste, and the Moral Sense. "I place Taste in the middle," said Poe, "because it is just this position which in the mind it occupies." Until someone can refute this admirable explanation, we shall retain the traditional structure. True, we have hinted that there may be another way of looking at it in which the middle world is not simply one of three but a trinity containing them all. But as yet the simpler conception has by no means exhausted its usefulness for us.

Similarly, we have portrayed the poetic symbol as intermediate between event and idea, example and precept, ritual and dream, and have finally displayed it as Aristotle's *ethos*, human nature and the human situation, between and made up of *mythos* and *dianoia*, which are verbal imitations of action and thought respectively. There is however still another aspect of the same diagram. The world of social action and event, the world of time and process, has a particularly close association with the ear. The ear listens, and the ear translates what it hears into practical conduct. The world of individual thought and idea has a correspondingly close association with the eye, and nearly all our expressions for thought, from the Greek *theoria* down, are connected with visual metaphors. Further, not only does art as a whole seem to be central to events and ideas, but literature seems in a way to be central to the arts. It appeals to the ear, and so partakes of the nature of music, but music is a much more concentrated art of the ear and of the imaginative perception of time. Literature appeals to at least the inner eye, and so partakes of the nature of the plastic arts, but the plastic arts, especially painting, are much more concentrated on the eye and on the spatial world. We notice that Aristotle gives a list of six elements of poetry, three of which, *mythos*, *ethos* and *dianoia*, we have been considering. The other three, *melos*, *lexis*, and *opsis* (spectacle), deal with this second aspect of the same diagram. Considered as a verbal structure, literature presents a *lexis* which combines two other elements: *melos*, an element analogous to or otherwise connected with music, and *opsis*, which has a similar connection with the plastic arts. The word *lexis* itself may be translated "diction" when we are thinking of it as a narrative sequence of sounds caught by the ear, and as "imagery" when we are thinking of it as forming a simultaneous pattern of meaning apprehended in an act of mental "vision." This second or rhetorical aspect of literature we must now turn to examine. It is an aspect which returns us to the "literal" level of narrative and meaning, the context that Ezra Pound has in mind when he speaks of the three qualities of poetic creation as *melopoeia*, *logopoeia*, and *phanopoeia*. The terms musical and pictorial are often employed figuratively in literary criticism, and we shall attempt among other things to see how much genuine sense they make as critical terms.

The word "rhetoric" reminds us of yet another triad: the traditional division of studies based on words into a "trivium" of grammar, rhetoric, and logic. While grammar and logic have become the names of specific sciences, they also retain something of a more general connection with the narrative and significant aspects respectively of all verbal structures. As grammar may be called the art of ordering words, there is a sense — a literal sense — in which grammar and narrative are the same thing; as logic may be called the art of producing meaning, there is a sense in which logic and meaning are the same thing. The second part of this sentence is more traditional, and hence more familiar. There is no historical justification for the first part, as the art of constructing narrative ("invention," "disposition," and the like) has traditionally formed a part of rhetoric. Let us, however, in spite of history, begin with an association between narrative and grammar, grammar being understood primarily as syntax or getting words in the right (narrative) order, and between logic and meaning, logic being understood primarily as words arranged in a pattern with significance. Grammar is the linguistic aspect of a verbal structure; logic is the "sense" which is the permanent common factor in translation.

What we have been calling assertive, descriptive, or factual writing tends to be, or attempts to be, a direct union of grammar and logic. An argument cannot be logically correct unless it is verbally correct, the right words chosen and the proper syntactical relations among them established. Nor does a verbal narrative communicate anything to a reader unless it has continuous significance. In assertive writing, therefore, there seems to be little place for any such middle term as rhetoric, and in fact we often find that among philosophers, scientists, jurists, critics, historians, and theologians, rhetoric is looked upon with some distrust.

Rhetoric has from the beginning meant two things: ornamental speech and persuasive speech. These two things seem psychologically opposed to each other, as the desire to ornament is essentially disinterested, and the desire to persuade essentially the reverse. In fact ornamental rhetoric is inseparable from literature itself, or what we have called the hypothetical verbal structure which exists for its own sake. Persuasive rhetoric is applied literature, or the use of literary art to reinforce the power of argument. Ornamental rhetoric acts on its hearers statically, leading them to admire its own beauty or wit; persuasive rhetoric tries to lead them kinetically towards a course of action. One articulates emotion; the other manipulates it. And whatever we decide about the ultimate literary status of oratory, there seems little doubt that ornamental rhetoric is the *lexis* or verbal texture of poetry. Aristotle remarks, when he comes to *lexis* in the *Poetics*, that that subject belongs more properly to rhetoric. We may, then, adopt the following tentative postulate: that if the direct union of grammar and logic is characteristic of non-literary verbal structures, literature may be described as the rhetorical organization of grammar and logic. Most of the features characteristic of literary form, such as rhyme, alliteration, metre, antithetical balance, the use of exempla, are also rhetorical schemata.

The psychology of creation is not our theme, but it must happen very rarely that a writer sits down to write without any notion of what he proposes to produce. In the poet's mind, then, some kind of controlling and coordinating power, what Coleridge called the "initiative," establishes itself very early, gradually assimilates every thing to itself, and finally reveals itself to be the containing form of the work. This initiative is clearly not a unit but a complex of factors. The theme is one such factor; the sense of the unity of mood which makes certain images appropriate and others not is another. If what is produced is to be a poem in a regular metre, the metre will be a third: if not, some other integrating rhythm will be present. We remarked earlier, too, that the poet's intention to produce a poem normally includes the genre, the intention of producing a specific kind of verbal structure. The poet thus is incessantly deciding that certain things, whether they can be critically accounted for by himself or not, belong in his structure, and that what he cuts out in revising does not, though it may be good enough in itself to belong somewhere else. But as the structure is complex, so these decisions relate to a variety of poetic elements, or a group of initiatives. Of these, theme and the choice of images engaged our attention in the previous essay; genre and the integrating rhythm concern us here.

We complained in our introduction that the theory of genres was an undeveloped subject in criticism. We have the three generic terms drama, epic, and lyric, derived from the Greeks, but we use the latter two chiefly as jargon or trade slang for long and short (or shorter) poems respectively. The middle-sized poem does not even have a jargon term to describe it, and any long poem gets to be called an epic, especially if it is divided into a dozen or so parts, like Browning's *Ring and the Book*. This poem takes a dramatic structure, a triangle of jealous husband, patient wife, and chivalrous lover involved in a murder trial with courtroom and death-house scenes, and works it all out through the soliloquies of the characters. It is an astounding *tour de force*, but we can fully appreciate this only when we see it as a generic experiment in drama, a drama turned inside out, as it were. Similarly, we call Shelley's *Ode to the West Wind* a lyric, perhaps because it is a lyric; if we hesitate to call *Epipsychidion* a lyric, and have no idea what it is, we can always call it the product of an essentially lyrical genius. It is shorter than the *Iliad*, and there's an end of it.

However, the origin of the words drama, epic, and lyric suggests that the central principle of genre is simple enough. The basis of generic distinctions in literature appears to be the radical of presentation. Words may be acted in front of a spectator; they may be spoken in front of a listener; they may be sung or chanted; or they may be written for a reader. Criticism, we note resignedly in passing, has no word for the individual member of an author's audience, and the word "audience" itself does not really cover all genres, as it is slightly illogical to describe the readers of a book as an audience. The basis of generic criticism in any case is rhetorical, in the sense that the genre is determined by the conditions established between the poet and his public.

We have to speak of the radical of presentation if the distinctions of acted, spoken, and written word are to mean anything in the age of the printing press. One may print a lyric or read a novel aloud, but such incidental changes are not enough in themselves to alter the genre. For all the loving care that is rightfully expended on the printed texts of Shakespeare's plays, they are still radically acting scripts, and belong to the genre of drama. If a Romantic poet gives his poem a dramatic form, he may not expect or even want any stage representation; he may think entirely in terms of print and readers; he may even believe, like many Romantics, that the stage drama is an impure form because of the limitations it puts on individual expression. Yet the poem is still being referred back to some kind of theatre, however much of a castle in the air. A novel is written, but when Conrad employs a narrator to help him tell his story, the genre of the written word is being assimilated to that of the spoken one.

The question of how we are to classify such a novel is less important than the recognition of the fact that two different radicals of presentation exist in it. It might be thought simpler, instead of using the term radical, to say that the generic distinctions are among the ways in which literary works are *ideally* presented, whatever the actualities are. But Milton, for example, seems to have no ideal of reciter and audience in mind for *Paradise Lost*; he seems content to leave it, in practice, a poem to be read in a book. When he uses the convention of invocation, thus bringing the poem into the genre of the spoken word, the significance of the convention is to indicate what tradition his work primarily belongs to and what its closest affinities are with. The purpose of criticism by genres is not so much to classify as to clarify such traditions and affinities, thereby bringing out a large number of literary relationships that would not be noticed as long as there were no context established for them.

The genre of the spoken word and the listener is very difficult to describe in English, but part of it is what the Greeks meant by the phrase *ta epe*, poems intended to be recited, not necessarily epics of the conventional jumbo size. Such "epic" material does not have to be in metre, as the prose tale and the prose oration are important spoken forms. The difference between metre and prose is evidently not in itself a generic difference, as the example of drama shows, though it tends to become one. In this essay I use the word "*epos*" to describe works in which the radical of presentation is oral address, keeping the word epic for its customary use as the name of the form of the *Iliad*, *Odyssey*, *Aeneid*, and *Paradise Lost*. *Epos* thus takes in all literature, in verse or prose, which makes some attempt to preserve the convention of recitation and a listening audience.

The Greeks gave us the names of three of our four genres: they did not give us a word for the genre that addresses a reader through a book, and naturally we have not invented one of our own. The nearest to it is "history," but this word, in spite of *Tom Jones*, has gone outside literature, and the Latin "scripture" is too specialized in meaning. As I have to have some word, I shall make an arbitrary choice of "fiction" to describe the genre of the printed page. I know that I used this word in the first essay in a different context, but it seems better to compromise with the present confused terminology than to increase the difficulties of this book by introducing too many new terms. The analogy of the keyboard in music may illustrate the difference between fiction and other genres which for practical purposes exist in books. A book, like a keyboard, is a mechanical device for bringing an entire artistic structure under the interpretive control of a single person. But just as it is possible to distinguish genuine piano music from the piano score of an opera or symphony, so we may distinguish genuine "book literature" from books containing the reduced textual scores of recited or acted pieces.

The connection between a speaking poet and a listening audience, which may be actual in Homer or Chaucer, soon becomes increasingly theoretical, and as it does so *epos* passes insensibly into fiction. One may even suggest, not quite seriously, that the legendary figure of the blind bard, which is used so effectively by Milton, indicates that the drift towards an unseen audience sets in very early. But whenever the same material does duty for both genres, the distinction between the genres becomes immediately apparent. The chief distinction, though not a simple one of length, is involved with the fact that *epos* is episodic and fiction continuous. The novels of Dickens are, as books, fiction; as serial publications in a magazine designed for family reading, they are still fundamentally fiction, though closer to *epos*. But when Dickens began to give readings from his own works, the genre changed wholly to *epos*; the emphasis was then thrown on immediacy of effect before a visible audience.

In drama, the hypothetical or internal characters of the story confront the audience directly, hence the drama is marked by the concealment of the author from his audience. In very spectacular drama, such as we get in many movies, the author is of relatively little importance. Drama, like music, is an ensemble performance for an audience, and music and drama are most likely to flourish in a society with a strong consciousness of itself as a society, like Elizabethan England. When a society becomes individualized and competitive, like Victorian England, music and drama suffer accordingly, and the written word almost monopolizes literature. In *epos*, the author confronts his audience directly, and the hypothetical characters of his story are concealed. The author is still theoretically there when he is being represented by a rhapsode or minstrel, for the latter speaks as the poet, not as a character in the poem. In written literature both the author and his characters are concealed from the reader.

The fourth possible arrangement, the concealment of the poet's audience from the poet, is presented in the lyric. There is, as usual, no word for the audience of the lyric: what is wanted is something analogous to "chorus" which does not suggest simultaneous presence or dramatic context. The lyric is, to go back to Mill's aphorism referred to at the beginning of this book, preeminently the utterance that is overheard. The lyric poet normally pretends to be talking to himself or to someone else: a spirit of nature, a Muse (note the distinction from *epos*, where the Muse speaks through the poet), a personal friend, a lover, a god, a personified abstraction, or a natural object. The lyric is, as Stephen Dedalus says in Joyce's *Portrait*, the poet presenting the image in relation to himself: it is to *epos*, rhetorically, as prayer is to sermon. The radical of presentation in the lyric is the hypothetical form of what in religion is called the "I-Thou" relationship. The poet, so to speak, turns his back on his listeners, though he may speak for them, and though they may repeat some of his words after him.

Epos and fiction make up the central area of literature, and are flanked by the drama on one side and by the lyric on the other. Drama has a peculiarly intimate connection with ritual, and lyric with dream or vision, the individual communing with himself. We said at the beginning of this book that there is no such thing as direct address in literature, but direct address is natural communication, and literature may imitate it as it may imitate anything else in nature. In *epos*, where the poet faces his audience, we have a *mimesis* of direct address. *Epos* and fiction first take the form of scripture and myth, then of traditional tales, then of narrative and didactic poetry, including the epic proper, and of oratorical prose, then of novels and other written forms. As we progress historically through the five modes, fiction increasingly overshadows *epos*, and as it does, the mimesis of direct address changes to a mimesis of assertive writing. This in its turn, with the extremes of documentary or didactic prose, becomes actual assertion, and so passes out of literature.

The lyric is an internal mimesis of sound and imagery, and stands opposite the external mimesis, or outward representation of sound and imagery, which is drama. Both forms avoid the mimesis of direct address. The characters in a play talk to each other, and are theoretically talking to themselves in an aside or soliloquy. Even if they are conscious of an audience, they are not speaking for the poet, except in special cases like the parabasis of Old Comedy or the prologues and epilogues of the rococo theatre, where there is an actual generic change from drama to *epos*. In Bernard Shaw the comic parabasis is transferred from the middle of the play to a separate prose preface, which is a change from drama to fiction.

In *epos* some kind of comparatively regular metre tends to predominate: even oratorical prose shows many metrical features, both in its syntax and in its punctuation. In fiction prose tends to predominate, because only prose has the continuous rhythm appropriate for the continuous form of the book. Drama has no controlling rhythm peculiar to itself, but it is most closely related to *epos* in the earlier modes and to fiction in the later ones. In the lyric a rhythm which is poetic but not necessarily metrical tends to predominate. We proceed to examine each genre in turn with a view to discovering what its chief features are. As in what immediately follows we are largely concerned with diction and linguistic elements, we must limit our survey mainly to a specific language, which will be English: this means that a good deal of what we say will be true only of English, but it is hoped that the main principles can be adapted to other languages as well.

THE RHYTHM OF RECURRENCE: EPOS

The regular pulsating metre that traditionally distinguishes verse from prose tends to become the organizing rhythm in epos or extended oratorical forms. Metre is an aspect of recurrence, and the two words for recurrence, rhythm and pattern, show that recurrence is a structural principle of all art, whether temporal or spatial in its primary impact. Besides metre itself, quantity and accent (or stress) are elements in poetic recurrence, though quantity is not an element of regular recurrence in modern English, except in experiments in which the poet has to make up his own rules as he goes along. The relation of accent or stress to metre needs, perhaps, a different kind of explanation from what is usually given it.

A four-stress line seems to be inherent in the structure of the English language. It is the prevailing rhythm of the earlier poetry, though it changes its scheme from alliteration to rhyme in Middle English; it is the common rhythm of popular poetry in all periods, of ballads and of most nursery rhymes. In the ballad, the eight-six-eight-six quatrain is a continuous four-beat line, with a "rest" at the end of every other line. This principle of the rest, or a beat coming at a point of actual silence, was already established in Old English. The iambic pentameter provides a field of syncopation in which stress and metre can to some extent neutralize one an other. If we read many iambic pentameters "naturally," giving the important words the heavy accent that they do have in spoken English, the old four-stress line stands out in clear relief against its metrical background. Thus:

- To bé, or nót to be: thát is the quéstion.
- Whéther 'tis nóbler in the mínd to súffer
- The slíngs and árrows of outrágeous fórtune,
- Or táke up árms against a séa of tróubles ...
- Of mán's fírst disobédience, and the frúit
- Of that forbídden trée, whose mórtal táste
- Brought déath into the wórld and áll our wóe,
- With lóss of Éden, till one gréater Mán
- Restóre us, and regáin the blíssful séat ...

The stopped couplet of Dryden and Pope, as we should expect, has a higher percentage of five-stress lines, but any rhythmical license such as a feminine caesura is likely to bring back the old beat:

- Forgét their hátred, and consént to féar. (Waller)
- Nor héll a fúry, like a wóman scórn'd. (Congreve)
- A líttle leárning is a dángerous thíng. (Pope)

Any period of metrical uncertainty or transition will illustrate the native strength of the four-stress line. After the death of Chaucer and the change from middle to modern English, we find ourselves in the strange metrical world of Lydgate, in which we are strongly tempted to apply to Lydgate himself what the Minstrel says to Death in the Danse Macabre:

- This newe daunce / is to me so straunge
- Wonder dyverse / and passyngli contrarie
- The dredful fotynge / doth so ofte chaunge
- And the mesures / so ofte sithes varie.

But there is a dance there all the same: let us look at the preceding stanza, Death's speech to the Minstrel:

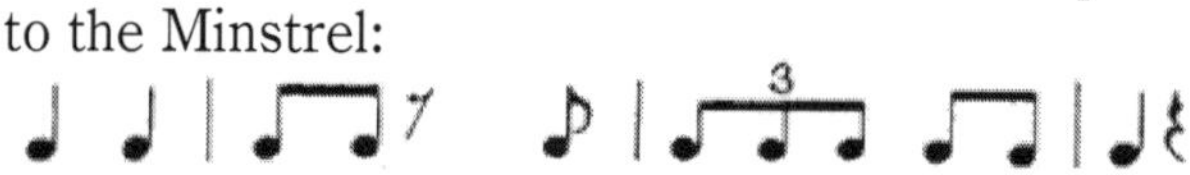

O thow minstral / that cannest so note and pype

Un-to folkes / for to do plesaunce

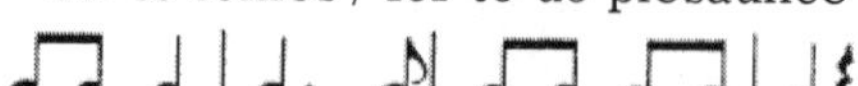

By the right honde (anoone) I shal the gripe

With these other / to go vp-on my daunce
Ther is no scape / nowther a-voydaunce
On no side / to contrarie my sentence
For yn musik / be crafte and accordaunce
Who maister is / show his science.

This stanza will give us a bad time if we try to analyze it as a pentameter stanza of Chaucer's ABC type: the last line, for instance, is not a pentameter at all. Read as a continuous four-beat line, it is fairly simple; and such a reading will bring out what the prosodic analysis could never do, the grotesque, leaping-skeleton lilt of the voice of Death ending in the measured irony of the last line. I do not claim to know the details of Lydgate's prosody, what e's he might have preferred to pronounce or elide or what foreign words he might have accented differently.

It is possible that neither Lydgate nor the fifteenth-century reader was entirely clear on all such points either; but a line with four main stresses and a variable number of syllables between the stresses is the obvious device for getting over such problems, as a good deal can be left to the individual reader's choice. In any case I am not indicating how the passage is to be read so much as how it may most easily be scanned: as with metrical scansion, every reader will make his own modification of the pattern.

The "Skeltonic" line is also usually a four-beat line: the spirited prelude to *Philip Sparowe* is a quick-march rhythm, with more rests and more accented beats coming close together than we found in Lydgate:

Placebo,
Who is there, who?
Di le xi,
Dame Margery;
Fa, re, my, my,

Wherefore and why, why?

For the sowle of Philip Sparowe,

That was late slayn at Carowe.

In short, the "new principle" on which Coleridge constructed Christabel was about as new as principles usually are in literature. It is clear too that the Finnish inspiration of Hiawatha was no more fundamentally exotic than such inspirations usually are. Hiawatha fits the four-stress pattern of English very snugly, which explains perhaps why it is one of the easiest poems in the language to parody. Meredith's *Love in the Valley*, also, is most easily scanned as a four-stress line very similar in its rhythmical make-up to Lydgate's:

Under yonder beech-tree single on the green-sward

Couched with her arms behind her golden head,

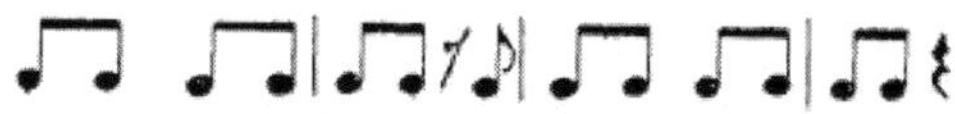

Knees and tresses folded to slip and ripple idly,

Lies my young love sleeping in the shade.

These examples have, perhaps, begun to illustrate already some thing of what the word "musical," Aristotle's *melos*, really means as a term in modern literary criticism. In the music contemporary with English poetry since Lydgate's time, we have had almost uniformly a stress accent, the stresses marking rhythmical units (measures) within which a variable number of notes is permitted. When in poetry we have a predominating stress accent and a variable number of syllables between two stresses (usually four stresses to a line, corresponding to "common time" in music), we have musical poetry, that is, poetry which resembles in its structure the music contemporary with it. We are speaking now of *epos* or extended poetry in a continuous metre: the music most closely analogous to such poetry is music in its more extended instrumental forms, in which the organizing rhythm has descended more directly from dance than from song.

This technical use of the word musical is very different from the sentimental fashion of calling any poetry musical if it sounds nice. In practice the technical and the sentimental uses are often directly opposed, as the sentimental term would be applied to, for example, Tennyson, and withdrawn from, for example, Browning. Yet if we ask the external but relevant question: Which of these two poets knew more about music, and was *a priori* more likely to be influenced by it? the answer is certainly not Tennyson. Here is a passage from Tennyson's Oenone:

O mother Ida, many-fountain'd Ida,
Dear mother Ida, harken ere I die.
I waited underneath the dawning hills,
Aloft the mountain lawn was dewy-dark,
And dewy dark aloft the mountain pine:
Beautiful Paris, evil-hearted Paris,
Leading a jet-black goat white-horn'd, white-hooved,
Came up from reedy Simois all alone.

And here is a passage from Browning's The Flight of the Duchess:

I could favour you with sundry touches
Of the paint-smutches with which the Duchess
Heightened the mellowness of her cheek's yellowness
(To get on faster) until at last her
Cheek grew to be one master-plaster
Of mucus and fucus from mere use of ceruse:
In short, she grew from scalp to udder
Just the object to make you shudder.

In the Browning passage speed is a positive factor: one has the sense of a metronome beat. Tennyson has tried to minimize the sense of movement; his passage should be read slowly and with much dwelling on the vowels. Both passages repeat sounds obtrusively, but the repetitions in Tennyson are there to slow down the advance of ideas, to compel the rhythm to return on itself, and to elaborate what is essentially a pattern of sound. In Browning the rhymes sharpen the accentuation of the beat and help to build up a cumulative rhythm. The speed and the sharp accent in Browning's poetry are musical features in it, and it is difficult to see what the words in parentheses can be except a musical direction, an English translation of *più mosso*.

Such phrases as "smooth musical flow" or "harsh unmusical diction" belong to the sentimental use of the word musical, and are perhaps derived from the fact that the word "harmony" in ordinary English, apart from music, means a stable and permanent relationship. In this figurative sense of the word harmony, music is not a sequence of harmonies at all, but a sequence of discords ending in a harmony, the only stable and permanent "harmony" in music being the final resolving tonic chord.

It is more likely to be the harsh, rugged, dissonant poem (assuming of course some technical competence in the poet) that will show in poetry the tension and the driving accented impetus of music. When we find a careful balancing of vowels and consonants and a dreamy sensuous flow of sound, we are probably dealing with an unmusical poet. Pope, Keats, and Tennyson are all unmusical. This term, I need hardly observe, is not pejorative: *The Rape of the Lock* is unmusical, just as it is a bad example of blank verse, because it is something else altogether. When we find sharp barking accents, crabbed and obscure language, mouthfuls of consonants, and long lumbering polysyllables, we are probably dealing with *melos*, or poetry which shows an analogy to music, if not an actual influence from it.

The musical diction is better fitted for the grotesque and horrible, or for invective and abuse. It is congenial to a gnarled intellectualism of the so-called "metaphysical" type. It is irregular in metre (because of the syncopation against stress), leans heavily on enjambement, and employs a long cumulative rhythm sweeping the lines up into larger rhythmical units such as the paragraph. The fact that Shakespeare shows an increasing use of *melos*as he goes on is the principle employed for dating his plays on internal evidence.

When Milton says that rhymed heroic verse is "of no true musical delight," because musical poetry must have "the sense variously drawn out from one verse into another," he is using the word musical in its technical sense. When Samuel Johnson speaks of "the old manner of continuing the sense ungracefully from verse to verse," he is speaking from his own consistently anti-musical point of view.

The Heretic's Tragedy is a musical poem; *Thyrsis* is not. *The Jolly Beggars* is; the *Ode on a Grecian Urn* is not. Pope's *Messiah* is not musical, but Smart's *Song to David*, with its pounding thematic words and the fortissimo explosion of its coda, is a musical *tour de force*.

Crashaw's hymns and Cowley's Pindarics are musical, with their fluent, variable, prevailingly four-stress lines and their relentless pushing enjambement; Herbert's stanzaic poems and Gray's Pindarics are not. Skelton, Wyatt, and Dunbar are musical; Gavin Douglas and Surrey are not. Alliterative verse is usually accentual and musical; elaborate stanza forms usually are not. The use of *melos* in poetry does not, of course, necessarily imply any technical knowledge of music on the part of the poet, but it often goes with it. Such a technically musical poem as Crashaw's *Musicks Duell* (a Baroque aria with instrumental accompaniment) is an example.

And occasionally it is at least conceivable that some exposure to music would have guided a tendency to *melos* in verse. One feels that Southey, for instance, never quite clarified his remarkable experiments in *epos* rhythm: if so, it may be instructive to set be side Milton's incisive list of the musical qualities of poetry the stammer and mumble of the preface to *Thalaba*: "I do not wish the improvisatore tune; — but something that denotes the sense of harmony, something like the accent of feeling, — like the tone which every poet necessarily gives to poetry." The conception of *melos*, too, may throw more light on what Wordsworth was trying to do in *Peter Bell* and *The Idiot Boy*. Wordsworth's remarks about metre as the source of excitement in verse apply more particularly to accent, in which the physical pulsation of the dance is present.

What metre in itself gives is rather the pleasure of seeing a relatively predictable pattern filling up with the inevitably felicitous words. Pope's "What oft was thought, but ne'er so well expressed" is a metrical conception: as we listen to his couplets, we have a sense of fulfilled expectation which is the opposite of obviousness. The greater violence in the imagery of Donne's satires is appropriate to the greater energy of a more accentually-conceived rhythm.

If we turn to the contrasting group of what we have called the unmusical poets, Spenser, Pope, Keats, Tennyson, we find slower and more resonant rhythms. Four-stress lines are much rarer in *The Faerie Queene* than in *Paradise Lost*, and the opposite tendency is marked by the recurrent Alexandrine. The practice of this group of poets is finely expressed by Johnson in his anti-musical dictum: "The musick of the English heroic line strikes the ear so faintly that it is easily lost, unless all the syllables of every line co-operate together; this co-operation can be obtained only by the preservation of every verse unmingled with another, as a distinct system of sounds." The implication is that as the only musical elements in poetry that Johnson is considering have been lost for good with the loss of pitch accent and quantity, English poetry should think in terms of sound-pattern rather than cumulative rhythm.

The relations between poetry and the visual arts are perhaps more far-fetched than those between poetry and music. Unmusical poets are often "pictorial" in a general sense: they frequently use their more meditative rhythms to build up, detail by detail, a static picture, as in the careful description of the nude Venus in *Oenone* or in the elaborate tapestry-like pageants in *The Faerie Queene*.

Where we do have something really analogous to *opsis*, however, is in the rhetorical device known as imitative harmony or onomatopoeia, as described and exemplified by Pope in the *Essay on Criticism*:

'Tis not enough no harshness gives offence,
The sound must seem an echo to the sense ...
When Ajax strives some rock's vast weight to throw,
The line too labours, and the words move slow;
Not so, when swift Camilla scours the plain,
Flies o'er th' unbending com, and skims along the main.

This device is easy to recognize, and has been remarked on ever since Aristotle, in his treatise on rhetoric, illustrated in Homer's line about the stone of Sisyphus the sound of a large stone rolling downhill:

Pope's translation renders this line "Thunders impetuous down, and smoaks along the ground," and won for once the approval of Johnson, Johnson being in general very doubtful about imitative harmony. He ridicules it in one of the *Idler* papers in the figure of Dick Minim the critic, who points out that the words bubble and trouble cause "a momentary inflation of the cheeks by the retention of the breath, which is afterwards forcibly emitted, as in the practice of blowing bubbles."

All that the ridicule really illustrates, however, is that onomatopoeia is a linguistic as well as a poetic tendency, and that the poet takes advantage of whatever his language offers as a matter of course. The English language has many excellent sound-effects, though it has lost a few: in Old English *The Wanderer* can express cold weather as a modern poem cannot:

Hreosan hrim ond snaw hagle gemenged

But because such devices are linguistic as well as literary, they are continually being recreated in colloquial speech. Colloquial speech, when good, is frequently called "picturesque" or "colourful," both words being pictorial metaphors. The narrative passages of *Huckleberry Finn* have an imitative flexibility about them that the narrative passages of *Tom Sawyer*, for instance, hardly attain to:

... Then there was a racket of ripping and tearing and smashing, and down she goes, and the front wall of the crowd begins to roll in like a wave.

The most remarkably sustained mastery of verbal opsis in English, perhaps, is exhibited in *The Faerie Queene*, which we have to read with a special kind of attention, an ability to catch visualization through sound. Thus in

The Eugh obedient to the bender's will,

the line has a number of weak syllables in the middle that makes it sag out in a bow shape. When Una goes astray the rhythm goes astray with her:

And Una wandring farre in woods and forrests ...

Part of the effect of this line is due to the weak rhyme of "forrests" against "guests." When the subject is wreckage, the rhythm is wrecked with the same kind of disappointment-rhyme:

For else my feeble vessell crazd, and crackt
Through thy strong buffets and outrageous blowes,
Cannot endure, but needs it must be wrackt
On the rough rocks, or on the sandy shallowes.

When Florimell finds her way difficult to scan, so does the reader:

Through the tops of the high trees she did descry ...

When the subject is harmony in music, we have an identical rhyme on one of the few appropriate words in the language:

To th' instruments diuine respondence meet:
The siluer sounding instruments did meet ...

When the subject is a "perillous Bridge," we have:

Streight was the passage like a ploughed ridge,
That if two met, the one mote needes fall ouer the lidge.

Renaissance readers had been put on the alert for such effects by their school training in rhetoric: a harmless looking line from Spenser's *January*, for instance, is promptly sandbagged by E. K. as "a prety Epanorthosis ... and withall a Paronomasia." The source of Pope's passage quoted above is Vida's *Art of Poetry*, which is earlier than Spenser. After Spenser the poet who showed the most consistent or persistent interest in imitative harmony was Cowley, who uses it so freely in *Davideis* as to draw a hoarse growl from Johnson that he saw no reason why a pine tree should be taller in Alexandrines than in pentameters. Some of Cowley's effects however are interesting enough, such as his use of the oracular hemistich. Here, for instance, three feet of a pentameter line are assigned to silent contemplation:

O who shall tell, who shall describe thy Throne,
Thou great Three-One?

The first line in the passage quoted from Pope ("Tis not enough no harshness gives offence") implies that a sharp discord or apparent bungle in the writing may often be interpreted as imitative decorum. Pope uses such intentional discords in the same poem when he gives horrible examples of practices he disapproves of, and Addison's discussion of the passage in *Spectator 253* shows how lively an interest such devices still aroused. Here, for example, is the way that Pope describes constipated genius:

And strains, from hard-bound brains, eight lines a year.

Spenser, naturally, employs the same device constantly. A tasteless misuse of alliteration marks a speaker (Braggadocchio) as a liar and hypocrite:

But minds of mortall men are muchell mard,
And mou'd amisse with massie mucks vnmeet regard.

and when the false Duessa tempts St. George, the grammar, rhythm, and assonance could hardly be worse: the worthy knight's ear should have warned him that all was not well:

Yet thus perforce he bids me do, or die.
Die is my dew; yet rew my wretched state
You ...

Certain imitative devices become standardized in every language, and most of them in English are too familiar to need recapitulation here: beheaded lines increase speed, trochaic rhythms suggest falling movement, and so on. The native stock of English words consists largely of monosyllables, and a monosyllable always demands a separate accent, however slight.

Hence long Latin words, if skilfully used, have the rhythmical function of lightening the metre, in contrast to the sodden unrhythmical roar that results "When ten low words oft creep in one dull line." A by-product of this latter phenomenon in English is more useful: the so-called broken-backed line with a spondee in the middle has since Old English times (when it was Sievers' type C) been most effective for suggesting the ominous and foreboding:

Thy wishes then dare not be told. (Wyatt)
Depending from on high, dreadful to sight. (Spenser)
Which tasted works knowledge of good and evil. (Milton)

Imitative harmony may of course be employed occasionally in any form of writing, but as a continuous effect it seems to adhere most naturally to *epos*in verse, where it takes the form of variants from a sustained normal pattern. Dramatists and prose writers use it very sparingly: in Shakespeare it occurs only for some definite reason, as when Lear calls to the storm on the heath in the accents of the storm itself. In lyrics its introduction has the effect of a *tour de force* which absorbs most of the interest and turns the poem into an epigram. An example is the brilliant little fourteenth-century poem *The Blacksmiths*, which uses the alliterative line to represent hammering:

Swarte smekyd smethes smateryd wyth smoke
Dryue me to deth wyth den of here dyntes ...

Recurrently in the history of rhetoric some theory of a "natural" relation between sound and sense turns up. It is unlikely that there is any such natural relation, but that there is an onomatopoeic element in language which is developed and exploited by the poet is obvious enough. It is simpler to think rather of imitative harmony as a special application of a rhetorical feature which is analogous to Classical quantity, but would be better described as "quality": the patterns of assonance made by vowels and consonants. It is not difficult to distinguish *epos* with a continuous "quality" or sound-pattern, such as*Hyperion*, from the *epos* of, say, *Red Cotton Nightcap Country*, where the sound exists primarily for the sake of the sense, and is consequently felt to be closer to prose. We have an indication that there is no consistent sound-pattern when there are two equally satisfactory versions of the same poem differing in texture, as in the Prologue to Chaucer's *Legend of Good Women*.

The main reason for the confused use of the term musical in literary criticism is that when critics think of music in poetry, they seldom think of the actual music contemporary with the poetry they are discussing, with its stress accent and dance rhythm, but of the (very largely unknown) structure of Classical music, which was presumably closer to song and to pitch accent. We have stressed imitative harmony because it illustrates the principle that while in Classical poetry sound-pattern or quantity, being an element of recurrence, is part of the *melos* of the poetry, it is part of the *opsis* in ours.

THE RHYTHM OF CONTINUITY: PROSE

In every poem we can hear at least two distinct rhythms. One is the recurring rhythm, which we have shown to be a complex of accent, metre, and sound-pattern. The other is the semantic rhythm of sense, or what is usually felt to be the prose rhythm. Exaggerating the former, in speaking poetry aloud, will produce sing-song; exaggerating the latter will produce "insanely pompous prose," to quote a remark of Bernard Shaw on the speaking of Shakespeare in his day. We have verse *epos* when the recurrent rhythm is the primary or organizing one, and prose when the semantic rhythm is primary. Literary prose results from the use within literature of the form used for discursive or assertive writing. Treatises in verse, however "unpoetical," are invariably classified as literary. The sixteenth century was a period of experiment, mainly in verse *epos* or running rhythm, to use Hopkins's term. The influence of *melos* developed blank verse; the influence of *opsis* the Spenserian stanza and

Drayton's hexameter (the fact that *Polyolbion* is a descriptive poem may account for Drayton's choice of this metre). As in all experimental periods, there were some comparative failures, such as poulterer's measure, which had a vogue and were then dropped. Prose *epos*, that is, prose which is conceived primarily as oratorical prose, reflects the cultural domination of *epos*: it is normally thought of as a subsidiary form of spoken expression, of which the highest form is verse. It is assigned to the low or at best the middle style, such metaphors as Milton's "sitting here be low in the cool element of prose" being typical. Hence any attempt to give literary dignity to prose is likely to give it some of the characteristics of verse.

Jeremy Bentham is reputed to have distinguished prose from verse by the fact that in prose all the lines run to the end of the page. Like many simple-minded observations, this has a truth that the myopia of knowledgeability is more apt to overlook. The rhythm of prose is continuous, not recurrent, and the fact is symbolized by the purely mechanical breaking of prose lines on a printed page. Of course every prose writer knows that the writing of prose is not as mechanical as the printing of it, and that it is possible for printing to injure or even spoil the rhythm of a sentence by putting an emphatic word at the end of a line instead of at the beginning of the next one, by hyphenating a strongly stressed word, and so on. But the prose writer is largely the prisoner of his luck, unless he is willing to make the kind of revolt against luck illustrated by Mallarmés *Coup des Dés*. The characteristics of Renaissance oratorical prose, with the many recurrent features in its rhythm, are often concealed by the continuous printing of typography. The antiphonal chant in which the character books are written is a good example.

He distastes religion as a sad thing,
and is six years elder for a thought of heaven.
He scorns and fears, and yet hopes for old age,
but dare not imagine it with wrinkles ...
He offers you his blood today in kindness,
and is ready to take yours tomorrow.
He does seldom anything which he wishes not to do again,
and is only wise after a misfortune ...
and is ready to take yours tomorrow.
He does seldom anything which he wishes not to do again,
and is only wise after a misfortune ...

Euphuism, again, employs every device known to the rhetoric books, including rhyme, metrical balance, and alliteration, which are usually thought of as the prerogative of verse. Ciceronian prose was based on a periodic rhythm and a balancing of clauses that was often a quasi-metrical balance. In prose works which are deliberate rhetorical exercises, such as Browne's *Urn Burial*, one can pick out recurring units of rhythm like the *clausulae* of Cicero: "handsome enclosure in glasses," "revengeful contentions of Rome," are anapestic examples. The 1611 Bible is frequently printed with each verse a separate paragraph: this is doubtless done primarily for the convenience of preachers, but it also gives a clearer idea of its prose rhythm than conventionally printed prose would do. The rhythm of some of Bacon's essays, especially the earlier and more aphoristic ones, would also emerge more clearly if each sentence were a separate paragraph.

By the seventeenth century the period of experiment in running rhythm had run its course, and a period of experiment in prose succeeded. This begins with the "Senecan amble" or Attic prose, the revolt in the direction of a natural speaking style against the formal half-metrical rhetoric of the Ciceronians. In Dryden the emancipating of prose from the domination of metre and the liberating of the distinctive semantic rhythm of prose is an accomplished fact. Thus Matthew Arnold was right in calling the period of Dryden and Pope an age of prose and reason, not because its poetry is prosaic, but because its prose is fully realized prose. One of the curious facts of literary history is that M. Jourdain's celebrated discovery in fact is a discovery, and one that a literature seems most often to make at a well advanced point in its development.

In saying that the distinctive rhythm of prose emerges more clearly from Dryden's time on, we are not, of course, saying that better prose was then written, though perhaps the reader needs no further warnings against premature value-judgements. But it becomes obvious that prose by itself is a transparent medium: it is at its purest that is, at its furthest from *epos* and other metrical influences when it is least obtrusive and presents its subject-matter like plate glass in a shop window. It goes without saying that such neutral clarity is far from dullness, as dullness is invariably opaque. Hence, while there is no literary reason why prose should not be as rhetorical as the writer pleases, rhetorical prose often becomes a disadvantage when prose is used for non-literary purposes. Something of this is expressed by the remark that it is impossible to tell the truth in Macaulay's style not that Macaulay is the best writer to attach the remark to. A highly mannered prose is not sufficiently flexible to do the purely descriptive work of prose: it continually oversimplifies and over-symmetrizes its material. Even Gibbon is not above sacrificing a necessary qualification of a fact to an antithesis. Some thing of the same principle can be seen within literature itself: in studying the euphuist romances, for example, one becomes aware of how difficult it is to get a story told in euphuist prose. Euphuism grew out of oratorical forms, and remains best adapted to harangue: the euphuist writer seizes every chance for relapsing into monologue that he can get.

Rhetorical prose, in short, is naturally best adapted to the two purposes of rhetoric, ornament and persuasion. But as these two purposes are a psychological contrast, persuasive prose is often neutralized in its effect by the very ornament that makes it delightfully persuasive. The beauty of Jeremy Taylor's devotional writing is a disinterested factor in it which has kept him in the permanent confines of literature instead of in the transient stream of kinetic persuasion. The principle involved is by no means confined to Taylor: even in the Anglo-Saxon congregation of Wulfstan there must have been a few secular-minded highbrows who were thinking less of their sins than of the preacher's mastery of alliterative rhythm:

Her syndan mannslagan ond maegslagan ond maesserbanan ond mynsterhatan, ond her syndan mansworan ond morthorwyrhtan, ond her syndan myltestran ond bearnmyrthran ond fule forlegene horingas manege, ond her syndan wiccan ond waelcyrian, ond her syndan ryperas ond reaferas ond worolstruderas, ond, hraedest is to cwethenne, mana ond misdaeda ungerim ealra,

We are concerned here with literary prose: an account of non-literary prose rhythm will be given later in the essay. A tendency to long sentences made up of short phrases and coordinate clauses, to emphatic repetition combined with a driving linear rhythm, to invective, to exhaustive catalogues, and to expressing the process or movement of thought instead of the logical word-order of achieved thought, are among the signs of prose *melos*. Rabelais is one of the greatest masters of *melos* in prose: the wonderful drinking party in the fifth chapter of the first book seems to me to be technically musical, Jannequin set to words, so to speak. In English we have Burton, who is said to have amused himself by going down to the Isis and listening to the bargemen swear. Perhaps his visits were professional, for the qualities of his style are essentially the qualities of good swearing: a swinging sense of rhythm, a love of invective and of catalogue, an unlimited vocabulary, a tendency to think in short accentual units, and an encyclopaedic knowledge of the two subjects relevant to swearing, theology and personal hygiene. All of these except the last are musical characteristics.

The prose of Milton, like his verse, is at its best full of "true musical delight," though of course of a very different kind. The enormous periodic sentences with their short barking phrases, the variations of speed within these sentences, the rhetorical accumulation of emotionally charged epithets, the roaring Beethovenish-coda perorations, are some of its features. Sterne, however, is the chief master of prose *melos* before the development of "stream of consciousness" techniques for presenting thought as a process revived it in our own day. In Proust this technique takes the form of a Wagnerian intertwining of leitmotifs. In Gertrude Stein a deliberate prolixity of language gives to the words something of the capacity for repetition that music has. But it is of course Joyce who has made the most elaborate experiments in *melos*, and the bar-room scene in Ulysses (the one called "Sirens" in the Stuart Gilbert commentary) is, if somewhat acrobatic, still good evidence that the prose techniques just discussed have an analogy to music which is not purely fanciful. The analogy is accepted in Wyndham Lewis, for example, whose *Men Without Art* is evidently intended as a manifesto in favor of *opsis*. Here and there we can discern a tendency to melos even in normally unmusical writers. When in the rhetoric of *Sartor Resartus*, for instance, we run across such a passage as "From amid these confused masses of Eulogy and Elegy, with their mad Petrarchan and Werterean ware lying madly scattered among all sorts of quite extraneous matter," we can see that some of the devices of euphuism are being used for linear accentuation instead of for parallel balance, as they would be in actual euphuism.

In prose, as in verse, the writers most frequently called musical in the sentimental sense are usually the ones most remote from actual music. The tendency to *opsis* in De Quincey, Pater, Ruskin, and Morris, to name a few at random, often includes a tendency to elaborate pictorial description and long decorative similes, but the second tendency does not define the first: we cannot judge a quality of style by choice of subject-matter. The real difference is rather in the conception of the sentence. The long sentences in the later novels of Henry James are containing sentences: all the qualifications and parentheses are fitted in to a pattern, and as one point after another is made, there emerges not a linear process of thought but a simultaneous comprehension. What is explained is turned around and viewed from all aspects, but it is completely there, so to speak, from the beginning. In Conrad, too, the dislocations in the narrative working backwards and forwards, as he put it are designed to make us shift our attention from listening to the story to looking at the central situation. His phrase "above all to make you see" contains a visual metaphor with much of its original meaning left in it. The dislocations of narrative in *Tristram Shandy* have the opposite effect: they take our attention away from looking at the external situation to listening to the process of its coming into being in the author's mind.

As prose is by itself a transparent medium, relatively few prose writers show a pronounced leaning to one side or the other. In general, when we are most conscious of a marked "style," or rhetorical idiosyncrasy of verbal structure, we are most likely to be in contact with either *melos* or *opsis*. Browne and Jeremy Taylor are as much inclined to *opsis* as Burton and Milton are to *melos*: the comment on Taylor made by a character in an O. Henry story, "Why doesn't someone write words to it?", refers to something analogous, not to music, but to a Tennysonian sound-pattern.

One may perhaps risk the generalization that the main weight of Classical influence falls on the *opsis* side, for the reason that an inflected language permits greater freedom in word order than Modern English or French, and so one tends to think of the sentence as containing all its parts at once. Even in Cicero, who is an orator, we are intensely aware of "balance," and balance implies a neutralizing of linear movement. In later Latin a new kind of linear propulsion begins to be perceptible, and one feels closer to the new Teutonic civilization with its alliterative line and its embryonic stress-accent music. Thus in Cassiodorus thematic words and alliterative accents echo and call and respond through the turgid sentences: Hinc etiam appellatam aestimamus chordam, quod facile corda moveat: ubi tenta vocum collecta est sub diversitate concordia, ut vicina chorda pulsata alteram faciat sponte contremiscere, quam nullam contigit attigisse.

THE RHYTHM OF DECORUM: DRAMA

In all literary structures we are aware of a quality that we may call the quality of a verbal personality or a speaking voice something different from direct address, though related to it. When this quality is felt to be the voice of the author himself, we call it style: *le style c'est l'homme* is a generally accepted axiom. The conception of style is based on the fact that every writer has his own rhythm, as distinctive as his handwriting, and his own imagery, ranging from a preference for certain vowels and consonants to a preoccupation with two or three archetypes. Style exists in all literature, of course, but may be seen at its purest in thematic prose: in fact it is the chief literary term applied to works of prose generally classified as non-literary. Style had its great period in late Victorian times, when the primary connection between writing and personality was a fundamental principle of criticism.

In a novel we are aware of a more complicated problem: dialogue has to speak with the voice of the internal characters, not the author, and sometimes dialogue and narrative are so far apart as to divide the book into two different languages. The suiting of style to an internal character or subject is known as decorum or appropriateness of style to content. Decorum is in general the poet's *ethical* voice, the modification of his own voice to the voice of a character or to the vocal tone demanded by subject or mood. And as style is at its purest in discursive prose, so decorum is obviously at its purest in drama, where the poet does not appear in person. Drama might be described, from our present point of view, as *epos* or fiction absorbed by decorum.

Drama is a mimesis of dialogue or conversation, and the rhetoric of conversation obviously has to be a very fluid one. It may range from a set speech to the kind of thrust and parry which is called stichomythia when its basis is metrical; and it has the double difficulty of expressing the speaker's character and speech rhythm and yet modifying them to the situation and the moods of other speakers. In Elizabethan drama the center of gravity, so to speak, is somewhere between verse *epos* and prose, so that it can move easily from one to the other depending on the requirements of decorum, which are chiefly the social rank of the character and the genre of the play. Comedy and lower ranks run to prose, and in later centuries, as *epos* gives way before fiction, comedy and prose exhibit a power of adaptation to the changed conditions that tragedy and verse *epos* conspicuously lack.

Yet even in prose comedy, where the lofty style of rhetoric demanded by ruling-class figures has largely disappeared, there still remains the technical problem of representing in prose the features that a verse drama would express by verse: such features as dignity, passion, witty imagery (probably the most important), and pathos. Prose comedy often meets such requirements by developing a mannered epigrammatic prose style, in which something of the antithetical and repetitive structure of rhetorical prose reappears. Nearly all the great writers of English comedy from Congreve to O'Casey have been Irishmen, and the rhetorical tradition survived longer in Ireland. The dramatic prose of Synge also ranks as literary mannerism, even if it does reproduce the speech rhythms of Irish peasantry. By contrast a verse rhythm like that of Browning in the nineteenth century or that of Eliot and Fry in this one seems to straddle the gap between *epos* and prose with much less effort. One wonders if there is not something to be said for Shaw's contention that it is actually easier to write a play in blank verse than in prose. The feeling of unnaturalness and strain in a good deal of modern verse drama would in that case be the result of attempting an inappropriate kind of rhetoric, one which is too far out of touch with normal conversational rhythms, in a way that Elizabethan drama, however elaborately stylized, very seldom is.

The attempt to find verse forms for conversational rhythms did not interest very many of the Romantics or Victorians. Students of English are often urged, in Romantic fashion, to use as many short words of native origin as possible, on the ground that they make one's vocabulary concrete, but a style founded on simple native words can be the most artificial of all styles. Samuel Johnson at his most bumbling is still colloquial and conversational compared to a William Morris romance. Standard educated English speech today, with its many long abstract and technical words and the heavy accent of its short ones, is a polysyllabic clatter which is much easier to fit to prose than to verse. Blake's Prophetic Books represent one of the few successful efforts to tackle conversational rhythm in verse so successful that many critics are still wondering if they are "real poetry." Blake's view that a longer line than the pentameter was needed to represent educated colloquial speech in verse may be compared with the experiments of Clough and Bridges in hexameters, which are also attempts to capture the same kind of rhythm, though at least in Clough one feels that a strict adherence to the metre gives a somewhat roller-coaster quality to the accent. In the verse rhythm of *The Cocktail Party*, which perhaps most clearly foreshadows the development of a new rhythmical center of gravity between verse and prose in modern speech, we go back to a rhythm very close to the old four-accent line. Perhaps what is taking shape here is a long six-or-seven-beat accentual line finally made practicable for spoken dialogue by being split in two.

The question of *melos* and *opsis* in drama is easily dealt with: *melos* is actual music and *opsis* visible scenery and costume.

THE RHYTHM OF ASSOCIATION: LYRIC

In the historical sequence of modes, each genre in turn seems to rise to some degree of ascendancy. Myth and romance express themselves mainly in *epos*, and in the high mimetic the rise of a new national consciousness and an increase of secular rhetoric bring the drama of the settled theatre into the foreground. The low mimetic brings fiction and an increasing use of prose, the rhythm of which finally begins to influence verse. Wordsworth's theory that apart from metre the *lexis* of poetry and of prose are identical is a low mimetic manifesto. The lyric is the genre in which the poet, like the ironic writer, turns his back on his audience. It is also the genre which most clearly shows the hypothetical core of literature, narrative and meaning in their literal aspects as word-order and word-pattern. It looks as though the lyric genre has some peculiarly close connection with the ironic mode and the literal level of meaning.

Let us take a line of poetry at random, say the beginning of Claudio's great speech in *Measure for Measure*:

Ay, but to die, and go we know not where:

We can hear of course the metrical rhythm, an iambic pentameter spoken as a four-stress line. We can hear the semantic or prose rhythm, and we hear what we may call the rhythm of decorum, the verbal representation of the horror of a man facing death. But we can also, if we listen to the line very attentively, make out still another rhythm in it, an oracular, meditative, irregular, unpredictable, and essentially discontinuous rhythm, emerging from the coincidences of the sound-pattern:

Ay:
But to die ...
and go
we know
not where ...

Just as the semantic rhythm is the initiative of prose, and as the metrical rhythm is the initiative of *epos*, so this oracular rhythm seems to be the predominating initiative of lyric. The initiative of prose normally has its center of gravity in the conscious mind: the discursive writer writes deliberately, and the literary prose writer imitates a deliberative process. In verse *epos* the choice of a metre prescribes the form of rhetorical organization: the poet develops an unconscious habitual skill in thinking in this metre, and is thereby set free to do other things, such as tell stories, expound ideas, or make the various modifications demanded by decorum. Neither of these by itself seems quite to get down to what we think of as typically the poetic creation, which is an associative rhetorical process, most of it below the threshold of consciousness, a chaos of paronomasia, sound-links, ambiguous sense-links, and memory-links very like that of the dream. Out of this the distinctively lyrical union of sound and sense emerges.

Like the dream, verbal association is subject to a censor, which (or whom) we may call the "plausibility-principle," the necessity of shaping itself into a form acceptable to the poet's and his reader's waking consciousness, and of adapting itself to the sign-meanings of assertive language well enough to be communicable to that consciousness. But associative rhythm seems to retain a connection with dream corresponding to the drama's connection with ritual. The associative rhythm, no less than the others, can be found in all writing: Yeats's typographical rearrangement of Pater which begins *The Oxford Book of Modem Verse* illustrates how it may be extracted from prose.

The most natural unit of the lyric is the discontinuous unit of the stanza, and in earlier periods most lyrics tended to be fairly regular strophic patterns, reflecting the ascendancy of *epos*. Stanzaic *epos*, such as we find in medieval romance, is usually much closer to the atmosphere of a dream world than linear *epos*. With the Romantic movement a sense that the "true voice of feeling" was unpredictable and irregular in its rhythm began to increase. Poe's*Poetic Principle* maintains that poetry is essentially oracular and discontinuous, that the poetic is the lyrical, and that verse *epos* consists really of lyrical passages stuck together with versified prose. This is a manifesto of the ironic age, as Wordsworth's preface was a low mimetic one, and announces the arrival of a third period of technical experiment in English literature, in which the object is to liberate the distinctive rhythm of lyric. The aim of "free" verse is not simply revolt against metre and *epos* conventions, but the articulation of an independent rhythm equally distinct from metre and from prose. If we do not recognize this third rhythm, we shall have no answer for the naive objection that when poetry loses regular metre it becomes prose.

The loosening of rhyme in Emily Dickinson and of stanzaic structure in Yeats are intended, not to make the metrical pattern more irregular, but to make the lyric rhythm more precise. Hopkins's term "sprung rhythm," too, has as close an affinity with lyric as running rhythm has with *epos*. Pound's theories and techniques, from his early imagism to the discontinuous pastiche of the *Cantos* (preceded by a half-century of French and English experiment in the "fragmentation" or lyricizing of *epos*) , are lyric-centered theories and techniques. The rhetorical analysis founded on ambiguity in new criticism is a lyric-centered criticism which tends, often explicitly, to extract the lyrical rhythm from all the genres. The most admired and advanced poets of the twentieth century are chiefly those who have most fully mastered the elusive, meditative, resonant, centripetal word-magic of the emancipated lyrical rhythm. In the course of this development the associative rhythm has be come more flexible, and has consequently moved from its Romantic basis in style to a new kind of subjectivized decorum.

The traditional associations of lyric are chiefly with music. The Greeks spoke of lyrics as *ta mele*, usually translated as "poems to be sung"; in the Renaissance, lyric was constantly associated with the lyre and the lute, and Poe's essay just referred to lays an emphasis on the importance of music in poetry which makes up in strength what it lacks in precision. We should remember, however, that when a poem is "sung," at least in the modern musical sense, its rhythmical organization has been taken over by music. The words of a "singable" lyric are generally neutral and conventional words, and modern song has the stress accent of music, with little if anything left of the pitch accent that marks the domination of music by poetry. We should therefore get a clearer impression of the lyric if we translated *ta mele* as "poems to be chanted," for chanting, or what Yeats called cantillation, is an emphasis on words as words. Modern poets who, like Yeats, want their poems chanted are often precisely those who are most suspicious of musical settings.

The history of music shows a recurrent tendency to develop elaborate contrapuntal structures which, in vocal music, almost annihilate the words. There has also been a recurrent tendency to reform and simplify musical structures in order to give the words more prominence. This has sometimes been the result of religious pressure, but literary influences have been at work too. We may take the madrigal, perhaps, as representing something close to a limit of the subservience of poetry to music. In the madrigal the poetic rhythm disappears as the words are tossed from voice to voice, and the imagery in the words is expressed by the devices of what is usually called programme music. We may find long passages filled up with non-sense words, or the whole collection may bear the subtitle "apt for voices or viols," indicating that the words can be dispensed with altogether. The dislike of poets for this trituration of their words can be seen in the support they gave to the seventeenth- century style of isolating the words on a single melodic line, the style which made the opera possible. This certainly brings us closer to poetry, though music still predominates in the rhythm. But the closer the composer moves towards emphasizing the verbal rhythm of the poem, the closer he comes to the chanting which is the real rhythmical basis of lyric. Henry Lawes made some experiments in this direction which won the applause of Milton, and the admiration that so many symbolistes expressed for Wagner was evidently based on the notion (if so erroneous a notion can be said to be a base) that he was also trying to identify, or at least closely associate, the rhythm of music and the rhythm of poetry.

But now that we have music on one boundary of lyric, and the purely verbal emphasis of cantillation in the center, we can see that lyric has a relation to the pictorial on the other side which is equally important. Something of this is present in the typographical appearance of a lyric on a printed page, where it is, so to speak, overseen as well as overheard. The arrangement of stanzas and indentations gives a visible pattern to a lyric which is quite distinct from *epos*, where the lines have approximately the same length, as well as of course from prose. In any case there are thousands of lyrics so intently focussed on visual imagery that they are, as we may say, set to pictures. In the emblem an actual picture appears, and the poet-painter Blake, whose engraved lyrics are in the emblem tradition, has a role in the lyric analogous to that of the poet-composers Campion and Dowland on the musical side. The movement called imagism made a great deal of the pictorial element in the lyric, and many imagistic poems could almost be described as a series of captions to invisible pictures.

In such emblems as Herbert's *The Altar* and *Easter Wings*, where the pictorial shape of the subject is suggested in the shape of the lines of the poem, we begin to approach the pictorial boundary of the lyric. The absorption of words by pictures, corresponding to the madrigal's absorption of words by music, is picture-writing, of the kind most familiar to us in comic strips, captioned cartoons, posters, and other emblematic forms. A further stage of absorption is represented by Hogarth's *Rake's Progress* and similar narrative sequences of pictures, in the scroll pictures of the Orient, or in the novels in woodcuts that occasionally appear. Pictorial arrangements of the visible basis of literature, which is alphabetical writing, have had a more fitful and sporadic existence, ranging from capitals in illuminated manuscripts to surrealist experiments in collage, and have not had much specifically literary importance. They would have had more, of course, if our writing had remained in the hieroglyphic stage, as in hieroglyphics writing and drawing are much the same art. We have previously glanced at Pound's comparison of the imagistic lyric to the Chinese ideogram.

We should expect that during the last century there would have been a good deal said about the relation of poetry to music on the one hand, and to painting on the other. In fact the attempts to bring words as near as possible to the more repetitive and emphatic rhythm of music or the more concentrated stasis of painting make up the main body of what is usually called experimental writing. It would make for clearer thinking if these developments were regarded as lateral explorations of a single phase of rhetoric, not, through a false analogy with science, as "new directions" portending a general advance of literary technique on all fronts. The reverse movement of the same progressive fallacy gives us the moral indignation that talks about "decadence." A question on which little has yet been said is the extent to which poetry may, so to speak, disappear into painting or music and come back with a different rhythm. This happened for example in the emergence of the "prosa" out of the sequence in medieval music, and it happens in a different way when a song becomes a kind of rhythmical reservoir for a number of different lyrics.

The two elements of subconscious association which form the basis for lyrical *melos* and *opsis* respectively have never been given names. We may call them, if the terms are thought dignified enough, babble and doodle. In babble, rhyme, assonance, alliteration, and puns develop out of sound-associations. The thing that gives shape to the associating is what we have been calling the rhythmical initiative, though in a free verse poem it would be rather a sense of the oscillations of rhythm within an area which gradually becomes defined as the containing form. We can see from the revisions poets make that the rhythm is usually prior, either in inspiration or in importance or both, to the selection of words to fill it up. This phenomenon is not confined to poetry: in Beethoven's notebooks, too, we often see how he knows that he wants a cadence at a certain bar before he has worked out any melodic sequence to reach it. One can see a similar evolution in children, who start with rhythmical babble and fill in the appropriate words as they go along. The process is also reflected in nursery rhymes, college yells, work songs, and the like, where rhythm is a physical pulsation close to the dance, and is often filled up with non-sense words. An obvious priority of rhythm to sense is a regular feature of popular poetry, and verse, like music, is called "light" whenever it has the rhythmical accentuation of a railway coach with a flat wheel.

When babble cannot rise into consciousness, it remains on the level of uncontrolled association. This latter is often a literary way of representing insanity, and Smart's *Jubilate Agno*, parts of which are usually considered mentally unbalanced, shows the creative process in an interesting formative stage:

For the power of some animal is predominant in every language.
For the power and spirit of a CAT is in the Greek.
For the sound of a cat is in the most useful preposition KO.T cv-
X*>
For the Mouse (Mus) prevails in the Latin.
For edi-mus, bibi-mus, vivi-mus — ore-mus ...
For two creatures the Bull and the Dog prevail in the English,
For all the words ending in ble are in the creature.
Invisi-ble, Incomprehensi-ble, ineffa-ble, A-ble ...
For there are many words under Bull ...
For Brook is under Bull. God be gracious to Lord Bolingbroke.

It is possible that similar sputters and sparks of the fusing intellect take place in all poetic thinking. The puns in this passage impress the reader as both outrageous and humorous, which is consistent with Freud's view of wit as the escape of impulse from the control of the censor. In creation the impulse is the creative energy itself, and the censor is what we have called the plausibility-principle. Paronomasia is one of the essential elements of verbal creation, but a pun introduced into a conversation turns its back on the sense of the conversation and sets up a self-contained verbal sound-sense pattern in its place.

There is a perilous balance in paronomasia between verbal wit and hypnotic incantation. In Poe's line "the viol, the violet and the vine," we have a fusion of two opposed qualities. Wit makes us laugh, and is addressed to the awakened intelligence; incantation by itself is humorlessly impressive. Wit detaches the reader; the oracle absorbs him. In dream-poems like Arthur Benson's *The Phoenix*, or in poems intended to represent dreaming or drowsy states, like the medieval *Pearl* and many passages in Spenser and Tennyson, we notice a similar insistence on hypnotically recurrent sound- patterns. If we were to laugh at the wit in such a line as Poe's, we should break the spell of his poem, yet the line is witty, just as *Finnegan's Wake* is a very funny book, although it never leaves the oracular solemnity of the dream world. In the latter, of course, the researches of Freud and Jung into the mechanisms of both dream and wit have been extensively drawn upon. There may well be buried in it some such word as "vinolent," intended to express everything in Poe's line at once. In fiction the associative process ordinarily shows itself chiefly in the names the author invents for his characters. Thus "Lilliputian" and "Ebenezer Scrooge" are associative names for midgets and misers respectively, because one suggests "little" and "puny" and the other "squeeze," "screw" and perhaps "geezer." Spenser says that a character of his has been named Malfont:

Eyther for th' euill, which he did therein,
Or that he likened was to a welhed,

Which implies that the second syllable of his name is to be derived both from *fons* and from *facere*. We may call this kind of associative process poetic etymology, and we shall say more about it later. The characteristics of babble are again present in doggerel, which is also a creative process left unfinished through lack of skill or patience, though the psychological conditions are of the opposite kind from those of *Jubilate Agno*. Doggerel is not necessarily stupid poetry; it is poetry that begins in the conscious mind and has never gone through the associative process.

It has a prose initiative, but tries to make itself associative by an act of will, and it reveals the same difficulties that great poetry has overcome at a subconscious level. We can see in doggerel how words are dragged in because they rhyme or scan, how ideas are dragged in because they are suggested by a rhyme-word, and so on. Deliberate doggerel, as we have it in Hudibras or German knittehers, can be a source of brilliant rhetorical satire, and one which involves a kind of parody of poetic creation itself, just as malapropism is a parody of poetic etymology. The difficulties in the way of giving prose itself something of the associative concentration of poetry are enormous, and not many prose writers, apart from Flaubert and Joyce, have consistently and resolutely faced them.

The first rough sketches of verbal design ("doodle") in the creative process are hardly separable from associative babble. Phrases are scribbled in notebooks to be used later; a first stanza may suddenly "come" and then other stanzas of the same shape have to be designed to go with it, and all the ingenuity that Freud has traced in the dream has to be employed in putting words into patterns. The elaborateness of conventional forms — the sonnet and its less versatile congeners the ballade, villanelle, sestina, and the like, together with all the other conventions that the individual lyric poet invents for himself — indicates how far removed the lyrical initiative really is from whatever a *cri de coeur* is supposed to be. Poe's essay on his own *The Raven* is a perfectly accurate account of what he did in that poem, whether he did it on the conscious mental level that the essay suggests or not, and this essay, like The *Poetic Principle*, anticipates the critical techniques of a new mode.

We may note that although of course lyrics in all ages are addressed to the ear, the rise of fiction and the printing press develops an increasing tendency to address the ear through the eye. The visual patterns of E. E. Cummings are obvious examples, but do not by any means stand alone. A poem of Marianne Moore's, *Camellia Sabina*, employs an eight-line stanza in which the rhyming words are at the end of the first line, at the end of the eighth line, and at the third syllable of the seventh line. I doubt if the most attentive listener could pick this last rhyme up merely from hearing the poem read aloud: one sees it first on the page, and then translates the visual structural pattern to the ear.

We are now in a position to find more acceptable words for babble and doodle, the radicals of lyrical *melos* and *opsis* respectively. The radical of *melos* is charm: the hypnotic incantation that, through its pulsing dance rhythm, appeals to involuntary physical response, and is hence not far from the sense of magic, or physically compelling power. The etymological descent of charm from *carmen*, song, may be noted. Actual charms have a quality that is imitated in popular literature by work songs of various kinds, especially lullabies, where the drowsy sleep-inducing repetition shows the underlying oracular or dream pattern very clearly. Invective or flyting, the literary imitation of the spell-binding curse, uses similar incantatory devices for opposite reasons, as in Dunbar's *Flyting with Kennedy*:

Mauch mutton, bytbuttoun, peilit gluttoun, air to Hilhous;
Rank beggar, ostir dregar, foule fleggar in the flet;
Chittirlilling, ruch rilling, like schilling in the milhous;
Baird rehator, theif of natour, fals tratour, feyindis gett ...

From here the line of descent is easy to the *melos* of physical absorption in sound and rhythm, the pounding movement and clashing noise which the heavy accentuation of English makes possible. Lindsay's *The Congo* and *Sweeney Agonistes* are modern examples of a tendency to ragtime in English poetry that can be traced back through Poe's *Bells* and Dryden's *Alexander's Feast* to Skelton and to Dunbar's *Ane Ballat of our Lady*. A more refined aspect of *melos* is exhibited in lyrics which combine accentual repetition with variations in speed. Thus Wyatt's sonnet:

I abide and abide and better abide,
And, after the olde proverbe, the happie daye:
And ever my ladye to me dothe saye,
"Let me alone and I will provyde."
I abide and abide and tarrye the tyde
And with abiding spede well ye maye:
Thus do I abide I wott allwaye,
Nother obtayning nor yet denied.
Aye me! this long abidyng
Semithe to me as who sayethe
A prolonging of a dieng dethe,

Or a refusing of a desyred thing.
Moche ware it bettre for to be playne,
Then to saye abide and yet shall not obtayne.

This lovely sonnet is intensely musical in its conception: there is the repeated clang of "abide" and the musical, though poetically very audacious, sequential repetition of the first line in the fifth. Then as hope follows expectancy, doubt hope, and despair doubt, the lively rhythm gradually slows down and collapses. On the other hand, Skelton, like Scarlatti after him, gets fidgety in a slow rhythm and is more inclined to speed up. Here is an *accelerando* in a rhyme royal stanza from *The Garland of Laurell*:

That long tyme blew a full tymorous blaste,
Like to the Boriall wyndes, whan they blowe,
That towres and tounes and trees downe cast,
Drove clouds together like dryftes of snowe;
The dredful dinne drove all the route on a row;
Som trembled, som girned, som gasped, som gased,
As people half pevissh or men that were mased.

In the same poem there is a curious coincidental link with music: the verses to Margery Wentworth, Margaret Hussey, and Gertrude Statham are miniature musical rondos of the *abaca* type.

We have several times noticed the close relation between the visual and the conceptual in poetry, and the radical of *opsis* in the lyric is *riddle*, which is characteristically a fusion of sensation and reflection, the use of an object of sense experience to stimulate a mental activity in connection with it. Riddle was originally the cognate object of read, and the riddle seems intimately involved with the whole process of reducing language to visible form, a process which runs through such by-forms of riddle as hieroglyphic and ideogram. The actual riddle-poems of Old English include some of its finest lyrics, and belong to a culture in which such a phrase as "curiously inwrought" is a favorite aesthetic judgement. Just as the charm is not far from a sense of magical compulsion, so the curiously wrought object, whether sword-hilt or illuminated manuscript, is not far from a sense of enchantment or magical imprisonment. Closely parallel to the riddle in Old English is the figure of speech known as the kenning or oblique description which calls the body the bone-house and the sea the whale-road.

In all ages of poetry the fusion of the concrete and the abstract, the spatial and the conceptual aspects of *dianoia*, has been a central feature of poetic imagery in every genre, and the kenning has had a long line of descent. In the fifteenth century we have "aureate diction," the use of abstract terms in poetry, then thought of as "colours" of rhetoric. When such words were new and the ideas represented by them exciting, aureate diction must have sounded far less dull and bumbling than it generally does to us, and have had much more of the sense of intellectual precision that we feel in such phrases as Eliot's "piaculative pence" or Auden's "cerebrotonic Cato." The seventeenth century gave us the conceit or intellectualized image of "metaphysical" poetry, typically Baroque in its ability to express an exuberant sense of design combined with a witty and paradoxical sense of the stress and tension underlying the design. The eighteenth century showed its respect for the categorizing power of abstract thought in its poetic diction, in which fish appear as the finny tribe. In the low mimetic period a growing prejudice against convention made poets less aware of the conventional phrases they used, but the technical problems of poetical imagery did not thereby disappear, nor did conventional figures of speech.

Two of these connected with the matter under discussion, the fusion of the concrete with the abstract, may be noted. An abstract noun in the possessive case followed by an adjective and a concrete noun ("death's dateless night" is a Shakespearean example) is a nineteenth-century favorite. In J. R. Lowell's Harvard Commemoration Ode of 1865 this figure is employed nineteen times, "life's best oil/' "Oblivion's subtle wrong" and "Fortune's fickle moon" being three examples. In the twentieth century it was succeeded in favor by another phrase of "the adjective noun of noun" type, in which the first noun is usually concrete and the second abstract. Thus: "the pale dawn of longing," "the broken collar-bone of silence," "the massive eyelids of time," "the crimson tree of love." I have made these up myself, and they are free to any poet who wants them, but on examining a volume of twentieth-century lyrics I find, counting all the variants, thirty-eight phrases of this type in the first five poems.

The fusion of the concrete and abstract is a special case, though a very important one, of a general principle that the technical development of the last century has exposed to critical view. All poetic imagery seems to be founded on metaphor, but in the lyric, where the associative process is strongest and the ready-made descriptive phrases of ordinary prose furthest away, the unexpected or violent metaphor that is called catachresis has a peculiar importance. Much more frequently than any other genre does the lyric depend for its main effect on the fresh or surprising image, a fact which often gives rise to the illusion that such imagery is radically new or un conventional. From Nashe's "Brightness falls from the air" to Dylan Thomas's "A grief ago," the emotional crux of the lyric has over and over again tended to be this "sudden glory" of fused metaphor.

SPECIFIC FORMS OF DRAMA

We have now to see whether this expansion of perspective, which enables us to consider the relation of the lexis or verbal pattern to music and spectacle, gives us any new light on the traditional classifications within the genres. The division of dramas into tragedies and comedies, for instance, is a conception based entirely on verbal drama, and does not include or account for types of drama, such as the opera or masque, in which music and scenery have a more organic place. Yet verbal drama, whether tragic or comic, has clearly developed a long way from the primitive idea of drama, which is to present a powerful sensational focus for a community, The scriptural plays of the Middle Ages are primitive in this sense: they present to the audience a myth already familiar to and significant for that audience, and they are designed to remind the audience of their communal possession of this myth.

The scriptural play is a form of a spectacular dramatic genre which we may provisionally call a "myth-play." It is a somewhat negative and receptive form, and takes on the mood of the myth it represents. The crucifixion play in the Towneley cycle is tragic because the Crucifixion is; but it is not a tragedy in the sense that Othello is a tragedy. It does not, that is, make a tragic point; it simply presents the story because it is familiar and significant. It would be non-sense to apply such tragic conceptions as hybris to the figure of Christ in that play, and while pity and terror are raised, they remain attached to the subject, and there is no catharsis of them. The characteristic mood and resolution of the myth-play are pensive, and pensiveness, in this context, implies a continuing imaginative subjection to the story. The myth-play emphasizes dramatically the symbol of spiritual and corporeal communion. The scriptural plays themselves were associated with the festival of Corpus Christi, and Calderon's religious plays are explicitly autos sacramentdes or Eucharist plays. The appeal of the myth-play is a curious mixture of the popular and the esoteric; it is popular for its immediate audience, but those outside its circle have to make a conscious effort to appreciate it. In a controversial atmosphere it disappears, as it cannot deal with controversial issues unless it selects its audience. In view of the ambiguities attaching to the word myth, we shall speak of this genre as the auto.

When there is no clear-cut distinction between gods and heroes in a society's mythology, or between the ideals of the nobility and the priesthood, the auto may present a legend which is secular and sacred at once. An example is the No drama of Japan, which with its unification of chivalric and otherworldly symbols and its dreamy un-tragic, un-comic mood so strongly attracted Yeats. It is interesting to see how Yeats, both in his theory of the anima mundi and in his desire to get his play as physically close to the audience as possible, reverts to the archaic idea of corporeal communion. In Greek drama, too, there is no sharp boundary line between the divine and the heroic protagonist. But in Christian societies we can see glimpses of a secular auto, a romantic drama presenting the exploits of a hero, which is closely related to tragedy, the end of a hero's exploit being eventually his death, but which in itself is neither tragic nor comic, being primarily spectacular.

Tamburlaine is such a play: there the relation between the hero's hybris and his death is more casual than causal. This genre has had varying luck: more in Spain, for instance, than in France, where the establishing of tragedy was part of an intellectual revolution. The two attempts in France to move tragedy back towards heroic romance, Le Cid and Hernani, each precipitated a big row.

In Germany, on the other hand, it is clear that the actual genre of many plays by Goethe and Schiller is the heroic romance, however much affected they have been by the prestige of tragedy. In Wagner, who expands the heroic form all the way back to a sacramental drama of gods, the symbol of communion again occupies a conspicuous place, negatively in Tristan, positively in Parsifal. In pro portion as it moves closer to tragedy and further from the sacred auto, drama tends to make less use of music. If we look at the earliest extant play of Aeschylus, The Suppliants, we can see that close behind it is a predominantly musical structure of which the modern counterpart would normally be the oratorio it is perhaps possible to describe Wagner's operas as fermented oratorios.

In Renaissance England the audience was too bourgeois for a chivalric drama to get firmly established, and the Elizabethan secular auto eventually became the history-play. With the history- play we move from spectacle to a more purely verbal drama, and the symbols of communion become much attenuated, although they are still there. The central theme of Elizabethan history is the unifying of the nation and the binding of the audience into the myth as the inheritors of that unity, set over against the disasters of civil war and weak leadership. One may even recognize a secular Eucharist symbol in the red and white rose, just as one may recognize in the plays that end by pointing to Elizabeth, like Peek's Arraignment of Paris, a secular counterpart of a mystery play of the Virgin. But the emphasis and characteristic resolution of the history play are in terms of continuity and the closing up both of tragic catastrophe and (as in the case of Falstaff) of the comic festival. One may compare Shaw's "chronicle play" of Saint Joan, where the end of the play is a tragedy, followed by an epilogue in which the rejection of Joan is, like the rejection of Falstaff, historical, suggesting continuity rather than a rounded finish.

The history merges so gradually into tragedy that we often can not be sure when communion has turned into catharsis. Richard II and Richard III are tragedies insofar as they resolve on those defeated kings; they are histories insofar as they resolve on Boling- broke and Richmond, and the most one can say is that they lean towards history. Hamlet and Macbeth lean towards tragedy, but Fortinbras and Malcolm, the continuing characters, indicate the historical element in the tragic resolution. There seems to be a far less direct connection between history and comedy: the comic scenes in the histories are, so to speak, subversive. Henry V ends in triumph and marriage, but an action that kills Falstaff, hangs Bardolph and debases Pistol is not related to comedy in the way that Richard II is related to tragedy.

We are here concerned only with tragedy as a species of drama. Tragic drama derives from the auto its central heroic figure, but the association of heroism with downfall is due to the simultaneous presence of irony. The nearer the tragedy is to auto, the more closely associated the hero is with divinity;

the nearer to irony, the more human the hero is, and the more the catastrophe appears to be a social rather than a cosmological event. Elizabethan tragedy shows a historical development from Marlowe, who presents his heroes more or less as demigods moving in a kind of social ether, to Webster, whose tragedies are almost clinical analyses of a sick society. Greek tragedy never broke completely from the auto, and so never developed a social form, though there are tendencies to it in Euripides. But whatever the proportions of heroism and irony, tragedy shows itself to be primarily a vision of the supremacy of the event or mythos. The response to tragedy is "this must be," or, perhaps more accurately, "this does happen": the event is primary, the explanation of it secondary and variable.

As tragedy moves over towards irony, the sense of inevitable event begins to fade out, and the sources of catastrophe come into view. In irony catastrophe is either arbitrary and meaningless, the impact of an unconscious (or, in the pathetic fallacy, malignant) world on conscious man, or the result of more or less definable social and psychological forces. Tragedy's "this must be" becomes irony's "this at least is," a concentration on foreground facts and a rejection of mythical superstructures. Thus the ironic drama is a vision of what in theology is called the fallen world, of simple humanity, man as natural man and in conflict with both human and non-human nature. In nineteenth-century drama the tragic vision is often identical with the ironic one, hence nineteenth-century tragedies tend to be either Schicksal dramas dealing with the arbitrary ironies of fate, or (clearly the more rewarding form) studies of the frustrating and smothering of human activity by the combined pressure of a reactionary society without and a disorganized soul within. Such irony is difficult to sustain in the theatre because it tends towards a stasis of action. In those parts of Chekhov, notably the last act of The Three Sisters, where the characters one by one withdraw from each other into their subjective prison-cells, we are coming about as close to pure irony as the stage can get.

The ironic play passes through a dead center of complete realism, a pure mime representing human life without comment and with out imposing any sort of dramatic form beyond what is required for simple exhibition. This idolatrous form of mimesis is rare, but the thin line of its tradition can be traced from Classical mime- writers like Herodas to their tranche-de-vie descendants in recent times. The mime is somewhat commoner as an individual performance, and, outside the theatre, the Browning monodrama is a logical development of the isolating and soliloquizing tendencies of ironic conflict. In the theatre we usually find that the spectacle of "all too human" life is either oppressive or ridiculous, and that it tends to pass directly from one to the other. Irony, then, as it moves away from tragedy, begins to merge into comedy.

Ironic comedy presents us of course with "the way of the world," but as soon as we find sympathetic or even neutral characters in a comedy, we move into the more familiar comic area where we have a group of humors outwitted by the opposing group. Just as tragedy is a vision of the supremacy of mythos or thing done, and just as irony is a vision of ethos, or character individualized against environment, so comedy is a vision of dianoia, a significance which is ultimately social significance, the establishing of a desirable society. As an imitation of life, drama is, in terms of mythos, conflict; in terms of ethos, a representative image; in terms of dianoia, the final harmonic chord revealing the tonality under the narrative movement, it is community.

The further comedy moves from irony, the more it becomes what we here call ideal comedy, the vision not of the way of the world, but of what you will, life as you like it. Shakespeare's main interest is in getting away from the son-father conflict of ironic comedy towards a vision of a serene community, a vision most prominent in The Tempest. Here the action is polarized around a younger and an older man working in harmony together, a lover and a benevolent teacher.

The next step brings us to the extreme limit of social comedy, the symposium, the structure of which is, as we should expect, clearest in Plato, whose Socrates is both teacher and lover, and whose vision moves towards an integration of society in a form like that of the symposium itself, the dialectic festivity which, as is explained in the opening of the Laws, is the controlling force that holds society together. It is easy to see that Plato's dialogue form is dramatic and has affinities with comedy and mime; and while there is much in Plato's thought that contradicts the spirit of comedy as we have outlined it, it is significant that he contradicts it directly, tries to kidnap it, so to speak. It seems almost a rule that the more he does this, the further he moves into pure exposition or dictatorial monologue and away from drama. The most dramatic of his dialogues, such as Euthydemus, are regularly the most in decisive in philosophical "position." In our own day Bernard Shaw has tried hard to keep the symposium in the theatre.

His early manifesto, The Quintessence of Ibsenism, states that a play should be an intelligent discussion of a serious problem, and in his preface to Getting Married he re marks approvingly on the fact that it observes the unities of time and place. For comedy of Shaw's type tends to a symposium form which occupies the same amount of time in its action that the audience consumes in watching it. However, Shaw discovered in practice that what emerges from the theatrical symposium is not a dialectic that compels to a course of action or thought, but one that emancipates from formulated principles of conduct. The shape of such a comedy is very clear in the bright little sketch In Good King Charles's Golden Days, where even the most highly developed human types, the saintly Fox and the philosophical Newton, are shown to be comic humors by the mere presence of other types of people. Yet the central symposium figure of the haranguing lover bulks formidably in Man and Superman, and even the renunciation of love for mathematics at the end of Back to Methusaleh is consistent with the symposium pirit.

The view of poetry which sees it as intermediate between history and philosophy, its images combining the temporal events of the one with the timeless ideas of the other, seems to be still involved in this exposition of dramatic forms. We can now see a mimetic or verbal drama stretching from the history-play to the philosophy-play (the act-play and the scene-play) , with the mime, the pure image, halfway between. These three are specialized forms, cardinal points of drama rather than generic areas. But the whole mimetic area is only a part, a semicircle, let us say, of all drama. In the misty and unexplored region of the other semicircle of spectacular drama we have identified a quadrant that we have called the auto, and we have now to chart the fourth quadrant that lies between the auto and comedy, and establish the fourth cardinal point where it meets the auto again. When we think of the clutter of forms that belong here, we are strongly tempted to call our fourth area "miscellaneous" and let it go; but it is precisely here that new generic criticism is needed.

The further comedy moves from irony, and the more it rejoices in the free movement of its happy society, the more readily it takes to music and dancing. As music and scenery increase in importance, the ideal comedy crosses the boundary line of spectacular drama and becomes the masque. In Shakespeare's ideal comedies, especially A Midsummer Night's Dream and The Tempest, the close affinity with the masque is not hard to see. The masque or at least the kind of masque that is nearest to comedy, and which we shall here call the ideal masque is still in the area of dianoia: it is usually a compliment to the audience, or an important member of it, and leads up to an idealization of the society represented by that audience. Its plots and characters are fairly stock, as they exist only in relation to the significance of the occasion.

It thus differs from comedy in its more intimate attitude to the audience: there is more insistence on the connection between the audience and the community on the stage. The members of a masque are ordinarily disguised members of the audience, and there is a final gesture of surrender when the actors unmask and join the audience in a dance. The ideal masque is in fact a myth-play like the auto, to which it is related much as comedy is to tragedy. It is designed to emphasize, not the ideals to be achieved by discipline or' faith, but ideals which are desired or considered to be already possessed. Its settings are seldom remote from magic and fairyland, from Arcadias and visions of earthly Paradise. It uses gods freely, like the auto, but possessively, and without imaginative subjection. In Western drama, from the Renaissance to the end of the eighteenth century, masque and ideal comedy make great use of Classical mythology, which the audience is not obliged to accept as "true."

The rather limited masque throws some light on the structure and characteristics of its two far more important and versatile neighbors. For the masque is flanked on one side by the musically organized drama which we call opera, and on the other by a scenically organized drama, which has now settled in the movie. Puppet-plays and the vast Chinese romances where, as in the movie, the audience enters and leaves unpredictably, are examples of pre-camera scenic masques. Both opera and movie are, like the masque, proverbial for lavish display, and part of the reason for it in the movie is that many movies are actually bourgeois myth-plays, as half a dozen critics suddenly and almost simultaneously discovered a few years ago. The predominance of the private life of the actor in the imaginations of many moviegoers may perhaps have some analogy with the consciously assumed disguise of the masque.

Opera and movie possess, unlike the masque, the power of producing spectacular imitations of mimetic drama. The opera can only do this by simplifying its musical organization, otherwise its dramatic structure will be blurred by the distortion of acting which the highly repetitive structure of music makes necessary. The movie similarly must simplify its spectacle. In proportion as it follows its natural bent for scenic organization, the movie reveals its affinities with other forms of scenic masque: with the puppet-play in Chaplin and others, with the commedia deir arte in recent Italian films, with the ballet and pantomime in musical comedies. When the movie succeeds in imitating a mimetic drama, the distinction between the two forms is not worth making, but the generic difference shows itself in other ways. Mimetic drama works towards an end which illuminates, by being logically connected with, the beginning: hence the parabola shape of the typical five-act mimetic structure, and hence the ideological quality in drama expressed by the term discovery. Spectacular drama, on the other hand, is by nature processional, and tends to episodic and piecemeal discovery, as we can see in all forms of pure spectacle, from the circus parade to the revue. In the auto too, on the other side of spectacular drama, the same processional structure appears in the long continued stories of Shakespearean history and scriptural pageant. In the rotating performance and casual attendance of the movie, and the sequence of arias forcibly linked to dramatic structure by recitative in the opera, one can see the strong native tendency to linear movement in spectacular forms. In Shakespeare's first experimental romance, Pericles, the movement towards processional structure, a sequence of scenes "dispersedly in various countries/ ' is very clear.

The essential feature of the ideal masque is the exaltation of the audience, who form the goal of its procession. In the auto, drama is at its most objective; the audience's part is to accept the story without judgement. In tragedy there is judgement, but the source of the tragic discovery is on the other side of the stage; and what ever it is, it is stronger than the audience. In the ironic play, audience and drama confront each other directly; in the comedy the source of the discovery has moved across to the audience itself. The ideal masque places the audience in a position of superiority to discovery. The verbal action of Figaro is comic and that of Don Giovanni tragic; but in both cases the audience is exalted by the music above the reach of tragedy and comedy, and, though as profoundly moved as ever, isn't emotionally involved with the discovery of plot or characters. It looks at the downfall of Don Juan as spectacular entertainment, much as the gods are supposed to look at the downfall of Ajax or Darius. The same sense of viewing the dramatic mimesis through a haze of spectacular exhilaration is also of central importance in the movie, as it is even more obviously in the puppet-play from which the movie is chiefly descended. We move from ironic to ideal comedy through the symposium, and we note that at the conclusion of Plato's Symposium the prophecy is made that the same poet should be able to write both tragedy and comedy, though the ones who have done so most successfully are those who, like Shakespeare and Mozart, have had a strong interest in spectacular forms.

For our next step we must return to the masque proper. The further comedy moves from irony, the less social power is allowed to the humors. In the masque, where the ideal society is still more in the ascendant, the humors become degraded into the uncouth figures of the Jonsonian antimasque, who are said to be descended from a dramatic form far older than the rest of the masque. Farce, being a non-mimetic form of comedy, has a natural place in the masque, though in the ideal masque its natural place is that of a rigorously controlled interlude. In The Tempest, a comedy so pro found that it seems to draw the whole masque into itself, Stephano and Trinculo are comic humors and Caliban an antimasque figure, and the group shows the transition very clearly. The main theme of the masque involves gods, fairies, and personifications of virtues; the figures of the antimasque thus tend to become demonic, and dramatic characterization begins to split into an antithesis of virtue and vice, god and devil, fairy and monster. The tension between them partly accounts for the importance of the theme of magic in the masque. At the comic end this magic is held by the benevolent side, as in The Tempest; but as we move further away from comedy, the conflict becomes increasingly serious, and the anti- masque figures less ridiculous and more sinister, possessed in their turn of powers of enchantment. This is the stage represented by Comus, which is very close to the open conflict of good and evil in the morality play. With the morality play we pass into another area of masque which we shall here call the archetypal masque, the prevailing form of most twentieth-century highbrow drama, at least in continental Europe, as well as of many experimental operas and unpopular movies.

The ideal masque tends to individualize its audience by pointing to the central member of it: even the movie audience, sitting in the dark in small units (usually of two) , is a relatively individualized one. A growing sense of loneliness is noticeable as we move away from comedy. The archetypal masque, like all forms of spectacular drama, tends to detach its settings from time and space, but in stead of the Arcadias of the ideal masque, we find ourselves frequently in a sinister limbo, like the threshold of death in Everyman, the sealed underworld crypts of Maeterlinck, or the nightmares of the future in expressionist plays. As we get nearer the rationale of the form, we see that the auto symbol of communion in one body is reappearing, but in a psychological and subjective form, and with out gods. The action of the archetypal masque takes place in a world of human types, which at its most concentrated becomes the interior of the human mind. This is explicit even in the old moralities, like Mankynd and The Castell of Perseveraunce, and at least implicit in a good deal of Maeterlinck, Pirandello, Andreyev, and Strindberg.

Naturally, with such a setting, characterization has to break down into elements and fragments of personality. This is why I call the form the archetypal masque, the word archetype being in this con text used in Jung's sense of an aspect of the personality capable of dramatic projection. Jung's persona and anima and counsellor and shadow throw a great deal of light on the characterization of modern allegorical, psychic, and expressionist dramas, with their circus barkers and wraith-like females and inscrutable sages and obsessed demons. The abstract entities of the morality play and the stock types of the commedia del? arte (this latter representing one of the primitive roots of the genre) are similar constructions.

A sense of confusion and fear accompanies the sense of loneliness: Maeterlinck's early plays are almost dedicated to fear, and the constant undermining of the distinction between illusion and reality, as mental projections become physical bodies and vice versa, splits the action up into a kaleidoscopic chaos of reflecting mirrors. The mob scenes of German expressionist plays and the mechanical fantasies of the Capeks show the same disintegration at work in a social context. From the generic point of view, one of the most interesting archetypal plays is Andreyev's powerful The Black Maskers, in which its author saw reflected not only the destruction of an individual's nobile castello, which is its explicit theme, but the whole social collapse of modern Russia. This play distinguishes two groups of dissociative elements of personality, one group connected with self-accusation and the other with the death-wish, and it exhibits the human soul as a castle possessed by a legion of demons. It is evident that the further the archetypal masque gets from the ideal masque, the more clearly it reveals itself as the emancipated antimasque, a revel of satyrs who have got out of control. The progress of sophisticated drama appears to be towards an anagnorisis or recognition of the most primitive of all dramatic forms.

At the far end of the archetypal masque, where it joins the auto, we reach the point indicated by Nietzsche as the point of the birth of tragedy, where the revel of satyrs impinges on the appearance of a commanding god, and Dionysos is brought into line with Apollo. We may call this fourth cardinal point of drama the epiphany, the dramatic apocalypse or separation of the divine and the demonic, a point directly opposite the mime, which presents the simply human mixture. This point is the dramatic form of the point of epiphany, most familiar as the point at which the Book of Job, after describing a complete circuit from tragedy through symposium, finally ends. Here the two monsters behemoth and leviathan replace the more frequent demonic animals. The Classical critics, from Aristotle to Horace, were puzzled to understand why a disorganized ribald farce like the satyr-play should be the source of tragedy, though they were clear that it was. In medieval drama, where the progression through sacred and heroic auto to tragedy is so much less foreshortened, the development is plainer. The most clearly epiphanic form of scriptural drama is the Harrowing of Hell play, which depicts the triumph of a divine redeemer over demonic resistance. The devils of that play are the Christian forms of figures very like the Greek satyrs, and dramatic groups generically very close to the satyrs are never far from any scriptural play that deals directly with Christ, whether tamed and awed as in the Secunda Pastorum, or triumphantly villainous, as in the crucifixion and Herod plays. And just as Greek tragedy retained and developed the satyr-play, so Elizabethan tragedy retains a satyric counterpoint in its clown scenes and the farcical under plots of Faustus and many later tragedies.

The same element pro vides those superb episodes of the porter in Macbeth, the grave-diggers in Hamlet, and the serpent-bearer in Antony and Cleopatra, which so baffled Classically-minded critics who had forgotten about the satyr-play. Perhaps we could make more dramatic sense out of Titus Andronicus if we could see it as an unharrowed hell, a satyr- play of obscene and gibbering demons.

The two nodes of the scriptural play are Christmas and Easter: the latter presents the triumphant god, the former the quiet virgin mother who gathers to herself the processional masque of the kings and shepherds. This figure is at the opposite end of the masque from the watching queen or peeress of an ideal masque, with the virtuous but paralyzed Lady of Comus halfway between.

A female figure symbolizing some kind of reconciling unity and order appears dimly at the end of the great panoramic masques of Faust and Peer Gynt, the "eternal feminine" of the former having some of its traditional links. Modern examples of the same epiphanic form range from Claudel's Annunciation play to Yeats's Countess Cathleen, where the heroine is really a female and Irish Jesus, sacrificing herself for her people and then cheating the devils by the purity of her nature, very much as in the pre-Anselm theory of the atonement. As Yeats remarks in a note, the story represents one of the supreme parables of the world.

SPECIFIC CONTINUOUS FORMS (PROSE FICTION)

In assigning the term fiction to the genre of the written word, in which prose tends to become the predominating rhythm, we collide with the view that the real meaning of fiction is falsehood or unreality. Thus an autobiography coming into a library would be classified as non-fiction if the librarian believed the author, and as fiction if she thought he was lying. It is difficult to see what use such a distinction can be to a literary critic. Surely the word fiction, which, like poetry, means etymologically something made for its own sake, could be applied in criticism to any work of literary art in a radically continuous form, which almost always means a work of art in prose. Or, if that is too much to ask, at least some protest can be entered against the sloppy habit of identifying fiction with the one genuine form of fiction which we know as the novel.

Let us look at a few of the unclassified books lying on the boundary of "non-fiction" and "literature/' Is Tristram Shandy a novel? Nearly everyone would say yes, in spite of its easygoing disregard of "story values." Is Gulliver's Travels a novel? Here most would demur, including the Dewey decimal system, which puts it under "Satire and Humor/' But surely everyone would call it fiction, and if it is fiction, a distinction appears between fiction as a genus and the novel as a species of that genus. Shifting the ground to fiction, then, is Sartor Resartus fiction? If not, why not? If it is, is The Anatomy of Melancholy fiction? Is it a literary form or only a work of "non-fiction" written with "style"? Is Sorrow's Lavengro fiction? Everyman's Library says yes; the World's Classics puts it under "Travel and Topography."

The literary historian who identifies fiction with the novel is greatly embarrassed by the length of time that the world managed to get along without the novel, and until he reaches his great deliverance in Defoe, his perspective is intolerably cramped. He is compelled to reduce Tudor fiction to a series of tentative essays in the novel form, which works well enough for Deloney but makes non sense of Sidney. He postulates a great fictional gap in the seventeenth century which exactly covers the golden age of rhetorical prose. He finally discovers that the word novel, which up to about 1900 was still the name of a more or less recognizable form, has since expanded into a catchall term which can be applied to practically any prose book that is not "on" something. Clearly, this novel-centered view of prose fiction is a Ptolemaic perspective which is now too complicated to be any longer workable, and some more relative and Copernican view must take its place.

When we start to think seriously about the novel, not as fiction, but as a form of fiction, we feel that its characteristics, whatever they are, are such as make, say, Defoe, Fielding, Austen, and James central in its tradition, and Borrow, Peacock, Melville, and Emily Bronte somehow peripheral. This is not an estimate of merit: we may think Moby Dick "greater" than The Egoist and yet feel that Meredith's book is closer to being a typical novel. Fielding's conception of the novel as a comic epic in prose seems fundamental to the tradition he did so much to establish. In novels that we think of as typical, like those of Jane Austen, plot and dialogue are closely linked to the conventions of the comedy of manners. The conventions of Wuthering Heights are linked rather with the tale and the ballad. They seem to have more affinity with tragedy, and the tragic emotions of passion and fury, which would shatter the balance of tone in Jane Austen, can be safely accommodated here. So can the supernatural, or the suggestion of it, which is difficult to get into a novel. The shape of the plot is different: instead of manoeuvering around a central situation, as Jane

Austen does, Emily Bronte tells her story with linear accents, and she seems to need the help of a narrator, who would be absurdly out of place in Jane Austen. Conventions so different justify us in regarding Wuthering Heights as a different form of prose fiction from the novel, a form which we shall here call the romance. Here again we have to use the same word in several different contexts, but romance seems on the whole better than tale, which appears to fit a somewhat shorter form.

The essential difference between novel and romance lies in the conception of characterization. The romancer does not attempt to create "real people" so much as stylized figures which expand into psychological archetypes. It is in the romance that we find Jung's libido, anima, and shadow reflected in the hero, heroine, and villain respectively. That is why the romance so often radiates a glow of subjective intensity that the novel lacks, and why a suggestion of allegory is constantly creeping in around its fringes. Certain elements of character are released in the romance which make it naturally a more revolutionary form than the novel The novelist deals with personality, with characters wearing their personcte or social masks. He needs the framework of a stable society, and many of our best novelists have been conventional to the verge of fussiness. The romancer deals with individuality, with characters in vacuo idealized by revery, and, however conservative he may be, something nihilistic and untamable is likely to keep breaking out of his pages.

The prose romance, then, is an independent form of fiction to be distinguished from the novel and extracted from the miscellaneous heap of prose works now covered by that term. Even in the other heap known as short stories one can isolate the tale form used by Poe, which bears the same relation to the full romance that the stories of Chekhov or {Catherine Mansfield do to the novel. "Pure" examples of either form are never found; there is hardly any modern romance that could not be made out to be a novel, and vice versa. The forms of prose fiction are mixed, like racial strains in human beings, not separable like the sexes. In fact the popular demand in fiction is always for a mixed form, a romantic novel just romantic enough for the reader to project his libido on the hero and his anima on the heroine, and just novel enough to keep these projections in a familiar world. It may be asked, therefore, what is the use of making the above distinction, especially when, though undeveloped in criticism, it is by no means unrealized. It is no surprise to hear that Trollope wrote novels and William Morris romances.

The reason is that a great romancer should be examined in terms of the conventions he chose. William Morris should not be left on the side lines of prose fiction merely because the critic has not learned to take the romance form seriously. Nor, in view of what has been said about the revolutionary nature of the romance, should his choice of that form be regarded as an "escape" from his social attitude. If Scott has any claims to be a romancer, it is not good criticism to deal only with his defects as a novelist. The romantic qualities of

The Pilgrim's Progress, too, its archetypal characterization and its revolutionary approach to religious experience, make it a well-rounded example of a literary form: it is not merely a book swallowed by English literature to get some religious bulk in its diet. Finally, when Hawthorne, in the preface to The House of the Seven Gables, insists that his story should be read as romance and not as novel, it is possible that he meant what he said, even though he indicates that the prestige of the rival form has induced the romancer to apologize for not using it.

Romance is older than the novel, a fact which has developed the historical illusion that it is something to be outgrown, a juvenile and undeveloped form. The social affinities of the romance, with its grave idealizing of heroism and purity, are with the aristocracy (for the apparent inconsistency of this with the revolutionary nature of the form just mentioned, see the introductory comment on the mythos of romance in the previous essay) . It revived in the period we call Romantic as part of the Romantic tendency to archaic feudalism and a cult of the hero, or idealized libido.

In England the romances of Scott and, in less degree, the Brontes, are part of a mysterious Northumbrian renaissance, a Romantic reaction against the new industrialism in the Midlands, which also produced the poetry of Wordsworth and Burns and the philosophy of Carlyle. It is not surprising, therefore, that an important theme in the more bourgeois novel should be the parody of the romance and its ideals. The tradition established by Don Quixote continues in a type of novel which looks at a romantic situation from its own point of view, so that the conventions of the two forms make up an ironic compound instead of a sentimental mixture. Examples range from Northanger Abbey to Madame Bovary and Lord Jim.

The tendency to allegory in the romance may be conscious, as in The Pilgrim's Progress, or unconscious, as in the very obvious sexual mythopoeia in William Morris. The romance, which deals with heroes, is intermediate between the novel, which deals with men, and the myth, which deals with gods. Prose romance first appears as a late development of Classical mythology, and the prose Sagas of Iceland follow close on the mythical Eddas. The novel tends rather to expand into a fictional approach to history.

The soundness of Fielding's instinct in calling Tom Jones a history is confirmed by the general rule that the larger the scheme of a novel becomes, the more obviously its historical nature appears. As it is creative history, however, the novelist usually prefers his material in a plastic, or roughly contemporary state, and feels cramped by a fixed historical pattern. Waverley is dated about sixty years back from the time of writing and Little Dorrit about forty years, but the historical pattern is fixed in the romance and plastic in the novel, suggesting the general principle that most "historical novels" are romances. Similarly a novel becomes more romantic in its appeal when the life it reflects has passed away: thus the novels of Trollope were read primarily as romances during the Second World War. It is perhaps the link with history and a sense of temporal con text that has confined the novel, in striking contrast to the world wide romance, to the alliance of time and Western man.

Autobiography is another form which merges with the novel by a series of insensible gradations. Most autobiographies are inspired by a creative, and therefore fictional, impulse to select only those events and experiences in the writer's life that go to build up an integrated pattern. This pattern may be something larger than him self with which he has come to identify himself, or simply the coherence of his character and attitudes. We may call this very important form of prose fiction the confession form, following St. Augustine, who appears to have invented it, and Rousseau, who established a modern type of it. The earlier tradition gave Religio Medici, Grace Abounding, and Newman's Apologia to English literature, besides the related but subtly different type of confession favored by the mystics.

Here again, as with the romance, there is some value in recognizing a distinct prose form in the confession. It gives several of our best prose works a definable place in fiction instead of keeping them in a vague limbo of books which are not quite literature be cause they are "thought," and not quite religion or philosophy because they are Examples of Prose Style. The confession, too, like the novel and the romance, has its own short form, the familiar essay, and Montaigne's livre de bonne joy is a confession made up of essays in which only the continuous narrative of the longer form is missing. Montaigne's scheme is to the confession what a work of fiction made up of short stories, such as Joyce's Dubliners or Boccaccio's Decameron, is to the novel or romance.

After Rousseau in fact in Rousseau the confession flows into the novel, and the mixture produces the fictional autobiography, the Kunstler-roman, and kindred types. There is no literary reason why the subject of a confession should always be the author himself, and dramatic confessions have been used in the novel at least since Moll Flanders. The "stream of consciousness" technique permits of a much more concentrated fusion of the two forms, but even here the characteristics peculiar to the confession form show up clearly. Nearly always some theoretical and intellectual interest in religion, politics, or art plays a leading role in the confession. It is his success in integrating his mind on such subjects that makes the author of a confession feel that his life is worth writing about. But this interest in ideas and theoretical statements is alien to the genius of the novel proper, where the technical problem is to dissolve all theory into personal relationships. In Jane Austen, to take a familiar instance, church, state, and culture are never examined except as social data, and Henry James has been described as having a mind so fine that no idea could violate it. The novelist who can not get along without ideas, or has not the patience to digest them in the way that James did, instinctively resorts to what Mill calls a "mental history" of a single character. And when we find that a technical discussion of a theory of aesthetics forms the climax of Joyce's Portrait, we realize that what makes this possible is the presence in that novel of another tradition of prose fiction.

The novel tends to be extroverted and personal; its chief interest is in human character as it manifests itself in society. The romance tends to be introverted and personal: it also deals with characters, but in a more subjective way. (Subjective here refers to treatment, not subject-matter. The characters of romance are heroic and there fore inscrutable; the novelist is freer to enter his characters' minds because he is more objective.) The confession is also introverted, but intellectualized in content. Our next step is evidently to discover a fourth form of fiction which is extroverted and intellectual.

We remarked earlier that most people would call Gulliver's Travels fiction but not a novel. It must then be another form of fiction, as it certainly has a form, and we feel that we are turning from the novel to this form, whatever it is, when we turn from Rousseau's Emile to Voltaire's Candide, or from Butler's The Way of All Flesh to the Erewhon books, or from Huxley's Point Counterpoint to Brave New World. The form thus has its own traditions, and, as the examples of Butler and Huxley show, has preserved some integrity even under the ascendancy of the novel. Its existence is easy enough to demonstrate, and no one will challenge the statement that the literary ancestry of Gulliver's Travels and Candide runs through Rabelais and Erasmus to Lucian. But while much has been said about the style and thought of Rabelais, Swift, and Voltaire, very little has been made of them as craftsmen working in a specific medium, a point no one dealing with a novelist would ignore. Another great writer in this tradition, Huxley's master Peacock, has fared even worse, for, his form not being understood, a general impression has grown up that his status in the development of prose fiction is that of a slapdash eccentric. Actually, he is as exquisite and precise an artist in his medium as Jane Austen is in hers.

The form used by these authors is the Menippean satire, also more rarely called the Varronian satire, allegedly invented by a Greek cynic named Menippus. His works are lost, but he had two great disciples, the Greek Lucian and the Roman Varro, and the tradition of Varro, who has not survived either except in fragments, was carried on by Petronius and Apulems. The Menippean satire appears to have developed out of verse satire through the practice of adding prose interludes, but we know it only as a prose form, though one of its recurrent features (seen in Peacock) is the use of incidental verse.

The Menippean satire deals less with people as such than with mental attitudes. Pedants, bigots, cranks, parvenus, virtuosi, enthusiasts, rapacious and incompetent professional men of all kinds, are handled in terms of their occupational approach to life as distinct from their social behavior. The Menippean satire thus resembles the confession in its ability to handle abstract ideas and theories, and differs from the novel in its characterization, which is stylized rather than naturalistic, and presents people as mouthpieces of the ideas they represent. Here again no sharp boundary lines can or should be drawn, but if we compare a character in Jane Austen with a similar character in Peacock we can immediately feel the difference between the two forms. Squire Western belongs to the novel, but Thwackum and Square have Menippean blood in them. A constant theme in the tradition is the ridicule of the philosophus gloriosus, already discussed. The novelist sees evil and folly as social diseases, but the Menippean satirist sees them as diseases of the intellect, as a kind of maddened pedantry which the philosophus gloriosus at once symbolizes and defines.

Petronius, Apuleius, Rabelais, Swift, and Voltaire all use a loose-jointed narrative form often confused with the romance. It differs from the romance, however (though there is a strong admixture of romance in Rabelais), as it is not primarily concerned with the exploits of heroes, but relies on the free play of intellectual fancy and the kind of humorous observation that produces caricature. It differs also from the picaresque form, which has the novel's interest in the actual structure of society. At its most concentrated the Menippean satire presents us with a vision of the world in terms of a single intellectual pattern. The intellectual structure built up from the story makes for violent dislocations in the customary logic of narrative, though the appearance of carelessness that results reflects only the carelessness of the reader or his tendency to judge by a novel-centered conception of fiction.

The word "satire,' in Roman and Renaissance times, meant either of two specific literary forms of that name, one (this one) prose and the other verse. Now it means a structural principle or attitude, what we have called a mythos. In the Menippean satires we have been discussing, the name of the form also applies to the attitude. As the name of an attitude, satire is, we have seen, a combination of fantasy and morality. But as the name of a form, the term satire, though confined to literature (for as a mythos it may appear in any art, a cartoon, for example), is more flexible, and can be either entirely fantastic or entirely moral. The Menippean adventure story may thus be pure fantasy, as it is in the literary fairy tale. The Alice books are perfect Menippean satires, and so is The Water-Babies, which has been influenced by Rabelais. The purely moral type is a serious vision of society as a single intellectual pattern, in other words a Utopia.

The short form of the Menippean satire is usually a dialogue or colloquy, in which the dramatic interest is in a conflict of ideas rather than of character. This is the favorite form of Erasmus, and is common in Voltaire. Here again the form is not invariably satiric in attitude, but shades off into more purely fanciful or moral discussions, like the Imaginary Conversations of Landor or the "dialogue of the dead." Sometimes this form expands to full length, and more than two speakers are used: the setting then is usually a cena or symposium, like the one that looms so large in Petronius. Plato, though much earlier in the field than Menippus, is a strong influence on this type, which stretches in an unbroken tradition down through those urbane and leisurely conversations which define the ideal courtier in Castiglione or the doctrine and discipline of angling in Walton. A modern development produces the country-house weekends in Peacock, Huxley, and their imitators in which the opinions and ideas and cultural interests expressed are as important as the love-making.

The novelist shows his exuberance either by an exhaustive analysis of human relationships, as in Henry James, or of social phenomena, as in Tolstoy. The Menippean satirist, dealing with intellectual themes and attitudes, shows his exuberance in intellectual ways, by piling up an enormous mass of erudition about his theme or in overwhelming his pedantic targets with an avalanche of their own jargon. A species, or rather sub-species, of the form is the kind of encyclopaedic farrago represented by Athenaeus' Deipnosophists and Macrobius' Saturnalia, where people sit at a banquet and pour out a vast mass of erudition on every subject that might conceivably come up in a conversation. The display of erudition had probably been associated with the Menippean tradition by Varro, who was enough of a polymath to make Quintilian, if not stare and gasp, at any rate call him vir Romanorum eniditissimus. The tendency to expand into an encyclopaedic farrago is clearly marked in Rabelais, notably in the great catalogues of torcheculs and epithets of codpieces and methods of divination. The encyclopaedic compilations produced in the line of duty by Erasmus and Voltaire suggest that a magpie instinct to collect facts is not unrelated to the type of ability that has made them famous as artists. Flaubert* s encyclopaedic approach to the construction of Bouvard et Pecuchet is quite comprehensible if we explain it as marking an affinity with the Menippean tradition.

This creative treatment of exhaustive erudition is the organizing principle of the greatest Menippean satire in English before Swift, Burton's Anatomy of Melancholy. Here human society is studied in terms of the intellectual pattern provided by the conception of melancholy, a symposium of books replaces dialogue, and the result is the most comprehensive survey of human life in one book that English literature had seen since Chaucer, one of Burton's favorite authors. We may note in passing the Utopia in his introduction and his "digressions,' which when examined turn out to be scholarly distillations of Menippean forms: the digression of air, of the marvellous journey; the digression of spirits, of the ironic use of erudition; the digression of the miseries of scholars, of the satire on the philosophus gloriosus. The word "anatomy" in Burton's title means a dissection or analysis, and expresses very accurately the intellectualized approach of his form. We may as well adopt it as a convenient name to replace the cumbersome and in modern times rather misleading "Menippean satire."

The anatomy, of course, eventually begins to merge with the novel, producing various hybrids including the roman a these and novels in which the characters are symbols of social or other ideas, like the proletarian novels of the thirties in this century. It was Sterne, however, the disciple of Burton and Rabelais, who combined them with greatest success. Tristram Shandy may be, as was said at the beginning, a novel, but the digressing narrative, the catalogues, the stylizing of character along "humor" lines, the marvellous journey of the great nose, the symposium discussions, and the constant ridicule of philosophers and pedantic critics are all features that belong to the anatomy.

A clearer understanding of the form and traditions of the anatomy would make a good many elements in the history of literature come into focus. Boethius' Consolation of Philosophy, with its dialogue form, its verse interludes and its pervading tone of contemplative irony, is a pure anatomy, a fact of considerable importance for the understanding of its vast influence. The Compleat Angler is an anatomy because of its mixture of prose and verse, its rural cena setting, its dialogue form, its deipnosophistical interest in food, and its gentle Menippean raillery of a society which considers everything more important than fishing and yet has discovered very few better things to do. In nearly every period of literature there are many romances, confessions, and anatomies that are neglected only because the categories to which they belong are unrecognized. In the period between Sterne and Peacock, for example, we have, among romances, Melmoth the Wanderer; among confessions, Hogg's Confessions of a Justified Sinner; among anatomies, Southey's Doctor, Amory's John Bundle, and the Noctes Ambrosianae.

To sum up then: when we examine fiction from the point of view of form, we can see four chief strands binding it together, novel, confession, anatomy, and romance. The six possible combinations of these forms all exist, and we have shown how the novel has combined with each of the other three. Exclusive concentration on one form is rare: the early novels of George Eliot, for instance, are influenced by the romance, and the later ones by the anatomy. The romance-confession hybrid is found, naturally, in the autobiography of a romantic temperament, and is represented in English by the extroverted George Borrow and the introverted De Quincey. The romance-anatomy one we have noticed in Rabelais; a later example is Moby Dick, where the romantic theme of the wild hunt expands into an encyclopaedic anatomy of the whale. Confession and anatomy are united in Sartor Resartus and in some of Kierkegaard's strikingly original experiments in prose fiction form, including Either/Or. More comprehensive fictional schemes usually employ at least three forms: we can see strains of novel, romance, and confession in Pamela, of novel, romance, and anatomy in Don Quixote, of novel, confession, and anatomy in Proust, and of romance, confession, and anatomy in Apuleius.

I deliberately make this sound schematic in order to suggest the advantage of having a simple and logical explanation for the form of, say, Moby Dick or Tristram Shandy. The usual critical approach to the form of such works resembles that of the doctors in Brob- dingnag, who after great wrangling finally pronounced Gulliver a lusus naturae. It is the anatomy in particular that has baffled critics, and there is hardly any fiction writer deeply influenced by it who has not been accused of disorderly conduct. The reader may be reminded here of Joyce, for describing Joyce's books as monstrous has become a nervous tic. I find "demogorgon," "behemoth," and "white elephant" in good critics; the bad ones could probably do much better. The care that Joyce took to organize Ulysses and Finnegans Wake amounted nearly to obsession, but as they are not organized on familiar principles of prose fiction, the impression of shapelessness remains. Let us try our formulas on him.

If a reader were asked to set down a list of the things that had most impressed him about Ulysses, it might reasonably be some what as follows. First, the clarity with which the sights and sounds and smells of Dublin come to life, the rotundity of the character-drawing, and the naturalness of the dialogue. Second, the elaborate way that the story and characters are parodied by being set against archetypal heroic patterns, notably the one provided by the Odyssey. Third, the revelation of character and incident through the searching use of the stream-of-consciousness technique. Fourth, the constant tendency to be encyclopaedic and exhaustive both in technique and in subject matter, and to see both in highly intellectualized terms. It should not be too hard for us by now to see that these four points describe elements in the book which relate to the novel, romance, confession, and anatomy respectively. Ulysses, then, is a complete prose epic with all four forms employed in it, all of practically equal importance, and all essential to one another, so that the book is a unity and not an aggregate.

This unity is built up from an intricate scheme of parallel contrasts. The romantic archetypes of Hamlet and Ulysses are like remote stars in a literary heaven looking down quizzically on the shabby creatures of Dublin obediently intertwining themselves in the patterns set by their influences. In the "Cyclops" and "Circe" episodes particularly there is a continuous parody of realistic patterns by romantic ones which reminds us, though the irony leans in the opposite direction, of Madame Bovary. The relation of novel and confession techniques is similar; the author jumps into his characters' minds to follow their stream of consciousness, and out again to describe them externally. In the novel-anatomy combination, too, found in the "Ithaca" chapter, the sense of lurking antagonism between the personal and intellectual aspects of the scene accounts for much of its pathos. The same principle of parallel contrast holds good for the other three combinations: of romance and confession in "Nausicaa" and "Penelope," of confession and anatomy in "Proteus" and "The Lotos-Eaters," of romance and anatomy (a rare and fitful combination) in "Sirens" and parts of "Circe."

In Finnegans Wake the unity of design goes far beyond this. The dingy story of the sodden HCE and his pinched wife is not contrasted with the archetypes of Tristram and the divine king: HCE is himself Tristram and the divine king. As the setting is a dream, no contrast is possible between confession and novel, between a stream of consciousness inside the mind and the appearances of other people outside it, Nor is the experiential world of the novel to be separated from the intelligible world of the anatomy. The forms we have been isolating in fiction, and which depend for their existence on the commonsense dichotomies of the daylight consciousness, vanish in Finnegans Wake into a fifth and quintessential form. This form is the one traditionally associated with scriptures and sacred books, and treats life in terms of the fall and awakening of the human soul and the creation and apocalypse of nature. The Bible is the definitive example of it; the Egyptian Book of the Dead and the Icelandic Prose Edda, both of which have left deep imprints on Finnegans Wake, also belong to it.

THE RHETORIC OF NON-LITERARY PROSE

Prose is, unlike verse, used also for non-literary purposes; it ex tends not only to the literary boundaries of melos and opsis, but to the outer worlds of praxis and theoria, social action and indi vidual thought themselves. Renaissance critics used to argue about what the greatest form for poetry was, and whether it was epic or tragedy. There is probably no answer to such a question, but one can learn a good deal about literary form by discussing it. Now if we ask the question: What is the greatest possible prose form? there is probably no answer to that question either, but the moment we ask it, a great number of works, the Bible, the dialogues of Plato, the meditations of Pascal in fact, all "great books" usually placed outside literature leap into a new literary significance, It is thus necessary for us at this point to consider what literary elements are involved in the verbal structures in which the literary or hypo thetical intention is not the primary one,

We are still thinking of literature as facing the world of social action on one side, and of individual thought on the other, so that the rhetoric of non-literary prose would tend to emphasize emotion and the appeal to action through the ear in the former area, and intellect and the appeal to contemplation based predominantly on visual metaphors in the latter. Let us begin with that extensive suburb of prose that is concerned with the technique of social or oratorical persuasion.

The most concentrated examples of this are to be found in the pamphlet or speech that catches the rhythm of history, that seizes on a crucial event or phase of action, interprets it, articulates the emotions concerned with it, or in some means employs a verbal structure to insulate and conduct the current of history. Areopa- gitica, Johnson's letter to Chesterfield, some sermons in the pe riod between Latimer and the Commonwealth, some of Burke's speeches, Lincoln's Gettysburg address, Vanzetti's death speech, Churchill's 1940 speeches, are a few examples that come readily to mind. None of these were designed with a primarily literary intention, and would have failed of their original purpose if they had been, but they are literary now, and data for the critic. Nearly all of them are marked by the emphatic patterns of repetition and anaphora characteristic of rhetorical prose.

The measured cadences of these historical oracles represent a kind of strategic withdrawal from action: they marshal and review the ranks of familiar but deeply-held ideas. The rhetoric of persua sion to action itself, which is the next stage of prose as we proceed from literature outwards into social life, is considerably stepped up in its rhythm. Here the repetitions are hypnotic and incantatory, aimed at breaking down customary associations of ideas and habitual responses, and at excluding any alternative line of action. Such a rhetoric may be heard in its purest form in the speech rhythms of a boy talking to a dog, with the object of persuading him to sit up or shake hands or otherwise move out of the normal line of canine endeavor. When addressed to a human audience, such rhetoric must follow the dialectic of rhetoric: it must have either a rallying point or a point of attack, or both. The rhetoric of attack or in vective is exemplified in the pulpit's crusade against sin and in the prosecutor's summing-up in the courtroom. The latter has produced the by-form of the philippic, the indictment of a social enemy. The rhetoric of eulogy, the so-called epideictic rhetoric of the Classical world, is in our day most clearly seen in advertising and publicity, although it has a more genuinely literary form in the type of "purple passage" prose, usually with a descriptive content, that attempts to communicate some kind of wordless emotion.

As these examples show, we are moving rapidly away from litera ture towards the direct verbal expression of kinetic emotion. The further we go in this direction, the more likely the author is to be, or to pretend to be, emotionally involved with his subject, so that what he exhorts us to embrace or avoid is in part a projection from his own emotional life. As this increases, a certain automatism comes into the writing: the verbal expression of infantile-centered hatreds, fears, loves, and objects of adoration. When Swinburne speaks of "the yelling Yahoos whom the scandalous and senseless license of our own day allows to run and roar about the country unmuzzled and unwhipped," we may not know what he is referring to, but a glance at the prose structure, with its automatic allitera tion and doubling of adjectives, makes it clear that whatever it is we hardly need to take it seriously. Such writing is a familiar and easily recognized phenomenon: it is tantrum prose, the prose of so much Victorian criticism, of several acres of Carlyle and Ruskin, of clerical denunciations of heresies or secular amusements, of totalitarian propaganda, and in fact of nearly all rhetoric in which we feel that the author's pen is running away from him, setting up a mechanical for an imaginative impetus. The metaphor of "in toxication" is often employed for the breakdown of rhetorical control.

The more incoherent this kind of rhetoric becomes, the more clearly it shows itself to be an attempt to express emotion apart from or without intellect. At this point we enter the area of emo tional jargon, which consists largely in an obsessive repetition of verbal formulas. Not far removed is the kind of vulgar inarticulate ness that uses one word, generally unprintable, for the whole rhetori cal ornament of the sentence, including adjectives, adverbs, epi thets, and punctuation. Finally, words disappear altogether, and we are back to a primitive language of screams and gestures and sighs. The whole sequence can of course be imitated within literature, Shakespeare giving us everything from Henry V's address before the walls of Harfleur to Othello's "goats and monkeys" speech. The imitation of emotional rhetoric in literary prose is a feature making for melos in the latter. Similarly in literature we occasionally run across a writer who uses such rhetorical material without being able to absorb or assimilate it: the result is pathological, a kind of literary diabetes, and may be studied in the novels of Amanda Ros.

The expression of conceptual thought in prose exhibits a parallel sequence of phenomena, moving in the opposite direction. Philos ophy is assertive or prepositional writing, and we notice in the history of philosophy a persistent attempt to isolate the rhythm of the proposition. Philosophy begins in proverbs and axioms/and at vari ous times it has produced the dialectic dialogue of Plato and the Upanishads, the closely related question-objection-answer scheme of St. Thomas, the quasi-mathematical arrangements of ideas in Spi noza, the aphorisms of Bacon (who remarks that aphorisms are a sign of vitality in philosophy) , and, in our day, the numbered prop ositions of Wittgenstein's Tractates. All of these are clearly at least in part endeavors to purify verbal communication of the emo tional content of rhetoric; all of them, however, impress the literary critic as being themselves rhetorical devices.

The implication is that there is a conceptual rhetoric aimed, like persuasive rhetoric, at separating emotion and intellect, but at tempting to throw away the emotional half. It seeks the book and the individual reader as its fellow seeks the audience; its goal is understanding as the goal of persuasion is action or emotional re sponse. A good deal of the strategy of teaching is rhetorical strategy, choosing words and images with great care in order to evoke the response: "I never thought of it that way before," or "Now that you put it that way, I can see it." What distinguishes, not simply the epigram, but profundity itself from platitude .is very frequently rhetorical wit. In fact it may be doubted whether we ever really call an idea profound unless we are pleased with the wit of its expres sion. Teaching, like persuasion, employs a dissociative rhetoric aimed at breaking down habitual response: the maddening prolixity of Oriental sutras results from this, and there are passages in the New Testament almost as dissociative as Gertrude Stein:

That which was from the beginning, which we have heard, which we have seen with our eyes, which we have looked upon, and our hands have handled, of the Word of life; (For the life was manifested, and we have seen it, and bear witness, and shew unto you that eternal life, which was with the Father, and was manifested unto us;) That which we have seen and heard de clare we unto you ...

Without trying to suggest that only good writers can be good philosophers, we may still observe that much of the difficulty in a philosophical style is rhetorical in origin, resulting from a feeling that it is necessary to detach and isolate the intellect from the emo tions, A sentence from James Mill's Essay on Government will il lustrate what I mean:

One caution, first of all, we should take along with us, and it is this: that all those persons who hold the powers of govern ment without having an identity of interests with the community, and all those persons who share in the profits which are made by the abuse of those powers, and all those persons whom the ex ample and representations of the two first classes influence, will be sure to represent the community, or a part having an identity of interest with the community, as incapable in the highest de gree of acting according to their own interest; it being clear that they who have not an identity of interest with the community ought to hold the power of government no longer, if those who have that identity of interest could be expected to act in any tolerable conformity with their interest.

This is finally discovered to mean, after one has worked it all out like a crossword puzzle, that those who have a stake in one form of government are likely to resist the introduction of another. The critic, searching for the reasons why, if James Mill meant that, he could not have said it, eventually realizes that the style is motivated by a perverse, bristly intellectual honesty. He will not condescend to employ any of the pretty arts of persuasion, sugar-coated illustra tions or emotionally-loaded terms; he will appeal only to the cold logic of reason itself reinforced, to be sure, by a peculiarly Vic torian sense that the more difficult the style, the tougher the moral and intellectual fibre one develops in wrestling with it.

We note that the basis of James Mill's rhetoric is the imitation of legal style, with its careful qualifying inclusiveness. The long containing sentences of the later Henry James already mentioned illustrate the literary use of similar devices. Passing over some inter mediate stages, we eventually arrive, in this pursuit of non-emo tional rhetoric, at conceptual jargon, otherwise known as gobble- dygook or officialese. This is a naive intensification of Mill's desire to speak with the voice, not of personality, but of Reason itself. The jargon of government reports, inter-office memoranda, and military instructions is motivated by a wish to be as impersonal as possible, to represent verbally the Institution or some anonymous cybernetic deity functioning in a state of "normalcy/' What it ac tually utters, of course, is the voice of the lonely crowd, the anxiety of the outward-directed conformist. Such jargon may be called, borrowing a term from medicine, benign jargon: it is unmistakably a disease of language, but not yet a cancerous disease like a dema gogue's oratory. It is found in most aspects of journalism and is the dress uniform of a large amount of professional writing, including that of humanists. That it could become malignant is indicated in 1984, where a further stage of it is caricatured as

"Newspeak," a pseudo-logical simplification of language which has, like emotional jargon, complete automatism as its goal. We are not surprised to find that the further we depart from literature, or the use of lan guage to express the completely integrated state of emotional con sciousness we call imagination, the nearer we come to the use of language as the expression of reflex. Whether we go in the emo tional or in the intellectual direction, we arrive at much the same point, a point antipodal to literature in which language is a run^ ning commentary on the unconscious, like a squirrel's chatter.

If there is such a thing as conceptual rhetoric, which is likely to increase in proportion as the discursive writer tries to avoid it, it seems as though the direct union of grammar and logic, which we suggested at the beginning of this essay might be the characteristic of the non-literary verbal structure, does not, in the long run, exist. Anything which makes a functional use of words will always be involved in all the technical problems of words, including rhetorical problems. The only road from grammar to logic, then, runs through the intermediate territory of rhetoric.

We notice in the first place that attempts to reduce grammar to logic, or logic to grammar, have not had the success they should have had if there were a large and important non-rhetorical com mon factor on which non-literary writing could be built. For a long time the prestige of the discursive reason fostered the notion that logic was the formal cause of language, that universal grammars on logical principles were possible, and that the entire resources of linguistic expression could fee categorized. We are now more ac- pustomed to think pf reasoning as one of many things that man does with words, a specialized function of language. There seems to be no evidence whatever that man learned to speak primarily because he wanted to speak logically.

The attempts to reduce logic to grammar are more recent, but not much more successful. Logic grows out of grammar, the un conscious or potential logic inherent in language, and we often find that the containing forms of conceptual thought are of gram matical origin, the stock example being the subject and predicate of Aristotelian logic. The fluid primitive linguistic conceptions often mentioned by anthropologists, such as the Polynesian mana or the Iroquois orenda, are participial or gerundive conceptions: they belong in a world where energy and matter have not been clearly separated, either in thought or into the verbs and nouns of our own less flexible language-structure. As energy and matter are not clearly separated in nuclear physics either, we might do worse than to re turn to such "primitive" words ourselves. The words atom and light, for example, being nouns, may be too material and static to be adequate symbols for what they now mean, and when they pass from the equations of a physicist into the linguistic apparatus of contemporary social consciousness, the grammatical difficulties in the translation show up clearly.

But there is still the scholar's mate in the argument for reducing logic to grammar: the fallacy of thinking that we have explained the nature of something by accounting for its origin in something else. Logic may have grown out of grammar, but to grow out of something is in part to outgrow it. For grammar may also be a hampering force in the development of logic, and a major source of logical confusions and pseudo-problems. These confusions ex tend much further than even the enormous brood of fallacies spawned by paronomasia, which is, like so many of our phenomena, a structural principle in literature and an obstacle in discursive writ ing. For instance, many long arguments may be annihilated by a grammatical change from definite articles and statements of identity to indefinite articles and active verbs. To say "reason is a function of the mind" is unlikely to lead to dispute; to say "reason is the function of the mind" involves one in a pointless struggle for the exclusive possession of an essence. To say "art communicates" is similarly to be content with an obvious plurality of functions: to say "art is communication" forces us into circular wrangling around a metaphor taken as an assertion. It is no wonder, then, that many logicians tend to think of grammar as something of a logical disease, some of them even maintaining that mathematics is the real source of coherence in logic. I have no opinion on this, except to repeat that anything which makes a functional use of words will always be involved in all the problems of words.

Grammar and logic both seem to develop through internal con flict. The humanist tradition has always, and rightly, stressed the importance of linguistic conflict in training the mind: if we do not know another language, we have missed the best and simplest op portunity of getting our ideas disentangled from the swaddling clothes of their native syntax. Similarly logic cannot develop prop erly without dialectic, the principle of opposition in thought. Now when people speaking different languages come into contact, an ideogrammatic structure is built up out of the efforts at communi cation. The figure 5 is an ideogram,- because it means the same num ber to people who call it five, cinq, cinque, flinf, and a dozen other things. Similarly, the purely linguistic associations of English "time" and French "temps" are different, but it is quite practicable to translate Proust or Bergson on time into English without serious risk of misunderstanding the meaning.

When two languages are in different cultural orbits, like English and Zulu, the ideogrammatic structure is more difficult to build up, but it always seems to be more or less possible. There are French equivalents for all English words and ideas, but obviously one cannot walk into a Polynesian or Iroquois society and ask: "What are your words for God, the soul, reality, knowledge?" They may have no such words or con cepts, nor can we give them our equivalents for mana and orenda. Yet it seems clear that we can eventually, with patient and sym pathetic study, find out what is going on in a Polynesian or Iroquois mind. The problems of communication between two people speak ing the same language may in some respects be even greater, be cause more difficult to become aware of, but even they can be ulti mately surmounted. It is out of such ideogrammatic inner struc tures, whether produced linguistically between two languages, or psychologically between two people speaking the same language, that the capacity to assimilate language to rational thought devel ops.

This ideogrammatic middle ground between two languages, or between two personal structures of meaning in the same language, must itself be a symbolic structure, not simply a bilingual dictionary. Hence the ideogram is neither purely grammatical nor purely logical: it is both at once, and rhetorical as well, for, like rhetoric, it brings an audience into being, and reinforces the language of con sciousness with that of association. The ideogram, in short, is a metaphor, the identification of two things of which each retains its own form, the realization that what you mean by X in this context is what I mean by Y. Such an ideogram may differ from the purely hypothetical metaphor of the poem, but the mental leap of met aphor away from the simple "this means that" sign is present in it.

Whether the reader agrees with all this or not, he may at any rate be willing to admit the possibility of links between grammar and rhetoric, and between rhetoric and logic, that have a neglected but crucial importance. Let us take the link of grammar and rhet oric first.

We remember that a good deal of verbal creation begins in asso ciative babble, in which sound and sense are equally involved. The result of this is poetic ambiguity, the fact that, as remarked earlier, the poet does not define his words but establishes their powers by placing them in a great variety of contexts. Hence the importance of poetic etymology, or the tendency to associate words similar in sound or sense. For many centuries this tendency passed itself off as genuine etymology, and the student was taught to think in terms of verbal association.

He learned to think of snow as coming ety- mologically as well as physically from clouds (nix a nubes), and of dark groves as derived from sunlight (the derivation by opposites which produced the famous lucus a non lucendo). When real etymology developed, this associative process was discarded as mum- bo-jumbo, which it is from one point of view, but it remains a fac tor of great importance in criticism. Here again we meet the prin ciple that an analogy between A and B (in this case two words) may still be important even if the view that A is the source of B is dropped. Whether or not one is etymologically justified in as sociating Prometheus with forethought or Odysseus with wrath, the poets have accepted such associations and they are data for the critic. Whether or not "new" critics make mistakes or anachronisms in explicating the texture of earlier poetry, the principle involved is defensible historically as well as psychologically.

We soon become aware, moreover, that verbal association is still a factor of importance even in rational thought. One of the most effective methods of conveying meaning in translation, for instance, is to leave a key word untranslated, so that the reader has to pick up its contextual associations in the original language from his own. Again, in trying to understand the thought of a philosopher, one often starts by considering a single word, say nature in Aristotle, substance in Spinoza, or time in Bergson, in the total range of its connotations. One often feels that a full understanding of such a word would be a key to the understanding of the whole system. If so, it would be a metaphorical key, as it would be a set of identifi cations made by the thinker with the word. The attempt to regard such connotative terms as invariably fallacious does not get us very far. Students are often graduated from college armed only with complaints that people will not define their terms, reason clearly, or argue about freedom or order without emotional attachments to those words.

It is perhaps more useful to shift our attention from what verbal communication is not to what it is, and what is com municated is usually some ambiguous and emotionally charged complex. In any case the notion that it is possible to reduce lan guage to sign-language, to make one word invariably mean one thing, is an illusion. After One has removed associative ambiguity from verbs and nouns, one has then the problem of adjectives and adverbs, which are universals by their very nature, and finally prepo sitions and conjunctions, which, being pure connectives, will always display a disconcerting semantic versatility. A glance at the N.E.D. entries for "to," "for," and "in" should discourage the brashest of verbal atomizers.

The link between rhetoric and logic is "doodle" or associative diagram, the expression of the conceptual by the spatial. A great number of prepositions are spatial metaphors, most of them de rived from the orientation of the human body. Every use of "up," "down," "besides," "on the other hand," "under" implies a sub conscious diagram in the argument, whatever it is. If a writer says "But on the other hand there is a further consideration to be brought forward in support of the opposing argument," he may be writing normal (if wordy) English, but he is also doing precisely what an armchair strategist does when he scrawls plans of battle on a tablecloth. Very often a "structure" or "system" of thought can be reduced to a diagrammatic pattern in fact both words are to some extent synonyms of diagram.

A philosopher is of great as sistance to his reader when he realizes the presence of such a dia gram and extracts it, as Plato does in his discussion of the divided line. We cannot go far in any argument without realizing that there is some kind of graphic formula involved All division and categori zation, the use of chapters, the topotropism (if I have constructed this correctly) signalled by "let us now turn to" or "reverting to the point made earlier/' the sense of what "fits" the argument, the feeling that one point is "central" and another peripheral, has some kind of geometrical basis.

It used to be said that, as all abstract words were originally con crete metaphors, something of the latter will always adhere to the word through all its semantic history. This view is discredited now, but it still has much truth in it: I question whether it is really pos sible to make B depend on A without in some measure hanging it on, or involve B with A without in some measure wrapping them up.

The only fallacy in it, I think, is the assumption that the at tached metaphor must necessarily be the one implied in the ety mology of the word. Of course a writer may give a word a meaning which has no recognizable connection with its origin. But it looks as though abstract words and ideas were on loan, so to speak, from a latent concrete formulation which is to be found, not in the history of the word used, but in the structure of the argument into which the word is fitted.

As soon as one starts to think of the role of association and dia gram in argument, one begins to realize how extraordinarily per vasive they are. I once heard a preacher advocate religion on the ground that science was too cold and dry to serve as a guide to life, while the heat of revolutionary zeal still left one thirsting for some thing more. The figures seemed commonplace, yet it was clear that the ancient diagram of the four principles of substance, hot, cold, moist, and dry, was the graphic formula of his argument, and that religion meant something wet to him, a fertilizing moisture that would warm the scientists and cool the radicals.

The same prin ciple of a graphic formula is found in such assumptions as: that the intellect is cool and sober and the emotions warm and drunk; that the practical sense walks and the imaginative one leaps; that facts are solid ("stubborn"), hypotheses liquid ("covering" facts), and theories gaseous; that whatever is "inside" the mind is dimly lit and whatever is "outside" it clear, and so on. Also in value-assump tions: that the concrete is better than the abstract, the active better than the passive, the dynamic better than the static, the unified better than the multiple, the simple better than the complex. Religious people think of heaven as "up"; psychologists think of the subconscious as "underneath" the consciousness, both words being obviously spatial metaphors.

We could go on for a long time, but by now it is surely clear that it is wiser simply to become aware of metaphor than to try to eradicate it. Attempts to analyze metaphor solely to debunk an argument or suggest that it is "nothing but" a metaphor are not to be encouraged.

What is to be encouraged is the analysis itself, in which there is, I think, an activity of considerable and increasing importance for literary critics, as the conclusion of this book will suggest.

The discursive reason has traditionally been given the place of honor in Western culture. In religion, no poetry outside Scripture is given the authority of the theologian's propositions; in philos ophy, the reason is the high priest of reality (unless there are spe cial features in the philosophy giving a peculiar importance to the arts, as there are in Schelling's); in science the same hierarchical diagram is even clearer. Hence the arts have been traditionally re garded as forms of "accommodation," their function being to es tablish a link between reason and whatever is put "below" it on the assumed diagram, such as the emotions or the senses.

It is thus no surprise to "find "accommodation" in verbal structures aimed at rousing emotion or at some form of kinetic persuasion. Such ac commodation has been recognized for centuries, as it is consistent with the traditional subordinating of rhetoric to dialectic. The no tion of a conceptual rhetoric raises new problems, as it suggests that nothing built out of words can transcend the nature and conditions of words, and that the nature and conditions of ratio, so far as ratio is verbal, are contained by oratio.

8

Anglo-American Literary Criticism

NEW CRITICISM OF ANGLO-AMERICAN LITERARY

New Criticism, post-World War I school of Anglo-American literary critical theory that insisted on the intrinsic value of a work of art and focused attention on the individual work alone as an independent unit of meaning. It was opposed to the critical practice of bringing historical or biographical data to bear on the interpretation of a work.

The primary technique employed in the New Critical approach is close analytic reading of the text, a technique as old as Aristotle's *Poetics*. The New Critics, however, introduced refinements into the method. Early seminal works in the tradition were those of the English critics I.A. Richards (*Practical Criticism*, 1929) and William Empson (*Seven Types of Ambiguity*, 1930). English poet T.S. Eliot also made contributions, with his critical essays "Tradition and the Individual Talent" (1917) and "Hamlet and His Problems" (1919). The movement did not have a name, however, until the appearance of John Crowe Ransom's *The New Criticism* (1941), a work that loosely organized the principles of this basically linguistic approach to literature. Other figures associated with New Criticism include Cleanth Brooks, R.P. Blackmur, Robert Penn Warren, and W.K. Wimsatt, Jr., although their critical pronouncements, along with those of Ransom, Richards, and Empson, are somewhat diverse and do not readily constitute a uniform school of thought. New Criticism was eclipsed as the dominant mode of Anglo-American literary criticism by the 1970s.

To the New Critics, poetry was a special kind of discourse, a means of communicating feeling and thought that could not be expressed in any other kind of language. It differed qualitatively from the language of science or philosophy, but it conveyed equally valid meanings. Such critics set out to define and formalize the qualities of poetic thought and language, utilizing the technique of close reading with special emphasis on the connotative and associative values of words and on the multiple functions of figurative language—symbol, metaphor, and image—in the work. Poetic form and content could not be separated, since the experience of reading the particular words of a poem, including its unresolved tensions, is the poem's "meaning." As a result, any rewording of a poem's language alters its content, a view articulated in the phrase "the heresy of paraphrase," which was coined by Brooks in his *The Well Wrought Urn* (1947).

HISTORY

New Criticism developed as a reaction to the older philological and literary history schools of the US North, which, influenced by nineteenth-century German scholarship, focused on the history and meaning of individual words and their relation to foreign and ancient languages, comparative sources, and the biographical circumstances of the authors. These approaches, it was felt, tended to distract from the text and meaning of a poem and entirely neglect its aesthetic qualities in favor of teaching about external factors. On the other hand, the literary appreciation school, which limited itself to pointing out the "beauties" and morally elevating qualities of the text, was disparaged by the New Critics as too subjective and emotional. Condemning this as a version of Romanticism, they aimed for newer, systematic and objective method.

It was felt, especially by creative writers and by literary critics outside the academy, that the special aesthetic experience of poetry and literary language was lost in the welter of extraneous erudition and emotional effusions. Heather Dubrow notes that the prevailing focus of literary scholarship was on "the study of ethical values and philosophical issues through literature, the tracing of literary history, and . . . political criticism". Literature was approached and literary scholarship did not focus on analysis of texts.

New Critics believed the structure and meaning of the text were intimately connected and should not be analyzed separately. In order to bring the focus of literary studies back to analysis of the texts, they aimed to exclude the reader's response, the author's intention, historical and cultural contexts, and moralistic bias from their analysis. These goals were articulated in Ransom's "Criticism, Inc." and Allen Tate's "Miss Emily and the Bibliographers."

Close reading (or *explication de texte*) was a staple of French literary studies, but in the United States, aesthetic concerns, and the study of modern poets was the province of non-academic essayists and book reviewers rather than serious scholars. But the New Criticism changed this. Though their interest in textual study initially met with resistance from older scholars, the methods of the New Critics rapidly predominated in American universities until challenged by Feminism and structuralism in the 1970s. Other schools of critical theory, including, post-structuralism, and deconstructionist theory, the New Historicism, and Receptions studies followed.

Although the New Critics were never a formal group, an important inspiration was the teaching of John Crowe Ransom of Vanderbilt University, whose students (all Southerners), Allen Tate, Cleanth Brooks, and Robert Penn Warren would go on to develop the aesthetics that came to be known as the

New Criticism. In his essay, "The New Criticism," Cleanth Brooks notes that "The New Critic, like the Snark, is a very elusive beast," meaning that there was no clearly defined "New Critical" manifesto, school, or stance. Nevertheless, a number of writings outline inter-related New Critical ideas.

In 1946, William K. Wimsatt and Monroe Beardsley published a classic and controversial New Critical essay entitled "The Intentional Fallacy", in which they argued strongly against the relevance of an author's intention, or "intended meaning" in the analysis of a literary work. For Wimsatt and Beardsley, the words on the page were all that mattered; importation of meanings from outside the text was considered irrelevant, and potentially distracting.

In another essay, "The Affective Fallacy," which served as a kind of sister essay to "The Intentional Fallacy" Wimsatt and Beardsley also discounted the reader's personal/emotional reaction to a literary work as a valid means of analyzing a text. This fallacy would later be repudiated by theorists from the reader-response school of literary theory. Ironically, one of the leading theorists from this school, Stanley Fish, was himself trained by New Critics. Fish criticizes Wimsatt and Beardsley in his essay "Literature in the Reader" (1970).

The hey-day of the New Criticism in American high schools and colleges was the Cold War decades between 1950 and the mid-seventies, doubtless because it offered a relatively straightforward and politically uncontroversial approach to the teaching of literature.. Brooks and Warren's *Understanding Poetry* and *Understanding Fiction* both became staples during this era.

Studying a passage of prose or poetry in New Critical style required careful, exacting scrutiny of the passage itself. Formal elements such as rhyme, meter, setting,characterization, and plot were used to identify the theme of the text. In addition to the theme, the New Critics also looked for paradox, ambiguity, irony, and tension to help establish the single best and most unified interpretation of the text.

Although the New Criticism is no longer a dominant theoretical model in American universities, some of its methods (like close reading) are still fundamental tools of literary criticism, underpinning a number of subsequent theoretic approaches to literature including poststructuralism, deconstruction theory, and reader-response theory.

CRITICISM

It was frequently alleged that the New Criticism treated literary texts as autonomous and divorced from historical context, and that its practitioners were "uninterested in the human meaning, the social function and effect of literature."

Indicative of the reader-response school of theory, Terence Hawkes writes that the fundamental close reading technique is based on the assumption that "the subject and the object of study—the reader and the text—are stable and independent forms, rather than products of the unconscious process of signification," an assumption which he identifies as the "ideology of liberal humanism," which is attributed to the New Critics who are "accused of attempting to disguise the interests at work in their critical processes." For Hawkes, ideally, a critic ought to be considered to "[create] the finished work by his reading of it, and [not to] remain simply an inert consumer of a 'ready-made' product." In response to critics like Hawkes, Cleanth Brooks, in his essay "The New Criticism" (1979), argued that the New Criticism was not diametrically opposed to the general principles of reader-response theory and that the two could complement one another. For instance, he stated, "If some of the New Critics have preferred to stress the writing rather than the writer, so have they given less stress to the reader—to the reader's response to the work. Yet no one in his right mind could forget the reader.

He is essential for 'realizing' any poem or novel. . .Reader response is certainly worth studying." However, Brooks tempers his praise for the reader-response theory by noting its limitations, pointing out that, "to put meaning and valuation of a literary work at the mercy of any and every individual [reader] would reduce the study of literature to reader psychology and to the history of taste." Another objection to the New Criticism is that it is thought to aim at making criticism scientific, or at least "bringing literary study to a condition rivaling that of science." However,René Wellek points out the erroneous nature of this criticism by noting that a number of the New Critics outlined their theoretical aesthetics in stark contrast to the "objectivity" of the sciences (though it should be noted that Ransom, in his essay "Criticism, Inc." did advocate that "criticism must become more scientific, or precise and systematic"). At times, Wellek defended the New Critics in his essay "The New Criticism: Pro and Contra" (1978).

BEGINNINGS IN ENGLAND, AMERICAN NEW CRITICISM

The New Criticism is the name given to the work of a school of formalist-oriented Anglo-American literary critics whose writings appeared in the years following World War I and came to prominence in the 1940s and 1950s. John Crowe Ransom (1888–1974) coined the moniker itself in his 1941 study *The New Criticism,* in which he provided an overview of the work of key "New" Critics, including I. A. Richards (1893–1979), T. S. Eliot (1888–1965), William Empson (1906–1984), and Yvor Winters (1900–1968). Other important critics associated with this school included F. R. Leavis (1895–1978), Kenneth Burke (1897–1993), Allen Tate (1899–1979), Cleanth Brooks (1906–1994), Robert Penn Warren (1905–1989), and René Wellek (1903–1995), to name a few. Arising, in part, as a response to earlier approaches such as comparative philology and biographical and impressionistic criticism, the New Criticism focused on the individual work of literature, usually the poem, as the sole object of study. These critics placed special emphasis on the formalistic aspects of the literary work, highlighting connotative and associative usage of words and the many figurative devices of language that functioned within the poem.

BEGINNINGS IN ENGLAND

The poet and critic T. S. Eliot gave shape to many of the concerns that would eventually coalesce as New Criticism. Eliot articulated a sense of literary tradition that wrenched criticism away from historical and biographical assessment. In essays such as "Tradition and the Individual Talent," rather than emphasizing the greatness of the individual poet, Eliot stressed the importance of directing criticism upon the poem itself. In turn, the tradition of poetry became the collective vessel through which cultural greatness was transmitted. By distinguishing levels of poetic appreciation, he stressed the benefit of technical appreciation as opposed to the more popular (and coarse) emotional. The aim of the critic was to mine "*significant* emotion, emotion which has its life in the poem and not in the history of the poet" (Eliot, p. 11). Eliot, then, was establishing a way of reading poetry that acknowledged Western tradition as a continuum dating back to Greek antiquity, in which "art never improves, but that material of art is never quite the same" (p. 6). In doing so, he sought a rigorous, formalist appreciation of art as a corrective to more popular modes of modern culture. Eliot, like later New Critics, hoped to cultivate an understanding of great literature as a countervailing force to the vulgar and degradative thrust of modern mass society.

The emphasis on rigorous technical understanding of the literary work would become the hallmark of New Criticism. Most practitioners generally eschewed explicit formulation of theoretical orientation but, rather, focused on the practical application of certain, specific ways of reading. This orientation was captured in the title of I. A. Richards's 1929 work *Practical Criticism,* in which the notion of criticism was allied with careful or "close" readings of poetic works. Richards used his Cambridge Honors students' responses to poetry to reveal the reading deficiencies of ostensibly well-trained readers. These misreadings allowed him to distinguish four distinct meanings that the critic needed to draw out in order to understand a poem: Sense, Feelings, Tone, and Intention. Such an emphasis on reading as a practice, whose focus was to be directed solely upon formal aspects of the literary object, would become a key trait of New Critical thought.

Indeed, the status of the literary object, isolated from historical and cultural context, would gain strength over the next two decades. The poem was the literary object par excellence, its condensed and intense use of language particularly conducive to close reading. For most of the New Critics poetry *was* literature, and they eschewed more lengthy and convoluted genres such as fiction and drama. In the 1920s, Richards had defined the poem as an autonomous and organic being whose unity as an aesthetic object was essential to its study. In the 1930s and 1940s, critics based in the American South would develop this idea further.

AMERICAN NEW CRITICISM

In the United States, several poets and critics based in the South would pick up on Richards's work. This group, associated with the Agrarian Revival, would elaborate upon close reading and the autonomy of the poem, eventually developing these principles into a full-fledged critical ethos. In the 1930s, John Crowe Ransom's writing on poetry positioned literature against the rapacious force of dehumanizing scientific logic. Considering the Revivalists' opposition to Southern industrialization, the turn to poetry as a means to maintain contact with a humanistic, organic, and agrarian tradition made sense. Most of the Agrarians shared a sense of distrust in technology and were religious and conservative in their social views. Ransom, Allen Tate, and others saw poetic knowledge as a remedy to an oppressive scientific modernity. For them, poetry offered access to means of human expression and communication that were not available in other, modern discourses.

Organic unity and the heresy of the paraphrase.

In the journal *Southern Review,* the editors Cleanth Brooks (1906–1994) and Robert Penn Warren (1905–1989) provided an influential platform for New Criticism. From 1935 to 1942, Brooks and Warren, in addition to raising the profile of Southern writers, also established New Critical principles of criticism as central to American literary studies. In his 1947 work *The Well Wrought Urn,* Brooks brought together many of his previous essays into a key text for the movement. Not only articulating its principles, Brooks also provided exemplary New Critical readings of poetry.

In positioning poetic against scientific knowledge, he argued that paradox was characteristic of the unique knowledge of the poem. Unlike science, which sought to eliminate paradox, the poetic work achieved its ontological status through contradictions, oppositions, and ambiguity. Brooks also described the "Heresy of the Paraphrase" in order to highlight the importance of the poetic object as a complete and unified whole. No part of the poem could be read outside of the whole, and the whole was constituted by each individual part. Thus, any summarization or paraphrase of a poem was grossly inadequate, as the internal multiplicities of the poem could not be reduced in such a way. Brooks would, in later work, elaborate upon William K. Wimsatt (1907–1975) and Monroe Beardsley's (1915–1985) concepts of the intentional fallacy and the affective fallacy to reaffirm the organic unity and autonomy of the poem. Aimed at biographical and impressionistic criticism, the former dismissed attempts to gauge the poet's intentions through examination of historical context, whereas the latter argued that the poem is not to be judged based upon its emotional impact on the reader.

DECLINE OF THE NEW CRITICISM AND CONTINUING INFLUENCE

In the years following World War II, New Criticism became a force in Anglo-American literary studies. Its rise was attributed not only to the focus it placed on literature as a discipline unto itself but also to its ease of pedagogical transmission. In an era when universities were flooded with returning soldiers, the New Criticism offered a clear and direct approach to the analysis and appreciation of literature as a rigorous, objective form of study. Several prominent literary critics challenged New Critical methods during its heyday. Alfred Kazin (1915–1998), in the early 1940s, charged that it fetishized formalism. In the latter part of the same decade, R. S. Crane (1886–1967) attacked Brooks and others for their “critical monism,” which was exemplified by their slavish adherence to poetry, and primarily lyrical poetry at that. While Brooks responded to this charge by setting his sights on fiction, he was forced to concede that historical context was an important component in the structure of the novel. But it was in the 1960s, with increasing social flux, when New Criticism began to see its influence diminish. Its ahistorical approach to the study of literature was faulted for depoliticizing literature and, thereby, upholding a political status quo. With increased interest paid to Marxist, hermeneutic, structuralist, and feminist criticism in the 1960s, New Criticism ceded ground to a variety of theoretical and historicist concerns. While in the early twenty-first century the New Criticism is faulted for its limitation of focus and methodological austerity, the impact it has had on the rise of a discipline of literary studies in the United States and that discipline’s underlying reliance upon various methods of “close” reading are lasting achievements.

9

Feminism and Literary Criticism

INTENTIONS OF FEMINIST CRITICISM

The main intentions of feminist criticism are:

- To unfold and widen the female tradition of writing
- To interpret symbolism of womens writing so that it will not be lost or ignored by the male point of view
- To help women's writings retain or gain a significant place even in the world of men
- To consider female writer and their writings from the perspective of a women
- To prevent sexism in literary texts
- To augment alertness regarding sexual politics of language and its approach

INTERNATIONAL WOMEN'S LIBERATION MOVEMENT

Feminist literary criticism started as part of the international women's liberation movement. The Feminine Mystique by Betty Friedan sparked a national debate about women's roles. According to The New York Times obituary of Friedan in 2006, it "ignited the contemporary women's movement in 1963 and as a result permanently transformed the social fabric of the United States and countries around the world" and "is widely regarded as one of the most influential nonfiction books of the 20th century". In the book, Friedan defines women's unhappiness as „„the problem that has no name, She pins the blame on an idealized image of femininity that she calls the feminine mystique.

FRIEDAN'S FOCUS

Friedan, women have been encouraged to confine themselves to the narrow roles of housewife and mother, foresaking education and career aspirations in the process. Betty Friedan attempted to demystify this false feminine mystique, which she described as "a world confined to her own body and beauty, the charming of man, the bearing of babies, and the physical care and serving of husband, children and home" in order to renew the women's fight for equal rights. "The only way for a woman, as for a man, to find herself, to know herself as a person, is by creative work of her own. There is no other way."

KATE MILLER

Kate Millet's Sexual Politics laid the foundation for subsequent feminist scholarship by showing how cultural discourse reflects a systematized subjugation and exploitation of women. Millet also introduces some of the fundamental terms, such as "patriarchal," which gained considerable significance in feminist literary studies. Millet "patriarchal" is a term where male-dominated structures and social arrangements elaborate the oppression of women. By definition it also exhibits androcentrism, meaning male centered. " Sexual Politics" soon became a cult book among feminist critics, especially with its politics of female representations in literature.

ELAINE SHOWALTER: FEMININE, FEMINIST AND FEMALE

Elaine Showalter, an American literary critic, feminist, and writer on cultural and social issues, is one of the founders of feminist literary criticism in United States academia, developing the concept and practice of gynocritics. Showalter coined the term 'gynocritics' to describe literary criticism based in a feminine perspective. Her A Literature of Their Own is a typical example. In her analysis of the historical development, Showalter presents three important stages of women's writing. First, the imitation of the mainstream literary tradition: second, the protest against the standards of this dominant tradition concerning social values and rights: and third, self-discovery which aims at a search for identity. Showalter identifies these stages as Feminine, Feminist and Female. The Feminine period covers the years between 1840-1889; the Feminist period 1890-1920, and the Female period starts in 1920 and comes to the 1960s.

It continues with its renewal of perspectives with the advent of the women's movement after the 1960s. Showalter's contribution to the feminist criticism centres on her rediscovery of the forgotten women writers falling into these stages. Feminists mission is to end all forms of exploitation and injustice against the women. They have a moral obligation to combat against tyranny and subjugation. In order to accomplish feminism's objectives it may be inevitable to oppose religion and economic exploitation, but not intrinsic. Their goal is only to oppose oppression, exploitation and injustice. Feminists advocate social, political and economical rights for women equal to men.

BELL HOOKS ARGUES

"Feminism, as liberation struggle, must exist apart from and as a part of the larger struggle to eradicate domination in all its forms. We must understand that patriarchal domination shares an ideological foundation with racism and other forms of group oppression, and that there is no hope that it can be eradicated while these systems remain intact. This knowledge should consistently inform the direction of feminist theory and practice." Hooks' approach describes that sexism is a particular form of oppression. Though there are also some other forms of oppression, *e.g.*, racism and homophobia. These forms of oppression require too much effort to dismantle like as sexism but feminists objective is to end only sexism against this view that women are subject to sexist oppression and that this is wrong.

MARY WOLLSTONECRAFT: THE RIGHTS OF WOMAN

The influence of Mary Wollstonecraft on over two hundred years of feminist enquiry cannot be overstated, who eloquently anticipated the concerns of second-wave feminism. At the heart of Wollstonecrafts work is an attack on the authority of Edmund Burke, John Milton and Jean-Jacques Rousseau, „fellow authors of a fictitious femininity, and patriarchal enemies in league against female emancipation in which Wollstonecraft exposed Burkes sentimental „aestheticisation of beauty, Rousseaus construction of an ideal, objectified woman, and the flawed misogynistic construction of Miltons Eve. Wollstonecraft reveals herself adept at the deployment of what would later be termed feminist critique. But this is not the limit of her achievement. Most notably in A Vindication of the Rights of Woman, Wollstonecraft argues that well-educated women will be good wives and mothers and ultimately contribute positively to the nation. Wollstonecraft argues that women ought to have an education commensurate with their position in society and then proceeds to redefine that position, claiming that women are essential to the nation because they educate their children and because they could be "companions" to their husbands rather than mere wives.

Instead of viewing women as ornaments to society or property to be traded in marriage, Wollstonecraft maintains that they are human beings deserving of the same fundamental rights as men. Large parts of the Rights of Woman respond vitriolically to conduct book writers such as James Fordyce and John Gregory and educational philosophers such as Jean-Jacques Rousseau, who wanted to deny women an education.

VIRGINIA WOOLF: FOUNDER OF MODERN FEMINIST LITERARY CRITICISM

Virginia Woolf is seen to be the founder of modern feminist literary criticism. As Jane Goldman demonstrates, Woolfs groundbreaking essay A Room of One's Own constitutes a „modern primer for feminist criticism, and her influence on later generations of feminist thought has been immense. Woolf matters to feminist literary criticism not simply as a writer and critic, but also as a subject of critical enquiry. The rescuing of Woolf from the apolitical prisons of Bloomsbury and madness was one of the formative projects of second-wave feminist literary criticism, giving rise to a constructive relationship between the writer, her criticism and her critics.

It is Woolf we must thank for the provocative concepts of thinking back through our mothers, the woman's sentence and the androgynous mind. It is Woolf who wrote of killing the angel in the house and demanded the adaptation of the book to the body. Goldman, in Woolf's creative contradictions and her disruptive boundary-crossing imagination, we find sources for the many, often conflicting, theoretical positions of contemporary feminist thought.

BEAUVOIR: A RICH LEXICON OF IMAGES AND IDEAS

Like Woolf, Beauvoir has left feminism with a rich lexicon of images and ideas, not least of which is her definitive assertion that „one is not born a woman. This concept is implicit in the work and debates surrounding all our protofeminists and pioneers, but in Beauvoir s The Second Sex this fundamental idea receives explicit articulation.

The recognition of the social construction of gender and the coercive nature of gendered subjectivities has been at the centre of feminist literary criticism, enabling it as a discourse to challenge humanist assumptions about identity, nature and progress, and to scrutinize the potent mythical formations of femininity and masculinity. From Kate Millett to Judith Butler, feminist critics have been inspired by Beauvoir, but, as Elizabeth Fallaize argues, the full substance of her monumental work is hardly known.

Since the 1990s, a new generation of feminist literary critics has been working to revise the limited perceptions of Beauvoirs work, and Fallaize contributes to this vital process through a study of Beauvoirs analysis of myth. Myth, claimed Beauvoir, was instrumental in „persuading women of the naturalness of their fate, and Fallaize traces her examination of feminine archetypes from Stendhal to Sade, in the process finding an ecumenical methodology that anticipates later literary-critical movements from Marxism to structuralism to psychoanalysis. The Second Sex prefaces the point at which A History of Feminist Literary Criticism more obviously begins and, as with Wollstonecraft and Woolf, the echoes of Beauvoirs influence will resonate throughout its pages.

SOCIAL CONSTRUCTION OF GENDER

Feminism is an umbrella term for range of views about injustices against women. There are some disagreements also among feminists about the nature of justice in general and the nature of sexism, in particular, the specific kinds of injustice or wrong women suffer; and the group who should be the primary focus of feminist efforts. But all the feminists agreed that there is some sense of "rights" on which achieving equal rights for women is a necessary condition for feminism to succeed.

As Kolodny also points out, there is a basic principle that unites feminist literary critics under one roof despite their plurality of methods:

- "What unites and repeatedly invigorates feminist literary criticism... is neither dogma nor method but an acute and impassioned attentiveness to the ways in which primarily male structures of power are inscribed within our literary inheritance: the consequences of that encoding for women - as characters, as readers, and as writers; and, with that, a shared analytic concern for the implications of that encoding not only for a better understanding of the past but also for an improved reordering of the present and future ".

HISTORICAL BACKGROUND OF FEMINISM CRITICISM

The history of feminism involves the story of feminist movements and of feminist thinkers. Depending on time, culture and country, feminists around the world have sometimes had different causes and goals. Most western feminist historians assert that all movements that work to obtain women's rights should be considered feminist movements, even when they did not apply the term to themselves. Other historians assert that the term should be limited to the modern feminist movement and its descendants. Those historians use the label "proto feminist" to describe earlier movements.

The history of the modern western feminist movements is divided into three "waves". Each is described as dealing with different aspects of the same feminist issues. The first wave refers to the movement of the 19th through early 20th centuries, which dealt mainly with suffrage, working conditions and educational rights for women and girls. The second wave dealt with the inequality of laws, as well as cultural inequalities and the role of women in society. The third wave of feminism, is seen as both a continuation of the second wave and a response to the perceived failures.

Introduction

The terms "feminism" or "feminist" first appeared in France and The Netherlands in 1872, Great Britain in the 1890s, and the United States in 1910. The Oxford English Dictionary lists 1894 for the first appearance of "feminist" and 1895 for "feminism".

The UK Daily News first introduced "feminist" to the English language, importing it from France and branding it as dangerous. "What our Paris Correspondent describes as a 'Feminist' group... in the French Chamber of Deputies". Prior to that time, "Woman's Rights" was probably the term used most commonly, hence Queen Victoria's description of this "mad, wicked folly of 'Woman's Rights'".

Defining feminism can be challenging, but a broad understanding of it includes the acting, speaking, writing, and advocating on behalf of women's issues and rights and identifying injustice to females in the social status quo.

Proto Feminism

People and activists who discussed or advanced women's issues prior to the existence of the feminist movement are sometimes labeled proto feminist. Some scholars, however, criticize the use of this term. Some argue that it diminishes the importance of earlier contributions, while others argue that feminism does not have a single, linear history as implied by terms such as proto feminist or pos tfeminist. Figures from the Italian writer of the 15th century, Christine de Pizan - the first woman to write about the relation of the sexes and the author of Epître au Dieu d'Amour, Christine de Pizan's work having been recognized by Simone de Beauvoir, Heinrich Cornelius Agrippa and Modesta di Pozzo di Forzi, who worked in the 16th century, up to and including the 17th century writers Hannah Woolley in England,Juana Inés de la Cruz in Mexico, Marie Le Jars de Gournay, Anne Bradstreet, and François Poullain de la Barre are sometimes described as protofeminist.

Eighteenth Century: The Age of Enlightenment

The Age of Enlightenment was characterised by secular intellectual reasoning, and a flowering of philosophical writing. Many Enlightenment philosophers defended the rights of women, including Jeremy Bentham, Marquis de Condorcet, and, perhaps most notably, Mary Wollstonecraft.

Jeremy Bentham

The remarkable utilitarian and classical liberal philosopher Jeremy Bentham said that it was the placing of women in a legally inferior position that made him choose the career of a reformist, at the age of eleven. Bentham spoke for a complete equality between sexes including the right to vote and to participate in the government, and opposed the strongly different sexual moral standards to women and men. In his Introduction to the Principles of Morals and Legislation Bentham strongly condemned the common practice in many countries to deny women's rights because of their allegedly inferior minds. Bentham gave many examples of able female regents.

Marquis de Condorcet

The mathematician, classical liberal politician, leading French revolutionary, republican and Voltairean anti-clericalist, Marquis de Condorcetwas a fierce defender of human rights, including the equality of women and the abolition of slavery, already on the 1780s. He advocated women's suffrage for the new government, writing an article for Journal de la Société de 1789, and by publishing De l'admission des femmes au droit de cité in 1790.

Wollstonecraft and a Vindication

Perhaps the most cited feminist writer of the time was Mary Wollstonecraft, often characterised as the first feminist philosopher. A Vindication of the Rights of Woman is one of the first works that can unambiguously be called feminist, although by modern standards her comparison of women to the nobility, the elite of society may at first seem dated as a feminist argument. Wollstonecraft identified the education and upbringing of women as creating their limited expectations based on a self-image dictated by the male gaze. Despite her perceived inconsistencies reflective of problems that had no easy answers, this book remains a foundation stone of feminist thought. Wollstonecraft believed that both genders contributed to inequality. She took it for granted that women had considerable power over men, but that both would require education to ensure the necessary changes in social attitudes. Her legacy remains in the continued need for women to speak out and tell their stories. Her own achievements speak to her own determination given her humble origins and scant education.

Wollstonecraft attracted the mockery of Samuel Johnson, who described her and her ilk as "Amazons of the pen". Given his relationship with Hester Thrale it would appear that Johnson's problem was not with intelligent educated women, but that they should encroach onto a male territory of writing. For many commentators, Wollstonecraft represents the first codification of "equality" feminism, or a refusal of the feminine, a child of the Enlightenment.

Other Important Writers

Other important writers of the time included Catherine Macaulay who argued in 1790 that the apparent weakness of women was caused by their miseducation. In other parts of Europe, Hedvig Charlotta Nordenflycht was writing in Sweden, and what is thought to be the first scientific society for women was founded in Middelburg, in the south of Holland in 1785. This was the Natuurkundig Genootschap der Dames. which met regularly to 1881, finally dissolving in 1887. Journals for women which focused on science became popular during this period as well. Other authors, however, point out that women have been scientists for 4,000 years.

Nineteenth Century

The Feminine Ideal

19th-century feminists reacted not only to the injustices they saw but also against the increasingly suffocating Victorian image of the "proper" role of women and their "sphere". This was the "feminine ideal" as typified in Victorian conduct books by Sarah Stickney Ellis or Mrs. Beeton. The Angel in the House and El ångel del hogar, bestsellers by Coventry Patmore and Maria del Pilar Sinués de Marco, came to symbolise the Victorian feminine ideal.

Feminism in Fiction

Just as Jane Austen had addressed the restricted lives women faced in the early part of the century, Charlotte Brontë, Anne Brontë, Elizabeth Gaskell and George Eliot depicted women's misery and frustration. In her autobiographical novel Ruth Hall, American journalist Fanny Fern describes her own struggle to support her children as a newspaper columnist after her husband's untimely death. Louisa May Alcott penned a strongly feminist novel, A Long Fatal Love Chase, that concerns a young woman's attempts to flee from her bigamist husband and become independent.

Some male authors, too, recognised the injustice women faced. The novels of George Meredith, George Gissing and Thomas Hardy, and the plays of Henrik Ibsen, also outlined the plight of women of the time. Meredith's Diana of the Crossways is an account of Caroline Norton's life. One critic later called Ibsen's plays "feministic propaganda".

Marion Reid and Caroline Norton

At the beginning of the 19th century, although individual women, and some men, were speaking out, it is doubtful how influential they were, other than to create awareness. There was little sign of change in the political or social order, nor any evidence of a recognizable women's movement. By the end of the century the voices of concern began to coalesce into something more tangible, paralleling the emergence of a more rigid social model and code of conduct, that Marion Reid would refer to as a "Womanliness"that admitted to "self-extinction". While the increasing emphasis on feminine virtue partly stirred the call for a woman's movement, the tensions that this role duality caused for women plagued many early 19th century feminists with doubt and worry, and fueled opposing views. In Scotland, Reid published her influential A plea for women in 1843 which set an agenda on both sides of the Atlantic, including voting rights for women.

Caroline Norton became active in advocating changes to British law. Upon entering into an abusive marriage she had become painfully aware that legally women were "non-existent".The publicity that she generated including her appeal to Queen Victoria helped change the situation for married women and child custody in England.

Florence Nightingale and Frances Power Cobbe

While many women including Norton were wary of organized movements, their actions and words often motivated and inspired such movements. Amongst these was Florence Nightingale whose conviction that women had all the potential of men but none of the opportunities drove her to a career that would make her a national figure as a scientist and administrator even if the popular image of her at the time emphasized her feminine virtues more. The paradox of the gulf between the achievements which we recognize now, and how she was portrayed underline the plight that women of talent and determination faced during the mid-1850s. Like all political movements, feminism knows several different ideological theories and opinions. Feminists could not always be supportive of each other's efforts, and also distanced themselves from others. British woman Harriet Martineau and many others dismissed Wollstonecraft's contributions as dangerous, and deplored Norton's candidness, but seized on the abolition of slavery campaign she had witnessed in the United States, as one that should logically be applied to women. Her Society in America was pivotal in that for the first time it caught the imagination of women who urged her to take up their cause.

Anna Doyle Wheeler had come under the influence of the Saint Simonian socialists while working in France, advocated suffrage and attracted the attention of Benjamin Disraeli, the Conservative leader, as a dangerous radical on a par with Jeremy Bentham. Later she was to be the inspiration for early socialist and feminist advocate William Thompson, author of the first work published in English to advocate full equality of rights for women, the 1825 "Appeal of One Half of the Human Race...".

Earlier centuries had concentrated on women's exclusion from education as the key to their being relegated to domestic roles and denied advancement. The education of women in the 19th century was no better, and Frances Power Cobbe was but one of many women who were calling for reform. But now many other issues were starting to gain attention including marital and property rights, and domestic violence. Nevertheless women like Martineau and Cobbe in Britain, and Margaret Fuller in America, were achieving journalistic employment which placed them in a position to influence other women. Women like Cobbe were referring to "Woman's Rights", not just in the abstract, but as an identifiable cause.

The ladies of Langham Place

Barbara Leigh Smith and her friends started to meet regularly during the 1850s in Langham Place in London to discuss the need for women to present a united voice to achieve reform. This earned them the name of the "Ladies of Langham Place", and included Bessie Rayner Parkes and Anna Jameson. They focused on education, employment and marital law. One of the causes they vigorously pursued became the Married Women's Property Committee of 1855. They collected thousands of signatures for petitions for legislative reform, some of which were successful. Smith had also attended the first women's convention in Seneca Falls, New York in America in 1848.

Smith and Parker wrote many articles, both separately and together, on education and employment opportunities, and like Norton in the same year, Smith summarized the legal framework for injustice in 1854 in her A Brief Summary of the Laws of England concerning Women. Playing an important role in the English Women's Journal, she was able to reach large numbers of women, and the response of women to this journal led to their creation of the Society for Promoting the Employment of Women. The Langham Ladies continued to provide inspiration, infrastructure and funding for much of the women's movement in England for the remainder of the century. Smith's Married Women's Property committee collected 26,000 signatures to change the law for all women including unmarried.

Harriet Taylor published her Enfranchisement in 1851, and wrote about the inequities of family law. In 1853 she married John Stuart Mill, providing him with much of the subject material for The Subjection of Women. Taylor's relatively low profile after her marriage has been a subject of speculation, but Mill was perhaps in a better position to translate theory into action.

Emily Davies was another woman who would encounter the Langham group, and with Elizabeth Garrett would help create branches of SPEW outside of London. While obtaining education remained largely a privilege rather than a right, the small group of women who were able to do so, were then able to campaign for women as a whole, realizing it was not just a portal to employment and financial self sufficiency but that the denial of education was tied to women's expectations and their self image of their potential and worth.

Educational Reform

The interrelated themes of barriers to education and employment continued to form the backbone of feminist thought in the 19th century, as described, for instance by Harriet Martineau in her 1859 article "Female Industry" in the Edinburgh Journal. The economy was changing but women's lot was not. Martineau, however, remained a moderate, for practical reasons, and unlike Cobbe, did not support the emerging call for the vote.

Slowly the efforts of women like Davies and the Langham group started to make inroads. Queen's College and Bedford College in London were starting to offer some education to women from 1848, and by 1862 Davies was establishing a committee to persuade the universities to allow women to sit for the recently established in 1858. Local Examinations, with partial success. A year later she published The Higher Education of Women. She and Leigh Smith founded the first higher educational institution for women, with 5 students, which became Girton College, Cambridge in 1869, followed by Newnham College, Cambridge in 1871 and Lady Margaret Hall at Oxford in 1879. Bedford had started awarding degrees the previous year. Despite these measurable advances, few could take advantage of them and life for women students was still difficult.

In the Ilbert Bill controversy in 1883, Bengali women who supported the bill responded by claiming that they were more educated than the English women opposed to the bill, and pointed out that more Indian women had degrees than British women did at the time.

As part of the continuing dialogue between British and American feminists, Elizabeth Blackwell, one of the first women in the US to graduate in medicine, lectured in Britain with Langham support. They also supported Elizabeth Garrett's attempts to assail the walls of British medical education against virulent opposition, eventually taking her degree in France. Garrett's very successful campaign to run for office on the London School Board in 1870 is another example of a how a small band of very determined women were starting to reach positions of influence at the level of local government and public bodies.

Women's Campaigns

Campaigns gave women the opportunity to test their new political skills, for disparate elements to come together, to join forces with other social reform groups. One had been the campaign for the Married Women's Property Act, eventually passed in 1882. Next was the campaign to repeal the Contagious Diseases Acts of 1864, 1866 and 1869, which brought together women's groups and utilitarian liberals such as John Stuart Mill.

Women in general were outraged by the inherent inequity and misogyny of the legislation and for the first time women in large numbers took up the rights of prostitutes. Prominent critics included Blackwell, Nightingale, and Martineau and Elizabeth Wolstenholme. Elizabeth Garrett did not support the campaign, though her sister Millicent did, later admitting the campaign had done good.

However, Josephine Butler, already experienced in prostitution issues, a charismatic leader and a seasoned campaigner, emerged as the natural leader of what became the Ladies National Association for the Repeal of the Contagious Diseases Acts. This demonstrated the potential power of an organised lobby group. The association successfully argued that the Acts not only demeaned prostitutes, but all women and men too by containing a blatant double sexual standard. Butler's activities resulted in the radicalisation of many moderate women. The Acts were repealed in 1886.

On a smaller scale was Annie Besant's campaign for the rights of match girls and against the appalling conditions under which they worked demonstrated how to raise public concern over social issues.

Waves of Feminism

First Wave

First-wave feminism refers to a period of feminist activity during the 19th and early 20th centuries especially in Europe and the Anglosphere; it focused primarily on gaining the right of women's suffrage, the right to be educated, better working conditions and double sexual standards. The term, "first-wave", was coined retrospectively after the term second-wave feminism began to be used to describe a newer feminist movement that focused as much on fighting social and cultural inequalities as further political inequalities.

In the U.S., leaders of the feminist movement campaigned for the abolition of slavery and Temperance prior to championing women's rights. American first-wave feminism involved a wide range of women, some belonging to conservative Christian groups, others resembling the diversity and radicalism of much of second-wave feminism. In the United States first-wave feminism is considered to have ended with the passage of the Nineteenth Amendment to the United States Constitution, granting women the right to vote.

The antislavery campaign of the 1830s provided a perfect cause for women to take up, identify with and learn political skills from. Attempts to exclude women only fuelled their convictions further. Sarah and Angelina Grimké moved rapidly from the emancipation of slaves to the emancipation of women. The most influential feminist writer of the time was the colourful journalist Margaret Fuller whose Woman in the Nineteenth Century was published in 1845. Her dispatches from Europe for the New York Tribune helped create a universality in the women's rights movement.

Elizabeth Cady Stanton and Lucretia Mott met in 1840 while en route to London where they were shunned as women by the male leadership of the firstWorld's Anti-Slavery Convention. In 1848, Mott and Stanton held a woman's rights convention in Seneca Falls, New York, where a declaration of independence for women was drafted. Lucy Stone helped to organize the first National Women's Rights Convention in 1850, a much larger event at which Sojourner Truth, Abby Kelley Foster and others spoke, and which sparked Susan B. Anthony to take up the cause of women's rights. Barbara Leigh Smith met with Mott in 1858, strengthening the link between the feminist movements on each side of the Atlantic.

Stanton and Matilda Joslyn Gage saw the church as a major obstacle to women's rights. They therefore welcomed the emerging literature on matriarchy, and both Gage and Stanton produced works on this topic: they collaborated on The Woman's Bible. Stanton wrote "The Matriarchate or Mother-Age" and Gage wrote "Woman, Church and State", neatly inverting Bachofen's thesis and adding a unique epistemological perspective, the critique of objectivity and the perception of the subjective.

Stanton made an astute observation regarding assumptions of female inferiority "The worst feature of these assumptions is that women themselves believe them". However this attempt to replace "androcentric" theological tradition with a "gynecentric" view made little headway in the women's movement which was dominated by religious elements, and she and Gage were largely ignored by subsequent generations.

By 1913, Feminism became widely known in the U.S. Major issues in the 1910s and 1920s included suffrage, economics and employment, sexualities and families, war and peace, and a Constitutional amendment for equality. Both equality and difference were seen as routes to women's empowerment.

Organizations at the time included theNational Woman's Party, suffrage advocacy groups such as the National American Woman Suffrage Association and the National League of Women Voters, career associations such as the American Association of University Women, the National Federation of

Business and Professional Women's Clubs, and the National Women's Trade Union League, war and peace groups such as the Women's International League for Peace and Freedom and the International Council of Women, alcohol-focused groups like the Woman's Christian Temperance Unionand the Women's Organization for National Prohibition Reform, and among organizations centered on race and gender the National Association of Coloured Women. Leaders and theoreticians then included Jane Addams, Ida B. Wells-Barnett, Alice Paul, Carrie Chapman Catt, Margaret Sanger, and Charlotte Perkins Gilman.

Suffrage

The fight for women's suffrage represents one of the most fundamental struggles of women, because explicitly denying them representation in the legislature and public governmental bodies gave an unambiguous message of second-class citizenship. No campaign has embedded itself so deeply in popular imagination than that of women's suffrage over the past 250 years. However it took a long time to work its way up the list of priorities to gradually become the dominant issue. The French Revolution accelerated this, with the assertions of Condorcet and de Gouges, and it was women that marched on Versailles. This reached its climax with the founding of the Society of Revolutionary Republican Women which included suffrage on its agenda, before being suppressed at the end of that year. However, this ensured that the issue was on the European political agenda.

German women were involved in the Vormärz, a prelude to the 1848 revolution. In Italy Clara Maffei, Cristina Trivulzio Belgiojoso and Ester Martini Currica were politically active in the events leading up to the events of 1848 there. In Britain suffrage emerged in the writings of Wheeler and Thompson in the 1820s, and Reid, Taylor and Anne Knight in the 1840s.

The Suffragettes

The Langham Place ladies again played a central role in women's suffrage, and set up a suffrage committee in 1866 at a meeting at Elizabeth Garrett's home, renamed the London Society for Women's Suffrage in 1867. Soon similar committees had spread across the country, raising petitions, and worked closely with JS Mill. Denied outlets by establishment periodicals, women like Lydia Becker started the Women's Suffrage Journal in 1870.

Other publications included Richard Pankhurst's Englishwoman's Review. Tactical disputes were the biggest problem, and the membership of various groups varied over time. One issue was whether men like Mill should be involved. As it was Mill also withdrew as the movement became more aggressive with each disappointment. The political pressure ensured debate, but year after year was defeated in parliament.

Despite this, the women benefited from their increasing political experience, which translated into slow progress at the level of local government and public bodies. However, the years of frustration took their toll, and many women became increasingly radicalised. Some refused to pay taxes, and the Pankhurst family emerged as the dominant influence of the movement, having also founded the Women's Franchise League in 1889.

International Suffrage

The Isle of Man was the first free standing jurisdiction to grant women the vote, followed by New Zealand in 1893, where Kate Sheppard had pioneered reform. Some Australian states had also granted women the vote. This included Victoria for a brief period, South Australia, and Western Australia. Australian women received the vote at the Federal level in 1902, Finland in 1906, and Norway initially in 1907.

Twentieth Century

Early Twentieth Century: The Edwardian Era

Women's Suffragists and the Prelude to War

The Edwardian era saw a loosening of Victorian rigidity and complacency; women had more employment opportunities, and were more active, leading to a relaxing of clothing restrictions.

Looking back from now, western women's rights movements seem to be dominated by the increasing clamour for political reform and votes for women. Books, articles, speeches, pictures and papers from the period however, show a diverse range of theme's being discussed in the public discours. In The Netherlands for instance, educational rights, rights to medical care, better working conditions, peace and double sexual standards were main feminist issues at the time. And feminists called themselves feminists without a lot of ado.

The charismatic and controversial Pankhursts took the political initiative, forming the Women's Social and Political Union in 1903. As Emmline Pankhurst put it, votes for women were seen then as no longer "a right, but as a desperate necessity". At the state level, Australia and the United States had already given the vote to some women, and American feminists such as Susan B Anthony visited Britain. While the WSPU is the best known suffrage group, it was only one of many, such as the Women's Freedom League and the National Union of Women's Suffrage Societies led by Millicent Garrett Fawcett. WSPU was largely a family affair, although externally financed. Christabel Pankhurst became the dominant figure and gathered friends such as Annie Kenney, Flora Drummond, Teresa Billington, Ethel Smythe, Grace Roe and Norah Dacre Fox later known as Norah Elam around her. Veterans such as Elizabeth Garrett also joined. In 1906, the Daily Mail first labeled these women 'suffragettes' as a form of ridicule, but the term was quickly embraced in Britain to describe a more militant form of suffragist, which were becoming increasingly visible with their marches and distinctive Green, Purple and White emblems, while the Artists' Suffrage League created dramatic graphics. Even underwear in WPSU colours appeared in stores.

They quickly learned new ways of exploiting the media and photography. The visual record they have left remains vivid, such as the 1914 photograph of Emmeline, shown here. As the movement became more active deep divisions appeared with older leaders of the movement parting company with the radicals. Sometimes the splits were ideological, and others tactical. Even Christabel's sister, Sylvia, was expelled.

Slowly but surely the protests became more vigorous and included heckling, banging on doors, smashing shop windows, and eventually, by 1914, arson. In 1913, one member of the group, Emily Davison, sacrificed herself on Derby Day, dying under the King's horse. These tactics produced mixed results of sympathy and alienation and many protesters were imprisoned, creating an increasingly embarrassing situation for the government.

Matters progressively worsened, with hunger strikes, then risky force feeding, and eventually the notorious Prisoners Act 1913, nicknamed the Cat and Mouse Act which allowed women to be released when their illness or injury became dangerously acute, but officers were then not prevented from arresting and charging these women again once they recovered. It could be argued, however, as did Reginald McKenna, the Home Secretary, that this was relatively humane, since a number of these women appeared ready to die for their cause.

If the aims were to reveal institutional sexism in British society, women's suffragists certainly created publicity around the issue. They also inadvertently drew attention to the brutality of the legal system at the time.

Feminist Science Fiction

At the beginning of the 20th century, feminist science fiction emerged as a sub-genre of science fiction which tends to deal with women's roles in society. Women writers in the utopian literature movement of the 19th century and early 20th century, at the time of first wave feminism, often addressed sexism. Charlotte Perkins Gilman did so in Herland, for example. The Sultana's Dream by Bengali Muslim feminist, Roquia Sakhawat Hussain, depicts a gender-reversed purdah in a futuristic world.

During the 1920s writers such as Clare Winger Harris and Gertrude Barrows Bennett published science fiction stories written from female perspectives and occasionally dealt with gender and sexuality-based topics. Meanwhile, much pulp science fiction published during 1920s and 1930s carried an exaggerated view of masculinity along with sexist portrayals of women. By the 1960s science fiction was combining sensationalism with political and technological critiques of society. With the advent of feminism, women's roles were questioned in this "subversive, mind expanding genre."

Feminist science fiction poses questions about social issues such as how society constructs gender roles, the role reproduction plays in defining gender and the unequal political and personal power of men and women. Some of the most notable feminist science fiction works have illustrated these themes using utopias to explore a society in which gender differences or gender power imbalances do not exist, or dystopias to explore worlds in which gender inequalities are intensified, thus asserting a need for feminist work to continue.

Mid-Twentieth Century: Interbellum

In the First World War women entered the labour market in unprecedented numbers, often in new sectors. They discovered that their work outside the home was now valued, but also left large numbers of women bereaved and with a net loss of household income. Meanwhile the large numbers of men killed and wounded created a major shift in demographic composition. War also split the feminist groups, with many opposed to the war, while other women became involved in the White Feather campaign.

Certain recent feminist scholars, such as Francoise Thebaud and Nancy Cott, also point out World War I's conservativizing effect in some countries, noting the reinforcement of traditional imagery as well as literature directed towards motherhood. These phenomena during World War I and between the two wars have been called the "nationalization of women."

In the years between the wars, women continued to fight discrimination and opposition to women's rights from the establishment and the media. In Virginia Woolf's A Room of One's Own, Woolf describes the extent of the backlash and her frustration at the waste of so much talent. Important writers of the time also included Rebecca West. Although the word "feminism" was now in use, the media and others gave it such a negative image, that women were afraid to embrace it. By 1938, Woolf was writing, in Three Guineas, "an old word...that has much harm in its day and is now obsolete". On another occasion she had to defend West, who had been attacked as a "feminist". Woolf also started to paint lesbian sexuality in a positive light "women...had almost always been seen in relation to men", and to examine the constructs of gender more minutely. West has perhaps best been remembered for her comment "I myself have never been able to find out precisely what feminism is: I only know that people call me a feminist whenever I express sentiments that differentiate me from a doormat, or a prostitute."

In the 1920s, the non-traditional styles and attitudes of flappers gained popularity among women in the U.S. and U.K.

Electoral Reform

Women's demand for the vote could no longer be ignored, and the Representation of the People Act 1918 enacted in February of that year gave men near-universal suffrage, and the vote to women over 30 years of age.

Representation of the People Act 1928 finally provided equal suffrage for men and women. It also shifted the socioeconomic make up of the electorate towards the working class, favouring the Labour Party who were more sympathetic to women's issues. The first election was held in December, and gave Labour the most seats in the house to date.

The electoral reforms also allowed women to run for parliament. Although Christabel Pankhurst narrowly failed to win a seat in 1918, in 1919 and 1920 bothLady Astor and Margaret Wintringham won seats for the Conservatives and Liberals respectively, by succeeding their husband's seats. Labour swept to power in 1924, including Ellen Wilkinson. Constance Markievicz was the first woman to be elected, in Ireland in 1918, but as an Irish nationalist, refused to take her seat. Astor's proposal to form a women's party in 1929 was unsuccessful, which some historians feel was a missed opportunity, and there were still only 12 women in parliament by 1940. Women gained considerable electoral experience over the next few years as a series of minority governments ensured almost annual elections. Close affiliation with Labour also proved to be a problem for NUSEC, which had little support in the Conservative party. However, their persistence with Prime Minister Stanley Baldwin was rewarded by the passage of the Representation of the People Act 1928.

Other Jurisdictions

Women received the vote in Denmark and Iceland in 1915, the USSR in 1917, Austria, Germany and Canada in 1918, and many countries including the Netherlands in 1919, and Turkey and South Africa in 1930. French women did not receive the vote till 1945. Liechtenstein was one of the last countries, in 1984.

The Women's Movement and Social Reform

As with many movements, women soon discovered that political change does not necessarily translate into a noticeable change in circumstances, and with economic recession they were the most vulnerable sector of the workforce. Some women who had held jobs prior to the war were obliged to give them up to returning soldiers, and many had been made redundant. With limited franchise, the NUWSS needed to change its role. The new organisation, the National Union of Societies for Equal Citizenship still advocated equality in franchise but extended its scope to examine equality in the social and economic area. Legislative reform was sought for those laws that were discriminatory, including family law andprostitution.

One area of division which is significant in the light of later developments was between equality and equity, which addressed accommodation to allow women to overcome barriers to fulfillment. In more recent years this has been referred to as the "equality vs. difference conundrum". Eleanor Rathbone, who became an MP in 1929, succeeded Millicent Garrett as president in 1919. She expressed the critical need for consideration of difference in gender relationships as "what women need to fulfill the potentialities of their own natures". A more formal split appeared with the 1924 Labour government's social reforms, with a splinter group of strict egalitarians forming the Open Door Council in May 1926.

This eventually became an international movement, and continued till 1965. Other important social legislation of this period included the Sex Disqualification Act 1919, and the Matrimonial Causes Act 1923. In 1932, NUSEC separated advocacy from education, and continued the former activities as the National Council for Equal Citizenship and education became the role of the Townswomen's Guild. The council continued until the end of the Second World War.

In 1921, Margaret Mackworth founded the Six Point Group which included Rebecca West. It was a political lobby group, whose aims were political, occupational, moral, social, economic and legal equality. Thus it was ideologically allied with the Open Door Council, rather than National Council. It also lobbied at an international level, such as theLeague of Nations, and continued its work till 1983. In retrospect both ideological groups were influential in advancing women's rights in their own way. Despite women being admitted to the House of Commons from 1918, Mackworth, a Viscountess in her own right, spent a lifetime fighting to take her seat in the House of Lords against bitter opposition, a battle which only achieved its goal in the year of her death. This revealed the weaknesses of the Sex Disqualification Act.

Mackworth also founded Time and Tide which became the group's journal, and to which West, Virginia Woolf, Rose Macaulay and many others contributed. A number of other women's periodicals also appeared in the 1920s, including Woman and Home, and Good Housekeeping, but whose content reflect very different aspirations. In 1925 Rebecca West wrote in Time and Tide something that reflected not only the movement's need to redefine itself post suffrage, but a continual need for re-examination of goals. "When those of our army whose voices are inclined to coolly tell us that the day of sex-antagonism is over and henceforth we have only to advance hand in hand with the male, I do not believe it."

Reproductive Rights

As feminism sought to redefine itself, new issues rose to the surface, one of which was reproductive rights. Even discussing the issue could be hazardous. Annie Besant had been tried in 1877 for publishing Charles Knowlton's Fruits of Philosophy, a work on family planning, under the Obscene Publications Act 1857. Knowlton had previously been convicted in the United States. She and her colleague Charles Bradlaugh were convicted but acquitted on appeal, the subsequent publicity resulting in a decline in the birth rate. Not discouraged in the slightest, Besant followed this with The Law of Population.

Similarly in America, Margaret Sanger was prosecuted for her Family Limitation under the Comstock Act 1873, in 1914, and fled to Britain where she met with Marie Stopes until it was safe for her to return. Sanger continued to risk prosecution, and her work was prosecuted in Britain. Stopes was never prosecuted but was regularly denounced for her work in promoting birth control. In 1917 Sanger started the Birth Control Review. In 1926, Sanger gave a lecture on birth control to the women's auxiliary of the Ku Klux Klan in Silver Lake, New Jersey.Even more controversial was the establishment of the Abortion Law Reform Association in 1936.

The penalty for abortion had been reduced from execution to life imprisonmentby the Offences against the Person Act 1861, although some exceptions were allowed in the Infant Life Act 1929. Following the prosecution of Dr. Aleck Bourne in 1938, the 1939 Birkett Committee made recommendations for reform, that like many other women's issues, were set aside at the outbreak of the Second World War.

In 1935 Germany amended its eugenics law, Law for the Prevention of Hereditarily Diseased Offspring, to promote abortion for women who have congenital and genetic disorders, or whose unborn fetuses have such hereditary disorders. Before the German law was passed, Rudin's "Eugenic Sterilization: An Urgent Need" article was published in the journal Margaret Sanger started.

In The Netherlands Aletta H. Jacobs, first Dutch female doctor, and Wilhelmina Drucker were frontwomen in discussing and taking action on the theme reproductive rights. Jacobs started to import pessaria from Germany and gave them out for free to poor women in her praxis.

1940s

The Second World War was involved double duty for many women—they retained their domestic chores and often added a paid job, especially one related to a war industry. Much more so than in the previous war, large numbers of women were hired for unskilled or semi-skilled jobs in munitions, and barriers against married women taking jobs were eased.The popular icon Rosie the Riveter became a symbol for a generation of working women. Some 300,000 women served in military uniform. With so many young men gone, sports organizers tried to set up pro women's teams, such as theAll-American Girls Professional Baseball League; it closed after the war. Indeed most munitions plants closed, and civilian plants replaced the new women with returning veterans, who had priority.

Second Wave

Second-wave feminism refers to a period of feminist activity beginning in the early '60s and through the late 1980s. Second Wave Feminism has existed continuously since then, and continues to coexist with what some people call Third Wave Feminism. Second wave feminism saw cultural and political inequalities as inextricably linked. The movement encouraged women to understand aspects of their personal lives as deeply politicized, and reflective of a sexist structure of power. If first-wavers focused on absolute rights such as suffrage, second-wavers were largely concerned with other issues of equality, such as the end to discrimination.

Betty Friedan, the Feminine Mystique, and the Rise of Women's Liberation

In 1963, Betty Friedan published her exposé The Feminine Mystique, giving a voice to the discontent and disorientation many women felt in being shunted into homemaking positions after graduating from college. In the book, Friedan explored the roots of the change in women's roles from essential workforce during World War II to homebound housewife and mother after the war, and assessed the forces that drove this change in perception of women's roles.

Over the following decade, the phrase and concept "Women's Liberation" began to be discussed.

While people sometimes use the expression "Women's Liberation" to refer to feminism throughout history, the term is relatively recent. "Liberation" has been associated with women's aspirations since 1895, and appears in the context of "women's liberation" in The Second Sex by Simone de Beauvoir in 1949 which was translated to English in 1953. The phrase "Women's Liberation" was first used in 1964, and appeared in print in 1966.

It was in use at the 1967 American Students for a Democratic Society convention, which held a panel discussion on it. By 1968, although the term Women's Liberation Front appeared in "Ramparts" it was starting to refer to the whole women's movement. In Chicago, women disillusioned with the New Left were meeting separately in 1967, and publishing Voice of the Women's Liberation Movement by March 1968. When the Miss America Pageant was held in September, the media referred to the demonstrations as Women's Liberation, and the Chicago Women's Liberation Union was formed in 1969. Similar groups with similar titles appeared in many parts of the United States. Bra-burning became associated with the movement, and the media coined other terms such as "libber." Women's Liberation, compared to various rival terms for the new feminism which co-existed for a while, captured the popular imagination and has persisted, although today the older term Women's Movement is used just as frequently.

1960s' feminism—and its theory and activism—was informed and fueled by the social, cultural, and political climate of that decade. This was a time when there was an increasing entry of women into higher education, the establishment of academic women's studies courses and departments and feminist thinking in many other related fields such as politics, sociology, history and literature, and a time when there was increasing questioning of accepted standards and authority.

It also became increasingly evident, almost from the beginning, that the Women's Liberation movement consisted of multiple "feminisms"—due to the diverse origins from which groups had coalesced and intersected, and the complexity and contentiousness of the issues involved. Starting in the 1980s, one of the most vocal critics of the whole movement has been bell hooks, who comments on lack of voice by the most oppressed women, glossing over of race and class as inequalities, and failure to address the issues that divided women.

Feminist Writing

Following the changes in women's consciousness provoked by Betty Friedan's The Feminine Mystique, in the 1970s new feminist activists took on more political and sexual issues in their writings.

Feminist writing in the early 1970s ranges from Gloria Steinem, to Kate Millett's Sexual Politics. Millett's uses her bleak survey of male writers and their attitudes and biases to demonstrates her thesis that sex is politics, and politics is power imbalance in relationships. Her pessimism is reflected in her description of "the desert we inhabit". From the same period come Shulamith Firestone's The Dialectic of Sex, Germaine Greer's The Female Eunuch, Sheila Rowbotham's Women's Liberation and the New Politicsand Juliet Mitchell's Woman's Estate, the following year. Firestone based her concept of revolution on Marxism, referred to the "sex war", and interestingly, in view of the debates over patriarchy, claimed that male domination dated to "back beyond recorded history to the animal kingdom itself". Co-founder of Redstockings, Firestone, considered a radical, put "feminism" back in the vocabulary.

Greer, Rowbotham and Mitchell represent an English perspective on the growing revolution, but as Mitchell argues, this should be seen as an international phenomenon, but taking on different manifestations relating to local culture. British women too, drew on left political backgrounds, and organised small local discussion groups. Much of this took Bartplace through the London Women's Liberation Workshop and its publications Shrew and the LWLW Newsletter. Although there were marches, the focus was on what Kathie Sarachild of Redstockings had called consciousness-raising. One of the functions of this was, as Mitchell describes it was that women would "find what they thought was an individual dilemma is social predicament". Women found that their own personal experiences were information that they could trust in formulating political analyses.

Meanwhile in the U.S., women's frustrations crystallised around the failure to ratify the Equal Rights Amendment during the 1970s. Against this background appeared Susan Brownmiller's Against Our Will in 1975, introducing a more explicit agenda directed against male violence, specifically male sexual violence in a treatise on rape. Perhaps her most memorable phrase was "pornography is the theory and rape the practice", creating a nexus that would cause deep fault lines to develop, largely around the concepts ofobjectification and commodification. Brownmiller's other major contribution is In our Time, a history of women's liberation. Less well known is Femininity a gentler deconstruction of a concept that has had an uneasy relationship with feminism.

Different Feminist Views on Pornography

One of the first women to develop the further implications of pornography was Susan Griffin in Pornography and Silence. Moving beyond Brownmiller and Griffin's positions areCatharine MacKinnon, and Andrea Dworkin with whom she collaborated. They took up a position that is generally regarded as the extreme end of the spectrum, and therefore not widely supported in the movement.

However, their influence in debates and activism on pornography and prostitution has been striking, in particular at the Supreme Court of Canada. Their position has been characterised as an extreme politicisation of sex, in which an individual woman's experience is generalised, so that women as a class are seen always to be victims. This is a position that many feminists, civil libertarians and jurists find uncomfortable and alienating.

MacKinnon, who is a lawyer, has a style considered to be frequently angry and acerbic. "To be about to be raped is to be gender female in the process of going about life as usual"She has described the perception of the inferiority of women as springing from misogyny, and is unconvinced that women ever express agency in their relationships with men. Sexual harassment, she says "doesn't mean that they all want to fuck us, they just want to hurt us, dominate us, and control us, and that is fucking us." To some radical feminists, she is a hero, the only person to truly express the pain of being woman in an unequal society, and to portray that reality through the experiences of the battered and violated, which she claims to be the norm. A useful evolution of this approach has been to transform the research and perspective on rape from an individual experience to a social problem.

Third Wave

The Third-wave of feminism began in the early 1990s. The movement arose as responses to what young women thought of as perceived failures of the second-wave. It was also a response to the backlash against initiatives and movements created by the second-wave. Third-wave feminism seeks to challenge or avoid what it deems the second wave's "essentialist" definitions of femininity, which over-emphasized the experiences of upper middle class white women. A post-structuralist interpretation of gender and sexuality is central to much of the third wave's ideology. Third wave feminists often focus on "micropolitics", and challenged the second wave's paradigm as to what is, or is not, good for females. In 1991, Anita Hill accused Clarence Thomas, an African-American man nominated to the Supreme Court, of sexual harassment that had allegedly occurred a decade earlier while Hill worked as his assistant at the U.S. Department of Education. Thomas denied the accusations and after extensive debate, the Senate voted 52-48 in favour of Thomas. In response to this case, Rebecca Walker published an article in a 1992 issue of Ms. titled "Becoming the Third Wave" in which she stated, "I am not a post-feminism feminist. I am the third wave." Hill and Thomas' case brought attention to the ongoing presence of sexual harassment in the workplace and reinstated a sense of concern and awareness in many people who assumed that sexual harassment and other second wave issues had been resolved.

The history of Third Wave feminism predates this and begins in the mid 1980s. Feminist leaders rooted in the second wave like Gloria Anzaldúa, bell hooks, Chela Sandoval, Cherríe Moraga, Audre Lorde, Luisa Accati, Maxine Hong Kingston, and many other feminists of colour, called for a new subjectivity in feminist voice. They sought to negotiate prominent space within feminist thought for consideration of race related subjectivities.

This focus on the intersection between race and gender remained prominent through the Hill-Thomas hearings, but began to shift with the Freedom Ride 1992. This drive to register voters in poor minority communities was surrounded with rhetoric that focused on rallying young feminists. For many, the rallying of the young is the emphasis that has stuck within third wave feminism.

Sexual Politics

Queer Sexuality

One challenge within second wave feminism was the increasing visibility of lesbianism within and without feminism. Lesbians felt sidelined by both gay liberation and women's liberation, where they were referred to as the "Lavender Menace", provoking The Woman-Identified Woman from the Radicalesbians in 1970. Jill Johnston's Lesbian Nation: The Feminist Solutionfollowed in 1973. Many lesbians felt that they should be central to the movement, representing a fundamental threat to male supremacy. In its extreme form this was expressed as the only appropriate choice for a woman. One of the more colourful lesbian feminist writers of this period was Rita Mae Brown. Eventually the lesbian movement was welcomed into the mainstream women's movement. The threat to male assumptions they represented turned out to be real in that their presence in the woman's movement became a target of the male backlash.

Reproductive Rights

One of the main fields of interest to these feminists was in gaining the right to contraception and birth control, which were almost universally restricted until the 1960s. With the development of the first birth control pill feminists hoped to make it as available as soon as possible. Many hoped that this would free women from the perceived burden of mothering children they did not want; they felt that control of reproduction was necessary for full economic independence from men. Access to abortion was also widely demanded, but this was much more difficult to secure because of the deep societal divisions that existed over the issue. To this day, abortion remains controversial in many parts of the world.

Many feminists also fought to change perceptions of female sexual behaviour. Since it was often considered more acceptable for men to have multiple sexual partners, many feminists encouraged women into "sexual liberation" and having sex for pleasure with multiple partners.

These developments in sexual behaviour have not gone without criticism by some feminists. They see the sexual revolution primarily as a tool used by men to gain easy access to sex without the obligations entailed by marriage and traditional social norms. They see the relaxation of social attitudes towards sex in general, and the increased availability of pornography without stigma, as leading towards greater sexual objectification of women by men.

Global Feminism

Immediately after the war a new global dimension was added by the formation of the United Nations. In 1946 the UN established a Commission on the Status of Women.Originally as the Section on the Status of Women, Human Rights Division, Department of Social Affairs, and now part of the Economic and Social Council. In 1948 the UN issued its Universal Declaration of Human Rights which protects "the equal rights of men and women", and addressed both the equality and equity issues. Since 1975 the UN has held a series of world conferences on women's issues, starting with the World Conference of the International Women's Year in Mexico City, heralding the United Nations Decade for Women.

These have brought women together from all over the world and provided considerable opportunities for advancing women's rights, but also illustrated the deep divisions in attempting to apply principles universally, in successive conferences in Copenhagen and Nairobi. However by 1985 some convergence was appearing. These divisions amongst feminisms included; First World vs. Third World, the relationship between gender oppression and oppression based on class, race and nationality, defining core common elements of feminism vs. specific political elements, defining feminism, homosexuality, female circumcision, birth and population control, the gulf between researchers and the grass roots, and the extent to which political issues were women's issues. Emerging from Nairobi was a realisation that feminism is not monolithic but "constitutes the political expression of the concerns and interests of women from different regions, classes, nationalities, and ethnic backgrounds. There is and must be a diversity of feminisms, responsive to the different needs and concerns of women, and defined by them for themselves.

This diversity builds on a common opposition to gender oppression and hierarchy which, however, is only the first step in articulating and acting upon a political agenda." The fourth conference was held in Beijing in 1995. At this conference a the Beijing Platform for Action was signed. This included a commitment to achieve "gender equality and the empowerment of women".

The most important strategy to achieve this was considered to be "gender mainstreaming" which incorporates both equity and equality, that is that both women and men should "experience equal conditions for realising their full human rights, and have the opportunity to contribute and benefit from national, political, economic, social and cultural development".

FEMINIST THEORY

Elaine Showalter's A Literature of Their Own, which describes three stages in the history of women's literature, also proposes a similar multi-part model of the growth of feminist theory. First, according to Showalter, comes an androgynist poetics.

Next, a feminist critique and female Aesthetic, accompanied by gynocritics, follows, and these are closely pursued by gynesic poststructuralist feminist criticism and gender theory.

Androgynist poetics, having relations and perhaps roots in mid-Victorian women's writing of imitation, contends that the creative mind is sexless, and the very foundation of describing a female tradition in writing was sexist. Critics of this vein found gender as imprisoning, nor believed that gender had a bearing in the content of writing, which, according to Joyce Carol Oates is actually culture-determined. Imagination is too broad to be hemmed in by gender.

However, from the 1970s on, most feminist critics reject the genderless mind, finding that the "imagination" cannot evade the conscious or unconscious structures of gender. Gender, it could be said, is part of that culture-determination which Oates says serves as inspiration. Such a position emphasizes "the impossibility of separating the imagination from a socially, sexually, and historically positioned self." This movement of thought allowed for a feminist critique as critics attacked the meaning of sexual difference in a patriarchal society/ideology. Images of male-wrought representations of women came under fire, as was the "'division, oppression, inequality, [and] interiorized inferiority for women.'"

The female experience, then, began to take on positive affirmations. The Female Aesthetic arose—expressing a unique female consciousness and a feminine tradition in literature—as it celebrated an intuitive female approach in the interpretation of women's texts. It "spoke of a vanished nation, a lost motherland; of female vernacular or Mother Tongue; and of a powerful but neglected women's culture." Writers like Virginia Woolf and Dorothy Richardson, emerging out of the Victorian period and influenced by its writings were perhaps the first women to recognize this. In "Professions for Women,"

Woolf discusses how a woman writer seeks within herself "the pools, the depths, the dark places where the largest fish slumber," inevitably colliding against her own sexuality to confront "something about the body, about the passions."

The French feminists of the day discussed this Mother Tongue, calling it l'écriture feminine. Accessible to men and women alike, but representing "female sexual morphology," l'écriture feminine sought a way of writing which literally embodied the female, thereby fighting the "subordinating, linear style of classification or distinction." Showalter finds that whether this clitoral, vulval, vaginal, or uterine; whether centered on semiotic pulsions, childbearing, or jouissance, the feminist theorization of female sexuality/textuality, and its funky audacity in violating patriarchal taboos by unveiling the Medusa, is an exhilarating challenge to phallic discourse.

There are problems with the Female Aesthetic, which feminist critics recognized. Even its most fervent fans avoided defining exactly what constituted the style of l'écriture feminine, as any definition would then categorize it and safely subsume it as a genre under the linear patriarchal structure. Its very restlessness and ambiguity defied identification as part of its identity. Needless to say, some feminists and women writers could feel excluded by the surreality of the Female Aesthetic and its stress on the biological forms of female experience, which, as Showalter says, also bears close resemblance to sexist essentialism. Men may try their hand at writing woman's bodies, but according to the feminist critique and Aesthetic, only woman whose very biology gave her an edge, could read these texts successfully—risking marginalization and ghettoization of both women's literature and theory. Lastly, the Female Aesthetic was charged with racism, as it rarely referred to racial or class differences between women and largely referred to a white woman's literary tradition.

Gynocritics, which developed shoulder-to-shoulder with the Female Aesthetic, attempted to resolve some of these problems, by agreeing that women's literature lay as the central concern for feminist criticism, but "rejected the concept of an essential female identity and style." One branch of gynocriticism sought to revise Freudian structures and take the edge off of an adversarial methodology of criticism. These critics emphasized a Pre-Oedipal phase wherein the daughter's bond to her mother inscribes the key factor in gender identity. Matriarchal values desolve intergenerational conflicts and build upon a female tradition of literature rather than the struggle of Oedipus and Lais at the crossroads.

Poststructuralism eventually influenced the course of feminist theory with the idea of a motherless as well as fatherless text. The female experience, as it relates to texts, only occurs in the feminine subjectivity of the reading process. "Gynesis" or "gynetic disruptions" occur in texts when the reader explores "the textual consequences and representations of 'the feminine.'" These considerations or interruptions in the discourse indicate a consideration or interruption of the patriarchal system.

Lastly and most recently are developments of an over-arching gender theory, which considers gender, both male and female, as a social construction upon biological differences. Gender theory proposes to explore "ideological inscription and the literary effects of the sex/gender system," and as many advantages, opening up the literary theory stage and bringing in questions of masculinity into feminist theory. Also, taking gender as a fundamental analytic category brings feminist criticism from the margin to the center, though risks depoliticizing the study of women.

10

The Foundations of English Literary Criticism

The foundations for a literary criticism which seeks to mediate between writers and readers belonging to different historical periods or social groupings. This makes it, among other things, a timely intervention in the postmodern "culture wars", though the theory put forward will be of interest not only to students of literature and culture, but also to linguists.

NEW CRITICISM

A literary movement that started in the late 1920s and 1930s and originated in reaction to traditional criticism that new critics saw as largely concerned with matters extraneous to the text, *e.g.*, with the biography or psychology of the author or the work's relationship to literary history. New Criticism proposed that a work of literary art should be regarded as autonomous, and so should not be judged by reference to considerations beyond itself. A poem consists less of a series of referential and verifiable statements about the 'real' world beyond it, than of the presentation and sophisticated organization of a set of complex experiences in a verbal form.

ARCHETYPAL/MYTH CRITICISM

A form of criticism based largely on the works of C. G. Jung (YOONG) and Joseph Campbell (and myth itself). Some of the school's major figures include Robert Graves, Francis Fergusson, Philip Wheelwright, Leslie Fiedler, Northrop Frye, Maud Bodkin, and G. Wilson Knight.

These critics view the genres and individual plot patterns of literature, including highly sophisticated and realistic works, as recurrences of certain archetypes and essential mythic formulae. Archetypes, according to Jung, are "primordial images"; the "psychic residue" of repeated types of experience in the lives of very ancient ancestors which are inherited in the "collective unconscious" of the human race and are expressed in myths, religion, dreams, and private fantasies, as well as in the works of literature (Abrams, p. 10, 112). Some common examples of archetypes include water, sun, moon, colours, circles, the Great Mother, Wise Old Man, etc. In terms of archetypal criticism, the colour *white* might be associated with innocence or could signify death or the supernatural.

MARXISM

A sociological approach to literature that viewed works of literature or art as the products of historical forces that can be analyzed by looking at the material conditions in which they were formed. In Marxist ideology, what we often classify as a world view (such as the Victorian age) is actually the articulations of the dominant class.

Marxism generally focuses on the clash between the dominant and repressed classes in any given age and also may encourage art to imitate what is often termed an "objective" reality. Contemporary Marxism is much broader in its focus, and views art as simultaneously reflective and autonomous to the age in which it was produced. The Frankfurt School is also associated with Marxism.

POSTCOLONIALISM

Literally, postcolonialism refers to the period following the decline of colonialism, *e.g.*, the end or lessening of domination by European empires. Although the term *postcolonialism* generally refers to the period after colonialism, the distinction is not always made. In its use as a critical approach, postcolonialism refers to "a collection of theoretical and critical strategies used to examine the culture (literature, politics, history, and so forth) of former colonies of the European empires, and their relation to the rest of the world". Among the many challenges facing postcolonial writers are the attempt both to resurrect their culture and to combat preconceptions about their culture. Edward Said, for example, uses the word Orientalism to describe the discourse about the East constructed by the West.

EXISTENTIALISM

Existentialism is a philosophy (promoted especially by Jean-Paul Sartre and Albert Camus) that views each person as an isolated being who is cast into an alien universe, and conceives the world as possessing no inherent human truth, value, or meaning. A person's life, then, as it moves from the nothingness from which it came towards the nothingness where it must end, defines an existence which is both anguished and absurd (Guerin). In a world without sense, all choices are possible, a situation which Sartre viewed as human beings central dilemma: "Man [woman] is condemned to be free." In contrast to atheist existentialism, Søren Kierkegaard theorized that belief in God (given that we are provided with no proof or assurance) required a conscious choice or "leap of faith."

PHENOMENOLOGY AND HERMENEUTICS

Phenomenology

Phenomenology is a philosophical method, first developed by Edmund Husserl (HUHSS-erel), that proposed "phenomenological reduction" so that everything not "immanent" to consciousness must be excluded; all realities must be treated as pure "phenomena" and this is the only absolute data from which we can begin. Husserl viewed consciousness always as intentional and that the act of consciousness, the thinking subject and the object it "intends," are inseparable. Art is not a means of securing pleasure, but a revelation of being. The work is the phenomenon by which we come to know the world.

Hermeneutics

Hermeneutics sees interpretation as a circular process whereby valid interpretation can be achieved by a sustained, mutually qualifying interplay between our progressive sense of the whole and our retrospective understanding of its component parts. Two dominant theories that emerged from Wilhelm Dilthey's original premise were that of E. D. Hirsch who, in accord with Dilthey, felt a valid interpretation was possible by uncovering the work's authorial intent (though informed by historical and cultural determinants), and in contrast, that of Martin Heidegger (HIGH-deg-er) who argued that a reader must experience the "inner life" of a text in order to understand it at all. The reader's "being-in-the-world" or *dasein* is fraught with difficulties since both the reader and the text exist in a temporal and fluid state. For Heidegger or Hans Georg Gadamer (GAH-de-mer), then, a valid interpretation may become irrecoverable and will always be relative.

STRUCTURALISM AND SEMIOTICS

Structuralism

Structuralism is a way of thinking about the world which is predominantly concerned with the perceptions and description of structures. At its simplest, structuralism claims that the nature of every element in any given situation has no significance by itself, and in fact is determined by all the other elements involved in that situation. The full significance of any entity cannot be perceived unless and until it is integrated into the structure of which it forms a part. Structuralists believe that all human activity is constructed, not natural or "essential."

Consequently, it is the systems of organization that are important (what we do is always a matter of selection within a given construct). By this formulation, "any activity, from the actions of a narrative to not eating one's peas with a knife, takes place within a system of differences and has meaning only in its relation to other possible activities within that system, not to some meaning that emanates from nature or the divine".

Semiology

Semiotics, simply put, is the science of signs. Semiology proposes that a great diversity of our human action and productions—our bodily postures and gestures, the the social rituals we perform, the clothes we wear, the meals we serve, the buildings we inhabit—all convey "shared" meanings to members of a particular culture, and so can be analyzed as signs which function in diverse kinds of signifying systems. Linguistics (the study of verbal signs and structures) is only one branch of semiotics but supplies the basic methods and terms which are used in the study of all other social sign systems.

LITERARY CRITICISM: DEFINITION, EXAMPLES AND FORMS

DEFINITION

All forms of art have their critics. We read film reviews in our daily newspapers, television reviews in weekly blogs and, of course, book reviews in magazines. Criticism is how we evaluate and interpret art. Critics let us know if a movie is worth spending our hard-earned money to see in a theater or whether we can wait for it on cable or even if we can skip the film all together.

Literary criticism goes all the way back to the days of Plato. Through the years, it has developed and grown, and ultimately provides us with parameters on how to study literature. Because there are a million different ways to dissect written works such as novels or poems, literary criticism provides some general guidelines to help us analyze, deconstruct, interpret and evaluate. We usually see literary criticism in a book review or critical essay; however, the Internet has made all forms of criticism readily available in everything from personal blogs to social media.

Why It's Important

Every one of us has taken at least one English class in our lives. Maybe we have been asked to analyze the works of Shakespeare, Faulkner or Poe. But whether or not we are reading a tragedy or a comedy, one of the most important things we learn from our English classes is how to read and discuss literature. Books and poems help us to expand our imaginations, while stories allow us to experience worlds other than our own.

By learning how to deconstruct literature through class discussions or in our reading, we get to experience how other people live. Literary criticism helps us to go inside of the text and understand the written work from many different viewpoints. Often times, these perspectives will not be readily apparent to us unless we delve into the work and learn how to look past the surface.

There are many different ways to evaluate literature. Some critics care about when and where an author was born, while other critics feel that information is irrelevant. Below are a few different approaches to literary criticism.

TRADITIONAL CRITICISM

Traditional critics feel that in order to truly evaluate an author's work, they must know some basic biographical information about the writer. They then look to see how that information reflects on the work. They ask questions like: When and where was the author born? Was he married? Where did he go to college (if he did go to college)?

Traditional critics also feel that it helps to be familiar with an author's past works - if there are any. They have determined that every writer has a unique style, a certain way with prose or structure that makes him or her different from everyone else. For example, Mark Twain used a lot of humor and satire in his writing. Besides Twain's major literary works, he penned numerous essays and short stories. In order to truly evaluate a work by an author like Twain, traditional critics would also probably recommend reading *Adventures of Huckleberry Finn* and *The Adventures of Tom Sawyer*.

SOCIOLOGICAL CRITICISM

As we can imagine, a little boy growing up in the American South at the height of the Civil War is going to have a lot of different life shape-experiences than a little boy growing up in Communist Russia in the 1980s. Sociological critics focus on how society and historical events shape a writer's work. They examine what sort of politics the author may draw from: Marxism, feminism, liberalism, socialism, etc.

SIR PHILIP SIDNEY: AN APOLOGIE FOR POETRIE

The *Apologie* was probably written about 1580; Gosson's pamphlet, which clearly suggested it, having appeared in 1579. Nothing need here be added to what has been said in the Introduction.

When the right virtuous Edward Wotton and I were at the emperor's court together, we gave ourselves to learn horsemanship of John Pietro Pugliano: one that with great commendation had the place of an esquire in his stable. And he, according to the fertileness of the Italian wit, did not only afford us the demonstration of his practice, but sought to enrich our minds with the contemplations therein, which he thought most precious. But with none I remember mine ears were at any time more laden, than when he exercised his speech in the praise of his faculty.

He said, soldiers were the noblest estate of mankind, and horsemen, the noblest of soldiers. He said, they were the masters of war, and ornaments of peace: speedy goers, and strong abiders, triumphers both in camps and courts. Nay, to so unbelieved a point he proceeded, as that no earthly thing bred such wonder to a prince, as to be a good horseman.

Skill of government was but a pedanteria in comparison: then would he add certain praises, by telling what a peerless beast a horse was. The only serviceable courtier without flattery, the beast of most beauty, faithfulness, courage, and such more, that, if I had not been a piece of a logician before I came to him, I think he would have persuaded me to have wished myself a horse. But thus much at least with his no few words he drove into me, that self-love is better than any gilding to make that seem gorgeous, wherein ourselves are parties. Wherein, if Pugliano his strong affection and weak arguments will not satisfy you, I will give you a nearer example of myself, who in these my not old years and idlest times, having slipped into the title of a poet, am provoked to say something unto you in the defence of that my unelected vocation; which if I handle with more good will than good reasons, bear with me, sith the scholar is to be pardoned that followeth the steps of his master.

And yet I must say that, as I have just cause to make a pitiful defence of poor poetry, which from almost the highest estimation of learning is fallen to be the laughing-stock of children, so have I need to bring some more available proofs: sith the former is by no man barred of his deserved credit, the silly latter hath had even the names of philosophers used to the defacing of it, with great danger of civil war among the muses.

And first, truly to all them that professing learning inveigh against poetry may justly be objected, that they go very near to ungratefulness, to seek to deface that which, in the noblest nations and languages that are known, hath been the first light-giver to ignorance, and first nurse, whose milk by little and little enabled them to feed afterwards of tougher knowledges: and will they now play the hedgehog that, being received into the den, drove out his host? or rather the vipers, that with their birth kill their parents? Let learned Greece in any of her manifold sciences, be able to show me one book, before Musaeus, Homer, and Hesiodus, all three nothing else but poets.

Nay, let any history be brought, that can say any writers were there before them, if they were not men of the same skill, as Orpheus, Linus, and some other are named: who having been the first of that country, that made pens deliverers of their knowledge to their posterity, may justly challenge to be called their fathers in learning: for not only in time they had this priority but went before them, as causes to draw with their charming sweetness the wild untamed wits to an admiration of knowledge.

So as Amphion was said to move stone with his poetry, to build Thebes. And Orpheus to be listened to by beasts indeed, stony and beastly people. So among the Romans were Livius Andronicus, and Ennius. So in the Italian language, the first that made it aspire to be a treasure-house of science were the poets Dante, Boccace, and Petrarch. So in our English were Gower and Chaucer.

After whom, encouraged and delighted with their excellent foregoing, others have followed, to beautify our mother tongue, as well in the same kind as in other arts. This did so notably show itself, that the philosophers of Greece durst not a long time appear to the world but under the masks of poets. So Thales, Empedocles, and Parmenides sang their natural philosophy in verses: so did Pythagoras and Phocylides their moral counsels: so did Tyrtaus in war matters, and Solon in matters of policy: or rather, they being poets, did exercise their delightful vein in those points of highest knowledge, which before them lay hid to the world. For that wise Solon was directly a poet, it is manifest, having written in verse the notable fable of the Atlantic Island, which was continued by Plato.

And truly, even Plato, whosoever well considereth, shall find, that in the body of his work, though the inside and strength were philosophy, the skin as it were and beauty depended most of poetry: for all standeth upon dialogues, wherein he feigneth many honest burgesses of Athens to speak of such matters, that if they had been set on the rack, they would never have confessed them. Besides, his poetical describing the circumstances of their meetings, as the well ordering of a banquet, the delicacy of a walk, with interlacing mere tales, as Gyges' ring, and others, which who knows not to be the flowers of poetry, did never walk into Apollo's garden.

And even historiographers have been glad to borrow both fashion, and perchance weight, of poets. So Herodotus entitled his history by the name of the nine Muses: and both he, and all the rest that followed him, either stole or usurped of poetry their passionate describing of passions, the many particularities of battles, which no man could affirm: or if that be denied me, long orations put in the mouths of great kings and captains, which it is certain they never pronounced.

So that truly, neither philosopher nor historiographer could at the first have entered into the gates of popular judgements, if they had not taken a great passport of poetry, which, in all nations at this day where learning flourisheth not, is plain to be seen: in all which they have some feeling of poetry. In Turkey, besides their law-giving divines, they have no other writers but poets. In our neighbour country Ireland, where truly learning goeth very bare, yet are their poets held in a devout reverence. Even among the most barbarous and simple Indians where no writing is, yet have they their poets, who make and sing songs which they call areytos, both of their ancestors' deeds, and praises of their Gods.

A sufficient probability, that, if ever learning come among them, it must be by having their hard dull wits softened and sharpened with the sweet delights of poetry. For until they find a pleasure in the exercises of the mind, great promises of much knowledge will little persuade them, that know not the fruits of knowledge. In Wales, the true remnant of the ancient Britons, as there are good authorities to show the long time they had poets, which they called bards: so through all the conquests of Romans, Saxons, Danes, and Normans, some of whom did seek to ruin all memory of learning from among them, yet do their poets, even to this day, last; so as it is not more notable in soon beginning than in long continuing. But since the authors of most of our sciences were the Romans, and before them the Greeks, let us a little stand upon their authorities, but even so far as to see what names they have given unto this now scorned skill.

Among the Romans a poet was called *vates*, which is as much as a diviner, fore-seer, or prophet, as by his conjoined words *vaticinium* and *vaticinari* is manifest: so heavenly a title did that excellent people bestow upon this heart-ravishing knowledge. And so far were they carried into the admiration thereof, that they thought in the chanceable hitting upon any such verses great foretokens of their following fortunes were placed. Whereupon grew the word of *Sortes Virgilianae*, when, by sudden opening Virgil's book, they lighted upon any verse of his making, whereof the histories of the emperors' lives are full: as of Albinus the governor of our island, who in his childhood met with this verse

Arma amens capio nee sat rationis in armis:

and in his age performed it; which although it were a very vain and godless superstition, as also it was to think that spirits were commanded by such verses, so yet serveth it to show the great reverence those wits were held in. And altogether not without ground, since both the oracles of Delphos and Sibylla's prophecies were wholly delivered in verses. For that same exquisite observing of number and measure in words, and that high-flying liberty of conceit proper to the Poet, did seem to have some divine force in it.

And may not I presume a little further, to show the reasonableness of this word *vates*? And say that the holy David's Psalms are a divine poem? If I do, I shall not do it without the testimony of great learned men, both ancient and modern: but even the name Psalms will speak for me; which being interpreted is nothing but songs. Then that it is fully written in metre, as all learned Hebricians agree, although the rules be not yet fully found. Lastly and principally, his handling his prophecy, which is merely poetical. For what else is the awaking his musical instruments? The often and free changing of persons? His notable prosopopeias, when he maketh you, as it were, see God coming in His majesty?

His telling of the beasts' joyfulness, and hills leaping, but a heavenly poesy: wherein almost he showeth himself a passionate lover of that unspeakable and everlasting beauty to be seen by the eyes of the mind, only cleared by faith? But truly now having named him, I fear me I seem to profane that holy name, applying it to poetry, which is among us thrown down to so ridiculous an estimation: but they that with quiet judgements will look a little deeper into it, shall find the end and working of it such as, being rightly applied, deserveth not to be scourged out of the Church of God.

But now, let us see how the Greeks named it, and how they deemed of it. The Greeks called him a poet, which name hath, as the most excellent, gone through other languages. It cometh of this word *poiein*, which is, to make: wherein I know not, whether by luck or wisdom, we Englishmen have met with the Greeks, in calling him a maker: which name, how high and incomparable a title it is, I had rather were known by marking the scope of other sciences, than by my partial allegation.

There is no art delivered to mankind, that hath not the works of nature for his principal object, without which they could not consist, and on which they so depend, as they become actors and players, as it were, of what nature will have set forth. So doth the astronomer look upon the stars, and by that he seeth, setteth down what order nature hath taken therein. So do the geometrician, and arithmetician, in their diverse sorts of quantities.

So doth the musician, in times, tell you which by nature agree, which not. The natural philosopher thereon hath his name, and the moral philosopher standeth upon the natural virtues, vices, and passions of man; and follow nature therein, and thou shalt not err. The lawyer saith what men have determined. The historian what men have done. The grammarian speaketh only of the rules of speech; and the rhetorician, and logician, considering what in nature will soonest prove and persuade, thereon give artificial rules, which still are compassed within the circle of a question, according to the proposed matter.

The physician weigheth the nature of a man's body, and the nature of things helpful, or hurtful unto it. And the metaphysic, though it be in the second and abstract notions, and therefore be counted supernatural, yet doth he indeed build upon the depth of nature: only the poet, disdaining to be tied to any such subjection, lifted up with the vigour of his own invention, doth grow in effect another nature, in making things either better than nature bringeth forth, or quite anew forms such as never were in nature, as the heroes, demigods, cyclops, chimeras, furies, and such like: so as he goeth hand in hand with nature, not inclosed within the narrow warrant of her gifts, but freely ranging only within the zodiac of his own wit.

Nature never set forth the earth in so rich tapestry, as divers poets have done, neither with pleasant rivers, fruitful trees, sweet-smelling flowers: nor whatsoever else may make the too much loved earth more lovely. Her world is brazen, the poets only deliver a golden: but let those things alone and go to man, for whom as the other things are, so it seemeth in him her uttermost cunning is employed, and know whether she have brought forth so true a lover as Theagenes, so constant a friend as Pylades, so valiant a man as Orlando, so right a prince as Xenophon's Cyrus: so excellent a man every way, as Virgil's Aneas.

Neither let this be jestingly conceived, because the works of the one be essential, the other, in imitation or fiction; for any understanding knoweth the skill of the artificer standeth in that idea or fore-conceit of the work, and not in the work itself.

And that the poet hath that idea, is manifest, by delivering them forth in such excellency as he hath imagined them. Which delivering forth also is not wholly imaginative, as we are wont to say by them that build castles in the air: but so far substantially it worketh, not only to make a Cyrus, which had been but a particular excellency, as Nature might have done, but to bestow a Cyrus upon the world, to make many Cyruses, if they will learn aright, why and how that maker made him.

Neither let it be deemed too saucy a comparison to balance the highest point of man's wit with the efficacy of Nature: but rather give right honour to the heavenly Maker of that maker: who, having made man to his own likeness, set him beyond and over all the works of that second nature, which in nothing he showeth so much as in poetry: when, with the force of a divine breath, he bringeth things forth far surpassing her doings, with no small argument to the incredulous of that first accursed fall of Adam; sith our erected wit maketh us know what perfection is, and yet our infected will keepeth us from reaching unto it. But these arguments will by few be understood, and by fewer granted. Thus much will be given me, that the Greeks, with some probability of reason, gave him the name above all names of learning.

Now let us go to a more ordinary opening of him, that the truth may be more palpable: and so I hope, though we get not so unmatched a praise as the etymology of his names will grant, yet his very description, which no man will deny, shall not justly be barred from a principal commendation.

Poesy, therefore, is an art of imitation, for so Aristotle termeth it in his word *Mimesis*, that is to say, a representing, counterfeiting, or figuring forth: to speak metaphorically, a speaking picture: with this end, to teach and delight; of this have been three several kinds. The chief both in antiquity and excellency, were they that did imitate the inconceivable excellencies of God. Such were David in his Psalms, Solomon in his Song of Songs, in his Ecclesiastes, and Proverbs: Moses and Deborah, in their hymns, and the writer of Job; which, beside other, the learned Emanuel Tremilius and Franciscus Junius do entitle the poetical part of Scripture. Against these none will speak that hath the Holy Ghost in due holy reverence.

In this kind, though in a full wrong divinity, were Orpheus, Amphion, Homer in his hymns, and many other, both Greeks and Romans: and this poesy must be used by whosoever will follow St. James his counsel, in singing psalms when they are merry: and I know is used with the fruit of comfort by some, when, in sorrowful pangs of their death-bringing sins, they find the consolation of the never-leaving goodness.

The second kind, is of them that deal with matters philosophical; either moral, as Tyrtaus, Phocylides, and Cato: or natural, as Lucretius and Virgil's *Georgics*; or astronomical, as Manilius, and Pontanus; or historical, as Lucan; which who mislike, the fault is in their judgements quite out of taste, and not in the sweet food of sweetly-uttered knowledge. But because this second sort is wrapped within the fold of the proposed subject, and takes not the course of his own invention, whether they properly be poets or no, let grammarians dispute; and go to the third, indeed right poets, of whom chiefly this question ariseth; betwixt whom and these second is such a kind of difference, as betwixt the meaner sort of painters and the more excellent; who, having no law but wit, bestow that in colours upon you which is fittest for the eye to see; as the constant, though lamenting look of Lucretia, when she punished in herself another's fault. Wherein he painteth not Lucretia whom he never saw, but painteth the outward beauty of such a virtue: for these third be they which most properly do imitate to teach and delight; and, to imitate, borrow nothing of what is, hath been, or shall be: but range, only reined with learned discretion, into the divine consideration of what may be, and should be. These be they that, as the first and most noble sort may justly be termed Vates, so these are waited on in the excellentest languages and best understandings, with the fore-described name of poets: for these indeed do merely make to imitate: and imitate both to delight and teach: and delight to move men to take that goodness in hand, which without delight they would fly as from a stranger: and teach, to make them know that goodness whereunto they are moved, which being the noblest scope to which ever any learning was directed, yet want there not idle tongues to bark at them.

These be subdivided into sundry more special denominations. The most notable be the heroic, lyric, tragic, comic, satiric, iambic, elegiac, pastoral, and certain others. Some of these being termed according to the matter they deal with, some by the sorts of verses they liked best to write in, for indeed the greatest part of poets have apparelled their poetical inventions in that numbrous kind of writing which is called verse: indeed but apparelled, verse being but an ornament and no cause to poetry: sith there have been many most excellent poets that never versified, and now swarm many versifiers that need never answer to the name of poets.

For Xenophon, who did imitate so excellently, as to give us*effigiem justi imperii* the portraiture of a just empire under the name of Cyrus, made therein an absolute heroical poem. So did Heliodorus in his sugared invention of that picture of love in Theagenes and Chariclea, and yet both these wrote in prose: which I speak to show, that it is not rhyming and versing that maketh a poet, no more than a long gown maketh an advocate: who, though he pleaded in armour, should be an advocate and no soldier. But it is that feigning notable images of virtues, vices, or what else, with that delightful teaching which must be the right describing note to know a poet by: although, indeed, the senate of poets hath chosen verse as their fittest raiment, meaning, as in matter they passed all in all, so in manner to go beyond them: not speaking words as they chanceably fall from the mouth, but peyzing each syllable of each word by just proportion according to the dignity of the subject.

Now, therefore, it shall not be amiss first to weigh this latter sort of poetry by his works, and then by his parts; and if in neither of these anatomies he be condemnable, I hope we shall obtain a more favourable sentence. This purifying of wit, this enriching of memory, enabling of judgement, and enlarging of conceit, which commonly we call learning, under what name soever it come forth, or to what immediate end soever it be directed, the final end is, to lead and draw us to as high a perfection, as our degenerate souls made worse by their clayey lodgings, can be capable of. This, according to the inclination of the man, bred many formed impressions; for some that thought this felicity principally to be gotten by knowledge, and no knowledge to be so high and heavenly as acquaintance with the stars, gave themselves to astronomy; others, persuading themselves to be demigods if they knew the causes of things, became natural and supernatural philosophers; some an admirable delight drew to music; and some the certainty of demonstration, to the mathematics. But all, one and other, having this scope to know, and by knowledge to lift up the mind from the dungeon of the body, to the enjoying his own divine essence.

But when by the balance of experience it was found, that the astronomer looking to the stars might fall into a ditch, that the inquiring philosopher might be blind in himself, and the mathematician might draw forth a straight line with a crooked heart: then lo, did proof the overruler of opinions make manifest that all these are but serving sciences, which, as they have each a private end in themselves, so yet are they all directed to the highest end of the mistress knowledge, by the Greeks called *Arkitektonike*, which stands in the knowledge of a man's self, in the ethic and politic consideration, with the end of well-doing, and not of well-knowing only; even as the saddler's next end is to make a good saddle: but his farther end, to serve a nobler faculty, which is horsemanship: so the horseman's to soldiery, and the soldier not only to have the skill, but to perform the practice of a soldier: so that the ending end of all earthly learning, being virtuous action, those skills that most serve to bring forth that, have a most just title to be princes over all the rest.

Wherein if we can show the poet's nobleness, by setting him before his other competitors, among whom as principal challengers step forth the moral philosophers, whom methinketh I see coming towards me with a sullen gravity, as though they could not abide vice by daylight, rudely clothed for to witness outwardly their contempt of outward things, with books in their hands against glory, whereto they set their names, sophistically speaking against subtlety, and angry with any man in whom they see the foul fault of anger; these men casting largess as they go, of definitions, divisions, and distinctions, with a scornful interrogative, do soberly ask, whether it be possible to find any path, so ready to lead a man to virtue, as that which teacheth what virtue is? and teacheth it not only by delivering forth his very being, his causes, and effects: but also, by making known his enemy vice, which must be destroyed, and his cumbersome servant passion, which must be mastered, by showing the generalities that contain it, and the specialities that are derived from it: lastly, by plain setting down, how it extendeth itself out of the limits of a man's own little world, to the government of families and maintaining of public societies.

The historian scarcely giveth leisure to the moralist, to say so much, but that he, laden with old mouse-eaten records, authorizing himself upon other histories, whose greatest authorities are built upon the notable foundation of hearsay, having much ado to accord differing writers, and to pick truth out of partiality, better acquainted with a thousand years ago than with the present age, and yet better knowing how this world goeth than how his own wit runneth, curious for antiquities and inquisitive of novelties, a wonder to young folks, and a tyrant in table-talk, denieth in a great chafe that any man, for teaching of virtue and virtuous actions, is comparable to him. I am *Lux vitae*, *Temporum Magistra*, *Vita memoriae*, *Nuncia vetustatis*, and c.

The philosopher teacheth a disputative virtue, but I do an active: his virtue is excellent in the dangerless academy of Plato, but mine showeth forth her honourable face in the battles of Marathon, Pharsalia, Poitiers, and Agincourt. He teacheth virtue by certain abstract considerations, but I only bid you follow the footing of them that have gone before you. Old-aged experience goeth beyond the fine- witted philosopher, but I give the experience of many ages. Lastly, if he make the songbook, I put the learner's hand to the lute; and if he be the guide, I am the light.

Then would he allege you innumerable examples, conferring story by story, how much the wisest senators and princes have been directed by the credit of history, as Brutus, Alphonsus of Aragon, and who not, if need be? At length the long line of their disputation maketh a point in this, that the one giveth the precept, and the other the example.

Now, whom shall we find to be moderator? Truly, as me seemeth, the poet; and if not a moderator, even the man that ought to carry the title from them both, and much more from all other serving sciences. Therefore compare we the poet with the historian and with the moral philosopher, and, if he go beyond them both, no other human skill can match him. For as for the divine, with all reverence it is ever to be excepted, not only for having his scope as far beyond any of these, as eternity exceedeth a moment, but even for passing each of these in themselves.

And for the lawyer, though *Jus* be the daughter of Justice, and Justice the chief of virtues, yet because he seeketh to make men good, rather *Formidine poenae* than *Virtutis amore* or to say righter, doth not endeavour to make men good, but that their evil hurt not others: having no care, so he be a good citizen, how bad a man he be. Therefore, as our wickedness maketh him necessary, and necessity maketh him honourable, so is he not in the deepest truth to stand in rank with these, who all endeavour to take naughtiness away, and plant goodness even in the secretest cabinet of our souls. And these four are all that any way deal in that consideration of men's manners, which being the supreme knowledge, they that best breed it deserve the best commendation.

The philosopher therefore and the historian are they which would win the goal: the one by precept, the other by example. But both not having both, do both halt. For the philosopher, setting down with thorny argument the bare rule, is so hard of utterance, and so misty to be conceived, that one that hath no other guide but him shall wade in him till he be old before he shall find sufficient cause to be honest; for his knowledge standeth so upon the abstract and general, that happy is that man who may understand him, and more happy that can apply what he doth understand.

On the other side, the historian wanting the precept is so tied, not to what should be, but to what is, to the particular truth of things, and not to the general reason of things, that his example draweth no necessary consequence, and therefore a less fruitful doctrine.

Now doth the peerless poet perform both: for whatsoever the philosopher saith should be done, he giveth a perfect picture of it in some one, by whom he presupposeth it was done. So as he coupleth the general notion with the particular example. A perfect picture, I say; for he yieldeth to the powers of the mind an image of that whereof the philosopher bestoweth but a wordish description: which doth neither strike, pierce, nor possess the sight of the soul so much as that other doth.

For as in outward things, to a man that had never seen an elephant or a rhinoceros, who should tell him most exquisitely all their shapes, colour, bigness, and particular marks; or of a gorgeous palace, the architecture; with declaring the full beauties, might well make the hearer able to repeat, as it were by rote, all he had heard, yet should never satisfy his inward conceits, with being witness to itself of a true lively knowledge: but the same man, as soon as he might see those beasts well painted, or the house well in model, should straightway grow without need of any description, to a judicial comprehending of them: so no doubt the philosopher with his learned definition, be it of virtue, vices, matters of public policy or private government, replenisheth the memory with many infallible grounds of wisdom: which, notwithstanding, lie dark before the imaginative and judging power, if they be not illuminated or figured forth by the speaking picture of poesy.

Tully taketh much pains and many times not without poetical helps, to make us know the force love of our country hath in us. Let us but hear old Anchises speaking in the midst of Troy's flames, or see Ulysses, in the fulness of all Calypso's delights, bewail his absence from barren and beggarly Ithaca. Anger, the Stoics say, was a short madness; let but Sophocles bring you Ajax on a stage, killing and whipping sheep and oxen, thinking them the army of Greeks, with their chieftains Agamemnon and Menelaus, and tell me if you have not a more familiar insight into anger, than finding in the schoolmen his genus and difference. See whether wisdom and temperance in Ulysses and Diomedes, valour in Achilles, friendship in Nisus and Euryalus, even to an ignorant man, carry not an apparent shining: and contrarily, the remorse of conscience in Odipus, the soon repenting pride of Agamemnon, the self-devouring cruelty in his father Atreus, the violence of ambition in the two Theban brothers, the sour-sweetness of revenge in Medea, and to fall lower, the Terentian Gnatho and our Chaucer's Pandar, so expressed, that we now use their names to signify their trades.

And finally, all virtues, vices, and passions so in their own natural seats laid to the view, that we seem not to hear of them, but clearly to see through them. But even in the most excellent determination of goodness, what philosopher's counsel can so readily detect a prince, as the feigned Cyrus in Xenophon? or a virtuous man in all fortunes, as Aneas in Virgil? or a whole commonwealth, as the way of Sir Thomas More's Utopia? I say the way; because where Sir Thomas More erred, it was the fault of the man and not of the poet; for that way of patterning a commonwealth was most absolute, though he perchance hath not so absolutely performed it: for the question is, whether the feigned image of poesy, or the regular instruction of philosophy, hath the more force in teaching; wherein if the philosophers have more rightly showed themselves philosophers than the poets have obtained to the high top of their profession, as in truth

Mediocribus esse poetis,
Non Di, non homines, non concessere columna:

it is I say again, not the fault of the art, but that by few men that art can be accomplished.

Certainly, even our Saviour Christ could as well have given the moral commonplaces of uncharitableness and humbleness, as the divine narration of Dives and Lazarus: or of disobedience and mercy, as that heavenly discourse of the lost child and the gracious Father; but that his through-searching wisdom knew the estate of Dives burning in hell, and of Lazarus being in Abraham's bosom, would more constantly inhabit both the memory and judgement. Truly, for myself, meseems I see before my eyes the lost child's disdainful prodigality, turned to envy a swine's dinner: which by the learned divines are thought not historical acts, but instructing parables. For conclusion, I say the philosopher teacheth, but he teacheth obscurely, so as the learned only can understand him: that is to say, he teacheth them that are already taught, but the poet is the food for the tenderest stomachs, the poet is indeed the right popular philosopher, whereof Asop's tales give good proof: whose pretty allegories, stealing under the formal tales of beasts, make many, more beastly than beasts, begin to hear the sound of virtue from these dumb speakers.

But now may it be alleged that, if this imagining of matters be so fit for the imagination, then must the historian needs surpass, who bringeth you images of true matters, such as indeed were done, and not such as fantastically or falsely may be suggested to have been done. Truly Aristotle himself in his discourse of poesy, plainly determineth this question, saying that poetry is *philosophoteron* and *spoudaioteron*, that is to say, it is more philosophical, and more studiously serious, than history. His reason is, because poesy dealeth with *katholou,* that is to say, with the universal consideration; and the history with*kathekaston,* the particular; now saith he, the universal weighs what is fit to be said or done, either in likelihood or necessity, and the particular only marks, whether Alcibiades did, or suffered, this or that. Thus far Aristotle: which reason of his is most full of reason. For indeed, if the question were whether it were better to have a particular act truly or falsely set down, there is no doubt which is to be chosen, no more than whether you had rather have Vespasian's picture right as he was, or at the painter's pleasure nothing resembling. But if the question be for your own use and learning, whether it be better to have it set down as it should be, or as it was: then certainly is more doctrinable the feigned Cyrus of Xenophon than the true Cyrus in Justin: and the feigned Aeneas in Virgil, than the right Aeneas in Dares Phrygius.

As to a lady that desired to fashion her countenance to the best grace, a painter should more benefit her to portrait a most sweet face, writing Canidia upon it, than to paint Canidia as she was, who, Horace sweareth, was foul and ill-favoured.

If the poet do his part aright, he will show you in Tantalus, Atreus, and such like, nothing that is not to be shunned. In Cyrus, Aeneas, Ulysses, each thing to be followed; where the historian, bound to tell things as things were, cannot be liberal of a perfect pattern: but as in Alexander or Scipio himself, show doings, some to be liked, some to be misliked.

And then how will you discern what to follow but by your own discretion, which you had without reading Quintus Curtius? And whereas a man may say, though in universal consideration of doctrine the poet prevaileth, yet that the history, in his saying such a thing was done, doth warrant a man more in that he shall follow; the answer is manifest: that if he stand upon that was; as if he should argue, because it rained yesterday, therefore it should rain to-day; then indeed it hath some advantage to a gross conceit: but if he know an example only informs a conjectured likelihood, and so go by reason, the poet doth so far exceed him, as he is to frame his example to that which is most reasonable: be it in warlike, politic, or private matters; where the historian in his bare Was, hath many times that which we call fortune, to overrule the best wisdom. Many times he must tell events, whereof he can yield no cause: or if he do, it must be poetical; for that a feigned example hath as much force to teach, as a true example, let us take one example, wherein a poet and a historian do concur.

Herodotus and Justin do both testify that Zopyrus, King Darius' faithful servant, seeing his master long resisted by the rebellious Babylonians, feigned himself in extreme disgrace of his king: for verifying of which, he caused his own nose and ears to be cut off: and so flying to the Babylonians, was received: and for his known valour so far credited, that he did find means to deliver them over to Darius. Much like matter doth Livy record of Tarquinius and his son. Xenophon excellently feigneth such another stratagem, performed by Abradates in Cyrus' behalf.

Now would I fain know, if occasion be presented unto you, to serve your prince by such an honest dissimulation, why you do not as well learn it of Xenophon's fiction, as of the others' verity: and truly so much the better, as you shall save your nose by the bargain: for Abradates did not counterfeit so far. So then the best of the historian is subject to the poet; for whatsoever action or faction, whatsoever counsel, policy or war stratagem, the historian is bound to recite, that may the poet with his imitation make his own; beautifying it both for further teaching, and more delighting, as it pleaseth him: having all, from Dante his heaven, to his hell, under the authority of his pen. Which if I be asked what poets have done so, as I might well name some, yet say I, and say again, I speak of the art, and not of the artificer.

Now to that which commonly is attributed to the praise of histories, in respect of the notable learning is gotten by marking the success, as though therein a man should see virtue exalted, and vice punished; truly that commendation is peculiar to poetry, and far off from history. For indeed poetry ever setteth virtue so out in her best colours, making fortune her well-waiting handmaid, that one must needs be enamoured of her. Well may you see Ulysses in a storm and in other hard plights; but they are but exercises of patience and magnanimity, to make them shine the more in the near-following prosperity. And of the contrary part, if evil men come to the stage, they ever go out so manacled, as they little animate folks to follow them. But the historian, being captived to the truth of a foolish world, is many times a terror from well-doing, and an encouragement to unbridled wickedness.

For see we not valiant Miltiades rot in his fetters? The just Phocion, and the accomplished Socrates, put to death like traitors? The cruel Severus live prosperously? The excellent Severus miserably murdered? Sulla and Marius dying in their beds? Pompey and Cicero slain then, when they would have thought exile a happiness?

See we not virtuous Cato driven to kill himself? and rebel Caesar so advanced, that his name yet after 1600 years, lasteth in the highest honour? And mark but even Caesar's own words of the fore-named Sulla, *literas nescivit*, as if want of learning caused him to do well. He meant it not by poetry, which not content with earthly plagues deviseth new punishments in hell for tyrants: nor yet by philosophy, which teacheth *occidendos esse*: but no doubt by skill in history: for that indeed can afford your Cypselus, Periander, Phalaris, Dionysius, and I know not how many more of the same kennel, that speed well enough in their abominable unjustice or usurpation. I conclude therefore that he excelleth history, not only in furnishing the mind with knowledge, but in setting it forward, to that which deserveth to be called and accounted good: which setting forward, and moving to well-doing, indeed setteth the laurel crown upon the poet as victorious, not only of the historian, but over the philosopher: howsoever in teaching it may be questionable.

For suppose it be granted that the philosopher, in respect of his methodical proceeding, doth teach more perfectly than the poet; yet do I think that no man is so much *philophilosophos*, as to compare the philosopher, in moving, with the poet.

And that moving is of a higher degree than teaching, it may by this appear: that it is well-nigh the cause and the effect of teaching. For who will be taught, if he be not moved with desire to be taught? and what so much good doth that teaching bring forth as that it moveth one to do that which it doth teach? for as Aristotle saith, it is not *Gnosis* but *Praxis* must be the fruit. And how *Praxis* cannot be, without being moved to practice, it is no hard matter to consider.

The philosopher showeth you the way, he informeth you of the particularities; as well of the tediousness of the way, as of the pleasant lodging you shall have when your journey is ended, as of the many by-turnings that may divert you from your way. But this is to no man but to him that will read him, and read him with attentive studious painfulness. Which constant desire, whosoever hath in him, hath already passed half the hardness of the way, and therefore is beholding to the philosopher but for the other half. Nay truly, learned men have learnedly thought, that where once reason hath so much overmastered passion, as that the mind hath a free desire to do well, the inward light each mind hath in itself is as good as a philosopher's book; seeing in nature we know it is well to do well, and what is well, and what is evil, although not in the words of art, which philosophers bestow upon us. For out of natural conceit, the philosophers drew it; but to be moved to do that which we know, or to be moved with desire to know,*Hoc opus, hic labour est*.

Now therein of all sciences, is our poet the Monarch. For he doth not only show the way, but giveth so sweet a prospect into the way, as will entice any man to enter into it. Nay, he doth as if your journey should lie through a fair vineyard, at the first give you a cluster of grapes: that, full of that taste, you may long to pass further. He beginneth not with obscure definitions, which must blur the margent with interpretations, and load the memory with doubtfulness: but he cometh to you with words sent in delightful proportion, either accompanied with, or prepared for the well enchanting skill of music; and with a tale forsooth he cometh unto you: with a tale which holdeth children from play, and old men from the chimney corner.

And pretending no more, doth intend the winning of the mind from wickedness to virtue: even as the child is often brought to take most wholesome things, by hiding them in such other as have a pleasant taste: which, if one should begin to tell them the nature of Aloes or Rhubarb they should receive, would sooner take their physic at their ears than at their mouth. So it is in men, glad they will be to hear the tales of Hercules, Achilles, Cyrus, and Aneas; and hearing them, must needs hear the right description of wisdom, valour, and justice; which, if they had been barely, that is to say philosophically, set out, they would swear they be brought to school again. That imitation, whereof poetry is, hath the most conveniency to Nature of all other, insomuch, that as Aristotle saith, those things which in themselves are horrible, as cruel battles, unnatural monsters, are made in poetical imitation delightful. Truly I have known men that, even with reading *Amadis de Gaule*, have found their hearts moved to the exercise of courtesy, liberality, and especially courage.

Who readeth Aneas carrying old Anchises on his back, that wisheth not it were his fortune to perform so excellent an act? Whom do not the words of Turnus move?

Fugientem hoec terra videbit; Usque adeone mori miserum est?

Where the philosophers, as they scorn to delight, so must they be content little to move: saving wrangling, whether virtue be the chief, or the only good: whether the contemplative, or the active life do excel: which Plato and Boethius well knew, and therefore made Mistress Philosophy very often borrow the masking raiment of poesy. For even those hard-hearted evil men, who think virtue a school name, and know no other good but *indulgere genio*, and therefore despise the austere admonitions of the philosopher, and feel not the inward reason they stand upon, yet will be content to be delighted: which is all the good fellow poet seemeth to promise: and so steal to see the form of goodness ere themselves be aware, as if they took a medicine of cherries. Infinite proofs of the strange effects of this poetical invention might be alleged; only two shall serve, which are so often remembered, as I think all men know them.

The one of Menenius Agrippa, who when the whole people of Rome had resolutely divided themselves from the Senate, with apparent show of utter ruin: though he were an excellent orator, came not among them upon trust of figurative speeches, or cunning insinuations: and much less, with far-fetched maxims of philosophy, which especially if they were Platonic, they must have learned geometry before they could well have conceived: but forsooth he behaves himself, like a homely, and familiar poet. He telleth them a tale, that there was a time, when all the parts of the body made a mutinous conspiracy against the belly, which they thought devoured the fruits of each other's labour; they concluded they would let so unprofitable a spender starve. In the end, to be short, with punishing the belly, they plagued themselves. This, applied by him, wrought such effect in the people, as I never read that ever words brought forth but then, so sudden and so good an alteration; for upon reasonable conditions, a perfect reconcilement ensued.

The other is of Nathan the prophet, who when the holy David had so far forsaken God, as to confirm adultery with murder: when he was to do the tenderest office of a friend, in laying his own shame before his eyes, sent by God to call again so chosen a servant: how doth he it but by telling of a man, whose beloved lamb was ungratefully taken from his bosom? the application most divinely true, but the discourse itself feigned: which made David, as in a glass, to see his own filthiness, as that heavenly psalm of mercy well testifieth.

By these therefore examples and reasons, I think it may be manifest, that the poet, with that same hand of delight, doth draw the mind more effectually than any other art doth; and so a conclusion not unfitly ensueth: that, as virtue is the most excellent resting-place for all worldly learning to make his end of, so poetry, being the most familiar to teach it, and most princely to move towards it, in the most excellent work is the most excellent workman.

But I am content not only to decipher him by his works, but more narrowly will examine his parts: so that though altogether he may carry a presence full of majesty and beauty, perchance in some one defectious piece we may find a blemish: now in his parts, kinds, or species, it is to be noted, that some poesies have coupled together two or three kinds, as tragical and comical, whereupon is risen the tragi-comical. Some in the like manner have mingled prose and verse, as Sanazzar and Boethius. Some have mingled matters heroical and pastoral. But that cometh all to one in this question; for if severed they be good, the conjunction cannot be hurtful. Therefore perchance forgetting some, and leaving some as needless to be remembered, it shall not be amiss in a word to cite the special kinds, to see what faults may be found in the right use of them.

Is it then the pastoral poem which is misliked? for perchance, where the hedge is lowest, they will soonest leap over. Is the poor pipe disdained, which sometime out of Melibeus's mouth, can show the misery of people under hard lords, or ravening soldiers?

And again, by Tityrus, what blessedness is derived to them that lie lowest from the goodness of them that sit highest? Sometimes, under the pretty tales of wolves and sheep, it can include the whole considerations of wrong-doing and patience. Sometimes show, that contention for trifles can get but a trifling victory. Where perchance a man may see that even Alexander and Darius, when they strave who should be cock of this world's dunghill, the benefit they got, was that the after-livers may say,

Hac memini et victum frustra contendere Thyrsin; Ex illo Corydon, Corydon est tempore nobis.

Or is it the lamenting Elegiac, which in a kind heart would move rather pity than blame, who bewails with the great philosopher Heraclitus the weakness of mankind, and the wretchedness of the world: who surely is to be praised, either for compassionate accompanying just causes of lamentation, or for rightly painting out how weak be the passions of woefulness. Is it the bitter, but wholesome Iambic, which rubs the galled mind, in making shame the trumpet of villany, with bold and open crying out against naughtiness; or the satirist, who

Omne vafer vitium ridenti tangit amico?

Who sportingly never leaveth, until he make a man laugh at folly, and at length ashamed, to laugh at himself: which he cannot avoid, without avoiding the folly. Who while

Circum pracordia ludit,

giveth us to feel, how many headaches a passionate life bringeth us to. How when all is done,

Est Ulubris, animus si nos non deficit aquus ?

No perchance it is the comic, whom naughty play-makers and stage-keepers have justly made odious. To the argument of abuse, I will answer after. Only thus much now is to be said, that the comedy is an imitation of the common errors of our life, which he representeth in the most ridiculous and scornful sort that may be. So as it is impossible that any beholder can be content to be such a one.

Now, as in geometry, the oblique must be known as well as the right: and in arithmetic, the odd as well as the even, so in the actions of our life, who seeth not the filthiness of evil, wanteth a great foil to perceive the beauty of virtue.

This doth the comedy handle so in our private and domestical matters, as with hearing it we get as it were an experience, what is to be looked for of a niggardly Demea: of a crafty Davus: of a flattering Gnatho: of a vainglorious Thraso: and not only to know what effects are to be expected, but to know who be such, by the signifying badge given them by the comedian.

And little reason hath any man to say that men learn evil by seeing it so set out: sith, as I said before, there is no man living but, by the force truth hath in nature, no sooner seeth these men play their parts, but wisheth them in Pistrinum: although perchance the sack of his own faults lie so behind his back, that he seeth not himself dance the same measure: whereto yet nothing can more open his eyes, than to find his own actions contemptibly set forth.

So that the right use of comedy will by nobody be blamed, and much less of the high and excellent tragedy, that openeth the greatest wounds, and showeth forth the vicers, that are covered with tissue: that maketh kings fear to be tyrants, and tyrants manifest their tyrannical humours: that, with stirring the effects of admiration and commiseration, teacheth the uncertainty of this world, and upon how weak foundations golden roofs are builded. That maketh us know,

Qui sceptra scevus duro imperio regit, Timet timentes, metus in auctorem redit.

But how much it can move, Plutarch yieldeth a notable testimony, of the abominable tyrant, Alexander Pheraus; from whose eyes, a tragedy well made and represented drew abundance of tears: who, without all pity, had murdered infinite numbers, and some of his own blood. So as he, that was not ashamed to make matters for tragedies, yet could not resist the sweet violence of a tragedy.

And if it wrought no further good in him, it was, that he in despite of himself withdrew himself from hearkening to that, which might mollify his hardened heart. But it is not the tragedy they do mislike: for it were too absurd to cast out so excellent a representation of whatsoever is most worthy to be learned. Is it the lyric that most displeaseth, who with his tuned lyre, and well accorded voice, giveth praise, the reward of virtue, to virtuous acts? who gives moral precepts and natural problems, who sometimes raiseth up his voice to the height of the heavens, in singing the lauds of the immortal God.

Certainly I must confess my own barbarousness, I never heard the old song of Percy and Douglas, that I found not my heart moved more than with a trumpet: and yet is it sung but by some blind crouder, with no rougher voice than rude style: which being so evil apparelled in the dust and cobwebs of that uncivil age, what would it work trimmed in the gorgeous eloquence of Pindar? In Hungary I have seen it the manner at all feasts and other such meetings, to have songs of their ancestors' valour; which that right soldier-like nation think the chiefest kindlers of brave courage.

The incomparable Lacedemonians did not only carry that kind of music ever with them to the field, but even at home, as such songs were made, so were they all content to be the singers of them, when the lusty men were to tell what they did, the old men what they had done, and the young men what they would do. And where a man may say that Pindar many times praiseth highly victories of small moment, matters rather of sport than virtue: as it may be answered, it was the fault of the poet, and not of the poetry; so indeed, the chief fault was in the time and custom of the Greeks, who set those toys at so high a price, that Philip of Macedon reckoned a horse-race won at Olympus, among his three fearful felicities. But as the inimitable Pindar often did, so is that kind most capable and most fit to awake the thoughts from the sleep of idleness, to embrace honourable enterprises.

There rests the heroical, whose very name should daunt all backbiters; for by what conceit can a tongue be directed to speak evil of that which draweth with it no less champions than Achilles, Cyrus, Aneas, Turnus, Tydeus, and Rinaldo? who doth not only teach and move to a truth, but teacheth and moveth to the most high and excellent truth? who maketh magnanimity and justice shine, throughout all misty fearfulness and foggy desires? who, if the saying of Plato and Tully be true, that who could see Virtue, would be wonderfully ravished with the love of her beauty, this man sets her out to make her more lovely in her holiday apparel, to the eye of any that will deign, not to disdain, until they understand. But if anything be already said in the defence of sweet poetry, all concurreth to the maintaining the heroical, which is not only a kind, but the best, and most accomplished kind of poetry.

For as the image of each action stirreth and instructeth the mind, so the lofty image of such worthies most inflameth the mind with desire to be worthy, and informs with counsel how to be worthy. Only let Aneas be worn in the tablet of your memory, how he governeth himself in the ruin of his country, in the preserving his old father, and carrying away his religious ceremonies: in obeying the god's commandment to leave Dido, though not only all passionate kindness, but even the humane consideration of virtuous gratefulness, would have craved other of him.

How in storms, how in sports, how in war, how in peace, how a fugitive, how victorious, how besieged, how besieging, how to strangers, how to allies, how to his enemies, how to his own: lastly, how in his inward self, and how in his outward government. And I think, in a mind not prejudiced with a prejudicating humour, he will be found in excellency fruitful: yea, even as Horace saith:

Melius Chrysippo et Crantore.

But truly I imagine, it falleth out with these poet-whippers, as with some good women, who often are sick, but in faith they cannot tell where. So the name of poetry is odious to them; but neither his cause, nor effects, neither the sum that contains him, nor the particularities descending from him, give any fast handle to their carping dispraise.

Sith then poetry is of all human learning the most ancient, and of most fatherly antiquity, as from whence other learnings have taken their beginnings: sith it is so universal, that no learned nation doth despise it, nor no barbarous nation is without it: sith both Roman and Greek gave divine names unto it, the one of prophesying, the other of making: and that indeed that name of making is fit for him; considering, that whereas other arts retain themselves within their subject, and receive, as it were, their being from it, the poet only bringeth his own stuff, and doth not learn a conceit out of a matter, but maketh matter for a conceit: sith neither his description, nor his end, containeth any evil, the thing described cannot be evil: sith his effects be so good as to teach goodness and to delight the learners: sith therein, he doth not only far pass the historian, but for instructing is well- nigh comparable to the philosopher: and for moving, leaves him behind him: sith the Holy Scripture, hath whole parts in it poetical: and that even our Saviour Christ vouchsafed to use the flowers of it: sith all his kinds are not only in their united forms, but in their severed dissections fully commendable, I think, the laurel crown, appointed for triumphing captains, doth worthily honour the poet's triumph. But because we have ears as well as tongues, and that the lightest reasons that may be, will seem to weigh greatly, if nothing be put in the counter-balance: let us hear, and as well as we can ponder, what objections may be made against this art, which may be worthy, either of yielding or answering.

First truly I note, not only in these *mysomousoi* poet-haters, but in all that kind of people, who seek a praise by dispraising others, that they do prodigally spend a great many wandering words, in quips, and scoffs; carping and taunting at each thing, which, by stirring the spleen, may stay the brain from a through beholding the worthiness of the subject. Those kind of objections, as they are full of very idle easiness, sith there is nothing of so sacred a majesty, but that an itching tongue may rub itself upon it: so deserve they no other answer, but instead of laughing at the jest, to laugh at the jester. We know a playing wit can praise the discretion of an ass; the comfortableness of being in debt, and the jolly commodity of being sick of the plague. So of the contrary side, if we will turn Ovid's verse:

Ut lateat virtus proximitate mali,

that good lie hid in nearness of the evil: Agrippa will be as merry in showingthe vanity of science, as Erasmus was in commending of folly. Neither shall any man or matter escape some touch of these smiling railers. But for Erasmus and Agrippa, they had another foundation than the superficial part would promise. Marry, these other pleasant fault-finders, who will correct the verb, before they understand the noun, and confute others' knowledge before they confirm their own: I would have them only remember, that scoffing cometh not of wisdom. So as the best title in true English they get with their merriments is to be called good fools: for so have our grave forefathers ever termed that humorous kind of jesters: but that which giveth greatest scope to their scorning humours is rhyming and versing.

It is already said it is not rhyming and versing that maketh poesy. One may be a poet without versing, and a versifier without poetry. But yet, presuppose it were inseparable truly it were an inseparable commendation. For if *oratio* next to *ratio*, speech next to reason, be the greatest gift bestowed upon mortality: that cannot be praiseless, which doth most polish that blessing of speech, which considers each word, not only by his forcible quality, but by his best measured quantity, carrying even in themselves, a harmony: without number, measure, order, proportion, be in our time grown odious. But lay aside the just praise it hath, by being the only fit speech for music: thus much is undoubtedly true, that if reading be foolish, without remembering, memory being the only treasurer of knowledge, those words which are fittest for memory, are likewise most convenient for knowledge. Now, that verse far exceedeth prose in the knitting up of the memory, the reason is manifest. The words, being so set, as one word cannot be lost, but the whole work fails: which accuseth itself, calleth the remembrance back to itself, and so most strongly confirmeth it. Besides, one word so as it were begetting another, as be it in rhyme or measured verse, by the former a man shall have a near guess to the follower. Lastly, even they that have taught the art of memory have showed nothing so apt for it, as a certain room divided into many places well and thoroughly known. Now, that hath the verse in effect perfectly: every word having his natural seat, which seat must needs make the words remembered. But what needeth more in a thing so known to all men?

Who is it that ever was a scholar, that doth not carry away some verses of Virgil, Horace, or Cato, which in his youth he learned, and even to his old age serve him for hourly lessons? But the fitness it hath for memory is notably proved by all delivery of arts: wherein for the most part, from grammar to logic, mathematic, physic, and the rest, the rules chiefly necessary to be borne away are compiled in verses. So that, verse being in itself sweet and orderly, and being best for memory, the only handle of knowledge, it must be in jest that any man can speak against it. Now then go we to the most important imputations laid to the poor poets; for aught I can yet learn, they are these: first, that there being many other more fruitful knowledges, a man might better spend his time in them, than in this. Secondly, that it is the mother of lies. Thirdly, that it is the nurse of abuse, infecting us with many pestilent desires: with a siren's sweetness, drawing the mind to the serpent's tail of sinful fancy.

And herein especially, comedies give the largest field to err, as Chaucer saith: how both in other nations and in ours, before poets did soften us, we were full of courage, given to martial exercises; the pillars of man-like liberty, and not lulled asleep in shady idleness with poets' pastimes. And lastly, and chiefly, they cry out with an open mouth, as if they outshot Robin Hood, that Plato banished them out of his commonwealth. Truly, this is much, if there be much truth in it. First to the first: that a man might better spend his time, is a reason indeed: but it doth but *petere principium*. For if it be as I affirm, that no learning is so good as that which teacheth and moveth to virtue; and that none can both teach and move thereto so much as poetry: then is the conclusion manifest, that ink and paper cannot be to a more profitable purpose employed.

And certainly, though a man should grant their first assumption, it should follow very unwillingly, that good is not good, because better is better. But I still and utterly deny that there is sprung out of earth a more fruitful knowledge. To the second, therefore, that they should be the principal liars; I answer paradoxically, but truly I think, truly; that of all writers under the sun, the poet is the least liar: and though he would, as a poet can scarcely be a liar, the astronomer, with his cousin the geometrician, can hardly escape, when they take upon them to measure the height of the stars.

How often, think you, do the physicians lie, when they aver things good for sicknesses, which afterwards send Charon a great number of souls drowned in a potion before they come to his ferry? And no less of the rest, which take upon them to affirm. Now, for the poet, he nothing affirms, and therefore never lieth. For, as I take it, to lie is to affirm that to be true which is false. So as the other artists, and especially the historian, affirming many things, can in the cloudy knowledge of mankind hardly escape from many lies. But the poet never affirmeth.

The poet never maketh any circles about your imagination, to conjure you to believe for true what he writes. He citeth not authorities of other histories, but even for his entry calleth the sweet Muses to inspire into him a good invention: in truth, not labouring to tell you what is or is not, but what should or should not be: and therefore, though he recount things not true, yet because he telleth them not for true, he lieth not, without we will say that Nathan lied in his speech, before alleged, to David. Which as a wicked man durst scarce say, so think I, none so simple would say, that Asop lied in the tales of his beasts: for who thinks that Asop wrote it for actually true, were well worthy to have his name chronicled among the beasts he writeth of.

What child is there, that coming to a play, and seeing Thebes written in great letters upon an old door, doth believe that it is Thebes? If then a man can arrive, at that child's age, to know that the poet's persons and doings are but pictures what should be, and not stories what have been, they will never give the lie to things not affirmatively, but allegorically and figuratively, written. And therefore as in history, looking for truth, they go away full fraught with falsehood: so in poesy, looking for fiction, they shall use the narration but as an imaginative groundplot of a profitable invention.

But hereto is replied that the poets give names to men they write of, which argueth a conceit of an actual truth, and so, not being true, proves a falsehood. And doth the lawyer lie, then, when under the names of John a stile and John a noakes, he puts his case? But that is easily answered. Their naming of men is but to make their picture the more lively, and not to build any history: painting men, they cannot leave men nameless. We see we cannot play at chess, but that we must give names to our chessmen; and yet methinks he were a very partial champion of truth that would say we lied for giving a piece of wood the reverend title of a bishop. The poet nameth Cyrus or Aneas no other way than to show what men of their fames, fortunes, and estates should do.

Their third is, how much it abuseth men's wit, training it to wanton sinfulness and lustful love; for indeed that is the principal, if not the only abuse I can hear alleged. They say the comedies rather teach than reprehend amorous conceits. They say the lyric is larded with passionate sonnets. The elegiac weeps the want of his mistress. And that even to the heroical, Cupid hath ambitiously climbed. Alas, Love! I would thou couldst as well defend thyself as thou canst offend others. I would those on whom thou dost attend could either put thee away or yield good reason why they keep thee. But grant love of beauty to be a beastly fault, although it be very hard, sith only man and no beast hath that gift, to discern beauty. Grant that lovely name of love to deserve all hateful reproaches: although even some of my masters the philosophers spent a good deal of their lamp-oil in setting forth the excellency of it. Grant, I say, whatsoever they will have granted; that not only love, but lust, but vanity, but scurrility, possesseth many leaves of the poet's books: yet think I, when this is granted, they will find their sentence may with good manners put the last words foremost; and not say that poetry abuseth man's wit, but that man's wit abuseth poetry.

For I will not deny but that man's wit may make poesy to be fantastic: which doth contrariwise infect the fancy with unworthy objects. As the painter, that should give to the eye either some excellent perspective or some fine picture fit for building or fortification, or containing in it some notable example, as Abraham sacrificing his son Isaac, Judith killing Holofernes, David fighting with Goliath, may leave those and please an ill-pleased eye with wanton shows of better hidden matters. But what, shall the abuse of a thing make the right use odious? Nay, truly, though I yield that poesy may not only be abused, but that, being abused by the reason of his sweet charming force, it can do more hurt than any other army of words: yet shall it be so far from concluding that the abuse should give reproach to the abused, that contrariwise it is a good reason that whatsoever being abused, doth most harm, being rightly used doth most good.

Do we not see the skill of physic, being abused, teach poison the most violent destroyer? Doth not knowledge of law, whose end is to even and right all things, being abused, grow the crooked fosterer of horrible injuries? Doth not God's word, abused, breed heresy? and His name abused, become blasphemy? Truly a needle cannot do much hurt, and as truly it cannot do much good. With a sword thou mayest kill thy father, and with a sword thou mayest defend thy prince and country. So that, as in their calling poets the fathers of lies they say nothing: so in this their argument of abuse they prove the commendation.

They allege herewith that, before poets began to be in price, our nation hath set their hearts' delight upon action and not upon imagination: rather doing things worthy to be written than writing things fit to be done. What that before time was, I think scarcely Sphinx can tell: sith no memory is so ancient that hath the precedence of poetry. And certain it is that, in our plainest homeliness, yet never was the Albion nation without poetry. Marry, this argument, though it be levelled against poetry, yet is it indeed a chain-shot against all learning, or bookishness, as they commonly term it. Of such mind were certain Goths, of whom it is written that, having in the spoils of a famous city taken a fair library, one hangman who had murdered a great number of bodies, would have set fire on it. "No", said another very gravely, "take heed what you do, for while they are busy about these toys, we shall with more leisure conquer their countries."

This indeed is the ordinary doctrine of ignorance, and many words sometimes I have heard spent in it; but because this reason is generally against all learning, as well as poetry; or rather, all learning but poetry: because it were too large a digression to handle, or at least too superfluous: I only with Horace, to him that is of that opinion,

Jubeo stultum esse libenter:

for as for poetry itself, it is the freest from this objection. For poetry is the companion of the camps.

I dare undertake, Orlando Furioso or honest King Arthur will never displease a soldier; but the quiddity of *ens* and *prima materia* will hardly agree with a corslet; and therefore, as I said in the beginning, even Turks and Tartars are delighted with poets. Homer, a Greek, flourished before Greece flourished. And if to a slight conjecture a conjecture may be opposed, truly it may seem that, as by him their learned men took almost their first light of knowledge, so their active men received their first motions of courage. Only Alexander's example may serve, who by Plutarch is accounted of such virtue that fortune was not his guide but his footstool; whose acts speak for him, though Plutarch did not: indeed, the Phoenix of warlike princes.

This Alexander left his schoolmaster, living Aristotle, behind him, but took dead Homer with him; he put the philosopher Calisthenes to death for his seeming philosophical, indeed mutinous stubbornness. But the chief thing he ever was heard to wish for was that Homer had been alive. He well found he received more bravery of mind by the pattern of Achilles than by hearing the definition of fortitude; and therefore, if Cato misliked Fulvius for carrying Ennius with him to the field, it may be answered that, if Cato misliked it, the noble Fulvius liked it, or else he had not done it. For it was not the excellent Cato Uticensis, but it was the former: in truth, a bitter punisher of faults, but else a man that had never well sacrificed to the Graces.

He misliked and cried out upon all Greek learning, and yet, being 80 years old, began to learn it. Belike, fearing that Pluto understood not Latin. Indeed, the Roman laws allowed no person to be carried to the wars but he that was in the soldiers' roll; and therefore, though Cato misliked his unmustered person, he misliked not his work. And if he had, Scipio Nasica, judged by common consent the best Roman, loved him. Both the other Scipio brothers, who had by their virtues no less surnames than of Asia and Affrick, so loved him that they caused his body to be buried in their sepulchre. So as Cato, his authority being but against his person, and that answered with so far greater than himself, is herein of no validity. But now, indeed, my burden is great; now Plato his name is laid upon me, whom I must confess, of all philosophers, I have ever esteemed most worthy of reverence, and with great reason, sith of all philosophers he is the most poetical. Yet if he will defile the fountain, out of which his flowing streams have proceeded, let us boldly examine with what reasons he did it.

First, truly, a man might maliciously object that Plato, being a philosopher, was a natural enemy of poets; for, indeed, after the philosophers had picked out of the sweet mysteries of poetry the right discerning true points of knowledge, they forthwith putting it in method, and making a school-art of that which the poets did only teach by a divine delightfulness, beginning to spurn at their guides like ungrateful 'prentices, were not content to set up shops for themselves, but sought by all means to discredit their masters. Which by the force of delight being barred them, the less they could overthrow them, the more they hated them. For, indeed, they found for Homer seven cities strove who should have him for their citizen: where many cities banished philosophers, as not fit members to live among them. For only repeating certain of Euripides' verses, many Athenians had their lives saved of the Syracusians: when the Athenians themselves thought many philosophers unworthy to live.

Certain poets, as Simonides and Pindarus had so prevailed with Hiero the first, that of a tyrant they made him a just king, where Plato could do so little with Dionysius, that he himself, of a philosopher, was made a slave. But who should do thus, I confess, should requite the objections made against poets, with like cavillation against philosophers; as likewise one should do, that should bid one read *Phaedrus* or*Symposium* in Plato, or the discourse of love in Plutarch, and see whether any poet do authorize abominable filthiness, as they do. Again, a man might ask out of what commonwealth Plato did banish them? in sooth, thence where he himself alloweth community of women: so as, belike, this banishment grew not for effeminate wantonness, sith little should poetical sonnets be hurtful, when a man might have what woman he listed. But I honour philosophical instructions, and bless the wits which bred them: so as they be not abused, which is likewise stretched to poetry.

St. Paul himself, who yet allegeth twice two poets, and one of them by the name of a prophet, setteth a watch-word upon philosophy, indeed upon the abuse. So doth Plato, upon the abuse, not upon poetry. Plato found fault, that the poets of his time filled the world with wrong opinions of the gods, making light tales of that unspotted essence; and therefore, would not have the youth depraved with such opinions.

Herein may much be said, let this suffice: the poets did not induce such opinions, but did imitate those opinions already induced. For all the Greek stories can well testify, that the very religion of that time stood upon many and many-fashioned gods, not taught so by the poets, but followed, according to their nature of imitation. Who list, may read in Plutarch, the discourses of Isis, and Osiris, of the cause why oracles ceased, of the divine providence: and see, whether the theology of that nation stood not upon such dreams, which the poets superstitiously observed, and truly, did much better in it than the philosophers, who, shaking off superstition, brought in atheism. Plato therefore, meant not in general of poets, in those words of which Julius Scaliger saith *qua auctoritate barbari quidam atque hispidi abuti velint, ad poetas e republica exigendos*: but only meant, to drive out those wrong opinions of the Deity perchance nourished by the then esteemed poets. And a man need go no further than to Plato himself, to know his meaning: who in his dialogue called *Ion*, giveth high, and rightly divine commendation to poetry.

So as Plato, banishing the abuse, not the thing, not banishing it but giving due honour unto it, shall be our patron, and not our adversary. For indeed I had much rather show their mistaking of Plato, than go about to overthrow his authority, whom the wiser a man is, the more just cause he shall find to have in admiration: especially, sith he attributeth unto poesy more than myself do; namely to be a very inspiring of a divine force, far above man's wit; as in the aforenamed dialogue is apparent.

Of the other side, who would show the honours have been by the best sort of judgements granted them, a whole sea of examples would present themselves. Alexanders, Caesars, Scipios, all favourers of poets. Lalius, called the Roman Socrates, himself a poet: so as part of *Heautontimorumenos* in Terence was supposed to be made by him. And even the Greek Socrates, whom Apollo confirmed to be the only wise man, is said to have spent part of his old time in putting Asop's fables into verses.

And therefore, full evil should it become his scholar Plato to put such words in his master's mouth against poets. But what need more? Aristotle writes the Art of Poesy: and why if it should not be written? Plutarch teacheth the use to be gathered of them, and how if they should not be read? And who reads Plutarch's either history or philosophy, shall find he trimmeth both their garments with guards of poesy. But I list not to defend poesy, with the help of her underling, historiography.

Let it suffice, that it is a fit soil for praise to dwell upon: and what dispraise may set upon it is either easily overcome, or transformed into just commendation. So that, sith the excellencies of it may be so easily and so justly confirmed, and the low-creeping objections, so soon trodden down; it not being an art of lies, but of true doctrine: not of effeminateness, but of notable stirring of courage: not of abusing man's wit, but of strengthening man's wit: not banished, but honoured by Plato: let us rather plant more laurels, for to engarland our poets' heads, than suffer the ill-favouring breath of such wrong-speakers, once to blow upon the clear springs of poesy.

But sith I have run so long a career in this matter, methinks, before I give my pen a full stop, it shall be but a little more lost time, to inquire, why England, should be grown so hard a step-mother to poets, who certainly in wit ought to pass all other: sith all only proceedeth from their wit, being indeed makers of themselves, not takers of others. How can I but exclaim,

Musa mihi causas memora, quo numine laso,

sweet poesy, that hath anciently had kings, emperors, senators, great captains, such as, besides a thousand others, David, Adrian, Sophocles, Germanicus, not only to favour poets, but to be poets; and of our nearer times, can present for her patrons, a Robert, king of Sicily, the great king Francis of France, King James of Scotland; such cardinals as Bembus, and Bibiena; such famous preachers and teachers, as Beza and Melancthon; so learned philosophers, as Fracastorius and Scaliger; so great orators, as Pontanus and Muretus; so piercing wits as George Buchanan; so grave counsellors, as besides many, but before all, that Hospital of France: than whom that realme never brought forth a more accomplished judgement: more firmly builded upon virtue; I say these, with numbers of others, not only to read others' poesies, but to poetise for others' reading: that poesy thus embraced in all other places, should only find, in our time, a hard welcome in England, I think the very earth lamenteth it, and therefore decketh our soil with fewer laurels than it was accustomed; for heretofore, poets have in England also flourished; and which is to be noted, even in those times, when the trumpet of Mars did sound loudest.

And now, that an over-faint quietness should seem to strew the house for poets, they are almost in as good reputation as the mountebanks at Venice. Truly even that, as of the one side it giveth great praise to poesy, which like Venus hath rather be troubled in the net with Mars, than enjoy the homely quiet of Vulcan: so serves it for a piece of a reason, why they are less grateful to idle England, which now can scarce endure the pain of a pen. Upon this necessarily followeth, that base men with servile wits undertake it: who think it enough, if they can be rewarded of the printer. And so as Epaminondas is said, with the honour of his virtue, to have made an office, by his exercising it, which before was contemptible, to become highly respected: so these, no more but setting their names to it, by their own disgracefulness, disgrace the most graceful poesy. For now, as if all the Muses were got with child, to bring forth bastard poets, without any commission, they do post over the banks of Helicon, till they make the readers more weary than post-horses: while in the mean time, they

Queis meliore luto finxit procordia Titan,

are better content, to suppress the outflowing of their wit, than by publishing them to be accounted knights of the same order. But I, that before ever I durst aspire unto the dignity am admitted into the company of the paper-blurrers, do find the very true cause of our wanting estimation, is want of desert: taking upon us to be poets, in despite of Pallas. Now, wherein we want desert were a thank-worthy labour to express: but if I knew, I should have mended myself. But I, as I never desired the title, so have neglected the means to come by it. Only overmastered by some thoughts, I yielded an inky tribute unto them. Marry, they that delight in poesy itself should seek to know what they do, and how they do; and especially, look themselves in an unflattering glass of reason, if they be inclinable unto it.

For poesy must not be drawn by the ears, it must be gently led, or rather, it must lead. Which was partly the cause, that made the ancient-learned affirm, it was a divine gift, and no human skill: sith all other knowledges lie ready for any that hath strength of wit: a poet no industry can make, if his own genius be not carried unto it: and therefore is it an old proverb, *orator fit; poeta nascitur*. Yet confess I always, that as the fertilest ground must be manured, so must the highest-flying wit have a Dadalus to guide him. That Dadalus, they say, both in this and in other, hath three wings, to bear itself up into the air of due commendation: that is, art, imitation, and exercise. But these, neither artificial rules, nor imitative patterns, we much cumber ourselves withal.

Exercise indeed we do, but that, very fore-backwardly: for where we should exercise to know, we exercise as having known: and so is our brain delivered of much matter, which never was begotten by knowledge. For, there being two principal parts, matter to be expressed by words, and words to express the matter, in neither, we use art, or imitation, rightly. Our matter is *quodlibet* indeed, though wrongly performing Ovid's verse,

Quicquid conabar dicere versus erat:

never marshalling it into an assured rank, that almost the readers cannot tell where to find themselves.

Chaucer undoubtedly did excellently in his *Troilus and Cresseid*; of whom, truly I know not whether to marvel more, either that he in that misty time, could see so clearly, or that we in this clear age walk so stumblingly after him. Yet had he great wants, fit to be forgiven, in so reverent antiquity. I account the *Mirror of Magistrates* meetly furnished of beautiful parts; and in the Earl of Surrey's *Lyrics*, many things tasting of a noble birth, and worthy of a noble mind.

The *Shepherd's Calendar* hath much poetry in his eclogues: indeed worthy the reading, if I be not deceived. That same framing of his style to an old rustic language I dare not allow, sith neither Theocritus in Greek, Virgil in Latin, nor Sannazar in Italian, did affect it. Besides these, do I not remember to have seen but few printed, that have poetical sinews in them: for proof whereof, let but most of the verses be put in prose, and then ask the meaning; and it will be found that one verse did but beget another, without ordering at the first, what should be at the last: which becomes a confused mass of words, with a tingling sound of rhyme, barely accompanied with reason.

Our tragedies and comedies, observing rules neither of honest civility nor of skilful poetry, excepting *Gorboduc*, which notwithstanding as it is full of stately speeches, and well-sounding phrases, climbing to the height of Seneca his style, and as full of notable morality, which it doth most delightfully teach, and so obtain the very end of poesy: yet in truth it is very defectious in the circumstances; which grieveth me, because it might not remain as an exact model of all tragedies. For it is faulty both in place and time, the two necessary companions of all corporal actions. For where the stage should always represent but one place, and the uttermost time presupposed in it should be, both by Aristotle's precept and common reason, but one day: there is both many days, and many places, inartificially imagined.

But if it be so in *Gorboduc*, how much more in all the rest? where you shall have Asia of the one side, and Africa of the other, and so many other under-kingdoms, that the player, when he cometh in, must ever begin with telling where he is: or else, the tale will not be conceived. Now ye shall have three ladies walk to gather flowers, and then we must believe the stage to be a garden. By and by, we hear news of shipwreck in the same place, and then we are to blame, if we accept it not for a rock.

Upon the back of that, comes out a hideous monster, with fire and smoke, and then the miserable beholders are bound to take it for a cave. While in the meantime, two armies fly in, represented with four swords and bucklers, and then what hard heart will not receive it for a pitched field? Now, of time they are much more liberal, for ordinary it is that two young princes fall in love. After many traverses, she is got with child, delivered of a fair boy, he is lost, groweth a man, falls in love, and is ready to get another child, and all this in two hours' space: which how absurd it is in sense, even sense may imagine, and art hath taught, and all ancient examples justified: and at this day the ordinary players in Italy will not err in. Yet will some bring in an example of *Eunuchus* in Terence, that containeth matter of two days, yet far short of twenty years. True it is, and so was it to be played in two days, and so fitted to the time it set forth.

And though Plautus hath in one place done amiss, let us hit with him, and not miss with him. But they will say, how then shall we set forth a story, which containeth both many places, and many times? And do they not know that a tragedy is tied to the laws of poesy, and not of history? not bound to follow the story, but having liberty, either to feign a quite new matter, or to frame the history to the most tragical convenience. Again, many things may be told, which cannot be showed, if they know the difference betwixt reporting and representing. As for example, I may speak of Peru, and in speech digress from that, to the description of Calicut: but in action, I cannot represent it without Pacolet's horse: and so was the manner the ancients took, by some *nuncius* to recount things done in former time, or other place.

Lastly, if they will represent a history, they must not begin *ab ovo*: but they must come to the principal point of that one action, which they will represent. By example this will be best expressed. I have a story of young Polydorus, delivered for safety's sake, with great riches, by his father Priamus to Polymnestor, king of Thrace, in the Trojan war time: he after some years, hearing the overthrow of Priamus, for to make the treasure his own, murdereth the child: the body is taken up by Hecuba: she the same day findeth a slight to be revenged most cruelly of the tyrant: where now would one of our tragedy writers begin, but with the delivery of the child? Then should he sail over into Thrace, and so spend I know not how many years, and travel numbers of places. But where doth Euripides?

Even with the finding of the body, leaving the rest to be told by the spirit of Polydorus. This need no further to be enlarged, the dullest wit may conceive it. But besides these gross absurdities, how all their plays be neither right tragedies, nor right comedies: mingling kings and clowns, not because the matter so carrieth it, but thrust in clowns by head and shoulders, to play a part in majestical matters, with neither decency nor discretion. So as neither the admiration and commiseration, nor the right sportfulness, is by their mongrel tragi-comedy obtained.

I know Apuleius did somewhat so, but that is a thing recounted with space of time, not represented in one moment: and I know, the ancients have one or two examples of tragi-comedies, as Plautus hath *Amphitryo*: but if we mark them well, we shall find, that they never, or very daintily, match hornpipes and funerals. So falleth it out, that having indeed no right comedy, in that comical part of our tragedy, we have nothing but scurrility, unworthy of any chaste ears: or some extreme show of doltishness, indeed fit to lift up a loud laughter, and nothing else: where the whole tract of a comedy should be full of delight, as the tragedy should be still maintained in a well-raised admiration. But our comedians think there is no delight without laughter, which is very wrong; for though laughter may come with delight, yet cometh it not of delight, as though delight should be the cause of laughter; but well may one thing breed both together: nay, rather in themselves, they have as it were a kind of contrariety: for delight we scarcely do, but in things that have a convenience to ourselves, or to the general nature: laughter almost ever cometh of things most disproportioned to ourselves and nature. Delight hath a joy in it, either permanent, or present. Laughter hath only a scornful tickling.

For example, we are ravished with delight to see a fair woman, and yet are far from being moved to laughter. We laugh at deformed creatures, wherein certainly we cannot delight. We delight in good chances, we laugh at mischances; we delight to hear the happiness of our friends, or country; at which he were worthy to be laughed at, that would laugh; we shall contrarily laugh sometimes, to find a matter quite mistaken, and go down the hill against the bias, in the mouth of some such men, as for the respect of them one shall be heartily sorry, yet he cannot choose but laugh; and so is rather pained, than delighted, with laughter. Yet deny I not, but that they may go well together; for as in Alexander's picture well set out we delight without laughter, and in twenty mad antics we laugh without delight: so in Hercules, painted with his great beard, and furious countenance, in woman's attire, spinning at Omphale's commandment, it breedeth both delight and laughter.

For the representing of so strange a power in love, procureth delight: and the scornfulness of the action stirreth laughter. But I speak to this purpose, that all the end of the comical part be not upon such scornful matters as stir laughter only: but mixed with it, that delightful teaching which is the end of poesy.

And the great fault even in that point of laughter, and forbidden plainly by Aristotle, is that they stir laughter in sinful things; which are rather execrable than ridiculous: or in miserable, which are rather to be pitied than scorned. For what is it to make folks gape at a wretched beggar, or a beggarly clown? or, against law of hospitality, to jest at strangers, because they speak not English so well as we do? what do we learn, sith it is certain

Nil habet infelix paupertas durius in se, Quam quod ridiculos homines facit:

but rather a busy-loving courtier; a heartless threatening Thraso; a self-wise-seeming schoolmaster; an awry-transformed traveller? These if we saw walk in stage names, which we play naturally, therein were delightful laughter, and teaching delightfulness: as in the other, the tragedies of Buchanan do justly bring forth a divine admiration.

But I have lavished out too many words of this play-matter. I do it because, as they are excelling parts of poesy, so is there none so much used in England, and none can be more pitifully abused. Which like an unmannerly daughter, showing a bad education, causeth her mother poesy's honesty to be called in question. Other sorts of poetry almost have we none, but that lyrical kind of songs and sonnets: which Lord, if he gave us so good minds, how well it might be employed, and with how heavenly fruit, both private and public, in singing the praises of the immortal beauty, the immortal goodness of that God, who giveth us hands to write, and wits to conceive, of which we might well want words, but never matter, of which we could turn our eyes to nothing, but we should ever have new budding occasions.

But truly many of such writings, as come under the banner of un-resistible love, if I were a mistress, would never persuade me they were in love: so coldly they apply fiery speeches, as men that had rather read lovers' writings, and so caught up certain swelling phrases, which hang together, like a man which once told me, the wind was at north, west, and by south, because he would be sure to name winds enough, than that in truth they feel those passions, which easily may be betrayed by that same forcibleness, or *energeia* of the writer. But let this be a sufficient, though short note, that we miss the right use of the material point of poesy.

Now, for the outside of it, which is words, or diction, it is even well worse. So is that honey-flowing matron eloquence apparelled, or rather disguised, in a courtezan-like painted affectation: one time with so far-fetched words, they may seem monsters, but must seem strangers to any poor Englishman; another time, with coursing of a letter, as if they were bound to follow the method of a dictionary: another time, with figures and flowers, extremely winter-starved.

But I would this fault were only peculiar to versifiers, and had not as large possession among prose-printers; and among many scholars; and among some preachers.

Truly I could wish, if at least I might be so bold to wish in a thing beyond the reach of my capacity, the diligent imitators of Tully and Demosthenes did not so much keep *Nizolian* paper-books of their figures and phrases, as by attentive translation devour them whole, and make them wholly theirs: for now they cast sugar and spice upon every dish that is served to the table; like those Indians, not content to wear earrings at the fit and natural place of the ears, but they will thrust jewels through their nose and lips because they will be sure to be fine.

Tully, when he was to drive out Catiline, as it were with a thunderbolt of eloquence, often used that figure of repetition, *Vivit? Vivit; immo in Senatum venit*, and c. Indeed, inflamed with a well-grounded rage, he would have his words double out of his mouth: and so do that artificially, which we see men do in choler naturally.

And we, having noted the grace of those words, hale them in sometime to a familiar epistle, when it were to too much choler to be choleric. Now for similitudes, in certain printed discourses, I think all herbarists, all stories of beasts, fowls, and fishes, are rifled up, that they come in multitudes, to wait upon any of our conceits: which certainly is as absurd a surfeit to the ears as is possible: for the force of a similitude, not being to prove anything to a contrary disputer, but only to explain to a willing hearer, when that is done, the rest is a most tedious prattling: rather over-swaying the memory from the purpose whereto they were applied, than any whit informing the judgement, already either satisfied, or by similitudes not to be satisfied.

For my part, I do not doubt, when Antonius and Crassus, the great forefathers of Cicero in eloquence, the one pretended not to know art, the other, not to set by it: because with a plain sensibleness they might win credit of popular ears; which credit is the nearest step to persuasion: which persuasion is the chief mark of oratory; I do not doubt but that they used these tracks very sparingly, which who doth generally use, any man may see doth dance to his own music: and so be noted by the audience more careful to speak curiously, than to speak truly.

Undoubtedly, I have found in divers smally learned courtiers a more sound style, than in some professors of learning: of which I can guess no other cause, but that the courtier, following that which by practice he findeth fittest to nature, therein doth according to art, though not by art: where the other, using art to show art, and not to hide art, flyeth from nature, and indeed abuseth art.

But what? methinks I deserve to be pounded, for straying from poetry to oratory: but both have such an affinity in this wordish consideration, that I think this digression will make my meaning receive the fuller understanding: which is not to take upon me to teach poets how they should do, but only finding myself sick among the rest, to show some one or two spots of the common infection, grown among the most part of writers: that, acknowledging ourselves somewhat awry, we may bend to the right use both of matter and manner; whereto our language giveth us great occasion, being indeed capable of any excellent exercising of it.

I know, some will say it is a mingled language. And why not so much the better, taking the best of both the other? Another will say it wanteth grammar. Nay, truly, it hath that praise, that it wanteth not grammar; for grammar it might have, but it needs it not; being so easy of itself, and so void of those cumbersome differences of cases, genders, moods, and tenses, which I think was a piece of the Tower of Babylon's curse, that a man should be put to school to learn his mother-tongue.

But for the uttering sweetly and properly the conceits of the mind, which is the end of speech, that hath it equally with any other tongue in the world: and is particularly happy, in compositions of two or three words together, near the Greek, far beyond the Latin: which is one of the greatest beauties can be in a language.

Now, of versifying there are two sorts, the one ancient, the other modern: the ancient marked the quantity of each syllable, and according to that framed his verse: the modern, observing only number, the chief life of it standeth in that like sounding of the words, which we call rhyme. Whether of these be the most excellent, would bear many speeches.

The ancient more fit for music, both words and tune observing quantity, and more fit lively to express divers passions, by the low and lofty sound of the well-weighed syllable.

The latter likewise, with his rhyme, striketh a certain music to the ear: and in fine, sith it doth delight, though by another way, it obtains the same purpose: there being in either sweetness, and wanting in neither majesty. Truly the English, before any other vulgar language I know, is fit for both sorts: for, for the ancient, the Italian is so full of vowels, that it must ever be cumbered with elisions. The Dutch, so of the other side with consonants, that they cannot yield the sweet sliding fit for a verse. The French, in his whole language, hath not one word, that hath his accent in the last syllable saving two, called*Antepenultima*, and little more hath the Spanish: and therefore, very gracelessly may they use *Dactyls*. The English is subject to none of these defects.

Now, for the rhyme, though we do not observe quantity, yet we observe the accent very precisely: which other languages either cannot do, or will not do so absolutely. That *Caesura*, or breathing place in the midst of the verse, neither Italian nor Spanish have; the French, and we, never almost fail of. Lastly, even the very rhyme itself, the Italian cannot put in the last syllable, by the French named the masculine rhyme, but still in the next to the last, which the French call the female, or the next before that, which the Italians termed *Sdrucciola*. The example of the former, is *Buono*, *Suono*; of the *Sdrucciola*, *Femina*, *Semina*.

The French, on the other side, hath both the male, as *Bon*, *Son*, and the female, as *Plaise*, *Taise*. But the *Sdrucciola* he hath not: where English hath all three, as *Due*, *True*, *Father*, *Rather*, *Motion*, *Potion* with much more which might be said, but that I find already, the triflingness of this discourse is much too much enlarged.

So that sith the ever-praiseworthy poesy is full of virtue-breeding delightfulness, and void of no gift, that ought to be in the noble name of learning: sith the blames laid against it are either false, or feeble: sith the cause why it is not esteemed in England, is the fault of poet-apes, not poets: sith lastly, our tongue is most fit to honour poesy, and to be honoured by poesy, I conjure you all, that have had the evil luck to read this ink-wasting toy of mine, even in the name of the nine Muses, no more to scorn the sacred mysteries of poesy: no more to laugh at the name of poets, as though they were next inheritors to fools: no more to jest at the reverend title of a rhymer: but to believe with Aristotle, that they were the ancient treasurers of the Grecians' Divinity.

To believe with Bembus, that they were first bringers in of all civility. To believe with Scaliger, that no philosopher's precepts can sooner make you an honest man, than the reading of Virgil.

To believe with Clauserus, the translator of Cornutus, that it pleased the heavenly Deity, by Hesiod and Homer, under the veil of fables, to give us all knowledge, logic, rhetoric, philosophy, natural and moral, and *Quid non?*

To believe with me, that there are many mysteries contained in poetry, which of purpose were written darkly, lest by profane wits it should be abused. To believe with Landin, that they are so beloved of the Gods, that whatsoever they write proceeds of a divine fury.

Lastly, to believe themselves, when they tell you they will make you immortal, by their verses.

Thus doing, your name shall flourish in the printers' shops; thus doing, you shall be of kin to many a poetical preface; thus doing, you shall be most fair, most rich, most wise, most all, you shall dwell upon superlatives. Thus doing, though you be *libertino patre natus*, you shall suddenly grow *Herculis proles*:

Si quid mea carmina possunt.

Thus doing, your soul shall be placed with Dante's Beatrix, or Virgil's Anchises.

But if you be born so near the dull making Cataphract of Nilus, that you cannot hear the planet-like music of poetry, if you have so earth-creeping a mind, that it cannot lift itself up, to look to the sky of poetry: or rather, by a certain rustical disdain, will become such a mome, as to be a *momus* of poetry: then, though I will not wish unto you the ass's ears of Midas, nor to be driven by a poet's verses to hang himself, nor to be rhymed to death, as is said to be done in Ireland: yet thus much curse I must send you, in the behalf of all poets, that, while you live, you live in love, and never get favour, for lacking skill of a sonnet: and when you die, your memory die from the earth, for want of an epitaph.

11

History and Development in Literary Critical Thought

DEFINING CRITICAL THINKING

Critical thinking is a rich concept that has been developing throughout the past 2500 years. The term "critical thinking" has its roots in the mid-late 20th century. We offer here overlapping definitions, together which form a substantive, transdisciplinary conception of critical thinking.

CRITICAL THINKING AS DEFINED BY THE NATIONAL COUNCIL FOR EXCELLENCE IN CRITICAL THINKING, 1987

A statement by Michael Scriven and Richard Paul, presented at the 8th Annual International Conference on Critical Thinking and Education Reform, Summer 1987.

Critical thinking is the intellectually disciplined process of actively and skillfully conceptualizing, applying, analyzing, synthesizing, and/or evaluating information gathered from, or generated by, observation, experience, reflection, reasoning, or communication, as a guide to belief and action. In its exemplary form, it is based on universal intellectual values that transcend subject matter divisions: clarity, accuracy, precision, consistency, relevance, sound evidence, good reasons, depth, breadth, and fairness.

It entails the examination of those structures or elements of thought implicit in all reasoning: purpose, problem, or question-at-issue; assumptions; concepts; empirical grounding; reasoning leading to conclusions; implications and consequences; objections from alternative viewpoints; and frame of reference.

Critical thinking — in being responsive to variable subject matter, issues, and purposes — is incorporated in a family of interwoven modes of thinking, among them: scientific thinking, mathematical thinking, historical thinking, anthropological thinking, economic thinking, moral thinking, and philosophical thinking.

Critical thinking can be seen as having two components: 1) a set of information and belief generating and processing skills, and 2) the habit, based on intellectual commitment, of using those skills to guide behavior. It is thus to be contrasted with: 1) the mere acquisition and retention of information alone, because it involves a particular way in which information is sought and treated; 2) the mere possession of a set of skills, because it involves the continual use of them; and 3) the mere use of those skills ("as an exercise") without acceptance of their results.

Critical thinking varies according to the motivation underlying it. When grounded in selfish motives, it is often manifested in the skillful manipulation of ideas in service of one's own, or one's groups', vested interest. As such it is typically intellectually flawed, however pragmatically successful it might be. When grounded in fairmindedness and intellectual integrity, it is typically of a higher order intellectually, though subject to the charge of "idealism" by those habituated to its selfish use.

Critical thinking of any kind is never universal in any individual; everyone is subject to episodes of undisciplined or irrational thought. Its quality is therefore typically a matter of degree and dependent on, among other things, the quality and depth of experience in a given domain of thinking or with respect to a particular class of questions. No one is a critical thinker through-and-through, but only to such-and-such a degree, with such-and-such insights and blind spots, subject to such-and-such tendencies towards self-delusion. For this reason, the development of critical thinking skills and dispositions is a life-long endeavor.

ANOTHER BRIEF CONCEPTUALIZATION OF CRITICAL THINKING

Critical thinking is self-guided, self-disciplined thinking which attempts to reason at the highest level of quality in a fair-minded way. People who think critically consistently attempt to live rationally, reasonably, empathically. They are keenly aware of the inherently flawed nature of human thinking when left unchecked. They strive to diminish the power of their egocentric and sociocentric tendencies. They use the intellectual tools that critical thinking offers – concepts and principles that enable them to analyze, assess, and improve thinking. They work diligently to develop the intellectual virtues of intellectual integrity, intellectual humility, intellectual civility, intellectual empathy, intellectual sense of justice and confidence in reason. They realize that no matter how skilled they are as thinkers, they can always improve their reasoning abilities and they will at times fall prey to mistakes in reasoning, human irrationality, prejudices, biases, distortions, uncritically accepted social rules and taboos, self-interest, and vested interest. They strive to improve the world in whatever ways they can and contribute to a more rational, civilized society. At the same time, they recognize the complexities often inherent in doing so.

They avoid thinking simplistically about complicated issues and strive to appropriately consider the rights and needs of relevant others. They recognize the complexities in developing as thinkers, and commit themselves to life-long practice towards self-improvement. They embody the Socratic principle: *The unexamined life is not worth living* , because they realize that many unexamined lives together result in an uncritical, unjust, dangerous world. ~ Linda Elder, September, 2007

WHY CRITICAL THINKING?

The Problem

Everyone thinks; it is our nature to do so. But much of our thinking, left to itself, is biased, distorted, partial, uninformed or down-right prejudiced. Yet the quality of our life and that of what we produce, make, or build depends precisely on the quality of our thought. Shoddy thinking is costly, both in money and in quality of life. Excellence in thought, however, must be systematically cultivated.

A Definition

Critical thinking is that mode of thinking - about any subject, content, or problem - in which the thinker improves the quality of his or her thinking by skillfully taking charge of the structures inherent in thinking and imposing intellectual standards upon them.

The Result

A Well Cultivated Critical Thinker:

- Raises vital questions and problems, formulating them clearly and precisely;
- Gathers and assesses relevant information, using abstract ideas to interpret it effectively comes to well-reasoned conclusions and solutions, testing them against relevant criteria and standards;
- Thinks openmindedly within alternative systems of thought, recognizing and assessing, as need be, their assumptions, implications, and practical consequences; and
- Communicates effectively with others in figuring out solutions to complex problems.

Critical thinking is, in short, self-directed, self-disciplined, self-monitored, and self-corrective thinking. It presupposes assent to rigorous standards of excellence and mindful command of their use. It entails effective communication and problem solving abilities and a commitment to overcome our native egocentrism and sociocentrism.

(Taken from Richard Paul and Linda Elder, *The Miniature Guide to Critical Thinking Concepts and Tools,* Foundation for Critical Thinking Press, 2008)

CRITICAL THINKING DEFINED BY EDWARD GLASER

In a seminal study on critical thinking and education in 1941, Edward Glaser defines critical thinking as follows "The ability to think critically, as conceived in this volume, involves three things: (1) an attitude of being disposed to consider in a thoughtful way the problems and subjects that come within the range of one's experiences, (2) knowledge of the methods of logical inquiry and reasoning, and (3) some skill in applying those methods. Critical thinking calls for a persistent effort to examine any belief or supposed form of knowledge in the light of the evidence that supports it and the further conclusions to which it tends. It also generally requires ability to recognize problems, to find workable means for meeting those problems, to gather and marshal pertinent information, to recognize unstated assumptions and values, to comprehend and use language with accuracy, clarity, and discrimination, to interpret data, to appraise evidence and evaluate arguments, to recognize the existence (or non-existence) of logical relationships between propositions, to draw warranted conclusions and generalizations, to put to test the conclusions and generalizations at which one arrives, to reconstruct one's patterns of beliefs on the basis of wider experience, and to render accurate judgements about specific things and qualities in everyday life.

A BRIEF HISTORY OF THE IDEA OF CRITICAL THINKING

The intellectual roots of critical thinking are as ancient as its etymology, traceable, ultimately, to the teaching practice and vision of Socrates 2,500 years ago who discovered by a method of probing questioning that people could not rationally justify their confident claims to knowledge. Confused meanings, inadequate evidence, or self-contradictory beliefs often lurked beneath smooth but largely empty rhetoric. Socrates established the fact that one cannot depend upon those in "authority" to have sound knowledge and insight. He demonstrated that persons may have power and high position and yet be deeply confused and irrational. He established the importance of asking deep questions that probe profoundly into thinking before we accept ideas as worthy of belief.

He established the importance of seeking evidence, closely examining reasoning and assumptions, analyzing basic concepts, and tracing out implications not only of what is said but of what is done as well. His method of questioning is now known as "Socratic Questioning" and is the best known critical thinking teaching strategy. In his mode of questioning, Socrates highlighted the need in thinking for clarity and logical consistency.

Socrates set the agenda for the tradition of critical thinking, namely, to reflectively question common beliefs and explanations, carefully distinguishing those beliefs that are reasonable and logical from those which — however appealing they may be to our native egocentrism, however much they serve our vested interests, however comfortable or comforting they may be — lack adequate evidence or rational foundation to warrant our belief.

Socrates' practice was followed by the critical thinking of Plato (who recorded Socrates' thought), Aristotle, and the Greek skeptics, all of whom emphasized that things are often very different from what they appear to be and that only the trained mind is prepared to see through the way things look to us on the surface (delusive appearances) to the way they really are beneath the surface (the deeper realities of life). From this ancient Greek tradition emerged the need, for anyone who aspired to understand the deeper realities, to think systematically, to trace implications broadly and deeply, for only thinking that is comprehensive, well-reasoned, and responsive to objections can take us beyond the surface.

In the Middle Ages, the tradition of systematic critical thinking was embodied in the writings and teachings of such thinkers as Thomas Aquinas (*Sumna Theologica*) who to ensure his thinking met the test of critical thought, always systematically stated, considered, and answered all criticisms of his ideas as a necessary stage in developing them. Aquinas heightened our awareness not only of the potential power of reasoning but also of the need for reasoning to be systematically cultivated and "cross-examined." Of course, Aquinas' thinking also illustrates that those who think critically do not always reject established beliefs, only those beliefs that lack reasonable foundations.

In the Renaissance (15th and 16th Centuries), a flood of scholars in Europe began to think critically about religion, art, society, human nature, law, and freedom. They proceeded with the assumption that most of the domains of human life were in need of searching analysis and critique. Among these scholars were Colet, Erasmus, and Moore in England. They followed up on the insight of the ancients.

Francis Bacon, in England, was explicitly concerned with the way we misuse our minds in seeking knowledge. He recognized explicitly that the mind cannot safely be left to its natural tendencies. In his book*The Advancement of Learning*, he argued for the importance of studying the world empirically. He laid the foundation for modern science with his emphasis on the information-gathering processes. He also called attention to the fact that most people, if left to their own devices, develop bad habits of thought (which he called "idols") that lead them to believe what is false or misleading. He called attention to "Idols of the tribe" (the ways our mind naturally tends to trick itself), "Idols of the market-place" (the ways we misuse words), "Idols of the theater" (our tendency to become trapped in conventional systems of thought), and "Idols of the schools" (the problems in thinking when based on blind rules and poor instruction). His book could be considered one of the earliest texts in critical thinking, for his agenda was very much the traditional agenda of critical thinking.

Some fifty years later in France, Descartes wrote what might be called the second text in critical thinking,*Rules For the Direction of the Mind*. In it, Descartes argued for the need for a special systematic disciplining of the mind to guide it in thinking. He articulated and defended the need in thinking for clarity and precision. He developed a method of critical thought based on the *principle of systematic doubt*. He emphasized the need to base thinking on well-thought through foundational assumptions. Every part of thinking, he argued, should be questioned, doubted, and tested.

In the same time period, Sir Thomas Moore developed a model of a new social order, *Utopia*, in which every domain of the present world was subject to critique. His implicit thesis was that established social systems are in need of radical analysis and critique. The critical thinking of these Renaissance and post-Renaissance scholars opened the way for the emergence of science and for the development of democracy, human rights, and freedom for thought.

In the Italian Renaissance, Machiavelli's *The Prince* critically assessed the politics of the day, and laid the foundation for modern critical political thought. He refused to assume that government functioned as those in power said it did. Rather, he critically analyzed how it did function and laid the foundation for political thinking that exposes both, on the one hand, the real agendas of politicians and, on the other hand, the many contradictions and inconsistencies of the hard, cruel, world of the politics of his day

Hobbes and Locke (in 16th and 17th Century England) displayed the same confidence in the critical mind of the thinker that we find in Machiavelli. Neither accepted the traditional picture of things dominant in the thinking of their day. Neither accepted as necessarily rational that which was considered "normal" in their culture. Both looked to the critical mind to open up new vistas of learning. Hobbes adopted a naturalistic view of the world in which everything was to be explained by evidence and reasoning. Locke defended a common sense analysis of everyday life and thought. He laid the theoretical foundation for critical thinking about basic human rights and the responsibilities of all governments to submit to the reasoned criticism of thoughtful citizens.

It was in this spirit of intellectual freedom and critical thought that people such as Robert Boyle (in the 17th Century) and Sir Isaac Newton (in the 17th and 18th Century) did their work. In his *Sceptical Chymist*, Boyle severely criticized the chemical theory that had preceded him. Newton, in turn, developed a far-reaching framework of thought which roundly criticized the traditionally accepted world view.

He extended the critical thought of such minds as Copernicus, Galileo, and Kepler. After Boyle and Newton, it was recognized by those who reflected seriously on the natural world that egocentric views of world must be abandoned in favor of views based entirely on carefully gathered evidence and sound reasoning.

Another significant contribution to critical thinking was made by the thinkers of the French Enlightenment: Bayle, Montesquieu, Voltaire, and Diderot. They all began with the premise that the human mind, when disciplined by reason, is better able to figure out the nature of the social and political world. What is more, for these thinkers, reason must turn inward upon itself, in order to determine weaknesses and strengths of thought. They valued disciplined intellectual exchange, in which all views had to be submitted to serious analysis and critique. They believed that all authority must submit in one way or another to the scrutiny of reasonable critical questioning.

Eighteenth Century thinkers extended our conception of critical thought even further, developing our sense of the power of critical thought and of its tools. Applied to the problem of economics, it produced Adam Smith's *Wealth of Nations.* In the same year, applied to the traditional concept of loyalty to the king, it produced the *Declaration of Independence*. Applied to reason itself, it produced Kant's *Critique of Pure Reason.*

In the 19th Century, critical thought was extended even further into the domain of human social life by Comte and Spencer. Applied to the problems of capitalism, it produced the searching social and economic critique of Karl Marx. Applied to the history of human culture and the basis of biological life, it led to Darwin's *Descent of Man*. Applied to the unconscious mind, it is reflected in the works of Sigmund Freud. Applied to cultures, it led to the establishment of the field of Anthropological studies. Applied to language, it led to the field of Linguistics and to many deep probings of the functions of symbols and language in human life.

In the 20th Century, our understanding of the power and nature of critical thinking has emerged in increasingly more explicit formulations. In 1906, William Graham Sumner published a land-breaking study of the foundations of sociology and anthropology, *Folkways*, in which he documented the tendency of the human mind to think sociocentrically and the parallel tendency for schools to serve the (uncritical) function of social indoctrination :

"Schools make persons all on one pattern, orthodoxy. School education, unless it is regulated by the best knowledge and good sense, will produce men and women who are all of one pattern, as if turned in a lathe. An orthodoxy is produced in regard to all the great doctrines of life.

It consists of the most worn and commonplace opinions which are common in the masses. The popular opinions always contain broad fallacies, half-truths, and glib generalizations (p. 630).

At the same time, Sumner recognized the deep need for critical thinking in life and in education:

"Criticism is the examination and test of propositions of any kind which are offered for acceptance, in order to find out whether they correspond to reality or not. The critical faculty is a product of education and training. It is a mental habit and power. It is a prime condition of human welfare that men and women should be trained in it. It is our only guarantee against delusion, deception, superstition, and misapprehension of ourselves and our earthly circumstances. Education is good just so far as it produces well-developed critical faculty. A teacher of any subject who insists on accuracy and a rational control of all processes and methods, and who holds everything open to unlimited verification and revision, is cultivating that method as a habit in the pupils. Men educated in it cannot be stampeded. They are slow to believe. They can hold things as possible or probable in all degrees, without certainty and without pain. They can wait for evidence and weigh evidence. They can resist appeals to their dearest prejudices. Education in the critical faculty is the only education of which it can be truly said that it makes good citizens" (pp. 632, 633).

John Dewey agreed. From his work, we have increased our sense of the pragmatic basis of human thought (its instrumental nature), and especially its grounding in actual human purposes, goals, and objectives. From the work of Ludwig Wittgenstein we have increased our awareness not only of the importance of concepts in human thought, but also of the need to analyze concepts and assess their power and limitations. From the work of Piaget, we have increased our awareness of the egocentric and sociocentric tendencies of human thought and of the special need to develop critical thought which is able to reason within multiple standpoints, and to be raised to the level of "conscious realization." From the massive contribution of all the "hard" sciences, we have learned the power of information and the importance of gathering information with great care and precision, and with sensitivity to its potential inaccuracy, distortion, or misuse. From the contribution of depth-psychology, we have learned how easily the human mind is self-deceived, how easily it unconsciously constructs illusions and delusions, how easily it rationalizes and stereotypes, projects and scapegoats.

To sum up, the tools and resources of the critical thinker have been vastly increased in virtue of the history of critical thought. Hundreds of thinkers have contributed to its development. Each major discipline has made some contribution to critical thought. Yet for most educational purposes, it is the summing up of base-line common denominators for critical thinking that is most important. Let us consider now that summation.

THE COMMON DENOMINATORS OF CRITICAL THINKING ARE THE MOST IMPORTANT BY-PRODUCTS OF THE HISTORY OF CRITICAL THINKING

We now recognize that critical thinking, by its very nature, requires, for example, the systematic monitoring of thought; that thinking, to be critical, must not be accepted at face value but must be analyzed and assessed for its clarity, accuracy, relevance, depth, breadth, and logicalness. We now recognize that critical thinking, by its very nature, requires, for example, the recognition that all reasoning occurs within points of view and frames of reference; that all reasoning proceeds from some goals and objectives, has an informational base; that all data when used in reasoning must be interpreted, that interpretation involves concepts; that concepts entail assumptions, and that all basic inferences in thought have implications. We now recognize that each of these dimensions of thinking need to be monitored and that problems of thinking can occur in any of them.

The result of the collective contribution of the history of critical thought is that the basic questions of Socrates can now be much more powerfully and focally framed and used. In every domain of human thought, and within every use of reasoning within any domain, it is now possible to question:

- Ends and objectives,
- The status and wording of questions,
- The sources of information and fact,
- The method and quality of information collection,
- The mode of judgement and reasoning used,
- The concepts that make that reasoning possible,
- The assumptions that underlie concepts in use,
- The implications that follow from their use, and
- The point of view or frame of reference within which reasoning takes place.

In other words, questioning that focuses on these fundamentals of thought and reasoning are now baseline in critical thinking. It is beyond question that intellectual errors or mistakes can occur in any of these dimensions, and that students need to be fluent in talking about these structures and standards.

Independent of the subject studied, students need to be able to articulate thinking about thinking that reflects basic command of the intellectual dimensions of thought: "Let's see, what is the most fundamental issue here? From what point of view should I approach this problem? Does it make sense for me to assume this?

From these data may I infer this? What is implied in this graph? What is the fundamental concept here? Is this consistent with that? What makes this question complex? How could I check the accuracy of these data? If this is so, what else is implied? Is this a credible source of information? Etc." (For more information on the basic elements of thought and basic intellectual criteria and standards, see Appendices C and D).

With intellectual language such as this in the foreground, students can now be taught at least minimal critical thinking moves within any subject field. What is more, there is no reason in principle that students cannot take the basic tools of critical thought which they learn in one domain of study and extend it (with appropriate adjustments) to all the other domains and subjects which they study. For example, having questioned the wording of a problem in math, I am more likely to question the wording of a problem in the other subjects I study.

As a result of the fact that students can learn these generalizable critical thinking moves, they need not be taught history simply as a body of facts to memorize; they can now be taught history as historical reasoning. Classes can be designed so that students learn to think historically and develop skills and abilities essential to historical thought. Math can be taught so that the emphasis is on mathematical reasoning. Students can learn to think geographically, economically, biologically, chemically, in courses within these disciplines. In principle, then, all students can be taught so that they learn how to bring the basic tools of disciplined reasoning into every subject they study. Unfortunately, it is apparent, given the results of this study, that we are very far from this ideal state of affairs. We now turn to the fundamental concepts and principles tested in standardized critical thinking tests.

CRITICAL THINKING DEVELOPMENT: A STAGE THEORY

Though most teachers aspire to make critical thinking a primary objective of their instruction, most also do not realize that, to develop as thinkers, students must pass through stages of development in critical thinking. That is, most teachers are unaware of the levels of intellectual development that people go through as they improve as thinkers. We believe that significant gains in the intellectual quality of student work will not be achieved except to the degree that teachers recognize that skilled critical thinking develops, only when properly cultivated, and only through predictable stages.

In this paper we shall set out a stage theory based on the nearly twenty years of research of the Center for Critical Thinking and explain some of the theory's implications for instruction. We shall be brief, concise, and to the point in our explanation with minimal theoretical elaboration. Furthermore, we believe that the "practicality" of the theory we explain here is best tested in the classroom and in everyday life. The reader should be expressly aware that we are approaching the human mind exclusively from an intellectual standpoint — not from a psychological standpoint. Each stage of intellectual development will be explained in terms of the following variables:

1. Defining Feature
2. Principal Challenge
3. Knowledge of Thinking
4. Skill in Thinking
5. Relevant Intellectual Traits
6. Some Implications for Instruction

Due to space limitations, we have made no attempt to be exhaustive with respect to any stage, nor to answer the many questions that might be raised concerning the development, reliability or validity of the stages. The basic intention is to provide a practical organizer for teachers interested in using a conceptual map to guide student thinking through developmental stages in the process of becoming critical thinkers. Once the stages are explained, and stage-specific recommendations are given, we close with some global implications for instruction.

We make the following assumptions: (1) that there are predictable stages through which every person who develops as a critical thinker passes, (2) that passage from one stage to the next is dependent upon a necessary level of commitment on the part of an individual to develop as a critical thinker, is not automatic, and is unlikely to take place "subconsciously," (3) that success in instruction is deeply connected to the intellectual quality of student learning, and (4) that regression is possible in development.

Before moving to the stages themselves, a brief overview of what we mean by critical thinking is in order. Our working definition is as follows: We define critical thinking as:

the ability and disposition to improve one's thinking by systematically subjecting it to intellectual self-assessment.

It is important to recognize that on this view, persons are critical thinkers, in the fullest sense of the term, only if they display this ability and disposition in all, or most, of the dimensions of their lives (*e.g.* as a parent, citizen, consumer, lover, friend, learner, and professional). We exclude from our concept of the critical thinker those who think critically in only one dimension of their lives. We do so because the quality of one's life is dependent upon high quality reasoning in all domains of one's life, not simply in one dimension.

The stages we will lay out are as follows:

- Stage One: The Unreflective Thinker
- Stage Two: The Challenged Thinker
- Stage Three: The Beginning Thinker
- Stage Four: The Practicing Thinker
- Stage Five: The Advanced Thinker
- Stage Six: The Accomplished Thinker

STAGE ONE: THE UNREFLECTIVE THINKER

Defining Feature: Unreflective thinkers are largely unaware of the determining role that thinking is playing in their lives and of the many ways that problems in thinking are causing problems in their lives. Unreflective thinkers lack the ability to explicitly assess their thinking and improve it thereby.

Knowledge of Thinking: Unreflective thinkers lack the knowledge that high quality thinking requires regular practice in taking thinking apart, accurately assessing it, and actively improving it. In fact, unreflective thinkers are largely unaware of thinking as such, hence fail to recognize thinking as involving concepts, assumptions, inferences, implications, points of view, etc. Unreflective thinkers are largely unaware of the appropriate standards for the assessment of thinking: clarity, accuracy, precision, relevance, logicalness, etc.

Skill in Thinking: Unreflective thinkers may have developed a variety of skills in thinking without being aware of them. However, these skills are inconsistently applied because of the lack of self-monitoring of thought. Prejudices and misconceptions often undermine the quality of thought of the unreflective thinker.

Some Implications for Instruction: We must recognize that in the present mode of instruction it is perfectly possible for students to graduate from high school, or even college, and still be largely unreflective thinkers. Though all students think, most students are largely unaware of how their thinking is structured or how to assess or improve it. Thus when they experience problems in thinking, they lack the skills to identify and "fix" these problems. Most teachers do not seem to be aware of how unaware most students are of their thinking. Little is being done at present to help students "discover" their thinking. This emphasis needs shifting.

STAGE TWO: THE CHALLENGED THINKER

Defining Features: Thinkers move to the "challenged" stage when they become initially aware of the determining role that thinking is playing in their lives, and of the fact that problems in their thinking are causing them serious and significant problems.

Principal Challenge: To become initially aware of the determining role of thinking in one's life and of basic problems that come from poor thinking.

Knowledge of Thinking: Challenged thinkers, unlike unreflective thinkers are becoming aware of thinking as such. They are becoming aware, at some level, that high quality thinking requires deliberate reflective thinking about thinking (in order to improve thinking). They recognize that their thinking is often flawed, although they are not able to identify many of these flaws. Challenged thinkers may develop an initial awareness of thinking as involving concepts, assumptions, inferences, implications, points of view, etc., and as involving standards for the assessment of thinking: clarity, accuracy, precision, relevance, logicalness, etc., though they have only an initial grasp of these standards and what it would take to internalize them. Challenged thinkers also develop some understanding of the role of self-deception in thinking, though their understanding is limited. At this stage the thinker develops some reflective awareness of how thinking operates for good or ill.

Skill in Thinking: Most challenged thinkers have very limited skills in thinking. However like unreflective thinkers, they may have developed a variety of skills in thinking without being aware of them, and these skills may (ironically) serve as barriers to development. At this stage thinkers with some implicit critical thinking abilities may more easily deceive themselves into believing that their thinking is better than it actually is, making it more difficult to recognize the problems inherent in poor thinking. To accept the challenge at this level requires that thinkers gain insight into the fact that whatever intellectual skills they have are inconsistently applied across the domains of their lives.

Relevant Intellectual Trait: The fundamental intellectual trait at this stage is intellectual humility, in order to see that problems are inherent in one's thinking.

Some Implications for Instruction: We must recognize the importance of challenging our students — in a supportive way — to recognize both that they are thinkers and that their thinking often goes awry. We must lead class discussions about thinking. We must explicitly model thinking (*e.g.*, thinking aloud through a problem). We must design classroom activities that explicitly require students to think about their thinking. We must have students examine both poor and sound thinking, talking about the differences. We must introduce students to the parts of thinking and the intellectual standards necessary to assess thinking. We must introduce the idea of intellectual humility to students; that is, the idea of becoming aware of our own ignorance. Perhaps children can best understand the importance of this idea through their concept of the "know-it-all," which comes closest to their recognition of the need to be intellectually humble.

STAGE THREE: THE BEGINNING THINKER

Defining Feature: Those who move to the beginning thinker stage are actively taking up the challenge to begin to take explicit command of their thinking across multiple domains of their lives. Thinkers at this stage recognize that they have basic problems in their thinking and make initial attempts to better understand how they can take charge of and improve it. Based on this initial understanding, beginning thinkers begin to modify some of their thinking, but have limited insight into deeper levels of the trouble inherent in their thinking. Most importantly, they lack a systematic plan for improving their thinking, hence their efforts are hit and miss.

Principal Challenge: To begin to see the importance of developing as a thinker. To begin to seek ways to develop as a thinker and to make an intellectual commitment to that end.

Knowledge of Thinking: Beginning thinkers, unlike challenged thinkers are becoming aware not only of thinking as such, but also of the role in thinking of concepts, assumptions, inferences, implications, points of view, etc. Beginning thinkers are also at some beginning stage of recognizing not only that there are standards for the assessment of thinking: clarity, accuracy, precision, relevance, logicalness, etc., but also that one needs to internalize them and thus begin using them deliberately in thinking. They have a beginning understanding of the role of egocentric thinking in human life. Skill in Thinking:

Beginning thinkers are able to appreciate a critique of their powers of thought. Beginning thinkers have enough skill in thinking to begin to monitor their own thoughts, though as "beginners" they are sporadic in that monitoring. They are beginning to recognize egocentric thinking in themselves and others.

Relevant Intellectual Traits: The key intellectual trait required at this stage is some degree of intellectual humility in beginning to recognize the problems inherent in thinking. In addition, thinkers must have some degree of intellectual confidence in reason, a trait which provides the impetus to take up the challenge and begin the process of active development as critical thinkers, despite limited understanding of what it means to do high quality reasoning. In addition, beginning thinkers have enough intellectual perseverance to struggle with serious problems in thinking while yet lacking a clear solution to those problems (in other words, at this stage thinkers are recognizing more and more problems in their thinking but have not yet discovered how to systematize their efforts to solve them).

Some Implications for Instruction: Once we have persuaded most of our students that much of their thinking — left to itself — is flawed and that they, like all of us, are capable of improving as thinkers, we must teach in such a way as to help them to see that we all need to regularly practice good thinking to become good thinkers. Here we can use sporting analogies and analogies from other skill areas. Most students already know that you can get good in a sport only if you regularly practice. We must not only look for opportunities to encourage them to think well, we must help them to begin to understand what it is to develop good HABITS of thinking. What do we need to do regularly in order to read well? What must we do regularly and habitually if we are to listen well? What must we do regularly and habitually if we are to write well. What must we do regularly and habitually if we are to learn well? We must recognize that students are not only creatures of habit, but like the rest of us, they are largely unaware of the habits they are developing. They are largely unaware of what it is to develop good habits (in general), let alone good habits of thinking. If our students are truly "beginning" thinkers, they will be receptive to the importance of developing sound habits of thought. We must emphasize the importance of beginning to take charge of the parts of thinking and applying intellectual standards to thinking. We must teach students to begin to recognize their native egocentrism when it is operating in their thinking.

STAGE FOUR: THE PRACTICING THINKER

Defining Feature: Thinkers at this stage have a sense of the habits they need to develop to take charge of their thinking. They not only recognize that problems exist in their thinking, but they also recognize the need to attack these problems globally and systematically. Based on their sense of the need to practice regularly, they are actively analyzing their thinking in a number of domains. However, since practicing thinkers are only beginning to approach the improvement of their thinking in a systematic way, they still have limited insight into deeper levels of thought, and thus into deeper levels of the problems embedded in thinking.

Principal Challenge: To begin to develop awareness of the need for systematic practice in thinking.

Knowledge of Thinking: Practicing thinkers, unlike beginning thinkers are becoming knowledgeable of what it would take to systematically monitor the role in their thinking of concepts, assumptions, inferences, implications, points of view, etc. Practicing thinkers are also becoming knowledgeable of what it would take to regularly assess their thinking for clarity, accuracy, precision, relevance, logicalness, etc. Practicing thinkers recognize the need for systematicity of critical thinking and deep internalization into habits. They clearly recognize the natural tendency of the human mind to engage in egocentric thinking and self-deception.

Skill in Thinking: Practicing thinkers have enough skill in thinking to critique their own plan for systematic practice, and to construct a realistic critique of their powers of thought. Furthermore, practicing thinkers have enough skill to begin to regularly monitor their own thoughts. Thus they can effectively articulate the strengths and weaknesses in their thinking. Practicing thinkers can often recognize their own egocentric thinking as well as egocentric thinking on the part of others. Furthermore practicing thinkers actively monitor their thinking to eliminate egocentric thinking, although they are often unsuccessful.

Relevant Intellectual Traits: The key intellectual trait required to move to this stage is intellectual perseverance. This characteristic provides the impetus for developing a realistic plan for systematic practice (with a view to taking greater command of one's thinking). Furthermore, thinkers at this stage have the intellectual humility required to realize that thinking in all the domains of their lives must be subject to scrutiny, as they begin to approach the improvement of their thinking in a systematic way.

Some Implications for Instruction: What are the basic features of thinking that students must command to effectively become practicing thinkers? What do they need to do to take charge of their thinking intellectually, with respect to any content? We must teach in such a way that students come to understand the power in knowing that whenever humans reason, they have no choice but to use certain predictable structures of thought: that thinking is inevitably driven by the questions, that we seek answers to questions for some purpose, that to answer questions, we need information, that to use information we must interpret it (*i.e.*, by making inferences), and that our inferences, in turn, are based on assumptions, and have implications, all of which involves ideas or concepts within some point of view. We must teach in such a way as to require students to regularly deal explicitly with these structures (more on these structure presently).

Students should now be developing the habit — whenever they are trying to figure something out — of focusing on: purpose, question, information, inferences, assumptions, concepts, point of view, and implications. The result of this emphasis in instruction is that students begin to see connections between all the subject matter they are learning. In studying history, they learn to focus on historical purposes and questions. When studying math, they clarify and analyze mathematical goals and problems. When studying literature, they reflect upon literary purposes and questions. They notice themselves making historical, mathematical, and literary assumptions. They notice themselves tracing historical, mathematical, and literary implications. Recognizing the "moves" one makes in thinking well is an essential part of becoming a practicing thinker.

Students should be encouraged to routinely catch themselves thinking both egocentrically and sociocentrically. They should understand, for example, that most of the problems they experience in learning result from a natural desire to avoid confusion and frustration, and that their inability to understand another person's point of view is often caused by their tendency to see the world exclusively within their own egocentric point of view.

STAGE FIVE: THE ADVANCED THINKER

Defining Feature: Thinkers at this stage have now established good habits of thought which are "paying off." Based on these habits, advanced thinkers not only actively analyze their thinking in all the significant domains of their lives, but also have significant insight into problems at deeper levels of thought. While advanced thinkers are able to think well across the important dimensions of their lives, they are not yet able to think at a consistently high level across all of these dimensions. Advanced thinkers have good general command over their egocentric nature. They continually strive to be fair-minded. Of course, they sometimes lapse into egocentrism and reason in a one-sided way.

Principal Challenge: To begin to develop depth of understanding not only of the need for systematic practice in thinking, but also insight into deep levels of problems in thought: consistent recognition, for example, of egocentric and sociocentric thought in one's thinking, ability to identify areas of significant ignorance and prejudice, and ability to actually develop new fundamental habits of thought based on deep values to which one has committed oneself.

Knowledge of Thinking: Advanced thinkers are actively and successfully engaged in systematically monitoring the role in their thinking of concepts, assumptions, inferences, implications, points of view, etc., and hence have excellent knowledge of that enterprise. Advanced thinkers are also knowledgeable of what it takes to regularly assess their thinking for clarity, accuracy, precision, relevance, logicalness, etc. Advanced thinkers value the deep and systematic internalization of critical thinking into their daily habits. Advanced thinkers have keen insight into the role of egocentrism and sociocentrism in thinking, as well as the relationship between thoughts, feelings and desires.

They have a deep understanding of the powerful role that thinking plays in the quality of their lives. They understand that egocentric thinking will always play a role in their thinking, but that they can control the power that egocentrism has over their thinking and their lives.

Skill in Thinking: Advanced thinkers regularly critique their own plan for systematic practice, and improve it thereby. Practicing thinkers regularly monitor their own thoughts. They insightfully articulate the strengths and weaknesses in their thinking. They possess outstanding knowledge of the qualities of their thinking. Advanced thinkers are consistently able to identify when their thinking is driven by their native egocentrism; and they effectively use a number of strategies to reduce the power of their egocentric thoughts.

Relevant Intellectual Traits: The key intellectual trait required at this stage is a high degree of intellectual humility in recognizing egocentric and sociocentric thought in one's life as well as areas of significant ignorance and prejudice. In addition the thinker at this level needs: a) the intellectual insight and perseverance to actually develop new fundamental habits of thought based on deep values to which one has committed oneself, b) the intellectual integrity to recognize areas of inconsistency and contradiction in one's life, c) the intellectual empathy necessary to put oneself in the place of others in order to genuinely understand them, d) the intellectual courage to face and fairly address ideas, beliefs, or viewpoints towards which one has strong negative emotions, e) the fair-mindedness necessary to approach all viewpoints without prejudice, without reference to one's own feelings or vested interests. In the advanced thinker these traits are emerging, but may not be manifested at the highest level or in the deepest dimensions of thought.

Some Implications for Instruction: For the foreseeable future most of our students will not become advanced thinkers — if at all — until college or beyond. Nevertheless, it is important that they learn what it would be to become an advanced thinker. It is important that they see it as an important goal. We can help students move in this direction by fostering their awareness of egocentrism and sociocentrism in their thinking, by leading discussions on intellectual perseverance, intellectual integrity, intellectual empathy, intellectual courage, and fair-mindedness.

If we can graduate students who are practicing thinkers, we will have achieved a major break-through in schooling. However intelligent our graduates may be, most of them are largely unreflective as thinkers, and are unaware of the disciplined habits of thought they need to develop to grow intellectually as a thinker.

STAGE SIX: THE ACCOMPLISHED THINKER

Defining Feature: Accomplished thinkers not only have systematically taken charge of their thinking, but are also continually monitoring, revising, and re-thinking strategies for continual improvement of their thinking. They have deeply internalized the basic skills of thought, so that critical thinking is, for them, both conscious and highly intuitive. As Piaget would put it, they regularly raise their thinking to the level of conscious realization. Through extensive experience and practice in engaging in self-assessment,accomplished thinkers are not only actively analyzing their thinking in all the significant domains of their lives, but are also continually developing new insights into problems at deeper levels of thought. Accomplished thinkers are deeply committed to fair-minded thinking, and have a high level of, but not perfect, control over their egocentric nature.

Principal Challenge: To make the highest levels of critical thinking intuitive in every domain of one's life. To internalize highly effective critical thinking in an interdisciplinary and practical way.

Knowledge of Thinking: Accomplished thinkers are not only actively and successfully engaged in systematically monitoring the role in their thinking of concepts, assumptions, inferences, implications, points of view, etc., but are also regularly improving that practice. Accomplished thinkers have not only a high degree of knowledge of thinking, but a high degree of practical insight as well.Accomplished thinkers intuitively assess their thinking for clarity, accuracy, precision, relevance, logicalness, etc. Accomplishedthinkers have deep insights into the systematic internalization of critical thinking into their habits. Accomplished thinkers deeply understand the role that egocentric and sociocentric thinking plays in the lives of human beings, as well as the complex relationship between thoughts, emotions, drives and behavior.

Skill in Thinking: Accomplished thinkers regularly, effectively, and insightfully critique their own use of thinking in their lives, and improve it thereby. Accomplished thinkers consistently monitor their own thoughts. They effectively and insightfully articulate the strengths and weaknesses inherent in their thinking.

Their knowledge of the qualities of their thinking is outstanding. Although, as humans they know they will always be fallible (because they must always battle their egocentrism, to some extent), they consistently perform effectively in every domain of their lives. People of good sense seek out master thinkers, for they recognize and value the ability of master thinkers to think through complex issues with judgement and insight.

Relevant Intellectual Traits: Naturally inherent in master thinkers are all the essential intellectual characteristics, deeply integrated.Accomplished thinkers have a high degree of intellectual humility, intellectual integrity, intellectual perseverance, intellectual courage, intellectual empathy, intellectual autonomy, intellectual responsibility and fair-mindedness. Egocentric and sociocentric thought is quite uncommon in the accomplished thinker, especially with respect to matters of importance. There is a high degree of integration of basic values, beliefs, desires, emotions, and action.

Some implications for Instruction: For the foreseeable future the vast majority of our students will never become accomplishedthinkers — any more than most high school basketball players will develop the skills or abilities of a professional basketball player or student writers the writing skills of a published novelist. Nevertheless, it is important that they learn what it would be to become an accomplished thinker. It is important that they see it as a real possibility, if practicing skills of thinking becomes a characteristic of how they use their minds day to day.

GENERAL IMPLICATIONS FOR INSTRUCTION

We believe that the thinking of students will remain "invisible" to them unless they are supportively challenged to discover the problems in their thinking. This is not possible unless they receive careful introduction into the intellectual workings of the human mind.. Thus it is vital that an intellectual vocabulary for talking about the mind be established for teachers; and that teachers lead discussions in class designed to teach students, from the point of view of intellectual quality, how their minds work, including how they can improve as thinkers.

Of course, teachers need to take students through stages of intellectual development. For example, in elementary school an essential objective would be that students become "beginning" thinkers, that is, that they will be taught so that they discover that they are thinkers and that their thinking, like a house, can be well or poorly constructed. This "discovery" stage—the coming to awareness that all of us are thinkers—needs to be given the highest priority. Middle school and High School, on this model, would aim at helping all students become, at least, "practicing" thinkers. Of course, students discover thinking only by discovering that thinking has "parts." Like learning what "Legos" are, we learn as we come to discover that there are various parts to thinking and those parts can be put together in various ways. Unlike Legos, of course, thinking well requires that we learn to check how the parts of thinking are working together to make sure they are working properly: For example, have we checked the accuracy of information? Have we clarified the question?

We are not advocating here that teachers withdraw from academic content. Rather we are suggesting that critical thinking provides a way of deeply embracing content intellectually. Within this view students come to take intellectual command of how they think, act, and react while they are learning...history, biology, geography, literature, etc., how they think, act, and react as a reader, writer, speaker, and listener, how they think, act, and react as a student, brother, friend, child, shopper, consumer of the media, etc. For example if we teach all courses with emphasis on the parts, or intellectual elements of thinking, we can help students discover content as a mode of thinking at the same time they are discovering their minds as thinkers. In fact, to effectively learn any subject in an intellectually meaningful way presupposes a certain level of command over one's thinking, which in turn presupposes understanding of the mind's processes.

DISCOVERING THINKING

Discovering the Parts of Thinking

What are the basic features of thinking that students need to know to effectively take charge of their thinking intellectually, with respect to any content? First, they must come to realize that whenever humans reason, they have no choice but to use certain elements, without which their thinking would be intellectually unintelligible. Consider.

Thinking is inevitably driven by the questions we seek to answer, and those questions we seek to answer for some purpose. To answer questions, we need information which is in fact meaningful to us only if we interpret it (*i.e.*, by making inferences). Our inferences, in turn, are based on assumptions and require that we use ideas or concepts to organize the information in some way from some point of view. Last but not least, our thinking not only begins somewhere intellectually (in certain assumptions), it also goes somewhere—that is, has implications and consequences.

Thus whenever we reason through any problem, issue, or content we are well advised to take command of these intellectual structures: purpose, question, information, inferences, assumptions, concepts, point of view, and implications. By explicitly teaching students how to take command of the elements of reasoning we not only help them take command of their thinking in a general way; we also provide a vehicle which effectively enables them to critically think through the content of their classes, seeing connections between all of what they are learning.

Of course, we are not implying that elementary school teachers would introduce all of these ideas simultaneously. Not at all. This vocabulary for talking about thinking needs to be learned slowly and progressively. And the process is the perfectly natural one of helping students to think better in context. For example, children come to school with their own goals and purposes and we as teachers have ours. For school to work, children have to enter into goals and purposes that they don't come to school with.

Young children do not come to school with the goal of learning numbers and letters, arithmetic, spelling, and reading. But they, like us, accomplish more when they know what they are trying to accomplish. The general goal of "figuring things out" is the essential goal intellectually. To become a good learner we have to learn how to figure things out: first numbers and letters and simple stories, and then eventually history, and novels and mathematical formulas. Whatever the "content" to be learned is, they need to learn to approach it in the spirit of "I can figure this out," "I can use my mind and thinking to understand this."

One way to begin to teach content as a mode of thinking is to recognize the fact that all content areas presuppose not only a particular purposes, but those purposes are connected to organized ways of figuring things out. If students understand the purpose of history, the purpose of literature, the purpose of government, etc., they can begin to learn that there are different things which we as learner try to figure out. Furthermore, they learn that when we want to figure something out, we have to ask particular questions about it. Hence, all subjects presuppose certain fundamental questions which guide thinking within a content area.

From the earliest stages of parenting and teaching, we can emphasize with our children what we are wanting them to figure out. We can focus instruction on key fundamental questions and make those questions explicit. When information is required, we can elicit student help in assembling that information. When it is appropriate to take the step of interpreting information, we can help students make their inferences explicit. When students make questionable inferences, we can call that to their attention and ask them what other inferences might be made. If they are making a questionable assumption, we can help them recognize that. We can emphasize the importance of their thinking through implications and consequences. We can introduce diverse point of view and make explicit we are doing that. We can help them to role play different ways of looking at things (using different characters in stories, etc.). There are many, many ways—almost endlessly different ways—to encourage students to discover and take command of their thinking. The central point is this, there are distinct advantages to helping students to discover thinking and begin to take charge of it. Let look at this in a broad and general way.

The Advantages of Critical Thinking

When teachers become advocates of quality thinking and learning, in keeping with this stage theory, they teach in such a way that students are regularly required to:

- State and explain goals and purposes,
- Clarify the questions they need to answer and the problems they need to solve,
- Gather and organize information and data,
- Explicitly assess the meaning and significance of information you give them,
- Demonstrate that they understand concepts,

- Identify assumptions,
- Consider implications and consequences,
- Examine things from more than one point of view,
- State what they say clearly,
- Test and check for accuracy,
- Stick to questions, issues, or problems; and not wander in their thinking,
- Express themselves precisely and exactly,
- Deal with complexities in problems and issues,
- Consider the point of view of others,
- Express their thinking logically,
- Distinguish significant matters from insignificant ones,

And as a result of such instruction, the students (in general):

- Learn content at a deeper and more permanent level
- Are better able to explain and apply what they learn,
- Are better able to connect what they are learning in one class with what they are learning in other classes,
- Ask more and better questions in class,
- Understand the textbook better,
- Follow directions better,
- Understand more of what you present in class,
- Write better,
- Apply more of what they are learning to their everyday life,
- Become more motivated learners in general,
- Become progressively easier to teach.

CLOSING

There are many ways to teach content so that students progress as thinkers. However if we are to do so, we must explicitly focus on the mind intellectually and grasp the stages that students must progress through. We and our students must recognize that we all develop incrementally as thinkers, and that the progress of any one of us is directly dependent on our level of intellectual knowledge and commitment. Put another way, if I am to develop my critical thinking ability I must both "discover" my thinking and must intellectually take charge of it. To do this I must make a deep commitment to this end.

Why is this so important? Precisely because the human mind, left to its own, pursues that which is immediately easy, that which is comfortable, and that which serves its selfish interests.

At the same time, it naturally resists that which is difficult to understand, that which involves complexity, that which requires entering the thinking and predicaments of others.

For these reasons, it is crucial that we as teachers and educators discover our own "thinking," the thinking we do in the classroom and outside the classroom, the thinking that gets us into trouble and the thinking that enables us to grow. As educators we must treat thinking—quality thinking—as our highest priority. It is the fundamental determinant of the quality of our lives. It is the fundamental determinant of the quality of the lives of our students. We are at some stage in our development as thinkers. Our students are at some stage in the development of theirs. When we learn together as developing thinkers, when we all of us seek to raise our thinking to the next level, and then to the next after that, everyone benefits, and schooling then becomes what it was meant to be, a place to discover the power of lifelong learning. This should be a central goal for all our students—irrespective of their favored mode of intelligence or learning style. It is in all of our interest to accept the challenge: to begin, to practice, to advance as thinkers.

CRITICAL THINKING IN LITERARY STUDIES

Defining critical thinking in Literature is difficult partly because of the nature of literary study itself. Literature isn't a natural subject area, in that what constitutes a literary text is the subject of much debate. The three genres that literary has traditionally focused on— drama, prose fiction, poetry—are central to literary studies because of an historical accident. There is no real reason why other genres, such as autobiography, film, or even weblogs should not be considered for literary analysis. Furthermore, different faculty members in any Literature department have radically different and frequently incommensurate epistemological positions on the nature of literary texts and the manner in which they should be studied. It is thus unlikely that all would agree on a single definition on critical thinking

In exploring critical thinking in literary studies, it is useful first to consider the origins of the discipline. Literature came into the university curricula of many nation-states in the nineteenth century, and became a central part of primary and secondary school curricula designed to foster a national culture. Initially, literary study was often combined with the study of national history and the national language. Thus Shakespeare's plays were discussed a representatively English, while American Literature claimed authors who were born well before the Declaration of Independence as key figures in a national tradition. Newly independent nations have also established a national literary canon in either English or a new national language: thus we have new templates for study such as Singaporean Literature or Indonesian Literature.

In early literary study in Britain, Europe, and America, an historical approach was supplemented by a concern with aesthetics. Students of literature would thus investigate the qualities that made good literature, the manner in which literature illuminated the human condition, and how literary texts fit into traditions, or developed from previous forms. In the early to middle twentieth century, stress was placed on the literary text itself, viewed in isolation from its background. In the late twentieth century, the influence of Philosophy, Political Science, Anthropology, and Sociology has led to the rise of what is sometimes, misleadingly perhaps, called "literary theory." The definition of a literary text has broadened to television serials, films, and other media, although much focus is still given to writings in more traditional media. In general, theoretical approaches will examine literary texts—and by extension all texts—as in some way structuring our perceptions of reality. Texts are the means by which we apprehend the real, the everyday, and the qualities of texts may help or hinder us in gaining a critical distance from the everyday. For instance, a novel about a maid in Singapore might reiterate and reinforce widely held societal prejudices about maids or it might, alternatively, offer readers the possibility of seeing things in a new light, of perceiving events from a maid's perspective and gaining a different apprehension of the reality they take for granted.

New approaches to literary studies have not displaced older ones, but rather entered into various forms of dialogue with them. What links all approaches to literary studies, however, is a stress on reading as a fundamental skill. Literary studies stresses in particular the ability to read slowly and carefully, and not merely for information.

Rather, we prize the ability to read with a double sight, to become aware of how the medium of writing, the nature of texts themselves—and also, by extension, of drama, film, or other media—shapes, transforms, or even contradicts the content.

A way I often illustrate this to students is by analogy with the visual arts. An engraving of a hare by Albrecht Dürer clearly looks lifelike: it seems to attempt to present reality almost photographically, so that the medium of the paper and ink vanishes. In contrast, a modernist painting by Paul Klee may have a title suggesting its content, but we must work hard to see a pictorial representation of the title in the image. The Klee painting foregrounds the medium, while the Dürer foregrounds the content. Yet in each case to appreciate the object we must understand the interplay between medium and content, even to the extent of ultimately finding the distinction between form and content problematic.

Critical reading thus involves a student paying close attention to formal features of the text—elements that American critics René Wellek and Austin Warren once called the "intrinsic elements" of the texts, and relating these to extrinsic elements, the manner in which the text relates to a larger world.

My own experience is that students often come to us from "A" levels without close-reading skills, and also with a non-theoretical understanding of the text which gives pride of place to unexamined "common sense"—received assumptions—about the way the world is.

Encouraging critical thinking thus first involves teaching students close reading skills through practice, allowing students to realize that there are frequently contradictions in texts, and that reading a text involves asking a number of questions, rather than moving too quickly to a solution.

As literary study develops, critical thinking is shown by a student's ability to use various conceptual frameworks to read texts, but also to realize how the nature of the texts questions the frameworks, and indeed the "common sense" of the worlds in which the text is produced and read. While pedagogical practice in literary studies often refers to the variety of frameworks or critical approaches as a "toolkit" or a "menu," my own feeling is that these are misleading analogies. The approaches are often mutually contradictory, and taking up one involves making certain epistemological assumptions about the way texts work. The notion of a "toolkit" may well encourage students to evaluate and compare different critical approaches from a position in which basic assumptions about the relationship of the text to the world are unexamined: working through the text through critical reading will often empower students to question the framework itself.

As an example of this process, I briefly discussed the poem "The Little Black Boy" by William Blake. It is a poem which often produces debate among students as to its final effect, as to whether it is a poem that condemns racism or whether it is a poem which is deeply racist. One's final answer may well depend on the epistemological framework one draws upon to read the poem. Within a historicist context, it is clear that Blake is arguing against racism and for a universal idea of humanity which informs early Romanticism. A reading informed by postcolonial criticism might note that despite the rhetoric of equality, the poem makes an opposition between images of whiteness and blackness, and whiteness is clearly the favoured term. A poststructuralist reading might note how this opposition itself breaks down in the poem. A new critical approach might ask one to stand back from the poem, to look at its form and the manner in which it develops rhetorically. Each approach offers different possibilities, and collectively they offer the possibility of cross-fertilisation and mutual interrogation. For me, critical thinking would occur when students use the poem and begin to ask questions—to which there are no easy answers—regarding the way the notion of race is put to use in their own lives. Students thus become aware of how their lives are mediated by texts, and begin to read their own lives as carefully as they would literary texts.

This form of critical thinking will likely take place as much outside the classroom as in it, but the literature classroom can be a place where it receives a new or a renewed impetus.

12

Ethical Criticism

ETHICAL CRITICISM'S FALL AND POSTMODERNISM'S RISE

For roughly 2500 years, ethical references constituted the starting point (and often the ending point) for most literary commentary. From Plato's attack on tragedy up through the Victorians' scandalized indignation over the work of Oscar Wilde and the Pre-Raphaelite poets, ethical criticism was the default position for most critics of literary art. However, like many long-lived positions not kept intellectually honest by ongoing criticism, ethical criticism over the centuries got fat, lazy, repetitive, shallow, doctrinaire, self-indulgent, platitudinous, and sometimes mean spirited. By the end of the 19th century, ethical criticism's fatuity had brought it to the lip of the very cliff over which it was about to be pushed by a great many intellectual and societal forces that it never saw coming. What began as a fairly local – that is, British – late 19th-century backlash against ethical criticism swelled throughout the 20th century into a tsunami of new ideas from all across Europe and America that swept ethical criticism away. At the academic and professional levels ethical criticism was killed, crushed, annihilated. I need to concede early on, however, that my own contribution here reflects on the critical debate about ethical criticism from a clearly Anglo-North-American perspective. As a consequence, some European positions go unmentioned (such as reception theory and hermeneutics). I am focusing on the history of and debate about ethical criticism that occurred mainly in England and America ranging from the late 19th-century to the present.

Persistently throughout the entire 20th century, the higher the prestige of other modes of criticism ascended – first, New Criticism, and, second, postmodernism – the lower the prestige of ethical criticism descended. Since, however, for today's disciplinarians even the history of this descent is hardly available, it may be useful here to string together a sketchy set of references to some of the most important 20th-century theories in criticism and philosophy that, in Cockney locution, ›did for‹ ethical criticism. The complete rout of such a centuries long mode as ethical criticism becomes intelligible only when one pulls all of these later views together and takes a moment to contemplate the credibility they claimed throughout most of the 20th century. These 20th-century theories did more than merely discredit ethical criticism of the arts; they tended to discredit ethics as a general human enterprise. I refer to such movements and theories as modernism, logical positivism, the writings of Karl Marx, the cultural aftermath of World Wars One and Two, the 20th-century elevation of scientific knowledge over humanistic inquiry, New Criticism, post-colonial studies, Freudianism, deconstruction, the work of Michel Foucault, anthropological relativism, changing views of human nature, and, finally, changing notions of truth.

Under the force and weight of all of these influences, ethical criticism bent and broke, and remained stuck for most of the 20th century in a literary criticism version of John Bunyan's Slough of Despond. A few critics made sidebar attempts to do something now and then that might have been called ethical criticism – some of the work of F. R. Leavis, Irving Babbit, Ivor Winters, Lionel Trilling, and Kenneth Burke comes to mind – but either this work proved completely ineffectual at refocusing the attention of academic and intellectual critics (Leavis, Babbit, and Winters) or the critics who took such lines of argument became well-known for *other* lines of argument, not their ethical criticism (Trilling and Burke).

It is curious, however – and, more than curious, it tells a compelling story about the inescapability of ethical concerns – to note that no matter how forcibly 20th-century critics tried to manage the house of criticism such that ethical criticism was kept locked in some Closet of Disrepute, the human concerns from which ethical criticism springs kept pushing it back into the middle of the room. During the nearly forty years of postmodern hegemony in criticism, it was considered almost an intellectual felony punishable by ridicule-unto-professional-death to introduce ethics in literary theory, yet*politics* played a vastly important role in theory during this entire period. The fact that political theory and the agendas of political policy are *always* nested inside ethical assumptions was an inconvenient fact that simply never got mentioned. As I put it in a previous publication,

Both within the academy and within society as a whole, someone is always claiming that a given novel, movie, or TV programme is either uplifting or degrading, inspiring or demeaning, should be read and seen by everyone or shouldn't disgrace either video airwaves or the shelves of the public library. Every time a feminist exposes Hemingway's complicity with the patriarchy, or every time an African-American critic recommends the retrieval of slave narratives because such narratives shame our past and help us shape the future, and every time a Judith Fetterley, a Terry Eagleton, or a Michel Foucault decries the dehumanizing effects of master narratives on subject-readers, such critics are deeply engaged in important versions of ethical criticism that are not at all diminished in robustness for being disguised as any kind of discourse but ethical criticism. (Gregory 1998, 195)

Allow me to offer one typical example of an important and well-known work of 20th-century criticism that, right in the middle of a critical discourse that ostensibly opposes ethical criticism, nevertheless deploys ethical commentary as an apparently unavoidable dimension of literary analysis. If this sounds self-contradictory, it is. I offer this one example here – and refer to other examples in a footnote – all of which stand in for a much larger range of examples that could be offered.

In one of the iconic, foundational texts of New Criticism, Cleanth Brooks's ›Irony as a Principle of Structure‹ (1949), Brooks performs a typical, New Criticism ›close reading‹ of a poem, Randall Jarrell's ›Eighth Air Force‹. After repeating intellectual gestures that we all recognize as the standard stuff of New Criticism (There are no superfluous parts, no dead or empty details, The Pontius Pilate metaphor, as the poet uses it, becomes a device for tremendous concentration. ibid., 1047), Brooks insists explicitly that the poem has nothing to do with ethics because it exists solely on an aesthetic plane – We do not ask a poet to bring his poem into line with our personal beliefs – still less to flatter our personal beliefs (1048) – yet at the end of his essay he introduces considerations that are unequivocally ethical, almost, one is tempted to say, against his will, if not against his better judgement.

Jarrell manages to bring us by an act of imagination, to the most penetrating insight. Participating in that insight, *we doubtless become better citizens. (One of the ›uses‹ of poetry, I should agree, is to make us better citizens.)* [...] Finding its proper symbol, defined and refined by the participating metaphors, *the theme becomes a part of the reality in which we live* – an insight, rooted in and growing out of concrete experience, many-sided, three-dimensional.

(ibid., emphasis added)

It is impossible to read this conclusion to Brooks's essay without being confused, or without thinking that Brooks himself is confused. Clearly, Brooks says, poetry has nothing to do with ethics, but, just as clearly, Brooks says, poetry has ways of engaging readers that make us better citizens . Evasively, Brooks does not say what he *means*by better citizen , but this notion makes sense only if it is based on (covert) ethical assumptions.

Regardless of whether one is reading Brooks's fellow New Critics such as Empson, Warren, and Ransom; or whether one is reading Sklovsky, Bakhtin, Todorov, Frye, Foucault, Fish, Derrida, or other prominent critics of the period, Brooks's confusion and inconsistency is typical of many literary critics of the 20th century. Ethical considerations get dragged in sideways, often at the end of an essay or book, and usually uttered in a parenthetical, passing, or oh-by-the-way tone. The point needing emphasis here, however, is that no matter how evasive or confused they are, *ethical considerations almost always do get dragged in one way or another*. Surely it is neither whimsical nor intellectually willful to insist that something both intellectually and culturally significant is occurring when one 20th-century critic after another who explicitly disesteems ethical considerations at one level cannot seem to help referring to such considerations at another level.

In this first decade of the 21st century, intellectual room for a renewed ethical criticism is expanding as the credibility of postmodernism is shrinking. To understand the see-saw relations of this dynamic, it will be helpful to discuss briefly three main reasons (both intellectual and cultural) that show why the credibility of postmodernism has shrunk so drastically. What is important about these reasons is how they help explain a new robustness in ethical criticism. The first two of these reasons occurred almost simultaneously near the end of the 20th century; the third reason occurred fourteen years later in the second year of the 21st century.

First, ethics came roaring back into criticism like an old-fashioned locomotive under a full head of steam at the end of 1987 with the explosive revelation of Paul de Man's collaborationist writings for the Nazis in occupied Belgium during World War Two. The postmodernists' claim that ethics has no place in literary criticism, a claim that de Man's own writings had not only strongly supported but, indeed, had made the most radical claims for, were suddenly trumped by the profound ethical shock that ran through the academy as de Man's duplicity came out in a series of articles first advanced by *The New York Times* in December, 1987 (cf. Anon. 1987).

During all the years that de Man had been granted the status of unimpeachable integrity by his American and European peers – with a fervency that was at times weirdly reverential – de Man had never made one single reference to these collaborationist writings, sitting on them in absolute silence, and, indeed, telling lies that misdirected anyone's potential interest in them. (de Man, when he adverted to his war years at all, told people that he'd gone to England and worked as a translator, or that he'd studied in Paris, or that he'd joined the underground in France – three palpable falsehoods. Lehman 1991, 160) The effect on the field of criticism was like an earthquake, and the academic equivalent of a guerilla war broke out in the pages of the *Times Literary Supplement* and the *Chronicle of Higher Education*, the *New Republic* and the *New Criterion*, the *Village Voice* and the *London Review of Books*. [...] One felt that one might just possibly be witnessing a crucial turning point in the history of an idea. (Lehman 161, emphasis added)

As tempting as it is to rehearse this entire story, the point of the story for my argument in this essay is that the fall of Paul de Man was a crucial turning point in the history of an idea, or, more accurately, a whole set of ideas that lay at the center of post-structuralism in particular and postmodernism in general. Paul de Man's fall created compelling grounds for the reintroduction into literary discourse of the very kinds of ethical considerations that, in a deeply ironic turnabout, de Man's own theories had been designed to forestall.

Second, and nearly simultaneously with de Man's downfall, a remarkable cluster of new publications beginning in the late 1980s and continuing into the present have provided a new set of arguments for not just the relevance of but the importance of ethical criticism. Some of these publications are, predictably, works in literary criticism, but others are works in philosophy, while some are works in science. Taken all together, with special credit for an unprecedented high level of argument going to Wayne Booth and Martha Nussbaum, these publications create a strong case *against* postmodernist assumptions that human beings are entirely creatures of ›social construction‹, and an equally strong case *for* the intrinsic importance of ethics to human beings. All of these works have done much to rehabilitate the dignity and value of thinking about ethics in relation to literature in particular, to narratives in general, and to the arts of all kinds, especially the representational arts. One of the earliest defectors from deconstruction was Frank Lentricchia, in whose *Criticism and Social Change* (1983) he paved the way for the reintroduction of ethical analysis into literary criticism with his assertion that politically, deconstruction translates into the passive kind of conservatism called quietism; it thereby plays into the hands of established power.

Deconstruction is conservatism by default – in Paul de Man it teaches the many ways to say that there is nothing to be done. The primary sources from which intellectual capital was invested in a ›new‹ ethical criticism of literature came, however, from Wayne Booth and Martha Nussbaum. In 1986 Nussbaum published *The Fragility of Goodness: Luck and Ethics in Greek Tragedy and Philosophy*, followed in 1988 by Wayne Booth's magisterial *The Company We Keep: An Ethics of Fiction*, followed two years later (1990) by another important Nussbaum book, *Love's Knowledge: Essays on Philosophy and Literature*. Two years later, in 1992, Frederick Crews published *The Critics Bear It Away*, which received much attention as a scorching attack on postmodernist inconsistencies and weaknesses.

At the same time these intense books focused on literature were appearing, philosophers such as Mark Johnson and Richard Eldridge were publishing works arguing that notions hitherto thought by many people to be exclusive to literary criticism, such as metaphor and other figures of speech, have instead a biological basis, and that, instead of human beings being creatures of social construction ›all the way down‹, human beings have a nature in which, not very far down at all, lies a vast network of inclinations, dispositions, neural programming, and perceptual protocols that come installed in every human being's brain as a part of our evolutionary heritage. In 1987 Mark Johnson published *The Body In the Mind: The Bodily Basis of Meaning, Imagination, and Reason*, while two years later Richard Eldridge published *On Moral Personhood: Philosophy, Literature,*

Criticism, and Self-Understanding. In 1991 Mary Midgley published *Can't We Make Moral Judgements?*, and in 1992 Robert Louden published *Morality and Moral Theory: A Reappraisal and Reaffirmation*, both of which argue that ethics comes neither from transcendental sources nor entirely from culture, but from intrinsic human needs that get mediated and tweaked by culture but that are not created by culture.

The next year, in 1993, two books appeared that argue strongly against the postmodern view of an infinitely malleable human nature entirely shaped by cultural forms of pressure and embodiment: James Q. Wilson's *The Moral Sense* and Mark Johnson's *Moral Imagination: Implications of Cognitive Science for Ethics*. In 1996 Steven Mithen published his ground breaking *The Prehistory of the Mind*, giving readers a sense of the vastness of time in which evolutionary pressures shaped the human brain, and, thus, also shaped many features of human cognition, emotion, perception, and interpersonal protocols, such as ethics. Also in 1996, Frans de Waal, a research scientist at the Yerkes Regional Primate Research Center at Emory University, published *Good Natured: The Origins of Right and Wrong in Humans and Other Animals*, arguing that some features of ethics are shared with other species of animals and that, while ethics is centrally important to human beings, it is not unique to human beings, a view that reinforces the notion that ethics is an intrinsic human orientation, not a product of culture entirely, and certainly not just a product of any particular set of cultural biases. Two years later, in 1998, E. O. Wilson published *Consilience: The Unity of Knowledge*, in which he asserts that the arts are not solely shaped by errant genius out of historical circumstances and idiosyncratic personal experience.

The roots of their inspiration date back in deep history to the genetic origins of the human brain, and are permanent. Lewis Wolpert's 1996 book, *Six Impossible Things Before Breakfast: The Evolutionary Origins of Belief*, takes a line of argument similar to Wilson's. In 1999 Geoffrey Galt Harpham published a searching inquiry into ethics, ethical criticism, and postmodernism, *Shadows of Ethics: Criticism and the Just Society*, a work that has received too little attention. In 2005 Jonathan Gottschall and David Sloan Wilson published an anthology of essays on the new approaches in criticism drawn from research done in the fields of cognitive science and evolutionary psychology, *The Literary Animal: Evolution and the Nature of Narrative* (with forewords by E. O. Wilson and Frederick Crews), but perhaps the two most well-known and influential books arguing for the value of applying the evolutionary perspective to the arts and ethics are Stephen Pinker's *The Language Instinct* (1994) and *The Blank Slate: The Modern Denial of Human Nature* (2002).My own book on ethical criticism,*Shaped By Stories: The Ethical Power of Narratives*, appeared in 2009.

I have not seen anywhere else the third point to which I now turn, but for nearly a decade it has seemed clear to me that an additional major blow to the cachet and swagger that postmodernism enjoyed for almost forty years was the attack on the Twin Towers in New York City on September 11, 2001. After 9/11, the typical postmodern ethos of mooning the establishment and indulging in a rhetoric of sophomoric naughtiness, subversion, and transgression ran distastefully counter to the emotional mood of the national moment (a ›moment‹ that is still ongoing, at least in America). To a nation in the throes of shock and grief, a discourse of subversion and paradox seemed profoundly deficient in gravitas. It was not a discourse that offered comfort or made sense out of tragedy, loss, grief, bewilderment, and fear. To many people, 9/11 made postmodernism seem cheap, cynical, and shallow. There was in fact a mood of national urgency about the need for a frankly ethical discourse, an urgency that helps explains why George W. Bush's simplistic attempt to meet that need by giving the nation an ethical discourse revolving around his accusation about an axis of evil collection of terrorist states (State of the Union speech, January 29, 2002) was met with general acceptance instead of being widely ridiculed for the feeble notion that it was. The nation's social and political context then (and now) was not a context in which postmodernism could continue to thrive.

ETHICAL CRITICISM'S SECOND CHANCE

So – ethical criticism is back, after a fashion if not exactly *in* fashion. At least it seems no longer despised. Does this matter? And if ethical criticism is going to get a second chance to make a lasting and valuable contribution to critical discourse in the academic and intellectual spheres, how is it going to avoid making the same mistakes that plagued it in the past: fatuity, doctrinaire shrillness, empty moralizing for the sake of moralizing, and fruitless debates with critical ›enemies‹ over the imputed ethical purity or ethical rot of one preferred or reviled work over another?

What's at stake in ethical criticism anyway? Ethical critics, regardless of the very long time they had to work out a decent theory, have in fact never clearly done so. Typical of the history of ethical criticism are infuriatingly evasive claims such as Matthew Arnold's statement near the end of ›Preface to *Poems*, 1853‹ that, I know not how it is, but their commerce with the ancients appears to me to produce, in those who constantly practice it, a steadying and composing effect upon their judgement, not of literary works only, but of men and events in general. (1968, 493) This claim is supported by no arguments or evidence and is left hanging, intellectually, by that frustrating clause, I know not how it is. This is the way ethical criticism was typically done until the late 20th-century work of Wayne Booth and Martha Nussbaum. As ethical critics now contemplate the possibility of reclaiming a hearing for their point of view, they *must* do better at developing real arguments rather than run on brainlessly and tediously about which works teach readers the ›right‹ lessons about ethics, ›right‹ usually referring to whatever ethical scheme the critic prefers.

What's at stake in ethical criticism is the centrality of both ethics and literary art to human beings' lives as morally deliberative, socially embedded, imaginatively fertile, and persistently emotional creatures who are capable, even if frequently unwilling and clumsy about doing so, of submitting their moral deliberations, their social relations, their imaginative constructions, and their emotional impulses to rational inspection, intellectual analysis, and ethical evaluation.

Ethics refers to all the ways that people perform the essentially important social and moral task of evaluating human beings' conduct as right or wrong, their own as well as others'. Literary art refers to those structures of language designed for the stimulation of aesthetic, imaginative, emotional, and ethical responses rather than for instrumental or utilitarian purposes. Artistic structures of language include the entire range of literary art: narratives, poems, chants, songs, movie scripts, TV scripts, and so on. The question for ethical criticism is whether there exists any space for enlightening and fruitful arguments about the dynamics between ethics and literary experience. There are more than 2000 years' worth of ›yes‹ answers to this question, but, frankly, these yes answers – despite the fact that they are often inspiring, erudite, and moving testimonials to critics' deep engagement with various texts – are seldom analytical in mode and seldom convincing as arguments. There have been about 130 years' worth of ›no‹ answers to this question, but, frankly, these answers are also unconvincing, not to mention inconsistent enough to give one intellectual whiplash.

Ethical criticism needs a new start. In the remainder of this essay I will be working towards a new ›yes‹ answer – yes, there is both space and need for fruitful and enlightening arguments about the dynamics between ethics and literary art – but this new ›yes‹ argument will entail rejection of most of what both traditional ethical critics*and* their detractors have had to say.

As an abstract concept or as an academic or intellectual topic of discussion, people with certain agendas may be able to *talk* themselves around ethics – this is what postmodern theorists who viewed ethics as a tool of oppression attempted to do – but they never manage to *live* their way around ethics, and most of the time (to their ethical credit if not to their intellectual consistency) they do not even attempt to do so.

For postmodernists as for all the rest of us, honesty counts – not just peripherally but centrally – in all arenas of real life (even if it does not count, curiously, in postmodern theory).

Ethics counts because ethics is an evolved adaptation that served the survival interests of the individuals among our ancient ancestors who figured out – behaviorally if not consciously – that a person's odds of survival were greater if everyone in the tribe observed certain injunctions about right and wrong, such as fairness in the distribution of resources, honesty in discussions about the adjudication of internal group conflicts, and compassion towards tribal members suffering from injury, illness, or loss.

In other words, ethics counts because the rights and wrongs of everyday life count, and they don't count just because we have not yet become sufficiently sophisticated in mind or manners to cease *letting* them count. They count not only because they have helped us survive, but because the rights and wrongs of everyday life have more to do with the quality of our lives than any other considerations. In everyday life at every level ethics is*the* central issue of human interactions because *nothing* is more important to us than whether other people treat us with honesty or deceit, kindness or cruelty, stinginess or generosity, compassion or callousness, contempt or charity, fairness or unfairness, respect or disrespect, and whether they acknowledge, apologize for, or offer restitution for any violations of these ethical standards they may have committed against us. Not only are these standards always crucial to our own quality of life, but they also carry an imperative of reciprocity. It *matters* to us not only how others treat us, but how we treat others.

The deep claim of ethics on human beings is illustrated clearly by the tenacity with which we hold on to some fundamental ethical standards despite the frequency with which they are violated. Cheating is common, for example, and so is deceit, but we never cease being shocked, angry, hurt, or outraged when our friends, family members, our bosses, or the politicians who represent us turn out to be cheaters and deceivers. The commonness of cheating and deceit never makes us blasé about being the object of these unethical behaviors. We cut off friends who lie to us and we vote politicians out of office or send them to jail for cheating. We may *talk* about ethics as an outmoded structure of moralistic injunctions, but the moment a spouse cheats or a child lies or a friend steals, it turns out that ethics *counts*.

The unavoidability of ethics explains why New Critics and postmodernists who *try* to ignore ethics in their discussions of literary art nevertheless keep trundling ethics back into their discussions like dieters who find themselves sneaking desserts at night right in the middle of their most determined efforts to lose weight. Human beings are built to like sweetness and they are also built to assess their interactions with each other by the application of ethical criteria. *Ethics is primal, not discretionary. Ethics lies at the center of and derives from the nature and requirements of sociability itself.* This does not mean that all human beings in all cultures share the same ethical standards for all human interactions, but what is less important than variations among ethical standards is the fact that there are no cultures in which ethical standards are not central to human interactions. As I put it in *Shaped By Stories*,

Every culture fills in the educational gaps left by first hand experience by means of stories. As Philip Sidney said so long ago (in 1583), ›poetry hath ever been the first light-giver to ignorance.‹ Stories' ethical visions enlighten our ignorance by giving us information that goes deeper than mere description. The real problem of life for human beings is not deciding on the one ›right‹ description of the world, because the truth is that we can live quite comfortably as the fervent believers of many (and sometimes vast) descriptive errors. You can live as complete and happy a life thinking that the world is flat as you can knowing that it's round, but if you cannot read other people's ethical dispositions – if you cannot tell whether other people are prone to help you or harm you, deceive you or tell you the truth, hate you or love you, be kind or unkind to you, be generous or stingy with you, and so on – then it won't matter if you think your world is flat or round because it will just be a mess. The real problem in life is knowing how to *judge* things, and this is a problem that, over and over, narratives' ethical visions help us think about in richer ways than if we had to rely solely on our own first hand experience.

But everything I have just said about ethics is also true of literary experience. Human beings are built for art, including literary art, as deeply as they are built for ethics. Both are human universals. There are no cultures without ethics and art, and both are coeval with the emergence of modern human beings. In *The Art Instinct*, Denis Dutton gives a vivid account of the immensely long period of evolutionary time during which human beings' behaviors and dispositions were shaped by adaptive pressures and the mechanisms of natural and sexual selection. It is only against the backdrop of this immense span of time that the shaping of the human brain into something that we might call a ›narrative brain‹ makes sense. According to Dutton,

The Pleistocene itself – the evolutionary theater in which we acquired the tastes, intellectual features, emotional dispositions, and personality traits that distinguish us from our hominid ancestors and make us what we are – was 80,000 generations long...[and only] a slight pressure over [only a few] thousands of generations can deeply engrave physical and psychological traits into the mind of any species. (2009, 42)

The Neanderthals disappeared in a mere 30 generations, in a mere 1000 years, which leads to the robust hypothesis that during the vast span of the Pleistocene's 1.6 million years, the socially cohesive functioning and imaginatively stimulating effects of story telling and poem making became indelible features of human consciousness through the slowly evolving brain functions of the survivors, our forebears, whose survival was in part the *consequence* of just those socially cohesive and imaginatively stimulating devices of counterfactual and ›as if‹ modes of thinking developed by literary art. Dutton relies on the work of two of the most well known researchers in the field of evolutionarypsychology, John Tooby and Leda Cosmides, to make the powerful point that

Where Kant claimed that a suspension of interest in the existence of an object was fundamental to a proper imaginative response to art, Tooby and

Cosmides argue more broadly that our imaginative lives are fundamental to our humanity, integrated into our nature by evolution. In particular, narrative art is for them an intensified, functionally adaptive extension of mental qualities that largely set us apart from other animals. [...] Fiction-making is an evolved adaptation. [...] By allowing us to confront the world not just as naïve realists who respond directly to immediate threats or opportunities (the general condition of other animals) but as supposition-makers and thought-experimenters, imagination gave human beings one of their greatest evolved cognitive assets. For Tooby and Cosmides, ›It appears as if humans have evolved specialized cognitive machinery that allows us to enter and participate in imagined worlds.‹

(Dutton 2009, 105–106)

In the evolution of modern human beings, then, the human, the ethical, and the narrative unfolded and developed inside of and around each other as integral components of a holistic, organic form. Poetry and story telling are no less primal and nondiscretionary than ethics. Also, as with ethics, what is less important than variations of literary art in different cultures is the fact that there are no cultures in which both ethical standards *and* story telling do not play crucially important roles in human psychology and individual socialization.

The importance to ethical criticism of contemporary work being done in the fields of cognitive science and evolutionary psychology can hardly be overstated. For 2500 years ethical critics have been making claims about the formative, shaping power of narratives and literary art, but such critics have never been able to support these claims with anything even remotely resembling deep psychological argument and empirical evidence – until now. Today, however, with the emergence of fMRI scanners and the development of cognitive science and evolutionary psychology as distinct fields, deep arguments *and* empirical evidence about how literary art makes its impact are beginning to emerge.

For the last fifteen years or so, one of the most exciting and significant terms in neural research and cognitive science is ›brain plasticity‹, a term that refers to contemporary notions of brain functioning and development that are radically different from older, traditional notions, especially the traditional notion that brain development is essentially completed, closed, and fixed by late adolescence. Brain plasticity refers to the brain's capacity to do two things, first, to continue developing until about age twenty-five, with judgement and decision-making functions the last to develop, and, second – and most significant for ethical criticism – the brain is now known to change physical structure and functioning on the basis not merely of physical input, such as the input from a brain injury, but on the basis of imaginative and hypothetical input, such as that stimulated by poetry, narratives, and story telling. Ethical criticism is ready to begin supplementing anecdotal storytelling and descriptive accounts of literary art with accounts that begin to blend these traditional modes of criticism with new modes of research in psychology and biology.

From Plato on, most philosophers, writers, and critics commenting on literary art, whether they are disposed to view literary art with favor or not, have founded their ruminations on the same deep intuition about its powerful educational potential. Turned into discourse, this intuition becomes the default assumption that defines an ethical critic: the assumption that literary representations have the power to influence people's character and conduct. The problem, however, as I showed in the case of Matthew Arnold, is that being an ethical critic by *default* does not make one an ethical critic by*argument*. The history of ethical criticism is marked by two kinds of ethical critics. First, there are ethical critics who, like Sidney and Shelley, wish to emphasize literary art's power to uplift the human spirit and improve readers' morality. Second, there are ethical critics who, like Plato and the Puritans and Richard Posner, wish to emphasize literary art's capacity for corrupting readers' moral character by making them believe a bunch of lies and by leading them into moral confusion. But instead of making analytical arguments that actually support their claims, both of these camps, whom we might call, respectively, the Ethical Critics of Uplift vs. the Ethical Critics of Skepticism, tend to operate like full-bore partisans rather than judicious critics. Like defence attorneys eager to show their client from every advantageous angle, Ethical Critics of Uplift obdurately deny that literary art could ever be morally suspect (Your honor, the book did not pull the trigger!). Simultaneously, the Ethical Critics of Skepticism operate like prosecution attorneys who are determined to show every weakness and wart the defendant has ever had, and obdurately recount the many literary representations of chaos, cruelty, and mayhem, or the many examples of literary artists who were feckless or immoral, as if piled up citations of literary art's representations of these terrible things constitute obvious proof that literature's ethical influence is always suspect.

ART AND ETHICAL CRITICISM

Over the past twenty or so years, both the philosophy of art and literary and art studies have progressively returned, albeit somewhat fitfully, to considering human subjects and the powers and interests they bring to the construction and reception of art. In the philosophy of art, Stanley Cavell and Arthur Danto called attention to the expressive and revelatory powers of art, helping us to overcome flatter institutional theories of art and one-sided obsession with the epistemological problem of the justification of judgements of taste. In literary studies, the New Critical formalism that reigned up through the mid-1960s was displaced first by deconstruction and then by various forms of sociohistorical analysis. Though much interesting and valuable work was done, a feeling began to emerge that this latter analysis scanted too much both the powers of authors to think productively and critically about their social circumstances and the powers of their audiences to follow their densely specific lines of thought. These two lines of disciplinary development have now begun to converge under the heading of *ethical criticism*: "criticism" because the philosophical thoughts about the powers and interest of literary art are often urged substantially via engagement with particular works, and "ethical" because it is oriented towards human subjects and what they might learn about values rather than towards generalizing sociohistorical explanation. A list of central figures in this line of development would include not only Cavell and Danto, but also Martha Nussbaum, Frank Farrell, Noël Carroll, John Gibson, and the present reviewer in philosophy, Wayne Booth, Charles Altieri, and Frank Kermode in literary studies and James Elkins and Michael Fried (all along) in the visual arts. In each case, the effort is to accept and incorporate, rather than deny, the insights afforded by deconstruction and sociohistorical criticism (beyond formalism) while focusing nonetheless centrally on the powers and interest of art as itself a form of productive critical thought.

A related but narrower line of thinking within philosophy has focused specifically on the question of the relation between the artistic value of a work and the moral value of a work. Does the fact that a given work embodies a noxious moral attitude detract from its artistic value, and does a praiseworthy moral attitude in a work add to its artistic value? Or is artistic value centrally formal and aesthetic, so that embodied moral attitudes have no implications for artistic value? Within discussions of these questions, Leni Riefenstahl and the Marquis de Sade are often under consideration. Important work on this topic has been done by Berys Gaut, Matthew Kieran, Marcia Eaton, Richard Posner, and Noël Carroll, among others. Jerrold Levinson's collection *Aesthetics and Ethics* provides a valuable overview of the various positions. A difficulty that has frequently been thought to attach to raising the topic of art and morality in just this way, however, is that it is not so clear how to distinguish the art-relevant features of a work sharply and exhaustively from its ethical features. Are Pynchon's manic wordplay or Powell's sympathetic reserve from overt judgement or Robbe-Grillet's geometric coolness artistic or moral features of their texts? Likewise for Francis Bacon's or David Hockney's ways of handling the painting of their human subjects. If it is hard to say with any assurance that these features are ethical rather than artistic (or vice versa), then it courts obtuseness to ask how *the ethical* affects *the artistic*.

Garry Hagberg's new anthology *Art and Ethical Criticism* consists of twelve new essays — ten by philosophers, one each by an art historian and a professor of French — together with a short foreword. The overall argument that emerges from these essays is that the first, broader topic (the powers and interest of art for human subjects) is more important than the second, narrower topic (the relation between artistic and moral value), and the essays are strongest exactly when they illuminate the powers and interest of art, precisely by not separating the artistic and ethical features of a work sharply from each other.

The Foreword announces that "ethical criticism" covers "the task of elucidating the ethical content of the arts, the character and viability of our ethical responses to them, and the nature of the moral benefit provided by a serious engagement with literature, the visual arts, and music" . It is, then, pretty much taken for granted that art, or at least successful art, matters ethically — matters, that is, to and for human subjects in thinking about values — and the central task is then elucidating how this is so. The elucidations on offer are ranged under roughly five headings: historical foundations, general conceptions of ethical content, literature, the visual arts, and music.

In the sole essay in Part I, Paul Guyer surveys the philosophies of art of Hutcheson, Shaftesbury, Wolff, Baumgarten, Sulzer, Diderot, Kames, and Kant in order to establish that *no* major 18th century thinker held that art is of purely formal interest without ethical significance. Taking the ethical stance manifested in a work into account when evaluating it was a commonplace practice, with purer formalisms (*e.g.* Clive Bell) emerging only in the late 19th and early 20th centuries. All this is surely right, and it is useful to have this terrain surveyed, especially to undo over-simplifications of Kant as a formalist.

Part II on Ethical Content contains essays by Joshua Landy, Mitchell Green, and Noël Carroll. Landy reads Chaucer's "The Nun's Priest's Tale" as "a parody of didacticism" . What falls out of this reading is that literary fiction never *teaches* moral values. "Literature cannot edify, but it can clarify" . That is, it cannot teach us any moral doctrines, but it can help us to become clearer about values we already have. Training in how to see complexities, where many values are in play, is more in view than overt instruction. This is a promising line of thought, though the full moral psychology that would be necessary in order to elucidate the relevant clarification and training is not present.

Mitchell Green begins to address this lack by drawing on a theory of artistic expression that he has developed elsewhere. After surveying various senses of "showing," including giving evidence for, making perceptible, proving, demonstrating a skill, and expressing a mood, feeling, or affect, Green settles on the account that expressing, as a species of showing, "makes knowledge available" , though audience uptake on a showing is required in order for it to take effect. In the literary arts, what is shown is predominantly an affect or mood ("how an emotion, mood, or experience appears or … feels"). (Here Green is close to work by Dorothy Walsh and Susan Feagin that he does not mention.) Such showings may further cultivate skill in empathizing. Missing in this rehearsal, however, are accounts of the moral significance of empathy and of why and how literature's formal devices are especially good at cultivating empathy where we need it. Just what sorts of things about the experiences of others are we prone not to feel, why does it matter to feel them, and how does literature help formally to cultivate apt feeling in morally significant ways?

Noël Carroll's essay, substantially the richest in Part II, addresses exactly these questions. Narratives, fictional and otherwise, Carroll argues (following Aristotle), are marked by their possession of *selected detail*. They thus combine particularity *and* generality, as details are selected for their significance, especially their significance in displaying attitudes and the affective colouration of an experience of a situation. The selection of details as attitudinally and affectively coloured matters because of the natures of virtues and vices. Virtues and vices are i) temporally extended dispositions to act or respond, ii) that have 'insides' or affective dimensions, and iii) that are displayed differently in different circumstances . A narrative is then able to show the interplay of outside (what is done in a context) and inside (attitude and feeling) over time . By following a narrative, we may then achieve fuller orientation in the development of our own dispositions (virtuous, one hopes) that are suffused with feeling. We may see how, in this new setting, to go on more coherently in the expression of our attitudes and commitments.

"The notion of a meaningful life," in which the sustained, coherent exercise of virtue is achieved, "is parasitic on the notion of a meaningful narrative" , for the relevant coherence just *is*essentially narratival. One might perhaps wish for a fuller, more historical account of exactly why we moderns are especially prone to forget the powers of narrative to present the universal (shared possibilities of life) in the particular, in favor of the presentations of more immediately sortal, measurement-related universals (mass, velocity, etc.) that are a central business of the natural sciences. This forgetting must have something to do both with the rise of modern science and with the development in modernity of (increasing awareness of) cultural diversity, so that we have, if anything, too many narratives on hand rather than too few, so that *general* revelatory power may be harder to discern. Given, however, Carroll's masterful constructive analysis of the powers of narrative, it would be churlish to complain much.

Part III on literature is focused on particular cases and, while advancing the overall argument, is somewhat slighter in weight than the overt theorizing of Part II on ethical content. Robert Solomon surveys the responses of the major characters of Camus's *The Plague* to the horrors of their situation, arguing unsurprisingly that "human responsibility emerges as its major theme" and that responsibility is best exercised in "doing something, [in] making life meaningful, despite its futility or its consequences, and quite apart from any moral 'principles' that might be operative" . Paisley Livingston reads Virginia Woolf's 1920 short story "Solid Objects" as a reduction of Clive Bell's formalism, showing that *it* is an absurd characterization of aesthetic experience as a self-sufficient pleasure in pure form. "Rapture does not suffice" ; there are "cognitive, ... content, ... and axiological conditions" for the proper experience of art. Catherine Wilson balances the thoughts, drawn from Bernard Williams, that risk is unavoidable in life and that no value obviously has categorical force in all circumstances of personal life against the thought that we moderns tend to accept some form of (political?) equality as an absolute value. The task is then to develop so far as possible institutions of equal political citizenship without self-piety and the refusal to recognize contingency and complexity. J. M. Coetzee's novel *Disgrace* usefully tracks the complexities and difficulties of this task.

The treatment of visual works of art in Part IV provides a useful counterpoint to the treatment of literature in Part III, since there are at least in some cases ethical questions about how we are to treat them, quite apart from how they may instruct us. In addition, the different modality of experience involved in dwelling in visual experience rather than reading alone brings different ethical complexities and possibilities to the fore. The essays by Ivan Gaskell and David Davies focus less on what we might learn ethically from works than on questions about how we are to treat them and about their differences as art from non-art objects. Gaskell considers primarily the display of Native American baskets in museums.

Though return of these objects to the descendents of their original makers and users is sometimes required, both morally and legally, that is not always and obviously the best course of action. Taking into account both moral and legal responsibilities, museum curators as members of the dominant culture must decide whether and, if so, how to display them. Since these objects are often sacred or at least have something numinous about them in 'speaking' of and for a whole way of life, it is a mistake to display them as "specimens alone" of the Native American basket in general. They are, rather, specifically Chitimacha or Hupa, for example, with distinct origins, uses, and aesthetic and expressive features. For any such object, we should "accord it historical and aesthetic standing" , letting it count in our experience as museum visitors as the specifically valuable thing it is. Curators can and should further this kind of experience through appropriate lighting, arrangement, and commentary.

Davies turns to the photographs of Diane Arbus, framed by Susan Sontag's criticism of them, in order to illuminate the interest of photographic art. Sontag notoriously charged that Arbus's images exploit their subjects and function pornographically to titillate their viewers and to desensitize them to the grotesqueries of their subjects' appearances. How, Davies wonders, could a photograph even be charged with doing such things? — Only if, contrary to Roger Scruton's reading of photographs as necessarily inartistic, merely causally engendered 'direct' transcriptions of their subjects, these images do embody thoughts about and attitudes towards their subjects. Since, however, the visually grotesque subjects are presented with striking directness as "confident and accepting of their lives" , and so presented, moreover, with their consent, the images are specifically *not* demeaning or horrible. In representing their subjects both *as subjects* and as subjects of thought, they are not pornographic, but rather successfully artistic. Here too, as with Landy and Green, one would like to hear more about how and why such artistic success matters ethically. It is clear that there is an achievement of art about which ethical questions have been raised (by Sontag) and settled (by Davies), but then how and why does this work really matter to viewers who do understand what is going on?

Carolyn Korsmeyer's essay, "Staying in Touch," is richer in dwelling more fully on what we have to learn from visual art. Beginning from considering the Gettysburg battlefield, Silesian House (Gestapo interrogation cells in Krakow, now part of its Historical Museum), and, especially, Frank Lloyd Wright's Darwin Martin House in Buffalo, New York, Korsmeyer argues that "genuineness is a feature that has both ethical and aesthetic valence" . It matters to us to know that this battlefield looks largely as it did in 1863, that it is just these walls on which prisoners scratched their names and prayers, and that restoration of this house used as many original elements as possible. Only a genuine article can "bear witness ... to a way of life and to a distinctive artistic achievement" . We want to stay literally in touch with the object, placing our hands on it or walking over it, as itself an inscription of the experience that went into *its* making, and no replica will suffice for this. Here the aesthetic dimension ("the affective understanding that issues from imaginative engagement") and the ethical dimension ("the meaning [of a situation involving] suffering, cruelty, loss; or valor, endurance, or achievement") are simply not separable from each other. This claim, compellingly presented through these examples, might well stand for the strongest line of thought in the collection as a whole. In the spirit of Dewey, it situates art objects and the making and apprehending of them within a wider field of human experiences and concerns, however formally distinctive they may also be.

In Part V, Stephen Davies and Garry Hagberg turn to music. Davies undertakes to explain why Guglielmo does not participate in the canon in the last act finale of *Cosi Fan Tuttì*. The answer is that*Cosi* is not (only) a simple, serial *opera buffa*, but (also) a large-scale dramatic musical form that Mozart deploys to show the development of individuals as they come "to appreciate their own virtues and vices" . The psychological journey towards this end is no simple matter, and Guglielmo's non-participation shows how "the inescapable autonomy of the individual [is set] against the common need for mutual acceptance and recognition" , in life as in art.

Garry Hagberg's extraordinarily rich concluding essay focuses on how jazz "improvisation simultaneously mimetically represents as well as exemplifies in action ... ethical content" . What is both exemplified and represented (or presented by being consciously exemplified for attentive understanding of its significance in other domains) falls under the broad heading of "'ear training' in the realm of humane acknowledgment" . That is, jazz improvisers must display such things as "a mindfulness of the labors and projects of others" , awareness of "the anti-atomistic nature of intentional action itself" , "the distinctive kind of mindfulness that morally significant intentional action demands" , and acknowledgment of "the autonomy of others" in mutually respectful musical dialogue. These claims are tellingly illustrated via specific references to Charlie Parker, Charles Mingus, Billie Holiday, Freddie Green, Bill Evans, and Lee Konitz, among others. I dare say that anyone who heard Lee Konitz play, as I have, and paid attention, was struck by the reflective clarity of his musical intelligence and responsiveness. Hagberg's account of Konitz's achievement, as of the achievements and failures of the other figures mentioned (*e.g.*, Mingus) is right on the mark. Once one fully sees the nature of improvisatory intelligence that is simultaneously musical and ethical, then, Hagberg argues, it seems obvious that utilitarian and deontological theories of right action at a moment are desperately over-simplified, inattentive to what responsiveness, respect, the avoidance of cliché, and the projection of a future out of a remembered past really involve. (I note, as Hagberg does in accepting the value of respect, that a Kantian morality of principle rather than narrow rule-mongering is wholly compatible with this thought.) The idea that one improvises intelligently in the moment, drawing on a background of both training and talk, so that one is able after the fact to give a learned, retrospective justification of what one did *by* specifying a process of reasoning that one *didn't*just then, in the moment, explicitly go through, further undoes the Cartesian picture of an action as consisting of a bodily movement plus an (explicit, inner, guiding) intention. *That* picture, like the utilitarian and deontological accounts of right action, both oversimplifies and misdescribes our (sometimes intelligent) being in the world and with others.

That conclusions such as these in ethics, metaphysics, and the philosophy of mind, echoed in many of the other essays and compellingly achieved, arise out of the consideration of various practices of art*ought* to undermine the more abstractly generalizing, science-inspired forms of theorizing about human life that prominently distinguish central precincts of philosophy from the other disciplines of the humanities, arts, and history, thus turning philosophy towards more substantial affiliation with these latter fields, at least where values are concerned. Entrenched disciplinary habits being what they are, it is not likely that any significant shift along these lines will take place very soon. These essays provide, nonetheless, important reasons why it ought to.

Bibliography

A.A. Khan and Anil Saxena: *Medieval English Literature*, Shree Publishers, Delhi, 2012.

Abraham Mathew: *The Making of English Literature*, Cyber Tech Pub, 2011.

Anju Saxena: *Role of Women in English Literature*, Sonali Pub, 2011.

Anurag Tyagi: *History of English Literature*, Ancient Publication, Delhi, 2011.

Avadhesh Kumar Singh: *Indian English Literature: Marginalized Voices*, Creative Books, Delhi, 2003.

B N Patil: *History of English Literature*, Peral Books, Delhi, 2007.

B.K. Jha: *The Long Journey of English Literature*, ALP Books, 2011.

B.P. Sinha: *Studies and Essays in English Literature*, Book Enclave, 2002.

Basavaraj Naikar: *Indian English Literature (2 Vols-Set)*, Atlantic Publication, Delhi, 2002.

Basavaraj Naikar: *Indian English Literature: Vol. IX*, Atlantic Publication, Delhi, 2011.

Basavaraj Naikar: *Indian English Literature: Vol. V*, Atlantic Publication, Delhi, 2004.

Bijay Kumar Das: *Postmodern Indian English Literature*, Atlantic, 2003.

Daniel Reed and Tim Horton: *Roots and Influences of English Literature*, Dominant Pub, 2010.

Father Abraham: *Review of English Literature*, ABD, 2007.

George Sampson: *The Concise Cambridge History of English Literature*, Cambridge Univ Press.

H A Taine: *Taine's Encyclopaedia of English Literature with Thirty Two Portraits (4 Vols-Set)*, Shubhi Publications, 2003.

Kishore Ram: *Post Modernism in English Literature*, Sonali Publications, 2011.

Krishna Avtar Agrawal: *Post-Colonial Indian English Literature*, Book Enclave, 2007.

L Joseph: *Readings in English Literature*; Cyber Tech Pub, 2009.

L. D'Souza: *Studies in Contemporary English Literature*, Cyber Tech, 2011.

M S Bhatnagar: *Romantic and Victorian English Literature*, Alfa Pub, 2008.

M.K. Bhatnagar and M. Rajeshwar: *Post-Modernism and English Literature*, Atlantic Pub, 2011.

M.R. Verma and K.A. Agrawal: *Reflections on Indian English Literature*, Atlantic, 2002.

Madan Sood: *Romanticism in English Literature*, Pearl Books, 2007.

Malcolm Godden and Michael Lapidge: *The Cambridge Companion to Old English Literature*, Cambridge Univ Press.

Nigamananda Das: *Matrix of Redemption: Contemporary Multi-Ethnic English Literature from Northeast India*, Adhyayan Publication, Delhi, 2011.

O.P. Budholia and K.A. Agrawal: *Indian English Literature: Retrospect and Prospect*, Book Enclave, Delhi, 2010.

P. Varghese and Anita Jacob: *Landmarks of English Literature*, Alfa Publications, Delhi, 2012.

Partha Kumar Mukhopadhyay: *Literary Spectrums: Recent Studies in English Literature*, Sarup and Sons, Delhi, 2007.

Pramod Kumar Singh and Sanju Kumari: *Indian English Literature: Issues and Trends*, Yking Books, Delhi, 2010.

R.K. Das: *Major Trends in English Literature*, Pearl Books, Delhi, 2012.

Rajesh Sharma: *Modern English Literature*, ABD Publication, Delhi, 2006.

Richard Garnett and Edmund Gosse: *Illustrated Encyclopaedia of English Literature (4 Vols-Set)*, Sonali Publication, Delhi, 2003.

Index